Monica Irving

PLAY PRODUCTION
Theory and Practice

PLAY PRODUCTION

Theory and Practice

by

BARNARD HEWITT
Professor of Theatre, Speech Department,
University of Illinois.

J. F. FOSTER
Technical Director, Brooklyn
College, and Teacher of Stagecraft,
Columbia University Summer Session.

and

MURIEL SIBELL WOLLE
Professor of Art and Former
Head of The Department of Fine Arts,
University of Colorado.

J. B. LIPPINCOTT COMPANY

CHICAGO · PHILADELPHIA · NEW YORK

This volume is based in part upon Barnard Hewitt's earlier text
Art and Craft of Play Production, *copyright 1940*

PREFACE ~~~~~~~~~~~~~~~~~~~~~~~~~~~~~

Some readers of my earlier book *The Art and Craft of Play Production* were good enough to suggest that it would be more widely usable, especially in elementary theatre courses, if the material were presented in a simpler manner, less concentrated, and with more detail. Others suggested that it should contain more specific information about how to make and how to do.

As a matter of fact, *The Art and Craft of Play Production* was written to meet the needs of a particular college course which I was teaching. The students were upperclassmen, most of whom had had some previous theatre training or experience, and the course was conducted largely by lecture, discussion, and demonstration. Since *Art and Craft* still seems to me well suited to that type of course, I have resisted the suggestion that I revise it, and have instead prepared the present book along the lines suggested by the criticism.

I have been fortunate in securing as collaborators in areas where their special training and experience is especially valuable Muriel Sibell Wolle, Professor of Art and, until recently, Head of the Department of Fine Arts of the University of Colorado and Professor J. F. Foster, Technical Director of the Brooklyn College Theatre and teacher of stagecraft in Columbia University summer sessions.

Mrs. Wolle has contributed Chapter 20, *Costume Design,* and illustrated it with her own designs for some of the many productions she has costumed at the University of Colorado.

Professor Foster has contributed Chapters 11, *Scene Design;* 12, *Scene Construction;* 13, *Lighting;* and 15, *Backstage Organization.*

In addition, both have made suggestions regarding my sections of this book. Professor Foster was able to be particularly helpful in this respect because we shared an office at Brooklyn College when the book was in preparation.

However, the general plan and organization are mine, and I am solely responsible for the remaining chapters. Readers familiar with *Art and Craft of Play Production* will recognize similarities to the earlier book in viewpoint and in the treatment of many sections. The entirely new matter includes the opening section on the aesthetics of play production, material on various types of theatres, and the practical material on sound effects, makeup, business, and publicity.

The new matter is not the only difference between this book and *Art and Craft.* In the eleven years between them some of my ideas

v

have changed or clarified, and this will appear particularly in my discussion of the written play, Chapters 3, 4, and 5.

Others who have studied under Professor A. M. Drummond of Cornell University will doubtless hear in this book many echoes of him, and I am happy to acknowledge a general indebtedness to the perceptive director and stimulating teacher under whom I served my theatre apprenticeship.

It is difficult to find enough good pictures to illustrate a book like this, so I wish to thank the following who were particularly helpful in that respect: George Blair, University of Chicago; Marian Stebbins, Mills College; Charles Shattuck, University of Illinois; Albert McCleery, then at Fordham University; Dr. Saul Colin, Dramatic Workshop of the New School, New York; Glenn Hughes, University of Washington; Dina Rees Evans, Cain Park Theatre, Cleveland Heights, Ohio; and Milton Smith, Columbia University.

Special acknowledgement is due also to the Board of Higher Education of the City of New York and to Chapman and Evans, Architects, for permission to reproduce the ground plan of the Brooklyn College Little Theatre.

BARNARD HEWITT

CONTENTS ......

INTRODUCTION

WHAT IS PLAY PRODUCTION?

CHAPTER I.

THEATRE ART

$\mathcal{P}$lay production is an art. Everyone agrees on that. However, there is little agreement about the nature of art. In fact, there are almost as many different definitions of art as there are writers on the subject. Rather than adopt any one of these definitions, let us consider the characteristics of art which are most meaningful for play production.

General Characteristics

CREATION

Art implies creation, or to put it in plainer language, art implies the making of something. The artist uses materials drawn from nature, but the product of his art is not an exact imitation or reproduction of a product of nature. Works of art differ considerably in the extent to which they resemble works of nature, mainly because of differences in the art medium. The Empire State Building is not likely to be mistaken for a geological formation, nor the Moonlight Sonata for a natural sequence of sounds. On the other hand, some paintings convey a strong illusion of real things: of flowers, of animals, of human beings; and Daniel French's statue in the Lincoln Memorial clearly resembles a particular man.

Under certain circumstances the production of a play, composed as it usually is of lifelike movement and speech, might be mistaken by the unsophisticated for life itself. However, even when the art medium requires or permits a close resemblance to nature, art does not reproduce life. A painting of a flower is not a flower but something made of paint and canvas. A statue of Lincoln is not the man himself, nor even an imitation of him, but a creation in stone or metal. A play in performance is not life or a reproduction of life, but something made by man for a purpose.

3

UTILITY

Man makes many things: chairs and tables, pots and dishes, automobiles and airplanes. He makes them primarily because they are useful in the practical activities of living. They are helpful in resting, or in eating, or in getting from place to place. Man also makes songs and sonatas, pictures and statues, sonnets and plays. The usefulness of these products is not so obvious, and some philosophers have made a sharp distinction between the practical arts or crafts and the "fine arts." To other philosophers, this distinction seems unwarranted, because the well-designed chair or dish or airplane is pleasurable as well as useful, and the good song, picture, or play is not only pleasurable but useful or profitable.

In the beginning the so-called "fine" arts were strongly utilitarian. Much primitive art was magic, designed to influence the forces of nature. The first songs were sung, the first sculptures cut, the first pictures drawn in order to bring rain after a drouth, to propitiate the spirit of the slain antelope, or to insure a good harvest. In addition, early art frequently aimed to convey information. The returning hunters sang of their hunt or pictured it on the walls of their caves not only to appease the spirit of the slain antelope but also to inform the rest of the tribe of their success and how they achieved it.

As man learned more about the world in which he lived, the "fine" arts lost the character of magic; they were no longer practiced in order to bring rain or insure fertility. But they have kept their usefulness as conveyers of information. This is most obvious in the language arts, in literature and play production, and in the more realistic paintings. From novels, poetry, plays, and pictures we can learn a good deal that is specific about life. This informative function of art is not so obvious in abstract painting and in music. But painting, whether it resembles nature or not, enriches our knowledge of form in space, and music enriches our knowledge of form in time. Some writers on art have attempted to define the fine arts, or at any rate some of them, as nonutilitarian, and it is true that some art works, including a good many plays, add little to our practical knowledge. Nevertheless, most works of art do convey knowledge, either in the specific or in the more general sense. And the best plays seem to be those which inform in both senses.

PLEASURE

Art is not only useful; it is also pleasurable, so much so that the usefulness of fine art is sometimes forgotten. To know, to understand, is a pleasure; for to know is to put things together, to find order in life.

To express that knowledge, that understanding, the artist must make something: a statue, a picture, a poem, a song, a play. The making itself is pleasurable, perhaps because in the process the artist creates a new order, which, in the limited field of his art, can be more complete than any order possible in the limitless field of life. The artist works, not only because he wants to express something, but also because the physical process of expression, the handling of the brush, or the chisel, or words, is fun.

His audience, too, gains pleasure as well as profit from the art work. As far as it is able to experience the knowledge and understanding of the artist, it shares his pleasure in finding order in life. The audience gains pleasure also from the order in the work itself, from the design, from the arrangement of forms and planes in sculpture, from the arrangement of line, mass and color in painting, and of tones in music. In addition, the audience, particularly when it is present during the process of creation, as at the performance of a dance or of a play, vicariously enjoys the actual physical process of the expression. The audience feels itself executing the movements or uttering the words with the artists, and so experiences some of the artist's pleasure in performance.

MEANING

The pleasure element is so strong in art, both for the artist and for the audience, that the element of utility has sometimes been neglected or even denied. This has been especially true since the tremendous development of science, which pursues knowledge of man and the universe by objective, rather than intuitive, methods. Consequently we find pictures and even plays in which utility is slight or entirely lacking. However, in play production, which makes use of language, utility in the broad sense of *content* or *meaning* is still frequently of major importance. Indeed, unless the production conveys the meaning of the written play, it will not be so pleasurable as it might be.

ECONOMY

Art is characterized by economy—economy of materials and economy of effort. The work of art will contain no more than is necessary to express the author's vision. Although the painter may labor over his preliminary sketches and the actor may struggle in rehearsals, the finished painting and the finished performance will seem to be effortless. The greatest art expresses the most by the simplest means. It does not waste a note, a line, a word, a movement.

ORDER

We have noted that man's knowledge and understanding of himself, the world, and the universe is a putting together of things that hitherto have seemed separate, unrelated. It is the discovery of order in life. The artist is, first of all, one who discovers order in life. To express this knowledge of life, the artist must create order in his art. The product of art will be characterized by *unity*.

Our satisfaction in knowledge apparently increases with its extent, with the number of individual elements which are found to be related. In the art work, too, the greater the *variety* within which unity is achieved, the greater the satisfaction.

Man has long felt in himself and in the world around him certain principles of relationship, and these he has used to achieve unity in art.

Rhythm. Perhaps the most obvious of these is rhythm, the more or less regular recurrence of similar phenomena. We think first of examples of rhythm in time: the pulse, breathing, night and day, the seasons, birth and death. But there are examples in line, mass, and form also: within the genus is repeated the general form of man, of animal, of fish; within man himself two eyes, two ears, etc.; forms are repeated in the leaves of trees and plants, and in the structure of crystals.

Rhythm in art, as in life, is one of the most important principles of relationship and therefore of expressing or creating unity. It is most obvious in the more abstract arts, in music and the dance, but it is important, too, in literature. The rhythms of poetry are usually obvious, but prose, too, has its rhythms. Rhythm is important in play production, especially in the movement and speech of the actors, in the play of light, and in the line, color, and mass of the setting.

Equality. A second principle of relationship is expressed in the terms *balance, proportion,* and *harmony. Balance* is an equalization of contending forces. When we consider that man is able to stand upright only because his will, operating through his nerves and muscles, balances the pull of gravity (when he loses consciousness, the balance is upset and he falls to the ground), it is not surprising that he feels balance to be a principle of order. In art, the term *balance* is most often applied in the visual field. A picture is said to have *balance* when the elements on one side of its vertical central line seem to equal the elements on the other side in emphasis, importance, or "weight."

The simplest form of such balance is *symmetry,* in which exactly equal forms are grouped on the two sides of a central line or plane. Exact symmetry is uncommon in nature, but it does occur, for instance, in the formation of crystals. Symmetry is static and is likely to be monotonous. *Asymmetrical balance* is consequently more common in art. The lever principle is well known: a lesser weight will balance a greater if it is set further from the fulcrum. Moreover, our feeling of the weight of visible objects is modified by their size, distance, brightness, color, and meaning, so that a complex and dynamic asymmetrical balance may be achieved by taking into account several of these factors. Balance is important to play production in the design of the setting, in the grouping of the actors, and in the design of the costumes and of the lighting.

Proportion is difficult to define in its essence. We see things in relation to one another. In some instances, this is explainable in terms of the expected. We say a very large head on a very short man is "out of proportion" because the normal relation between the size of the head and the rest of the body seems to have been violated. Why we prefer one relationship to another in other instances, is difficult to say. The line cut in unequal parts is more interesting than the bisected line. The rectangle is more interesting than the square. Yet if the two sections of line are too unequal, and if the rectangle is very long and narrow, the effect is no longer pleasing. Probably both the desire for variety and the desire for balance are involved in our feeling for proportion.

In play production, proportion is an important unifying principle in all the visible elements. Proper proportion in the relation of one actor to another—in the relation of the actor to the furniture and to the forms in the setting, in the relation of the pieces of furniture to each other and to the forms in the setting—will help to unify the stage picture.

Harmony is a word describing the same kind of relationships between tone and tone or color and color as balance and proportion describe between forms. To the occidental ear at any rate, tones with similar frequencies of pitch, permitting easy blending of sound, are pleasant or harmonious. Tones with such dissimilar frequencies of pitch that they do not easily blend to the ear are unpleasant, unharmonious, or dissonant. Since in play production we deal ordinarily with a single pattern of sound, not with co-ordinate patterns as in the performance of choral or orchestral music, we are not much concerned with harmony in sound. However, it is a consideration in the relation between dialogue and incidental music.

Harmony in color, on the other hand, is of great importance in play production. The physical basis for our feeling about relationships in color is not clearly known. Although individuals differ in sensitiveness to color, it is possible to say that some colors seem to belong together or to harmonize, and some colors seem not to belong together, or to clash. Colors similar in hue, value, and intensity seem to harmonize. Other combinations are likely to clash. The large part which color plays in costume, setting, and light makes harmony in color a major principle of unity in play production.

Balance, proportion, and harmony are all words which express some kind of equality, and they have been grouped together as describing different aspects or manifestations of a second principle of order in life and in art.

EMPHASIS

There is a third principle of unity which involves relationships based not on equality, but on inequality or subordination. This is the principle of *emphasis*. In order to perceive any group of things as a whole, we must find among them a focus, a point of emphasis. This is most obvious in vision. When we look out of a window, we do not see with equal clarity all that is within our field of vision; the eyes select a point on which they concentrate, and we see everything else in the field as subordinate to this focal point.

To the ear, a regularly repeated and unvarying rhythm in the beating of a drum does not give as strong a sense of unity as does a rhythm which, while maintaining a fundamental beat, slowly increases in speed and loudness, and then grows slower and softer again to stop as it started.

Emphasis is an important principle for achieving unity in the visible elements of play production. The setting must be designed so as to provide a focus or several focuses for the eye of the spectator. Each grouping of the actors, each *tableau,* must provide such a focus. In the development of the performance in time also, there must be emphasis, the subordination of one part to another. The terms *climax* and *crisis* are descriptive of the principle of emphasis as applied to the written play, and to the play in performance.

Special Characteristics

THE MEDIUM

The different arts have different mediums, different means and materials of expression. The composer expresses himself in arrangements of tones, which he represents by notes and other musical symbols on paper. The painter expresses himself in paint on canvas, the sculptor in forms carved out of stone or wood.

The medium of play production is mixed. It permits expression through a combination of the movement and speech of the actors, through costume and makeup worn by the actors, and through scenery, light, sound effects, and sometimes music. The large number of materials is a limiting factor. Only opera uses more. And the marked differences in the materials present special problems. The actor permits expression both for the eye, through his posture and movement, and for the ear, through his speech. Costumes, makeup, scenery, and light permit expression for the eye. Sound effects and music permit expression for the ear. The actor's body, and through it costume and makeup, are mobile, permitting expression simultaneously in space and in time. So does light. Scenery, on the other hand, is static, permitting expression only in space, and the actor's speech, sound effects, and music permit expression only in time. The actor is three-dimensional; scenery is sometimes built in three dimensions and sometimes painted in two dimensions. Light, although it is very mobile, capable of change in intensity, color, direction, and area, is expressive only as it falls on the actor and the scenery.

CONDITIONS

Unlike some of the other arts, painting and sculpture for example, play production is performed in the presence of its audience. A rehearsal, no matter how perfect, is not the same as a performance before an audience. The work of the actor is obviously influenced by the size and responsiveness of the particular audience. Some producers regard the audience's contribution as so important that they include the audience as a collaborator in play production, and there can be no doubt that the presence of the audience is one of the major conditions affecting the practice of play production.

Usually a play is performed not once, but several or many times, each time for a different audience, and each time at a particular, fixed hour. Thence arise certain problems, particularly for the actor.

The presence of the audience has had much to do also with molding the theatre building. Originally, play production required only a place for the audience and a place for the actors. Our present theatre building was developed not only to house the materials of production and the machinery invented to facilitate their use, but also to house the spectators—to provide a permanent place from which they may see and hear in comfort and safety. The theatre building, once it has become permanent, presents a whole set of conditions which affect play production. Its size, its shape, the relation it sets up between playing space and audience space, all help to determine the forms which play production may take.

RELATION TO LIFE

Realism. We have noted that all art contains both lifelike and unlifelike, realistic and conventional or formal elements, and that the proportion of the realistic to the conventional depends to a large extent on the nature of the particular art medium. Music, which is expression in tones drawn from an arbitrary sound scale and placed in strongly rhythmic combinations, is probably the most conventional of the arts. Even when allied to language, as in song, the conventional pattern dominates. Dance is more realistic, because it is expression in the movement of the human body. And yet, since the dance is traditionally performed to music, it develops relatively conventional, formalized patterns of movement.

Play production tends to be more realistic than conventional because it is based upon language rather than on music and because its most important material is the actor. Costume and makeup, as accessories to the actor, necessarily share his bias toward realism. The other materials of production—scenery, light, nonvocal sound, and even music—are indirectly affected. The need for unity makes them tend to conform to the realistic patterns set up by the actor.

Convention. Nevertheless, in spite of its relative realism, play production is full of elements that are unlifelike, unrealistic, or conventional. Conventions are necessary to expression. The most realistic production of the most realistic play will still contain many conventions. The front curtain in our theatre is a convention which performs a number of expressive functions. Its rise indicates the beginning of the production; its final fall, the end. Between times it falls and rises to indicate change of place, lapse of time, or merely to allow the audience ten minutes of relaxation. The proscenium arch is a convention of our theatre. It frames the playing space like a picture, setting it off from the rest of the theatre building. And it nourishes another convention—namely, that the play is going on independently

The modern Greek-type open-air theatre at Mills College, Oakland, California, has many of the features of the original Greek theatre, although the architectural style is not Greek. Note the orchestra half-circle, the seats rising sharply from the orchestra, and the permanent stagehouse with its central door.

of the audience, which is permitted to observe the performance through an invisible fourth wall.

The conventions of play production are not fixed. They develop, fall into disuse, and are replaced by others. There was no front curtain in the Greek theatre. None was possible as long as the audience sat around the greater part of the playing space in a roofless stadium. The beginning of a play was marked by the first entrance of the actors and the end by their final exit. As long as there was no proscenium arch separating stage from audience, the convention of the fourth wall was impossible, probably inconceivable. Consequently, the actor in Shakespeare's time recognized the presence of the audience, and he could tell the audience directly what he was thinking and feeling in so-called *soliloquies* and *asides*. With the development of the proscenium arch and the growth of the convention that the presence of the audience should be ignored, the soliloquy and aside were discarded. More recently, Eugene O'Neill has re-

This is Shakespeare's theatre as reconstructed for the Laurence Olivier film *Henry V*. Note the large apron in the midst of the spectators (some of whom actually sit on one side of it) and the curtained inner stages flanked by permanent doors and windows. The boy with the sign may not be historically accurate.

vived them and used them to express man's newly discovered subconscious.

The conventions of play production at any particular time are dictated by what is to be expressed, by the materials available, and by the conditions under which they must be used.

INTERPRETATION

Play production, like the performance of music, is an interpretative art. Except in rare instances, as in the popular theatre of seventeenth-century Italy, a play is not composed spontaneously in the theatre. The play is first conceived by a *playwright*, who sets it down on paper in the form of dialogue and stage directions. The play in its written form may be read, appreciated, and criticized as literature, but it does not become a work of theatre art until it has been realized on the stage: until director, actors, and scenic artists have given it life in time and space before an audience. Even when the playwright stages his own play, designing scenery, costumes, lighting, and makeup, and acts a leading role himself, he still must call on other actors for the other roles, and their work is interpretative.

The production of a play has frequently been likened to the performance of a symphony. The latter is an interpretation of the composer's score; the former is an interpretation of the playwright's written play or *script*. An important difference is that musical symbols provide a more exact guide for the orchestra than language symbols do for the actors. Because play production is an interpretative art, it presents special problems in analyzing the script to secure as complete an understanding as possible of the playwright's intention.

COLLABORATION

Because of the number and variety of materials used in play production, it is necessarily a collaborative or group art. It requires a number of actors, each interpreting a particular role. It requires a designer of costumes, scenery, and light. Sometimes this may be one person, but sometimes the work is divided among two or three. Carpenters, painters, and stagehands are needed to construct and shift the scenery; an electrician or two to set up and manipulate the lights; dressmakers to construct the costumes; a technician to operate the sound effects; perhaps a composer of incidental music, and musicians to play it; and a stage manager to keep the whole show running smoothly in performance.

Many of these are properly called workers or craftsmen, who merely execute the designs of others, but the actor is traditionally regarded as an artist in his own right, and the settings (and frequently the costumes) are designed by an independent artist. The co-ordination of the work of all these collaborating artists and craftsmen, so that play production may achieve a unified expression of the playwright's script, is probably the principal problem of theatre art.

Questions

1. What is meant by the statement: "Art is creation"? How can it be applied to the art of play production?
2. How does the usefulness of *Hamlet* differ from the usefulness of a well-designed railroad engine?

3. What is meant by the statement: "Primitive art was magic"?
4. What are the sources of pleasure in art for the artist? For the audience?
5. Cite some examples of rhythm in nature other than those mentioned in the text.
6. Name and describe the sources of unity in art.
7. Describe the varieties of the principle of *equality*.
8. Distinguish between the two types of balance.
9. Give further examples from life of our feeling for proportion.
10. What is meant by harmony in color? In sound?
11. Give an example of the use of emphasis in the field of advertising.
12. How does play production differ from the dance as a medium of expression? How are the two mediums similar?
13. Why is play production a comparatively realistic art?
14. What are some of the common conventions of play production today?
15. What is meant by the statement: "Play production is an interpretative art"?

Exercises

1. Find out what you can about the origins of play production in ancient Greece and make a report on them in the light of this chapter.
2. Look up the beginnings of play production in the Middle Ages and report on them in the light of this chapter.
3. Find out what you can about dramatic performances in primitive tribes and make a report on them.
4. Make a report comparing the conventions of play production in Greek times with conventions of play production today.
5. Report on the conventions in the production of classic Chinese or Indian (oriental) plays.

Bibliography

The Beginnings

Batchelder, E. A., *Design in Theory and Practice*, New York: The Macmillan Company, 1910.

Harrison, Jane Ellen, *Ancient Art and Ritual*, New York: The Home Library of Modern Knowledge, c. 1913.

Havemeyer, Loomis, *The Drama of Savage Peoples*, New Haven: Yale University Press, 1916.

Theory of Art

Bosanquet, Bernard, *A History of Aesthetic,* London: S. Sonnenchein, 1904.

Fry, Roger, *Vision and Design,* London: Chatto & Windus, 1920.

Geddes, Norman Bel, *Horizons,* Boston: Little, Brown & Company, 1937.

Stein, Leo, *The A-B-C of Aesthetics,* New York: Boni & Liveright, 1927.

Teague, Walter Dorwin, *Design This Day,* New York: Harcourt, Brace & Company, 1940.

Theatre Aesthetics

Craig, Edward Gordon, *On the Art of the Theatre,* Boston: Small, Maynard & Company, 1925.

Jones, Robert Edmond, *The Dramatic Imagination,* New York: Duell, Sloan, & Pearce, 1941.

Simonson, Lee, *The Stage Is Set,* New York: Harcourt, Brace & Company, 1932.

Older Theatre Forms

Bieber, Margarete, *History of the Greek and Roman Theater,* Princeton: Princeton University Press, 1939.

Cheney, Sheldon, *The Theatre,* New York: Longmans, Green & Company, 1929.

Flickinger, Roy, *The Greek Theatre and Its Drama,* Chicago: The University of Chicago Press, 1918.

Freedley, George, and John A. Reeves, *A History of the Theatre,* New York: Crown Publishers, 1941.

Stevens, Thomas Wood, *From Athens to Broadway,* New York: D. Appleton-Century-Crofts, Inc., 1932.

Zucker, Adolph E., *The Chinese Theatre,* Boston: Little, Brown & Company, 1925.

CHAPTER 2.

THE THEATRE ARTIST

*O*bviously, if all the necessary collaborators are to work smoothly together, play production requires a supervising artist, or artist-in-chief, who can stand in the place both of the playwright and of the audience as a guide to the co-operating artists and craftsmen.

Sometimes in the past, in the great period of the Greek theatre for instance, the playwright himself was the artist-in-chief, supervising the production of his own plays. Molière produced his own plays, and in our own day George S. Kaufman, John Van Druten, George Kelly, and Lillian Hellman supervise the production of their own plays, or at any rate select and direct the actors. In the eighteenth and nineteenth centuries, the leading actor was frequently the artist-in-chief. David Garrick and Henry Irving are famous examples of the actor-manager. Since about 1880, the theatre has been dominated by the producer-director as artist-in-chief. David Belasco, Max Reinhardt, Jed Harris, George Abbott, and Herman Shumlin are examples of producers who have directed the actors and co-ordinated all the departments of production. Sometimes a producer, while he retains control over all departments of production, will delegate responsibility for rehearsing the actors to a stage director, just as he will delegate responsibility for designing and supervising the construction and painting of the settings to a scene designer. Such is the practice of the Shuberts.

In the nonprofessional theatre, the artist-in-chief is nearly always the producer-director. For convenience, we shall call him hereafter the *director*. This book is written primarily from the director's point of view.

The Director and the Playwright

Usually it is the director who selects the play to be produced. In order to make the best selection possible, he should be thoroughly familiar with dramatic literature. The more plays he knows, the better choice he should be able to make. This is particularly true in the nonprofessional theatre which depends largely upon published plays, but even in the professional theatre a knowledge of dramatic literature is useful—the more a director knows about old plays, the better able he should be to judge new ones.

When the play has been selected, it is the director's responsibility to see that the playwright's purpose is realized in the theatre for the audience. He will study the written play. In addition he may draw on his knowledge of the playwright's life and other writings. He may look up reviews of other productions, and study the comments of dramatic and literary critics. If the play is not a relatively recent one, he may need to know something of the political, social, and economic conditions under which it was written, and of the theatrical conditions under which it was first produced.

FREEDOM OF INTERPRETATION

There is room in many plays for differences of interpretation, and the plays which live any length of time are bound to be reinterpreted by different generations of artists, each of which will understand them somewhat differently. However, there are limits beyond which the director cannot go with impunity in tailoring a script to suit himself. Max Reinhardt was criticized adversely for distorting in his productions a number of the great plays of the past, and Orson Welles tried hard to make an anti-dictator play out of Shakespeare's *Julius Caesar.* Deliberate distortion, such as this, is hard to justify. If the director cannot find a play which will express his idea without cracking at the seams, he probably ought to write his own play.

MOLDING THE NEW SCRIPT

The director of a *new* script is in a somewhat different situation. The playwright is usually available to explain his intentions, so there is little danger of misunderstanding. However, the unproduced play, especially one by an inexperienced playwright, is seldom completely finished before it goes into rehearsal. There is a saying that "plays are not written but rewritten," and a lot of the rewriting is done in the course of production. Scenes which on paper seemed to achieve their purpose fail to do so when performed by actors. Some lines or even scenes are revealed as superfluous; the need for additional lines and scenes becomes apparent.

The director can and should help the playwright make the improvements indicated in the course of rehearsals and the first performances. No major changes, however, should be made without the playwright's consent. And the director should not take advantage of his superior knowledge of the theatre and of his position of authority to coerce the playwright into accepting changes of which he disapproves.

The Director and the Collaborating Artists

In the ideal arrangement for play production, all the collaborating artists (director, actors, scene designer, and composer, if one is needed) study the script and arrive at an agreement on its meaning, the form it is to take in the theatre, and in a general way the means by which the theatrical form is to be created. The director should be capable of stimulating each of the specialists to do his best and should act as arbiter when there is disagreement.

In practice, the director, with little or no consultation, frequently decides on the meaning of the play and dictates to each of the collaborating artists what each shall contribute to the expression of that meaning in the theatre. This happens in the professional theatre because the director holds the purse strings; the collaborating artists are his employees. It happens in the nonprofessional theatres also, but because the actors and the other theatre workers frequently are not far enough advanced in their respective branches of play production to be capable of creative contribution. In such cases, the director *must* dictate the interpretation of the script and the means by which it is to be realized in the theatre.

Whatever the relationship between the director and the collaborating artists in the professional theatre, the more he knows about each of their respective departments the more likely he is to succeed. He need not be an actor himself, but he should know the possibilities and the problems of acting. He need not be a costume designer, a scene designer, or a lighting engineer, but he should know as much as possible about what may be accomplished in each of those departments. The more he knows about each of them the better able he will be to inspire each collaborator to his best work, and unless he knows a good deal about each of them he cannot be a fair and effective arbiter among them.

If his aim is to achieve an expression not of the group interpretation but of his own, this knowledge is just as important. Ignorance of a particular field leaves him at the mercy of the expert he has hired. If he knows nothing of lighting, for instance, the electrician may say certain effects the director wants are impossible, and he will be unable to tell whether or not the electrician is telling the truth.

In the nonprofessional theatre, it is even more important for the director to know as thoroughly as possible each of the departments of production, for he usually has to teach them to his collaborators. He should be able to teach acting, as well as to direct actors, and he should be able to teach makeup, stagecraft, stage lighting, and costuming, or as many of these as possible.

The Director and the Actors

The director's general relation to the actors has been indicated above, but because the director works more closely and intensively with the actors than he does with the other collaborating artists, this relationship requires a more detailed analysis. The two extremes of this relation are well illustrated by the Moscow Art Theatre and by Meyerhold's theatre. In the Moscow Art Theatre, except in its earliest years, the productions have been largely an expression of the actors' interpretation of the plays. The director has been inspiration, guide, and arbiter. In Meyerhold's theatre, the director's interpretation dominated. Meyerhold even acted out each of the parts in rehearsals, and the best actor was the one who could best imitate the director. It is easier to achieve a unified production by the Meyerhold method, but frequently unity is achieved at the expense of true vitality. The production is likely to be lifeless, mechanical. The completely collaborative method on the other hand runs the risk of confusion. A nice balance between anarchy and dictatorship seems to be the ideal relation between director and actor.

Even when he is dealing with inexperienced actors, the director will find that his conception of the performance will be modified by the actors. Usually this is negative; the actors will be unable to execute movements or read lines as the director has imagined them. But even inexperienced actors sometimes make positive contributions also: a movement, a piece of business, or the reading of a line, which, although the director had not thought of it, yet illumines the part or the play. The director should not be so intent on his preconceived pattern that he fails to recognize such contributions when the actors are able to make them.

The Director and the Theatre

Because play production takes place in a theatre, the director, in order to plan his production intelligently, must know the dimensions, arrangement of space, stage machinery, and lighting equipment of the particular theatre which is to house it. The form of the production will be to a great extent determined by these physical factors. He should know the size and shape of the auditorium, the sightlines, the height and width of the proscenium opening, the stage depth, the amount of wing room, the fly space, the equipment for shifting scenery, the number of stage-lighting circuits, the location of electrical outlets, and the facilities for lighting control, to name some of the most important items.

It is useful for him to know also how this particular theatre differs from the general run of theatres today. Lack of fly space, for instance, will make it necessary for him to find some other method of setting a nineteenth-century melodrama like *Ten Nights In A Bar Room,* which was written for scenery painted on drops and wings.

Unless he is to produce only modern plays, he should know the major theatres of the past: the Greek theatre, the several forms of the medieval theatre, the Elizabethan theatre, the Renaissance theatre, and the theatre of Restoration England. He must know the forms that play production took in these theatres, if he is to find equivalents for them in terms of the modern theatre and its machinery.

The Director and the Audience

We have noted that the director stands in place of the playwright, but he stands in place of the audience also, for no matter how well the collaborating artists may grasp the playwright's conception and how conscientiously they may labor to realize it in the materials of play production, all will be in vain if the result does not have the intended effect upon the audience. So he must know his audience. Is it big or small, young or old, naïve or sophisticated? What are its likes and dislikes?

In choosing a play for production, the producer must consider his audience. All through the planning of the production—setting, lighting, costumes, casting—and through the whole course of preparation, he will think in terms of audience attention and interest.

He will be concerned with bringing the audience into the theatre through publicity and the sale of tickets. He will be concerned with the program as a means of preparing the audience for the particular play. He will plan ahead of time for the comfort of the audience in house management, in the sale and taking of tickets, in the ushering, in the ventilation, and so on.

The director should never forget that the production must come alive for the audience. Anything which interferes with the proper effect on the audience, whether it be poor casting, bad groupings, awkward movements, inadequate settings, noise in the lobby, or poor ventilation, may weaken or destroy the play in the theatre.

List of Playwrights

Below is a minimal list of the playwrights with whose plays the director should be familiar. To be really well equipped the director should extend his reading to include the works of many more playwrights, both old and new.

CLASSIC

Aeschylus
Sophocles
Euripides
Aristophanes
Plautus
Terence
Shakespeare

Lope de Vega
Calderon
Molière
Congreve
Sheridan
Goldoni

MODERN

American

Maxwell Anderson
Philip Barry
S. N. Behrman
Marc Connelly
Owen Davis
Paul Green
Lillian Hellman
Sidney Howard
George S. Kaufman
Sidney Kingsley
John Howard Lawson
Arthur Miller
Eugene O'Neill
Clifford Odets
Elmer Rice
Lynn Riggs
William Saroyan
Irwin Shaw
Robert Sherwood
Robert Turney
Thornton Wilder
Tennessee Williams

Scandinavian

Henrik Ibsen
August Strindberg

English

Oscar Wilde
J. M. Barrie
T. S. Eliot
John Galsworthy
Bernard Shaw
H. Granville-Barker
Somerset Maugham
St. John Ervine
A. A. Milne
John Van Druten
J. B. Priestley
Noel Coward
James Bridie

Italian

Luigi Pirandello

Russian

Nikolai Gogol
Leo Tolstoi
Anton Chekhov
Maxim Gorki
Leonid Andreyev

German, Austrian, Czech

Gerhart Hauptmann
Georg Kaiser
Frank Wedekind
Ernst Toller
Bertolt Brecht
Arthur Schnitzler
Ferenc Molnar
Franz Werfel
Karel and Josef Çapek

French

Henri Becque
Edmond Rostand
Maurice Maeterlinck
Paul Claudel
J. J. Bernard
H. R. Lenormand
Jean Giraudoux
Jules Romains
André Obey
Jean Anouilh
Jean-Paul Sartre

Spanish

José Echegaray
Benito Pérez-Galdós
Jacinto Benevente
Seraphin and Joaquin Quintero
Gregorio Martinez-Sierra
Federico Garcia-Lorca

Irish

J. M. Synge   Lennox Robinson
W. B. Yeats   Sean O'Casey
                       Paul Vincent Carroll

Questions

1. Who, in your opinion, is likely to make the best theatre artist-in-chief: the playwright, the actor, the director, or the scene designer? Why?
2. What are the qualifications for a good director?
3. How can the director help to improve a new play?
4. To what extent should the director feel free to "interpret" the written play?
5. What seems to you the best relationship between the director and the scene designer? Why? Between the director and the actors? Why?
6. Why should the director know his audience?
7. What does the director need to know about the theatre in which he is to produce?

Exercises

1. Report on "Playwrights as Theatre Directors."
2. Report on "Actors as Theatre Directors."
3. Report on Reinhardt's method of directing the actors. On Meyerhold's method.
4. Report on the relation of the director and the actor in the Moscow Art Theatre.
5. Report on Gordon Craig's conception of the function of the director.

Bibliography

Houghton, Norris, *Moscow Rehearsals,* New York: Harcourt, Brace & Company, 1936.

Sayler, Oliver M., *Max Reinhardt and His Theatre,* New York: Brentano's, 1924.

———, *Inside the Moscow Art Theatre,* New York: Brentano's, 1925.

Stanislavski, Constantin, *My Life in Art,* Boston: Little, Brown & Company, 1928.

Books by Cheney, Craig, Freedley, Simonson and Stevens listed in the Bibliography to Chapter 1.

Articles in *Theatre Arts, Quarterly Journal of Speech,* and *Educational Theatre Journal.*

PART ONE

THE FOUNDATION
OF PRODUCTION:
The Written Play

CHAPTER 3.~~~~~~~~~~~~~~~~~~~~~

BASIC CHARACTERISTICS

~~~~~~~~~~~~~~~~~~~~~~~~~~~~~

*S*ince the aim of play production is to realize as fully as possible the playwright's conception, a full understanding of the written play is essential to the director and to all the collaborators in theatre art. This and the following three chapters present a basis for studying particular plays in their written form preliminary to production.

Many attempts have been made to define a play in its written form, some by picking out the essential element, some by describing the form. Most of these definitions have proved too narrow to include easily all the plays which have succeeded in the theatre. Since we are concerned with practical problems of producing particular plays, it seems best to begin not with one of these restrictive definitions, but with a definition broad enough to include all the written compositions with which we are likely to have to deal. This very general skeleton can then be filled out with descriptions of the most important general characteristics to be found in plays and by more specific descriptions or definitions of different types of plays.

As a starting point then, we may say that *the written play is a composition in dialogue form, sometimes with interpolated description (stage directions), designed to express something to an audience when performed by actors.* The playwright has an idea or feeling about life which finds expression in an imagined picture of characters who live a life of their own, a life which is capable of being realized for an audience through the materials of the theatre: actors, setting, light, and so on. This complex vision he expresses not directly in theatrical terms, but on paper in the restricted form of dialogue and stage directions.

Literary Elements

Evidently, a play exists on several planes, or at any rate literary, dramatic, and theatrical elements are involved in the play

26

considered from the point of view of production. Since from this point of view the play in its written form constitutes a plan of production, let us consider first the two fundamental literary elements: dialogue and stage directions.

DIALOGUE

Of the two, dialogue is by far the more important means of expression for the playwright. From the dialogue, the characters and their actions should be readily imaginable. A good many of the older plays have few or no stage directions, so that the director must depend on the dialogue alone to stimulate his imagination. From an intensive study of what the characters say should come a vivid picture of what they look like, how they move, and what they do.

Dialogue differs greatly from play to play. The most obvious difference is between prose dialogue and verse dialogue, but there are important differences within the two general categories. Some prose dialogue resembles closely the speech used by real people in life, other prose dialogue departs more or less obviously from the speech of ordinary life. There are important differences also between the blank verse of Shakespeare and the blank verse of Maxwell Anderson, and even between the blank verse of *Romeo and Juliet* and the blank verse of *The Tempest*. The director should be aware of these differences. They are fundamental to a realization in production of the playwright's vision.

Dialogue is always important in production, but it seems to be especially important in plays of idea and in plays of wit. The play of idea, the philosophical play, if it is a good one, will embody its fundamental idea in the dramatic action, but it is likely to express many auxiliary ideas largely or entirely in what some of the characters say. This is true of Sartre's *The Flies,* and of Pirandello's *Six Characters in Search of an Author*. Wit is the expression of comedy in language—through the choice of words, through the turn of phrase—so it is only natural that dialogue assumes an added importance also in witty plays like Wilde's *The Importance of Being Earnest.*

STAGE DIRECTIONS

In the stage directions the playwright is free to relax and tell us what the characters look like, what they think and feel, how they speak and move, and what they do. He is able to tell us directly in the stage directions what kind of environment he has imagined for his characters, and to describe how scenery, light, properties, music, and sound effects may be used to create that environment.

As we have noted, a good many of the older plays have few or no stage directions. The director will have to build up his picture of their production from the dialogue alone. However, most modern plays have stage directions, and some, for instance those of J. M. Barrie and George Bernard Shaw, have many long and detailed stage directions. These are worth careful study, not with the aim of reproducing them faithfully in the production (an aim usually impossible of achievement) but as a help to understanding the total effect intended by the playwright.

Acting versions, such as are published for nonprofessionals by Samuel French, Walter Baker, and others, are likely to contain very full stage directions. In all probability these were not written by the playwright but are a record of the pattern of movement used in the play's first professional production. These are worth study also, but they can no more be taken as a literal guide for a new production than can the elaborate essays which Shaw and Barrie have interpolated as stage directions in the trade editions of their plays. Each new production is molded by the particular conditions under which it takes place.

Dramatic Elements

The dialogue and stage directions are the playwright's means of expressing for the reader beings or characters, characters which are alive and involved in action. Since action must occur somewhere, they express also the place of the action, its environment.

CHARACTER

Through characters, to be represented by actors in costume and makeup, the playwright expresses most of what he thinks and feels. The speech and action of the characters is the largest part of most plays in production. Usually the characters are more or less like real human beings, but sometimes they are clearly types, or personifications of human qualities, and sometimes they are animals, or insects, or even ordinarily inanimate objects which have been endowed with life by the playwright's imagination. The extent to which the characters resemble real persons is a basis for one of the useful classifications of plays.

The characters are conceived not to be talked about but to be presented in action, and the pattern of their action is known as *plot*. Dramatic critics are not in agreement about the relative importance of character and plot. Aristotle placed plot first, at any rate in tragedy, and character second, apparently on the grounds that character can be expressed dramatically only through action. Modern critics tend to place character ahead of plot. In the more significant plays character certainly seems more important, and even in those lesser plays in which plot is clearly paramount, character may yet do much to make the plot credible and effective. Character is undoubtedly of basic importance in all plays.

The relative importance of character and plot provides another basis for distinguishing between certain types of plays.

PLOT

One may say perhaps that character is the flesh and body of a play, but that plot is the skeleton or bony structure which gives a play its fundamental dramatic form. Plays differ considerably, not only in the relative importance of plot, but also in the type of plot: in the selection of the incidents of which the plot is composed and in the means by which these incidents are bound together. These differences in plot construction provide another useful basis for the classification of plays.

The incidents which make up the plot of a play are selected and arranged not only for their value in revealing the characters, but also for their *dramatic* value. The words *drama* and *dramatic* are sometimes used to describe works of art in other mediums, but they are generally recognized as pertaining particularly to plays. An understanding of them is essential to play analysis and production. The words are used also to describe certain phenomena in life, and an examination of these will throw some light on the *dramatic* as it is found in plays.

Conflict. Situations in life are likely to strike us as dramatic if they are characterized by struggle, contest, or conflict. When two major league baseball teams near the end of the season with only a game or two separating them, when two runners come down the homestretch neck and neck, when two evenly matched debaters face each other on opposite sides of a vital question, we say the situation is "dramatic."

There can be no doubt that such conflict is one of the principal sources of the dramatic in plays. One thinks of the conflict between Macbeth and Duncan, between Hamlet and Claudius, between Katharine and Petruchio, or between Mr. and Mrs. Craig in *Craig's Wife*. Most plays contain some elements of conflict, if not between one character and another, or between a character and his environment, then *within* a character, as in *Othello* between the hero's love for Desdemona and the terrible suspicion planted and cultivated by Iago.

Indeed, conflict is characteristic in one way or another of so many plays that attempts have been made to define a play in terms of conflict alone. In a number of successful plays, however, conflict is clearly subordinate to other elements, and in a few successful plays it appears in so attenuated a form as hardly to be worthy of the name. Conflict appears here and there in Thornton Wilder's *Our Town* but it is hardly the dominant element. Some of our most powerful plays are built on a story of deception and betrayal in which conflict cannot play a major part because the hero is unaware of the plot against him until too late. This is true of *Agamemnon*. The hero returns triumphant from the Trojan War and goes unwittingly to his death at the hands of Clytemnestra and Aegisthus.

Tension or suspense. In plays like *Agamemnon,* the primary dramatic element is not conflict but suspense or tension, not the suspense of a mystery story which conceals the solution until the end, but the suspense which arises from the spectacle of the inexorable approach of catastrophe. The terrible deed with which *Agamemnon* is to conclude is foreshadowed in the very beginning by the Watchman's misgivings, and tension is built up steadily by the revelation of Clytemnestra's hatred for her husband, by the fears of the Chorus, and by Cassandra's vague but ominous prophecy, until it explodes in the expected murder. In *Othello* it is the growth of the hero's horrible suspicions until they culminate in the murder of Desdemona which holds an audience, even more than the conflict within Othello, himself.

Suspense or tension is generated by conflict, as between Hamlet and Claudius, but it may be generated also by any unstable situation, whether or not it is characterized by obvious conflict. Agamemnon's return makes an intolerable situation for Clytemnestra, and she acts with violence to alter it.

Action. Neither conflict nor suspense will be dramatic for long without the aid of action. Conflict between two evenly matched teams is likely to result in a scoreless tie, a stalemate. To be dramatic, one side must score a touchdown, or at any rate come close. Suspense must find relief in action.

The fact is that action itself is dramatic, even action on a limited scale; for action is change, action is often growth. We recognize this in life when we speak of a drowning or murder, a rescue, or a narrow escape from death or injury as *dramatic*. Such events are dramatic in plays also, but the more subtle pattern of action is dramatic too, and violent action itself is more dramatic if it comes as a result of gradually mounting tension, growing either out of conflict or out of some other unstable situation.

Contrast. Although conflict, suspense, and violent action are perhaps the most common dramatic elements, contrast too may be dramatic. We speak of the *dramatic* contrast between a tenement and a luxurious apartment standing side by side, or between a broad plain and the high mountain rising abruptly from it. In one sense contrast or change is the result of most action. Action dissolves one situation and creates another, different from the first. But contrast appears in plays even more obviously between characters. It is most marked when it leads to conflict, as between Goneril and Regan and their sister, Cordelia, in *King Lear*. But it can be important also when it does not result in conflict, as between Othello and Iago, and subtly between Macbeth and Lady Macbeth. *The Silver Cord* is a play of strong contrasts. Not only is Mrs. Phelps contrasted with Christina, but Christina is contrasted with Hester, and David with Robert.

In its broadest sense, *variety,* contrast is essential even to the play which expresses weakness or monotony. The effect of monotony is achieved through a variety of minor actions within a limited range, the effect of weakness through the variety of its manifestations.

One of the fundamental responsibilities of the director is to discover these dramatic elements—conflict, suspense or tension, action, and contrast—in the plot of the written play and to recreate them in the production.

ENVIRONMENT

Although what the playwright has to say is expressed largely through the speech and action of the characters, environment as it is presented through scenery, light, sound effects, and music may be expressive also, most often indirectly as the place of the action, but sometimes directly and more or less independently of characters and action.

Plays differ greatly in the use they make of environment and of the different materials available for projecting it. Setting and light are not essential to Greek drama nor to many of the plays of Shakespeare and of Molière, but a number of these older plays seem to require music. Many modern plays, on the other hand, depend strongly on scenery and light to build up a lifelike environment or an atmosphere expressing a particular emotion. Other modern plays, like *The Glass Menagerie* and *Death of a Salesman,* use music to build up the emotional environment of their action.

Theatrical Elements

Since the playwright has imagined character, action, and environment not in the abstract, but as he hopes they will be realized in production for an audience, what he writes is inevitably influenced by what he knows of the abilities of actors and scenic artists, and also by the form of production prevalent in his time.

He imagines the characters represented by actors in a definite form of acting space which is capable of a particular kind and degree of expression as environment. And he imagines the whole production in relation to an audience. Since all of these conditions—the conventions of acting, the form of the acting space, the expressive value of the other materials of production, and the relation of the production to the audience—have varied considerably through the history of theatre art, these differences will be reflected in the written play. They provide a basis for classifying plays according to theatrical form.

Content

This complex organism of imagined characters involved in action to be presented by actors for an audience exists for one purpose: to express the playwright's ideas and feelings about life. Therefore, the director in building up from the written play his own imaginative recreation of the author's vision must see characters, action, and environment and their theatrical realization in terms of *idea* and *emotion*.

IDEA

Every play, no matter how light, how much it is designed to entertain, contains some dominant idea, often a simple idea. Irwin Shaw's *Bury The Dead* expresses the idea that war is unnecessary and avoidable. Maxwell Anderson's *Winterset* is built on the idea that the desire for revenge is self-destroying. Mary Coyle Chase's *Harvey* is built on the idea that much of life is either tiresome or burdensome. Many plays express other ideas also, most of them related in some way to the dominant idea, and some plays express a great many ideas woven together into a unified pattern. The importance of idea and ideas differs greatly from play to play, but the director must discover in the particular play the pattern of ideas and how it is expressed through character, plot, and environment.

EMOTION

Idea is fundamental, but it is expressed in plays as in other works of art very largely through emotion. Even epic drama and theatre, which claim a purely didactic purpose—the dissemination of scientific truth—do their teaching with passion. And plays differ so markedly in the emotions which they express, that these differences are the basis for the oldest and most familiar classification of plays as tragedy, comedy, etc.

Therefore, the director will study intensively the written play in order to draw from the dialogue and the stage directions a vivid picture of the characters, plot, and environment which the playwright has imagined. He will see the characters in terms of the particular actors with whom he must work and their environment in terms of the particular theatre and theatre materials available to him. He will see characters, plot, and environment recreated in a particular theatrical form, carefully designed to express for a particular audience what the playwright thought and felt about life.

Questions

1. What, in your opinion, is the dominant idea in one of the following: Shaw's *Heartbreak House*, Behrman's *The Second Man*, Barry's *Holiday*, Kelly's *Craig's Wife*, Hellman's *The Little Foxes*, Green's *In Abraham's Bosom*, Williams' *The Glass Menagerie*, Saroyan's *My Heart's in the Highlands*, Rice's *Street Scene*, Odets' *Awake and Sing*?
2. What is the dominant mood or emotion of the play you selected for the first question?
3. Name a play in which setting is of little importance. Why? Name a play in which setting is of great importance. Why?
4. Name a play in which sound effects are of great importance. Why?
5. Name a play in which lighting is of great importance. Why?
6. What are four dramatic elements?

Exercises

1. Compare the dialogue of a play by Eugene O'Neill with that of a play by Bernard Shaw, Clifford Odets, or William Saroyan.
2. Compare a passage of verse dialogue from Maxwell Anderson with a passage of verse dialogue from Shakespeare.
3. Compare the stage directions in a play by Bernard Shaw with the stage directions in a play by Ibsen.
4. Compare the stage directions in the acting edition and in the library or reading edition of the same play.
5. Select a well-known modern play and analyze it for (*a*) conflict, (*b*) suspense or tension, (*c*) action, and (*d*) contrast.

Bibliography

Theory

Brunetière, Ferdinand, *The Law of the Drama*, New York: Dramatic Museum of Columbia University, 1914. The original exposition of the "conflict" theory.

Clark, Barrett H., *European Theories of the Drama*, New York: Crown Publishers, rev. ed., 1947. An invaluable reference book on many aspects of dramatic theory.

Egri, Lajos, *The Art of Dramatic Writing*, New York: Simon & Schuster, 1946. The contemporary version of the conflict theory: dramatic dialectic.

Gassner, John, *Producing the Play*, New York: The Dryden Press, 1941.

Gaw, Allison, "Centers of Interest in Drama, Dramatic Tension, and Types of 'Dramatic Conflict,'" *Schelling Anniversary Papers*, New York: The Century Company, 1923.

Hamilton, Clayton, *The Theory of the Theatre*, New York: Henry Holt & Company, Inc., 1939. Contrast and other dramatic elements.

Anthologies of Plays

Chandler, Frank W., and Richard A. Cordell, *Twentieth Century Plays*, New York: Thomas Nelson & Sons, Inc., 1934.

Coe, Kathryn, and William H. Cordell, *The Pulitzer Prize Plays: 1918–1934*, New York: Random House, 1935.

Dickinson, Thomas H., *Chief Contemporary Dramatists*, Series 1, 2, and 3, Boston: Houghton Mifflin Company, 1915, 1921, 1930.

Gassner, John, *Twenty Best Plays of the Modern American Theatre*, Series 1 and 2, New York: Crown Publishers, 1939, 1947.

————, *Twenty-five Best Plays of the Modern American Theatre*, Early Series, New York: Crown Publishers, 1949.

————, *A Treasury of the Theatre (From Henrik Ibsen to Arthur Miller)*, New York: The Dryden Press, 1950 (rev. ed. for colleges).

Moses, Montrose J., *Dramas of Modernism*, Boston: Little, Brown & Company, 1931.

Theatre Guild, *Theatre Guild Anthology*, New York: Random House, 1936.

Tucker, S. Marion, *Twenty-five Modern Plays*, New York: Harper & Brothers, 1931.

Whitman, Charles H., *Representative Modern Dramas*, New York: The Macmillan Company, 1939.

CHAPTER 4.~~~~~~~~~~~~~~~~~~~~~~~~~~~~~~~

STYLE AND THEATRICAL FORM

~~~~~~~~~~~~~~~~~~~~~~~~~~~~~~~~~~~~~

$\mathcal{T}$he playwright, like any other artist, draws his material from life, but he cannot use this material unaltered if he is to express anything. If he is to hold the attention of an audience and succeed in expressing his own ideas and feelings about life, he must select, rearrange, and sometimes transform what he has observed. Plays differ considerably in the degree of transformation the playwright has worked in his materials, and consequently in the closeness with which the characters, action, and environment resemble those of actual life. We shall call these differences differences in *style*. They arise from differences in the playwright's handling of his materials in an effort to express himself under the general conditions of theatre art.

The playwright is affected not only by the general conditions of theatre art, but also by the particular conditions under which theatre art is practiced in his time, by the form which plays are given in production, and especially by the relation between the production and the audience. Consequently, plays differ in what we shall call theatrical *form*.

Differences in style and in theatrical form are both evident in written plays, and should result in corresponding differences in production.

Style: The Play and Life

Since style is perhaps more fundamental than theatrical form, let us consider first the different types of plays which may be distinguished on the basis of the playwright's selection, arrangement, or transformation of his material. First, however, it is necessary to dispel the confusion which often surrounds the use of the term *symbolism* in this connection.

Some writers, in classifying plays on the basis of their resemblance to life, have used the term *symbolism* as the opposite of *realism*. This is likely to be confusing, because it implies that

36

realistic or lifelike plays do not employ symbols. But (as we have seen in Chapter 1) all art is symbolic; expression is possible only through symbols. The words which make up the written play are symbols selected and arranged to express something to the reader; the speech and movement of the actors, the setting, the costumes, and so on are symbols selected and arranged to express something to the audience.

Mrs. Phelps in *The Silver Cord* is no less symbolic than Mr. Zero in *The Adding Machine,* and the sequence of actions through which Mrs. Phelps loses one son and holds the other is no less symbolic than the episodes which chronicle Mr. Zero's suffering, death, and damnation. *Ghosts* is no less symbolic than *Peer Gynt.*

In *Ghosts* Ibsen selected and arranged his symbols not only to express his meaning but also to create an illusion of real life. In *Peer Gynt* he selected and arranged his symbols only to express his meaning. Thus plays differ not according to whether or not they contain symbols, or according to the amount of symbolism they contain, but according to the selection and arrangement of the symbols.

REALISM

The playwright, in selecting and arranging the elements from his experience, may employ symbols in a pattern which closely follows patterns already recognized in life. If he does, his play will be lifelike or *realistic.* In this book, the term *realism* rather than *naturalism* is used to describe all plays which present a pattern resembling life. The term *naturalism* is sometimes used in this sense, but it has been used also to describe plays which present only the most sordid aspects of experience in a lifelike pattern, as for instance *Tobacco Road.* This is classification on the basis of subject matter and is of little significance in play production today. Some examples of realistic plays are Ibsen's *A Doll's House,* Gorki's *The Lower Depths,* Howard's *The Silver Cord,* Kingsley's *Dead End,* Rice's *Street Scene,* Miller's *All My Sons,* and Hellman's *The Little Foxes.*

However, as we have noted in Chapter 1, even the most realistic play is not an exact imitation or reproduction of life. If it were, it could convey no meaning. The playwright has selected, condensed, and arranged his experience of life in patterns which

Richard Redden

A realistic play gives the effect of eavesdropping on real life. This scene from *The Little Foxes,* staged by George Blair for the University of Chicago Theatre illustrates also the onstage focus of all representational drama.

are recognizable as lifelike but which, unlike life itself, are meaningful. The inept playwright may fail here and there to achieve a lifelike pattern, and his work will be criticized as unrealistic. On the other hand, he may use lifelike elements and fail to work them into a meaningful pattern, so that they remain distracting.

The problem of producing the realistic play is similar to the problem of writing it. Just as the playwright must select, condense, and arrange the stuff of life to express his meaning without seeming to do so, so the producer must find patterns of movement and speech, of form, light, color, and sound which express the playwright's meaning and at the same time create an illusion of real life. The unlifelike conventions necessary to play production must be minimized, the realistic elements emphasized. Nevertheless, lifelike elements should not be employed just because they are lifelike; they should be used only if they help to express the play's meaning. Detailed realism for its own sake is either boring or shocking.

ABSTRACTION

In seeking to express his meaning, the playwright may pay little attention to creating an illusion of real life; he may select his symbols and arrange them in patterns which have no very close resemblance to ordinary life, but rather appear generalized or abstract. The Greek tragedies, the medieval morality plays,

Abstraction for comic effect is shown in a scene from the American Repertory Theatre production of *Androcles and the Lion.*

Saroyan's *The Time of Your Life,* Shaw's *Androcles and the Lion,* and Sartre's *The Flies* are examples of plays which are more or less abstract.

The problem of producing the abstract play is to achieve in the acting and in the other elements of production the same kind and degree of abstraction which the playwright has employed. On the whole, because the realistic style dominates our theatre, there is a tendency to produce abstract plays in the realistic style. Shakespeare's tragedies are sometimes provided with realistic stage business, for instance, which is not merely unnecessary but, because it has no relation to the dialogue, is actively distracting.

FANTASY

The playwright may go further; he may select his symbols and arrange them in patterns which obviously depart from the patterns of real life so that his play becomes *fantasy.* Some examples of fantastic plays are: Aristophanes' *The Birds,* Maeterlinck's *The Bluebird,* Ibsen's *Peer Gynt,* Čapek's *The Insect Comedy,* Rice's *The Adding Machine,* Wilder's *The Skin of Our Teeth,* and Giraudoux' *The Madwoman of Chaillot.*

In producing such plays, the problem is to achieve, in a

Fantasy is shown in the troll scene from *Peer Gynt* as produced by the Fordham University Little Theatre. Albert McCleery, director.

theatre strongly conditioned to realistic production, patterns of sound, form, light, and color which depart from those of real life in the same way and to the same degree as does the written play. Habits of actors, production staff, and audience may have to be overcome.

MIXED STYLES

The above classifications, like all others, are not hard and fast. Some plays will not fit easily into any one of them. The borderline between realism and abstraction, and the borderline between abstraction and fantasy are not clearly defined. Strindberg's *The Father,* for all its apparent realism, borders on the abstract, and Saroyan's *The Beautiful People* hovers between abstraction and fantasy. Some plays which are largely realistic contain some fantasy, for instance Barrie's *Dear Brutus* and Wilder's *Our Town.* And some plays which are predominantly fantastic contain some realistic scenes. In fact, a fantasy is frequently provided with a realistic frame; for example, Hauptmann's *Hannele* and Kaufman and Connelly's *Beggar on Horseback.*

The problem in producing such plays of mixed styles is to create in production the different styles, to keep them distinct, and yet to maintain an over-all unity.

Form: The Play and the Theatre

The playwright is necessarily influenced in his selection and arrangement of elements from his experience of life by the materials of play production and by the conditions under which it is practiced in his time. As we have already noted, because the actor is the principal material of play production, playwriting must remain relatively realistic. There are definite limits to the distortion possible in the movement and speech of the actor. This has been true in all times and places.

But the other materials of play production and the conditions under which it is practiced have not been always and everywhere the same. In Sophocles' Greece and in Shakespeare's England a minimum of scenery was used. Consequently, we find that the physical action of their plays depends little on setting (in the sense of realistic environment) and that when setting is important for atmosphere it is described by the characters. Molière's plays provide an example of the influence of theatre conditions on playwriting. His ballet plays, written for production at court where expense was no item, depend heavily on setting, but his comedies written for production in the public theatres, ill-equipped and without royal subsidy, require the minimum of scenery. In the nineteenth century settings were usually painted on sets of wings, borders, and backdrops, quickly and easily shifted by simple machinery with which most theatres were equipped. A play like *Uncle Tom's Cabin,* which calls for twenty-nine changes of setting, could be written only for such a theatre.

The theatre of our own day, as we shall see more particularly in the chapters on setting, is characterized by certain practices in the use of scenery which influence the contemporary playwright. He may conform to the limitations these practices place upon his writing as have the majority, or he may rebel against them (at the risk that his plays may not be produced) and perhaps force them to be changed, as Eugene O'Neill has frequently done.

REPRESENTATION

The physical arrangement of the theatre building is a major factor affecting the writing of plays, and the ordinary theatre of today is arranged to separate the audience from the production. The audience is seated in an auditorium facing the stage where the production takes place. The stage is framed by the proscenium arch, and it can be cut off completely from the auditorium by the front curtain. Even if the stage floor projects somewhat into the auditorium, the custom is to keep the production behind the line of the proscenium arch. Thus it is natural for the playwright to think of his play as separate from the audience, and easy for him to think of it as distinct also from the theatre.

The term *representation* is useful to describe playwriting of this type. The representational play attempts to express its meaning by creating an illusion of life—realistic, abstract, or fantastic—which is being lived behind the proscenium. The audience is permitted to look at this "life" through the transparent fourth wall of the proscenium arch.

Most plays written since about 1860, when this form of production approached its full development, have been representational. Ibsen's *The Wild Duck,* Shaw's *Heartbreak House,* Chekhov's *The Seagull,* and Rice's *Street Scene* are examples of realistic plays which are representational; but Saroyan's abstract *The Time of Your Life,* and Maeterlinck's fantastic *Pelleas and Melisande* are representational also.

The problem of producing the representational play is a relatively simple one. As we have seen, today's theatre is arranged to make representational production easy. Moreover, actors, production workers, and audience all are accustomed to this form of production. The production must be kept behind the proscenium arch, and the actors must not let their legitimate urge to be expressive spread their focus beyond the stage. On the other hand, expression in acting must not be sacrificed to the illusion of reality. The actor must be seen and heard without appearing to be aware of the presence of the audience.

PRESENTATION

Our proscenium arch form of theatre first appeared in Italy in the early Renaissance, but its spread over the continent and eventually to England was slow. As we have noted, it did not reach full flower until the latter half of the nineteenth century. In the theatres which preceded it, there was no marked separation between stage or production place and auditorium or audience place.

In the Greek theatre the major playing space was a circle from three-fifths of whose circumference rose tiers of seats for the audience. In the Roman theatre the spectators sat in a semicircle facing a raised stage, but there was no proscenium arch or front curtain to separate stage from auditorium.[1] Medieval plays were produced on temporary platforms set up in a public square or on a village green, or on wagons drawn by horses to the various places of performance. The audience crowded around at least three sides of these platforms. In Shakespeare's theatre the major playing space extended out into the auditorium, and although there were inner stages which could be shut off with curtains, most of the acting was done on the forestage in the midst of the audience. The Laurence Olivier moving picture *Henry V* gives an excellent idea of the close relation between production and audience in Shakespeare's theatre. See the illustration on page 13.

Plays written for these earlier theatres instead of pretending to ignore the audience take the presence of the audience for granted. They frequently address the audience directly through the characters, and they use the materials of production much more directly for expression than do most plays written for the modern theatre. The term *presentation* is useful to describe this form of written play. Besides the earlier plays, Restoration and eighteenth-century comedy, and nineteenth-century melodrama belong to this category.

The representational form of play and production had hardly become established before the revolt against it began. Strindberg, who had helped to perfect representational drama in plays like *Miss Julia* and *The Father*, turned away from it in *The Dream Play*. The rebellion reached its height after the first World War in a movement called *expressionism*. So-called expressionistic plays such as O'Neill's *The Hairy Ape*, Rice's *The Adding Machine*, and Kaiser's *From Morn to Midnight* are presentational; they recognize the presence of the audience.

These plays differ from the earlier presentational plays such as *Oedipus Rex, Everyman, Hamlet,* and *The School for Scandal*

---

[1] There is some evidence of a curtain which could be dropped into a slot at the front of the stage, but this seems to have been used only to reveal the stage at the beginning of the performance.

Audience focus and painted scenery are shown in the presentational play *Aaron Slick of Punkin Crik* as produced by the Fordham University Little Theatre. Albert McCleery, director.

in their self-consciousness. The earlier playwrights accepted the presence of the audience as a normal condition of play production. O'Neill, Rice, and Kaiser were consciously rebelling against the accepted practice of their day. Consequently, they did not just speak to the audience; they shouted at it. Even a recent presentational play like *The Skin of Our Teeth* shows some of the self-conscious violence typical of expressionism in its heyday.

The problem of producing presentational plays is to create in the production the direct expression which is in the script. Actors and production artists and workers must abandon the habits of the illusionistic form and think in terms of expression. The audience also will need to be educated to accept the conventions of an unfamiliar form.

MIXED FORMS

Of course, some plays are not satisfactorily classified either as representational or as presentational. Particularly in periods of transition a play is likely to contain both representational and presentational elements. Wilder's *Our Town* is a good example of this mixture of theatrical forms. In that play the Stage Manager is wholly presentational: he addresses the audience, explaining the setting, introducing the characters, and so on; he sets up the stage properties; he even acts a character or two in the play proper. There is no scenery; the properties are the properties of a rehearsal. This too is presentational. On the other hand, most of the characters are conceived as separate from the audience, behaving so as to give an illusion of independent life.

The problem in producing such plays is to keep the representational elements distinct from the presentational elements and yet to achieve an over-all unity of production.

Questions

1. Explain and illustrate the statement, "All plays are symbolic."
2. What is meant by *realism* in drama? Illustrate.
3. What is the problem of producing the realistic play?
4. What is meant by *abstraction* in drama? Give an example.
5. What is the problem of producing the abstract play?
6. What is meant by *fantasy* in drama? Give an example.
7. What is the problem of producing the fantastic play?
8. What is meant by the representational form of drama? By the presentational form?
9. State the principal problem of producing the representational play.
10. State the principal problem of producing the presentational play.
11. What is meant by *expressionism* in drama?
12. How does the modern expressionistic drama differ from the older presentational drama?

Exercises

1. Analyze a realistic play, showing how lifelike elements have been selected and arranged by the playwright to convey his meaning.
2. Analyze an abstract play, showing in what ways the playwright has removed his material from everyday life. How might this be expressed in production?
3. Analyze a fantastic play, showing how the playwright has distorted material from life. How might this distortion be realized in production?

4. Analyze a play which combines realism and fantasy (*Dear Brutus, Beggar on Horseback, The Emperor Jones, Our Town, Hannele*), and suggest methods of combining the two styles satisfactorily in production.
5. Compare a representational play and a presentational play, pointing out fundamental differences in the way they were intended to be produced.
6. Analyze an expressionistic play, pointing out its presentational characteristics.

Bibliography

Theory

Bakshy, Alexander, *The Theatre Unbound,* London: Cecil Palmer, 1923. A plea for the presentational form.

Dickinson, Thomas H., *An Outline of Contemporary Drama,* Boston: Houghton Mifflin Company, 1927.

Dickinson, Thomas H. ed., *The Theatre in a Changing Europe,* New York: Henry Holt & Company, Inc., 1934.

Dolman, John, *The Art of Play Production,* New York: Harper & Brothers, rev. ed. 1946. The representational form.

Fülöp-Miller, René and Joseph Gregor, *The Russian Theatre,* Philadelphia: J. B. Lippincott Company, 1930.

Goldberg, Isaac, *The Drama of Transition,* Cincinnati: Stewart Kidd Company, 1922.

Gorelik, Mordecai, *New Theatres for Old,* New York: Samuel French, 1940.

Miller, Anna Irene, *The Independent Theatre in Europe,* New York: Long & Smith, 1927.

Plays

See the anthologies listed in the Bibliography to Chapter 3.

CHAPTER 5.~~~~~~~~~~~~~~~~~~~~~~

MOOD

~~~~~~~~~~~~~~~~~~~~~~~~~~~~~~~~~~~

*P*lays differ so greatly in their emotional content, and consequently in the emotions they arouse in an audience that these differences are the principal basis for the traditional classification of plays into tragedy, serious drama, melodrama, comedy, and farce.

Tragedy

Aristotle said that tragedy arouses in an audience the emotions of pity and fear in such a way as to effect a special purging away and relief of these emotions. *Pity* he defined as what we feel when a man suffers misfortune out of proportion to his faults, and *fear* as what we feel when we see misfortune fall upon a person like ourself.

CATHARSIS

This idea of the proper catharsis of the tragic emotions has long been the subject of dispute. *Pity* and *fear* do not seem entirely adequate terms for the emotions aroused by tragedy, and the notion of *purgation* grows out of a primitive quantitative concept of emotion. However, the tragic effect remains the same, whether we describe it in terms of Aristotle's psychology or of the psychology of our own day. *Tragedy arouses in the spectator the deepest emotions, but it allays them also, so that in the end the spectator is left in a state of exaltation and of calm.*

The exaltation appears to derive either from admiration for the human spirit triumphant over tyrannical or capricious Fate, or else from a renewed belief in the strength and ultimate triumph of the human spirit over its own weakness, folly, and wickedness. The calm comes from an acceptance of the inevitability of the conclusion, which usually requires the physical destruction of the hero. As James Feibleman says, "Tragedy

Here is the great tragedy, *Oedipus Rex,* as produced by the Old Vic Company of London.

affirms the infinite value of the world through the endorsement of the remorseless logic of events."

THE TRAGIC HERO

In the oldest tragedies, the hero with superhuman courage and fortitude wrestles with the gods or with an unjust fate. Such is the character of Prometheus who defies Zeus in the cause of human freedom. The spectacle of such a heroic conflict, if the audience can be made to believe in it, is bound to arouse the deepest emotions, and Prometheus' triumph in defeat leaves the audience in a state of calm exaltation. On a more human plane, Oedipus, if one is content with a logical analysis of his story, appears in hopeless conflict with a malignant fate.

However, *Oedipus Rex* already belongs emotionally to a newer type of tragedy, the type in which the hero suffers triumph and defeat in conflict with his own weakness, folly, or wickedness. The hero of this type of tragedy is a man essentially good and admirable, who incurs misfortune through some shortcom-

ing or error in judgment, the *tragic flaw* or "blindness of heart"
of Aristotle's theory. Sometimes this may be merely a lack of
insight which at critical points in the hero's career leads him
to mistaken action. In *Oedipus Rex* the flaw is the hero's hasty
temper which leads him unwittingly to kill his father. This
temper seems a slight fault, indeed, and of no account when
weighed against the fate which has been laid upon him by the
gods. However, Oedipus accepts his own responsibility without
question and punishes himself horribly.

Shakespeare provides us with examples of this type of tragic
hero in a purer form. Macbeth is destroyed by his own ambition, Othello by his jealousy, and Hamlet by his disillusion.

For the fully tragic effect, this type of tragedy must maintain
a balance between the faults of the hero and the catastrophe
which falls upon him. If he suffers through no fault of his own,
through weakness only, the play is likely to arouse only pity and
indignation. Shakespeare's *Richard II* is an example.

At the other end of the scale is the villain-hero, such as Shakespeare's *Richard III*. He is so bad that he appears wholly un-
sympathetic to the audience, and his destruction seems merely
poetic justice. Neither indignant pity nor a feeling that full
justice has been done is the effect of tragedy.

Some plays depend for their tragic effect upon the interpretation, the emphasis given in production. Macbeth and Hedda
Gabler are dangerously close to being villains. Macbeth can
easily appear a treacherous, cruel, ambitious man, who in the
end receives only his just deserts. For the tragic effect he must
be presented as a brave and essentially good man who is led by
ambition to perform deeds which he knows to be bad. Similarly
Hedda Gabler can very easily appear a woman of evil, alluring
but diabolical, whose suicide is simply poetic justice. Nazimova
played the part that way. But unless Hedda is presented as a
woman of extraordinary charm and will power, which for lack
of a proper sense of values are horribly misdirected, the tragic
effect will not be achieved.

The acceptance on the part of the audience of the catastrophe
in this type of tragedy results from a recognition of the hero's
responsibility for his fate, and the effect of exaltation appears
to come in many instances from the enlightenment of the hero.
The scales fall from his eyes. He sees clearly once more and
shoulders responsibility for the destruction he has brought upon

himself. This is obviously true of Oedipus and of Othello. Hamlet's enlightenment is not so obvious. When he discovers that the queen is dying of the drink that was meant for him and that both he and Laertes are mortally wounded with the poisoned rapier, he shakes off the paralysis which has gripped him and kills the king. Once his duty has been performed, it is as if a cloud lifts from his spirit, and he dies happy. In Lear the change is a growth rather than a sudden enlightenment. Blow after blow is rained upon the head of the old man, and by suffering he is gradually purged of his vanity, pride, and selfishness, and he is left in the end a humble, loving, good-hearted man.

Modern tragedies that reflect scientific knowledge of the importance of heredity and environment in molding the individual have tended to reject the notion that man is responsible even in part for what happens to him. The forces of heredity and environment take the place held by the gods or by Nemesis in the earliest tragedies, and man is represented as oppressed by or rebelling against the forces of heredity and environment, just as the hero of the earliest tragedies was oppressed by or rebelled against the gods or Nemesis. The whole point of many modern tragedies is that the principal characters are victims of forces beyond their control. That is the effect of Maeterlinck's *Pelleas and Melisande,* of Chekhov's *The Cherry Orchard,* and of Odets' *Paradise Lost.* In these plays, the effect of inevitability comes from the magnitude and power of the forces which beset the characters. And the suffering of the characters is not merely pathetic or shocking, because it is represented not as accidental but as the inevitable fate of human beings in an unfriendly or a hostile world.

When the catastrophe is due to such outside forces, no enlightenment of the hero is possible, but if he appears to rise triumphant in spirit over the forces which destroy him physically or economically, the effect of exaltation may be achieved. No such spiritual triumph is vouchsafed the hero and heroine of Maeterlinck's play. However, in *The Cherry Orchard* some of Trophimof's speeches provide a glimpse of a stronger, better generation to come, and in *Paradise Lost* Leo Gordon's final speech expresses hope for a new and better life.

Although most tragedies have an individual hero, or a hero and heroine, there are a number in which the hero is a group— for example, Euripides' *The Trojan Women,* Hauptmann's

The Weavers, and Odets' *Paradise Lost.* What has been said about the individual hero applies to the group hero as well.

UNIVERSALITY

Tragedy always deals with the universal and the fundamentally significant. Consequently the hero of tragedy must appear more than ordinarily important; he must somehow be endowed with universal significance. Sometimes the hero of tragedy is significant because he wields power over his fellow beings. Thus in the older plays the hero is likely to be a king, or prince, or general. Today we may expect to find him a dictator, a revolutionary leader, or an industrial magnate.

However, power is not the only source of this universal significance. The tragic hero may be endowed with more than ordinary courage or capacity for love or for self-sacrifice. Or the playwright may somehow make him seem typical of a society, a class, or of the whole human race.

Sometimes the playwright achieves an effect of universal significance in part by repetition. The fact that in *King Lear* Shakespeare presents two stories, that of Lear and his daughters and that of Gloucester and his sons, both on the theme of filial ingratitude and parental blindness, helps make these traits appear universal. Another type of repetition designed to produce the same effect appears in the use of the group hero. The fact that all the characters in *The Cherry Orchard* are weak-willed or impractical in one way or another goes far to make them appear typical of a whole class and a whole society.

THE GROTESQUE

Some tragedies, particularly the tragedies of Shakespeare, contain scenes which, if considered by themselves, might be called comic. The term *comic relief* frequently applied to such scenes suggests that their function is to offer a brief diversion from the tragic action and to relieve the tension by relaxation in laughter. Some scenes of real *comic relief* may occur in tragedy, but those which are most frequently cited serve quite a different purpose. The drunken porter in *Macbeth,* the gravediggers in *Hamlet,* the jesting Fool in *King Lear* do not divert attention from the tragic action, nor do they relax the tension.

Quite the contrary. The gravediggers are digging a grave for Ophelia, pathetic victim of the play's tragic action, and their rude jokes about death are grim, not laughable. In *Macbeth* the porter's drunken fooling postpones the inevitable discovery of the murder of Duncan, and far from decreasing the tension, increases it. Shakespeare was clearly aware of this for he has the porter imagine he is keeping Hell Gate and that the knocking announces the arrival of more human souls doomed to eternal damnation.

The way in which the juxtaposition of serious and comic elements may be used to intensify the serious emotions is well illustrated by the scene between Lear and the Fool on the heath. Lear is on the verge of madness, and the Fool, terribly aware of his master's plight, strives pitifully with his jokes to stem the rising tide of insanity. No one could laugh at these jokes; they intensify our pity.

This juxtaposition of the comic and the pathetic or the terrible is properly termed the *grotesque,* and the effect of the grotesque is best termed *irony*. Such scenes should be played not for laughs but for the irony, pitiful or terrible, which is their essential characteristic.

REALISM

Tragedies, particularly the old tragedies, are filled with physical suffering, bloodshed, and violent death. Othello smothers Desdemona; Macduff kills Macbeth in single combat; Oedipus tears out his own eyes. Too much emphasis on these elements through extreme realism in production and acting may arouse too much horror. An audience finds relief from extreme horror in hysterical laughter, which is not one of the effects tragedy should arouse.

In producing tragedy, the director is concerned primarily with creating and maintaining by means of acting, setting, light, and the other materials of production a mood in which the serious emotions can arise in the audience. He will seek to present clearly on the stage the action or actions through which the tragic catastrophe is reached. He will see that the admirable characteristics of the hero are emphasized and the blindness which leads him to destruction is suggested. He will see that the grotesque scenes are presented so as to intensify the tragic emotions, and that scenes of horror and physical suffering are not presented with too great realism. He will seek to emphasize, by every possible means, whatever elements the play provides to express in the end the spiritual victory of the hero.

The rhythm of tragedy is on the whole a slow and solemn rhythm, one which increases slowly in intensity until it breaks into violent action, to subside swiftly into a slow and peaceful march at the conclusion. It might be likened to the movement of a leaf, floating gently on the surface of a stream, which is drawn slowly into the orbit of a whirlpool. The leaf revolves first slowly, then faster and faster, until it is sucked into the vortex. Finally it is cast out to float gently down the stream once more.

Serious Drama

Many serious plays, particularly modern serious plays, either do not attempt the tragic effect, or if they do, fail to achieve it. The French call such plays *drames*. In English we have no one word to denote the play which does not achieve the effect of tragedy, and yet which is not comic either. The best we can do is to call such a play a *serious drama*. The term is awkward but it is useful to denote the play which deals seriously with dramatic material, but which fails to achieve the tragic effect, either because it stirs the sentiments rather than the deeper emotions, or because it does not reach a catastrophe, or because it leaves the audience aroused rather than calm, or for some other reason.

O'Neill's *The Iceman Cometh* seems to fail of the tragic effect because of the insignificance of the characters. In *The Wild Duck,* the principal character achieves no spiritual victory. *The Glass Menagerie* stirs our sentiments, not our more profound emotions. Paul Green's *Hymn to the Rising Sun* leaves the audience aroused at the end, indignant against the penal work camps of the South.

In the serious play, the producer will seek to discover the purpose of the play and the theme and mood by which it is expressed and to create them in the theatre with the materials of production. *The Iceman Cometh* aims to show that it is impossible to live without illusion. *The Wild Duck* shows that truth can be destructive. And *The Glass Menagerie* aims to arouse our pity for ordinary people caught and oppressed by circumstances with which they are unfit to cope.

Just as there is great variety in theme and mood in serious plays, so is there great variety also in rhythm. *The Iceman Cometh* has a slow, heavy rhythm like the labored breathing of drunken sleep, punctuated by hysterical nightmare-like outbursts. *The Wild Duck* has a very complex rhythm: the fundamental beat, heavy with catastrophe, is balanced and sometimes obscured by the crisp rhythm of laughter at the follies of men. The total effect is one of profound irony. The rhythm of *The Glass Menagerie* flutters with pathetic hopes, writhes with pain, and sinks with disappointment, but the whole is toned down, muted by memory.

Melodrama

The term *melodrama* is usually applied to plays which have no other purpose than to arouse the maximum of terror and suspense, relaxing the taut nerves of the audience in the end by providing a happy ending, or at least adequate punishment for the evil characters. Boucicault's *The Octoroon;* Mrs. Wood's *East Lynne; The Front Page* by Hecht and MacArthur; and Patrick Hamilton's *Angel Street* are examples of melodrama.

PLOT

The melodrama usually presents a complicated series of incidents chosen to surprise and shock, knit together in such a way as to arouse the maximum of suspense. It does not pretend to be seriously concerned with human character and the problems of life. It necessarily presents human characters involved in the problems of life, but the characters are not fully rounded and the problems are arbitrarily contrived and arbitrarily solved. Both are presented primarily for the sake of the action, which must move rapidly and with many surprises if it is to hold the attention of the audience. Chance and coincidence play a great part in melodrama.

CHARACTER

Some critics of the drama have said that character is paramount in tragedy and plot in melodrama. This is perhaps mis-

Richard Redden

East Lynne produced in appropriately presentational form and in an abstract style which burlesques the melodramatic acting of the nineteenth century. Staged by Albert Hibbs for the University of Chicago Theatre. George Blair, supervising director.

leading, at any rate in regard to tragedy, for character cannot be dramatically presented except through plot or action. The real difference is that the plot or action of tragedy appears to arise inevitably out of fully drawn characters, while the plot of melodrama seems somewhat arbitrarily imposed on characters drawn only fully enough to provide an excuse for the action. The characters of melodrama, consequently, are likely to be types, more or less two-dimensional, and sharply differentiated into good and bad.

POETIC JUSTICE

Since the aim of melodrama is not serious, it is likely to have a happy ending, characterized by *poetic justice;* happiness for the good characters and punishment for the villains. In *The Front Page,* Hildy Johnson eventually wins out in his duel with Walter Burns and goes off with his girl to happiness in the advertising business, but a surprise twist at the end shows that Burns is not yet beaten. In *Angel Street* the heroine is relieved of her suffering, and her villainous husband is headed for the gallows. In *The Octoroon,* the heroine had to die, because audiences would not accept the marriage of a white man and a girl with Negro blood, but Boucicault gave her a beautiful death in compensation.

COMIC RELIEF

As we have noted, suspense plays a very strong part in melodrama, and suspense is difficult to maintain over long periods of time. Consequently one often finds in melodrama real *comic relief*. Scenes of mounting tension and violent action are often separated by relatively unrelated scenes of pure comedy which allow the audience to relax before being harrowed once more. The stupid policeman, the timid sheriff, and the ribald reporters provide such true comic relief in *The Front Page*.

The producer will be mainly concerned in melodrama with the creation and intensification of suspense and with achieving surprise and shock. He must therefore emphasize the plot structure with every means at his command. The main source of suspense lies in the pattern of dramatic situations each of which grows more tense until it reaches a crisis and is resolved in action. Suspense must be built up in each of these situations and surprise achieved in each crisis. In order not to exhaust the audience, the producer will make full use of such scenes of comic relief as the play offers, being sure, however, that when a comic scene is over, the serious mood is at once re-established.

All in all, melodrama requires an effect of speed which may be achieved not so much through a rapid tempo in the acting as through wide variety and sharp changes in tempo. The rhythm of melodrama is a nervous rhythm.

Comedy

It has been said that comedy, like tragedy, deals with universal truths, but that "tragedy affirms the infinite value of the world by endorsing the remorseless logic of events," while comedy criticizes the actual order of events in terms of an ideal or infinite value, of which the actual world constantly falls short. This is

A realistic production of Gogol's comedy *The Inspector-General* by the Dramatic Workshop of the New School, New York. Erwin Piscator, director.

true of some comedies, perhaps of the greatest. In Molière's *Tartuffe,* the hero's pretended piety is weighed against an ideal of real goodness, and Orgon's impetuous love for the pious hypocrite is weighed against a rational mode of behavior expounded by Cleante.

However, authors of comedy are not all equally perceptive of infinite value, and they have frequently used their talents to criticize the new, regardless of its real value, in terms of the old and established, regardless of its defects. Such is very largely the effect of Aristophanes' *The Frogs,* in which Bacchus is made to choose the older dramatist, Aeschylus, rather than the younger and more revolutionary dramatist, Euripides. It is true that W. S. Gilbert poked fun at some of the ways of Victorian England, but in *Patience* he ridiculed Oscar Wilde and W. B. Yeats for cherishing new and unfamiliar values. Today Wilde and Yeats appear to have had a better perception of ideal value than had Gilbert.

What seems to be true is that comedy always expresses some

kind of judgment, and that this judgment is based upon a comparison. A mode of behavior, by comparison direct or implied, is found foolish, stupid, or wicked. It involves people in minor calamities at which we are invited to laugh. A comedy then presents so as to arouse laughter minor calamities arising from the folly, stupidity, or wickedness of human beings. Molière's *The Miser* and Sidney Howard's *The Late Christopher Bean* ridicule greed. Çapek's *Adam the Creator* ridicules pride and conceit, and a number of other human weaknesses as well.

Since comedy depends upon comparison or contrast, incongruity is the principal source of the ridiculous. The incongruity may be between what a character declares himself to be and what he is, for example Tartuffe, or between what he is and what he ought to be, for example Orgon.

The judgment that is required for the creation and appreciation of such incongruity requires the operation of reason, and in contrast to tragedy, which is characterized by faith and intuition, comedy is rational and logical. From the rational point of view, man is never completely adapted to the requirements of life, and consequently he is constantly suffering more or less minor calamities which excite only laughter. He slips on a banana peel; he absent-mindedly puts on his socks inside-out; he tries to make a million dollars and loses his shirt.

In order that one may laugh at suffering and calamity, the emotions must be kept largely in abeyance. It seems to be true also that in order to laugh, there must be created a playful attitude, a feeling of fun, and this is characteristic to a greater or less degree of all comedies.

TYPES OF COMEDY

Comedy in its purest form ridicules the folly, stupidity, and vice of men, but it does so without animus, in a spirit of acceptance surprisingly like that to be found in tragedy. The comic spirit recognizes that men will continue to be foolish, stupid, and vicious regardless of the dictates of reason.

Satire. However, all comedy is not without animus. An author may hate the defects he sees in men, and this hatred may appear in his writing. He may make his characters so monstrous

A scene of grotesque comedy is shown when Tiger Brown brings Mackie the Knife some final consolation in *Three-Penny Opera* by Bertolt Brecht and Kurt Weill, Illini Theatre Guild, University of Illinois. Charles Shattuck, director.

that we can no longer laugh at them with entire freedom. The term *satire* is frequently used to describe comedy which has this undertone of seriousness. Jonson's *Volpone* and Gay's *The Beggar's Opera* are examples. In the field of the novel, Aldous Huxley's *Antic Hay* and *Point Counterpoint* are good examples. The author ridicules his characters not with tolerant amusemen but with acid contempt and disgust.

Humor. At the other end of the comic scale, the attitude of rational criticism is diluted with sentiment and affection. The author sees the faults of men and women, and he laughs at them, but their importance is minimized. The sharp edge of criticism is blunted by affection or pity. The term *humor* is usually applied to this type of comedy.

Falstaff in the *Henry* plays is lazy, gluttonous, drunken, cowardly, and boastful, and yet he is so presented that although we laugh at him we do not condemn him. Indeed, like Prince Hal, we become fond of him. *Ah! Wilderness* is a comedy of humor. We laugh at Richard Miller's adolescent struggles with love and sex and at the painful efforts of his father to set him straight, but we feel that the faults of the characters are unimportant; they are so presented as to arouse our sympathy.

CHARACTER AND PLOT

In comedy, as in tragedy, plot springs inevitably out of the characters, and it is important not for itself but as an expression of the characters and of the theme of the play.

REALISM

It is frequently said that comedy is more realistic than tragedy. In one sense this is true, for comedy deals more with the surface customs and conventions of everyday living than does tragedy. Moreover, comedy frequently ridicules pretentious spirituality and empty idealism by contrasting them with ordinary animal activities like eating and drinking. Hjalmar Ekdal spouts windily of ideals and the need for truth—with his mouth full of bread and butter. There is little eating and drinking in tragedies.

Nevertheless, comedy has its own kind of conventionalization. The comedy of humor is the most realistic, because it maintains in the characters a balance between defect and merit, between vice and virtue. In pure comedy, the characters are so conventionalized that we are able to laugh at them in tolerant amusement, neither sympathizing with them in their misfortunes nor condemning them for their vices. In satire, the conventionalization is most marked. Each character is likely to be the mere embodiment of a single folly, weakness, or vice, which is represented with extreme exaggeration.

SURPRISE

We have noted that inevitability is a major characteristic of tragedy. Surprise on the other hand is a principal characteristic of comedy. A character expects one thing and is confronted with its opposite. The audience expects the entrance of one character and is given the entrance of another. In *Twelfth Night,* Aguecheek is persuaded to fight the timorous "Cesario" and is soundly beaten by Sebastian. In *Adam the Creator,* Adam, out of patience with God's bungled job, creates the ideal man and woman—and they scorn him. In *The Doctor in Spite of Himself,* Geronte is anxious to have his daughter cured of her dumbness. She is cured—and at once overwhelms him with such a torrent of rebellious speech that he pleads with the doctor to make her dumb again. Repetition, which in tragedy is a means of emphasis and a source of the feeling of inevitability, is used frequently in comedy to arouse laughter through surprise. It is a favorite device of Molière. The master beats the servant, and is in turn beaten by someone who takes him for a servant.

In pure comedy, the producer will seek to present the characters fully and to make the action flow logically from them, while exploiting the element of surprise to the full. He will see that the characters and action are presented in a spirit of fun so that the audience is free to laugh. In life, vicious, stupid, or foolish people are a danger, a care, or an irritation to people who must deal with them. Weakness and vice on the stage must not appear to injure innocent persons. We must feel that in the end they injure only themselves or those who through equal folly deserve it. The talkative bore is not amusing off the stage—he is a pest. On the stage he can be the cause of hearty laughter if the audience is not forced to sympathize with his victim. If comedy is acted too realistically in this respect, the comic mood is lost. The play becomes a serious drama, a problem play. The rhythm of pure comedy is that of a light-hearted, high-spirited romp.

In satirical comedy, the characters and the action are more

Alfred J. Balcombe

Exaggeration for comic effect is shown in a scene from *The Imaginary Invalid,* Dramatic Workshop of the New School, New York. Erwin Piscator, director.

conventionalized so that greater exaggeration in acting and staging is likely to be required. The rhythm of satirical comedy is heavier than that of pure comedy, energetic, even violent, rather than gay.

The comedy of humor requires the most realism in acting and

production. The rhythm is slower, gentler; it is the rhythm of pleasant remembrance rather than that of direct perception.

These categories, of course, are not at all hard and fast. Elements of pure comedy, satire, and humor frequently appear in the same play.

Farce

The boundary between *comedy* and *farce* is not clearly defined. *The Importance of Being Earnest,* for example, is sometimes classified as comedy, sometimes as farce. Farce, like comedy, is primarily designed to arouse laughter through the presentation of minor human calamities, but whereas in comedy these calamities arise naturally out of the folly, stupidity, or vice of the characters, in farce they seem to be more or less arbitrarily imposed on the characters. Accident and coincidence play a greater part in farce than in comedy.

The characters of farce are more simplified than those of comedy, the situations more unusual, the action more startling, and the plot more complex. Farce is characterized, too, by many physical misfortunes. Beatings, falls, and so on, typical of farce are known as *slapstick*.

Shakespeare's *Comedy of Errors,* Molière's *The Doctor in Spite of Himself,* Kesselring's *Arsenic and Old Lace,* Kaufman's *You Can't Take It With You,* and Coward's *Blithe Spirit* are plays usually classified as farces. Aristophanes' satirical comedies have many farcical characteristics.

REALISM

Farce, like comedy, can be destroyed by excessive realism in the acting. The characters of farce are even more conventionalized than those of comedy, and unless this conventionalization is realized in the acting, they are likely to appear disagreeable rather than amusing. The shrewish, domineering, sharp-tongued woman, for example, appears in many farces. She is Jeanette in *The Doctor in Spite of Himself* and Kate in *The Taming of the Shrew*. If she is represented as a shrew usually appears in life: a mean, bitter, neurotic woman who takes malicious pleasure in dominating and tormenting others, one feels sorry for her victims, and the play is tiresome. On the other hand, if she is represented as a vital, strong-minded, high-spirited woman who enjoys a battle with her equals, or who assumes that everyone will do what she tells them without protest, she can be highly amusing.

SLAPSTICK

The physical violence of farce is not intended to give an effect of real suffering and so raise implications of sadism or masochism. The playwright sometimes takes special pains to indicate this. In *The Doctor in Spite of Himself,* Valère and Lucas beat Sganarelle until he admits that he is a doctor, but they do this only as a last resort and with the greatest reluctance, when he stubbornly (as they think) persists in declaring that he is not a doctor.

PLOT

Although an extravagant plot is sometimes embellished with witty lines, as in *The Importance of Being Earnest,* plot, however absurd, is never unimportant in farce. The plot must be projected, if the witty lines are to be as amusing as they can be. Just as in life the spontaneous pun or epigram is more amusing than one dragged in by main force, so on the stage wit is doubly amusing if it grows out of situation and action.

CHARACTER

Although farce is by definition a play of plot rather than of character, few farces are entirely lacking in some elements of comic characterization. The more the action seems to spring from the characters, the more entertaining it will be. For instance, in *Blithe Spirit* the plot is to a large extent arbitrarily imposed upon the characters, particularly upon Charles and Ruth, but there are indications in Charles of an egotism, which if realized in the acting, makes his reactions to the situations infinitely funnier.

The producer of farce will be concerned with creating and maintaining the effect of good humor, high spirits, and boundless energy without which farce becomes extremely dull. He will seek to achieve in the acting a proper conventionalization which will keep the characters and the action on a plane where they can arouse laughter. In many plays he will need to invent farci- cal *business* appropriate to the dialogue and to the plot. He will use all the materials of production to create a robust, lively rhythm through marked changes in tempo, volume, pitch, and quality in the acting; through sharp contrast and brilliant colors in setting and costume; and through high illumination.

Questions

1. What is meant by the *tragic catharsis?*
2. What are three types of the tragic hero?
3. What is meant by the *tragic flaw?*
4. What is Lear's tragic flaw?
5. What is meant by *poetic justice* in drama? How does it differ from the tragic conclusion?
6. What are some of the sources of the effect of universality in tragedy?
7. Distinguish between the *grotesque* and *comic relief.*
8. What are some of the problems of producing tragedy?
9. What is meant by the term *serious drama?*
10. What is a *melodrama?*
11. What is the relation of character to plot in tragedy? In melo- drama?
12. What is comedy?
13. What is meant by the statement, "Comedy is rational; tragedy is intuitive"?
14. Differentiate between pure comedy, satire, and humor.
15. Briefly discuss "realism in comedy."
16. Describe some of the problems in the production of comedy.
17. What is farce?
18. What is the relation between character and plot in farce?

Exercises

1. Analyze a tragedy on the basis of the material in this chapter, pointing out the sources of its tragic effect.
2. Analyze a tragedy on the basis of Aristotle's discussion in the *Poetics.*
3. Analyze a serious drama, showing why it does not create the tragic effect.
4. Analyze an example of melodrama for suspense and surprise.
5. Describe the sources of laughter in a particular comedy.

6. Analyze a comedy for elements of satire and humor.
7. Analyze a comedy for its use of *surprise*.
8. Analyze an example of farce.

Bibliography

Theory

Anderson, Maxwell, *The Essence of Tragedy,* Washington, D. C.: Anderson House, 1939.

Bradley, A. C., *Shakespearian Tragedy,* London: The Macmillan Company, rev. ed. 1932.

Bergson, Henri, *Laughter,* tr. by Cloudesley Brereton and Frederick Rothwell, London: The Macmillan Company, 1911.

Clark, Barrett H., *European Theories of the Drama,* New York: Crown Publishers, rev. ed. 1947.

Cooper, Lane, *Aristotle on the Art of Poetry,* New York: Harcourt, Brace & Company, 1913.

Feibleman, James, *In Praise of Comedy,* New York: The Macmillan Company, 1939. Summarizes and criticizes the various theories

Nicoll, Allardyce, *The Theory of Drama,* London: George G. Harrap & Company, Ltd., 1931. Useful survey.

Thompson, Alan Reynolds, *The Anatomy of Drama,* Berkeley: University of California Press, 1946. Interesting analysis.

Plays

See anthologies listed in Bibliography to Chapter 3.

CHAPTER 6. ~~~~~~~~~~~~~~~~~~~~~~

STRUCTURE

$\mathcal{E}$very play has a dramatic structure, a skeleton which gives it fundamental form and unity. This structure should be discernible in the written play, and it must be realized in production. If this skeleton is not translated into theatre terms, the play will not stand up on the stage. It will appear dull and uninteresting, or confused and meaningless. However, the skeleton is not the same in every play. Plays differ in structure just as they differ in resemblance to life, in theatre form, and in emotion. The director must be able to recognize these differences in structure, if he is to realize them in production.

Logical Structure

A great many plays have a logical structure; that is, a skeleton of situations and actions related by cause and effect. The logically constructed play begins with a dramatic situation, a situation which is unstable, in which the relation between the characters or between the characters and their environment is strained. This situation grows more and more strained, more and more unstable, until the tension finds relief in action. Action results in a new situation, usually one more unstable than the first. Once more tension grows until it again finds relief in action.

This pattern of unstable situation leading to action is repeated, with on the whole increasing tension, until an action occurs which results in a stable situation.

CLIMAX AND CRISIS

The series of steps by which the logically constructed play develops from the opening situation to the point of highest tension is often called the *climax* or *rising action,* an appropriate term because it comes from the Greek meaning *stairway* or *ladder.*

Richard Redden

This is a scene from *Ghosts,* one of the greatest of the logically constructed plays, as staged by Caroline Rose and Christian Rohlfing for the University of Chicago Theatre. George Blair, supervising director.

The point of greatest tension, the peak of the rising action, is called the *crisis.* In a serious illness doctors speak of the crisis, the turning point in the body's struggle with disease, the point at which the balance is even between life and death. In a play

too, the crisis is the turning point, the point of maximum conflict, of highest tension, which must result in decisive action.

Moreover, each situation in the rising action has its own structure of increasing tension leading to minor crisis.

DENOUEMENT AND FALLING ACTION

The decisive action or series of actions which spring from the
play's crisis are called the *denouement,* literally the *untieing* or
resolution. Sometimes, particularly in the well-written one-act
play, the denouement is simple, resulting quickly in a stable situation on which the curtain can come down.

In long plays the decisive action is likely to be complex, reaching a stable situation in easy stages. In *Hamlet* the principal
situation is resolved when Hamlet stabs Claudius. He has performed his duty; he has avenged his father's murder. But the
queen, though poisoned, has yet to die. Laertes wishes to join
Hamlet in death and must be persuaded to live on that Hamlet's
story may be told. Denmark must not be left without a ruler;
Hamlet has to name the new king before he can die and complete stability be reached. Thus we have a complex denouement
which constitutes a falling action, reversing in brief the rising
action of the climax. With each step in the falling action a remainder of the tension generated in the rising action is dissipated.

Logically constructed plays are found in every period; Sophocles' *Oedipus Rex,* Shakespeare's *Macbeth,* Molière's *The
Miser,* Sheridan's *The School for Scandal,* Ibsen's *A Doll's
House,* Howard's *The Silver Cord,* Hellman's *The Watch on
the Rhine,* and Miller's *All My Sons* are examples.

ACT DIVISIONS

Most logically constructed plays are divided into acts and are
likely to have a secondary structure based on the act divisions.
That is, in a three-act play, the first act will have its own climax
and major crisis, the second act a climax which builds to a
higher point of tension to reach a crisis, and the play's highest
point of tension will be the crisis near the end of the third act.
The older five-act form (this does not include Shakespeare's
plays) is likely to have only a very mild crisis in the first act and

the major crisis at the end of the fourth act, with a short fifth act devoted to the falling action.

THE "SCENE"

The basic structural unit of the logically constructed play is the *scene*, in the acting sense. We have noted that the logically constructed play is made up of a chain of dramatic situations linked together by their resultant actions. Regardless of whether or not the curtain falls or the place changes, each one of these situations with its climax and crisis is a *scene*. French plays recognize this to an extent by indicating a new scene each time an important character enters or exits, for such an entrance or exit nearly always marks the end of one such structural unit and the beginning of another. Of course, analysis on the basis of entrances and exits may be incomplete; more than one *scene* in this structural sense may be developed without the entrance or exit of a major character.

POINT OF ATTACK

As we have seen, the logically constructed play presents a logically connected sequence of events. The whole sequence constitutes a *story*. However, because of the time limits of the play form, the playwright usually does not begin his play at the beginning of the story.

Late. The most tightly constructed plays have a *late* point of attack; that is, they begin late in the story's sequence of events, close in time to the major crisis. Such plays present only the events immediately leading up to the major crisis. The audience is informed by other means of events which occurred before the play begins. Such plays are likely to be written in few settings with few characters and are likely to engender a strong sense of inevitability and to create a powerful effect.

Oedipus Rex is the classical example of the late point of attack. The story of the play goes back to before the hero's birth, but the play does not begin until Oedipus is a mature man, married, and a king. In *Ghosts,* the modern counterpart of *Oedipus,* the story begins in the early days of Mrs. Alving's marriage, but

the play does not begin until her husband is dead and her son
a grown man.

Medium. Few plays have such a late point of attack as that of
Oedipus and *Ghosts.* The story of Sidney Howard's *They Knew
What They Wanted* begins when Tony sends Joe's picture instead of his own to Amy, the bride he is wooing by mail. The
major crisis is Tony's discovery that Amy's son is not his. The
play does not begin near the turning point, nor yet at the beginning, but somewhere in between, when preparations are being
made for Amy's arrival.

Hamlet begins not with the death of Hamlet's father, which
is the beginning of the story, nor yet with Hamlet's unexpected
return from England, which is the beginning of the major climax, but somewhere in between, after Gertrude has married
Claudius.

Early. Shakespeare's point of attack is sometimes very early.
In *King Lear* the beginning of the play coincides with the beginning of the story—Lear's division of his kingdom. In *Romeo
and Juliet* Shakespeare begins with events which, although they
contribute to our understanding of the story, are not part of the
story itself. The street fight between the followers of the house
of Montague and the followers of the house of Capulet shows us
vividly the enmity between the two families, and the Duke's
decree creates a condition which is to affect the story, but the
story itself does not begin until Romeo and Juliet meet. Likewise, the dramatic first act of *Othello,* although it reveals much
that we need to know about Iago, Othello, and Desdemona, is
not a part of the story. The story begins not in Venice but in
Cyprus when Iago begins to stir up in Othello suspicion of
Desdemona.

An early point of attack sometimes results in a play with two
major crises. *Macbeth* is an example; the first crisis comes at the
end of Act II with the murder of Duncan, the second at the end
of Act V with the death of Macbeth. *Julius Caesar* also has two
major crises, the first early in Act III with the assassination of
Caesar and the outbreak of civil war, the second at the end of
Act V with the defeat of the armies of Cassius and Brutus.

Plays with a very early point of attack almost inevitably require many lapses of time and changes of place, and consequently are likely to be constructed on the basis of the scene instead of on the basis of the act. This is particularly true of plays written for performance without intermission. The act divisions in Shakespeare's plays are believed to be the additions of editors after Shakespeare's death. Study of his plays indicates that the scene is the unit of construction and that an unbroken flow of action from scene to scene with contrast and repetition of mood through the entire play is what Shakespeare intended, rather than an action broken into three, four, or five distinct parts.

The play with an early point of attack is likely to have much greater variety but to be less concentrated in its total effect than the play which begins close to the major crisis.

EXPOSITION

Whenever the play's point of attack is later than the beginning of the story, the preceding events must be explained to the audience, and the later the point of attack the more there is to be explained. Sometimes events essential to the story occur during the time of the play, but *offstage,* and so have to be reported to the audience. The presentation of such essential information is called *exposition.* When a play begins before the story, the antecedent events presented likewise have the effect of exposition.

Direct narration. The logically constructed play requires the most exposition at the beginning. A good many of the older plays achieve some of the necessary exposition by direct narration. Thus at the beginning of *Romeo and Juliet* an actor addresses the audience,

> Two households, both alike in dignity,
> In fair Verona, where we lay our scene,
> From ancient grudge break to new mutiny,
> Where civil war makes civil hands unclean.
> From forth the fatal loins of these two foes
> A pair of star-crossed lovers take their life;
>
> .   .   .   .

The School for Scandal has a Prologue, which begins,

> A School for Scandal! Tell me, I beseech you,
> Needs there a school this modish art to teach you?

and goes on to cue the audience to the mood and central theme of the play. The direct narrative method of exposition fell into disuse, partly because of the adoption of printed programs and partly because of the rise of the representational form of writing and production. However, it is still used occasionally, in *The Glass Menagerie,* for example, which begins with Tom address-ing the audience. He explains who the characters are, the time and place of the action, the mood and form of the play.

Dialogue. In many plays, similar information is conveyed by dialogue between the characters, and frequently this dialogue is no more an integral part of the story than is the Prologue to *Romeo and Juliet.* The first scene of *Twelfth Night* is an ex-ample of this. Nothing happens in this scene, except that we learn that the Duke is in love with Olivia and that she will not receive his suit because she is in mourning for her brother. George Kelly's *Craig's Wife* begins with such an expository scene of static dialogue. Usually the playwright attempts to give to such dialogue some dramatic tension by making one of the characters very eager to find out what the audience must know or by building up a little conflict between two characters which results in airing the necessary information.

Action. "Actions speak louder than words" is an old adage that is especially true on the stage. Consequently we find in plays which begin before the beginning of the story that much of the introductory material is presented in action rather than in static dialogue. *Romeo and Juliet* provides a good example of this exposition in action. The first scene shows us the Capulets and the Montagues in physical conflict. Followers of the warring houses meet on the street, exchange insults, then blows, and in a twinkling we are watching a violent street fight, which is halted only by the arrival of the Duke who decrees,

> If ever you disturb our streets again,
> Your lives shall pay the forfeit of the peace.

The whole first act of *Othello* is devoted to Iago's rousing of Brabantio against Othello and to the trial before the Senate—actions which are entirely expository in relation to the main story of the play.

Integration. A few playwrights have been able to integrate earlier events so completely with the events presented in their plays that it is possible to distinguish little or no opening exposition distinct from the development of the action itself. In *Oedipus Rex,* for example, after a very brief expository action in which the citizens of plague-stricken Thebes pray for relief, Oedipus begins an investigation into the murder of his predecessor. As each fact is dug out of the past, it causes him to fear that he is himself the criminal—or to hope that he is not. Thus the disclosure of the past creates the climax and the crisis in the present. This is almost equally true of Ibsen's *Ghosts.* Each of the characters is ignorant of much that happened before the play opened, and as the past is gradually revealed to them they react in various ways to produce the pattern of climax and crisis that is the action of the play.

Not all the exposition comes at the beginning of a play. Unless the action is continuous in time, there will be more exposition at the beginning of each act. The audience must be informed of any essential action that has occurred between acts or scenes or offstage. However, unless there is a long time-lapse, as between Act III and Act IV in *The Winter's Tale,* the amount of this essential information is likely to be less and to be handled by the playwright in a more dynamic fashion. Once the dramatic action is under way, the playwright finds it easier to integrate essential information with the development of that action.

In producing the logically constructed play the producer will be concerned with realizing on the stage through all the materials of production, but especially through the acting, the logical structure of dramatic situation mounting in tension to crisis and action and a new dramatic situation, until the major crisis is reached and the tension is relaxed in the denouement. The over-all structure of the play can be realized only if the structure of each scene and its relation to the next are fully presented. The play with the late point of attack presents the fewest difficulties, but the producer must be sure that the revelations of the past have their full impact on the characters. Unless the dynamic quality of these revelations is fully realized, the play will not come to life. The rhythm of this type of play is like that of a symphony, which increases in speed and intensity until the major crisis is reached, when it returns rapidly to peaceful progress.

The early point of attack presents greater problems. The logical connection between one scene and another will not be so obvious, and greater care will be needed to realize this, particularly in the acting. It is especially important that the opening exposition be presented so that the audience grasps all the essential information, and that the lapses in time from act to act and from scene to scene are bridged as firmly as possible. In plays like *Macbeth* and *Julius Caesar* particular pains will be required if the second major crisis is not to appear anticlimactic, less exciting than the first. Plays of this type are more varied in rhythm and will be realized in the theatre through greater variety in tempo, volume, quality, and pitch in the acting and greater variety in color, form, and light in setting and costume.

Episodic Structure

Some plays present a sequence of dramatic situations and actions which do not have a logical, causal relationship. One does not lead inevitably to the next, and the whole does not form a causally connected sequence expressing the playwright's meaning.

Some such plays, to be sure, have a simple framework of causally connected actions to which the body of episodes is attached. Aristophanes' *The Frogs* is an example: Bacchus, dissatisfied with the state of tragedy in Athens, visits the underworld to bring back Euripides, but because Euripides is bested in poetic contest by Aeschylus, he brings back Aeschylus instead. However, the framework is simple, and the episodes are selected not because one leads logically to the next, but because each is amusing and holds up to ridicule certain aspects of Athenian life.

In *The Cherry Orchard,* we learn at the beginning that the Ranevsky estate, against the wishes of the family, is to be sold. At the end it is sold without a single attempt being made to prevent the sale. The whole point of the play is that the characters are incapable of such an attempt, and the episodes which fill out the simple framework are selected not because one leads to another, but because each illustrates in some fashion the weakness of the characters.

Alfred J. Balcombe

Chorus of Old Men in *Lysistrata*, episodic comedy by Aristophanes, as produced by the Dramatic Workshop of the New School, New York. Erwin Piscator, director.

Some episodic plays deal primarily with the life of a single character, for example *Richard III* and *Victoria Regina*, but as Aristotle long ago pointed out this gives only a superficial unity.

Since concentration on a single character is inadequate, and since in the episodic play the causal relation between events is too weak to provide a firm skeleton, we must look elsewhere for sources of unity.

SOURCES OF UNITY

Unity in the episodic play is to be found in the way the playwright has selected and arranged his material and in the particular emphasis he has given to certain dramatic elements.

Intensification. Although this type of play lacks a causally connected plot, it frequently displays a pattern of gradual intensification which constitutes a kind of *climax,* not unlike the climax of a logically constructed play, and which contributes to an effect of unity. In *The Cherry Orchard* as we learn more and more about the characters, their pathos increases, until it reaches its maximum with the departure of the family and the locking up of the house. *The Lower Depths* begins with small examples of man's inhumanity to man and progresses through more and more violent examples to the fight between Wassilissa and Natasha and the suicide of the Actor. *From Morn to Midnight* begins with the Cashier's revolt on a small scale and ends with the massive scene in the Salvation Army hall.

Idea. The theme or idea, which is the end product of the logically constructed play, is often a principal source of unity in the episodic play. Each apparently unrelated episode is selected because it illustrates some aspect of the central theme. *The Lower Depths,* which at first reading may seem a chaotic representation of life in a Russian flophouse, takes on form when one discovers that each incident, little as well as big, illustrates one half or the other of Gorki's thesis: treat men like animals and they will snarl and bite you; treat them like human beings and they will behave well. Most of Saroyan's plays are held together very largely by the idea that all men yearn for love or for beauty or for both.

Mood. Atmosphere or mood is another common source of unity in the episodic play. The mood of warm and loving pity which pervades most of Chekhov's plays is a major source of unity, just as the mood of seething violence is a source of unity in *From Morn to Midnight.*

Contrast. On the other hand, in some episodic plays *contrast,* achieved through a pattern of alternating moods, may be a source of unity. *I Remember Mama* tends to alternate pathetic and humorous incidents.

Repetition. Another common source of unity in the episodic play is *repetition.* Any such play in which the episodes are chosen to illustrate a theme uses repetition in a subtle form. In

From Morn to Midnight the Cashier breaks the bonds of his cashier's cage by stealing some money. Thereafter he seeks complete freedom: first in the home, where the chains of domesticity are heavy; then at the races, where apparently unbridled emotion yet bows to authority; then in the night club, where the dancer turns out to have a wooden leg; and finally at the Salvation Army hall, where religion proves a slave to money, and where death fastens on him the final, unbreakable bonds.

Repetition is much more obviously a source of unity in Thornton Wilder's episodic one-act play *The Long Christmas Dinner*. The play represents, through an uninterrupted Christmas dinner, ninety years in the life of a household. Characters enter the household, and die, or go away. The births and deaths, the arrivals and departures provide repetition in the major actions, and the business of eating, drinking, and serving provides repetition in the minor actions. The lines about Christmas, dinner, the weather, and so on, many of which are repeated word for word, provide a real continuity.

EXPOSITION

Because the episodic play does not tell a complex story, it seldom has any extensive passage of exposition such as the logically constructed play is likely to exhibit. Instead, each incident or episode is likely to have its own brief bit of exposition, presented through direct narration (as in *Our Town* by the Stage Manager), through static dialogue, or through action. Since the amount of exposition to be presented at any one time is small, it does not present a particular problem. However, its importance to the scene must be felt by the actors.

Most episodic plays are characterized by great variety, if not of place and of character, then of action, and consequently the principal problem in producing them is to find the sources of unity in intensification, theme, mood, contrast, and repetition, and to realize these fully by means of all the materials of production. Variety is the great value of the episodic play, but there must be unity also.

Episodic plays vary greatly in rhythm—depending largely on their mood and theme.

Rhythm

We have made some generalizations about rhythm in connection with the classification of plays according to mood and to structure, but the phenomenon now requires more detailed discussion. Not only does rhythm appear in the dialogue and in the action, in the individual character and in the group, in the scene and in the act, but it seems to be composed of idea, mood, climax, crisis, repetition, and contrast, and to constitute the play's characteristic structure.

IN DIALOGUE

Rhythm is perhaps most easily recognized in the dialogue. Compare the dialogue of *Romeo and Juliet* with the dialogue of *Pelleas and Melisande*. When Romeo in the Capulet orchard sees Juliet appear at the window he says,

> But soft! What light through yonder window breaks?
> It is the east and Juliet is the sun.
> Arise, fair sun, and kill the envious moon,
> Who is already sick and pale with grief,
> That thou her maid art far more fair than she.

When Pelleas looks up and sees Melisande combing her hair at one of the windows of the castle, he says,

> What art thou doing here at the window, singing
> like a bird that is not native here?

Melisande replies:

> I am doing my hair for the night . . .

And Pelleas says:

> Is it that I see upon the wall? . . . I thought
> you had some light.

Both of these plays are about fatal love, but the vigorous leaping rhythm of Romeo's speech is appropriate to this tragedy of unbridled hate and impetuous, youthful love, while the melancholy rhythm of the speech of Pelleas and Melisande is appropriate to their tragedy of fatality, in which the pale lovers flutter weakly in the overwhelming current which sweeps them to their doom.

Compare the dialogue of *From Morn to Midnight* with the dialogue of *Our Town:*

> CASHIER. . . . Frost and damp breed chills.
> Before you know it you've got a fever
> and that weakens the will—a man loses
> control of his actions if he's in bed
> sick. He's easily tracked. (Throws
> cuffs to the ground) Lie There! You'll be
> missed in the wash! Lamentations fill
> the kitchen! A pair of cuffs is missing!
> A castastrophe in the tubs! Chaos! . . .[1]

and

> STAGE MANAGER:
> Three years have gone by.
> Yes, the sun's come up over a thousand times.
> Summers and winters have cracked the mountains a little
> bit more and the rains have brought down some of the dirt
> Some babies that weren't even born before have begun
> talking regular sentences already; . . .[2]

The staccato, machine-like rhythm of the former expresses the anarchy and feverish pursuit of freedom which is the theme of Kaiser's play. The quiet, cheerful rhythm of the latter expresses the acceptance and appreciation of ordinary life which is the theme of Wilder's play.

IN ACTION

In *Romeo and Juliet,* the leaping rhythm of the dialogue is characteristic also of the action. Before the curtain has been up five minutes a violent street fight has broken out between the Montagues and the Capulets. In the very next scene Romeo and Benvolio resolve to crash a party at the home of their archenemies, the Capulets. At the party, Romeo, who has come in search of his beloved Rosaline, sees Juliet and instantly falls head over

[1] From Scene III of *From Morn to Midnight,* a Play in Seven Scenes by Georg Kaiser, translated by Ashley Dukes. Copyright 1922, 1933, by Coward-McCann, Inc.

[2] From *Our Town,* a Play by Thornton Wilder. Copyright 1938 by Coward-McCann, Inc. No performance of any kind whatsoever may be given without permission in writing from Samuel French, Inc., 25 West 45th Street, New York 19.

heels in love with her, and she with him. Then, instead of going safely home, Romeo climbs the wall of the Capulet garden, and the lovers not only plight their troth but plan to be married. And so it goes—the secret marriage, the fight provoked by Tybalt, Mercutio killed by Tybalt, Tybalt killed by Romeo, the decree of banishment—on to the final catastrophe. Not only the young, not only Romeo, Juliet, Tybalt, and Mercutio act impetuously. Old Capulet rushes his daughter into marriage with Paris, and Friar Lawrence, although he counsels prudence ("Wisely and slow: they stumble that run fast"), assists the lovers in the most imprudent fashion.

Thus, from the beginning, the play presents spurts of action which grow more violent as it goes on. The spurts are punctuated and set off in the early part of the play by interludes of comedy or displays of wit and fancy. Later the interludes take the form of obstacles to action, so the rhythm is like that of a torrent plunging down a rocky canyon which is halted momentarily by a makeshift dam. The waters pile against the obstacle until they burst over and through it, plunging on once more with redoubled force.

Totally different is the rhythm of Maeterlinck's *The Intruder.* A group of people, including an old, blind man, are seated in a dimly lighted room waiting for a visit from a relative. It is night, and all is still. The little movements, the words which are spoken fall like tiny pebbles in a deep, dark pool. They make little sound, but they send out ripples that widen, dimly seen on the surface of the water. Out of this slow, halting rhythm grows a feeling of extraordinary expectancy heavy with vague dread. An infant screams offstage. A nurse opens the door and announces that the child's mother is dead. Not the relative but death has paid a visit.

IN PRODUCTION

Each line of dialogue, of course, has its own rhythm, as well as its place in the rhythmic structure of the whole play. And every movement has its own rhythm. Every character has a rhythm of his own, which expresses his personality and meaning and plays a major part in the structure of the whole. Each scene has its own rhythm built up out of the repetition and variation of action, and out of the introduction, intensification, and dying away of emotion. It is the orchestration of the rhythms of the characters, the dialogue, the action, and their variations in the different scenes which provides the rhythmic structure of the play as a whole. A good production will re-create this rhythm in the materials of the theatre.

Questions

1. What is the unifying principle of the logically constructed play?
2. What is a "dramatic situation"?
3. What is the major crisis in *Othello?*
4. Distinguish between *climax* and *crisis.*
5. What is the *denouement?* Give an example.
6. What is *falling action?* Give an example.
7. What is meant by "point of attack"? Illustrate.
8. What is *exposition* in drama? Describe three methods of exposition and give an example of each.
9. What particular problem does the exposition raise in producing a play?
10. What are some of the problems to be solved in producing the ordinary logically constructed play?
11. What is meant by *episodic* construction? Give an example.
12. What are some of the sources of unity in the episodic play?
13. What are some of the problems which must be solved in producing the episodic play?
14. What do you understand by the term *rhythm* applied to a play?

Exercises

1. Analyze the sequence of major dramatic situations and crises in a logically constructed play.
2. Divide one act of a logically constructed play into scenes on the basis of entrances and exits and equate them with the sequence of dramatic situations.
3. Analyze the structure of a play with a late point of attack.
4. Analyze the structure of a play with an early point of attack.
5. Analyze an episodic play pointing out the elements which give it unity.
6. Describe the rhythm of a play whose structure you have analyzed.

Bibliography

Theory

Archer, William, *Playmaking,* New York: Dodd, Mead & Company, 1912.

Baker, George Pierce, *Dramatic Technique,* Boston: Houghton Mifflin Company, 1919.

Egri, Lajos, *The Art of Dramatic Writing,* New York: Simon & Schuster, 1946.

Lawson, John Howard, *Theory and Technique of Playwriting and Screenwriting,* New York: G. P. Putnam's Sons, 1949.

Rowe, Kenneth Thorpe, *Write That Play,* New York: Funk & Wagnalls Company, 1939.

Selden, Samuel, *An Introduction to Playwriting,* New York: D. Appleton-Century-Crofts, Inc., 1947.

Wilde, Percival, *The Craftsmanship of the One-Act Play,* Boston: Little, Brown & Company, 1923.

And Gassner's *Producing the Play,* cited in the Bibliography to Chapter 3.

Plays

See anthologies listed in the Bibliography to Chapter 3.

CHAPTER 7.

CHOOSING THE PLAY
and
PLANNING THE PRODUCTION

*A*ll the director's knowledge of written plays, of their dramatic qualities, their style, form, structure, and rhythm is brought to bear on the problem of selecting a play for production, and on the preliminary planning which is essential to effective production.

Choosing the Play

Usually it is the director's responsibility to choose the play or plays to be produced. Sometimes he does this with the advice of a play-reading committee elected by the producing organization. Sometimes the choice is made by a committee, and the director is hired to stage a play already selected. Whatever the arrangement, no director should be required to produce a play which does not interest him.

On the whole, the fewer persons involved in play selection the better. Relatively few people in any producing organization are likely to have the wide knowledge of plays necessary to making a good selection, and the more people involved the longer time will be required for discussion. If the choice must be supported by the whole membership, it should be presented with a slate of two or three plays recommended by a play-reading committee and the final choice made by vote of the membership.

No matter whether the selection is made by one person or by a committee, a good choice can be made only if certain considerations are kept in mind.

SHORT-RANGE CONSIDERATIONS

Play quality. The first question certainly should be: "Is this a good play?" In the nonprofessional theatre there is no excuse

for producing plays of little or no merit. The popularity of
cheap farces and melodramas with some audiences is insuffi-
cient reason. If an audience cannot be found for the good play
it is probably better not to produce at all. Of course, the producer, or whoever is doing the selecting, should have a broad
recognition of *quality* in drama. His own preference should not
be limited to one or two types of plays, to serious drama or to
comedy, to the latest plays or to the classics. He should be able
to recognize quality in melodrama as well as in tragedy, in farce
as well as in comedy.

This is not to say that audience taste and audience preference
should be ignored in play production. Most productions, even
in the nonprofessional theatre, must pay for themselves at the
box office. It is foolish to try to force on an audience a play
which there is reason to believe will be disliked. On the other
hand, it is not easy to predict what an audience will like. Attempts to poll audience preference usually reveal a wide variety
of opinion, or seem to indicate that the audience prefers only
the lighter plays. Regardless of such indicated preference, the
experience of nonprofessional producers shows that most audiences will enjoy a good production of any good play.

There are perhaps some communities in which it is impossible to muster an audience for a serious play. In such a community, it would be foolish to produce *Ghosts* or *Winterset*. A
farce or a melodrama is the obvious choice. However, even if the
audience appears to like the cheaper farces and melodramas
well enough, that is no reason why it should not be given *You
Can't Take It With You* or *Arsenic and Old Lace*. For a full
discussion of audience preferences see in Chapter 8 the section
headed "What the Audience Wants."

Acting requirements. Selection should be made, if possible,
with the actors in mind. Although some plays require particular
physical types, experience is probably the chief consideration.
Greater experience is desirable for the acting of serious plays
and comedies which depend more upon characterization. Melodrama and farce which depend more on plot present fewer difficulties to inexperienced actors. Age is another consideration.
The play of strong emotion or of sophisticated manners presents
particular difficulties for young and immature actors. Whatever
the group to be drawn upon, the question is: "Are the actors

available who can be expected to give the play a reasonably good performance?''

Theatre requirements. In most cases, the producer will know before the play is selected in what theatre it is to be produced and what scenery and lighting equipment are available. Another major question then is: "Can this play be produced adequately in this particular theatre with the equipment available or procurable?"

Most modern realistic plays lose much of their effect in a very large theatre. Realistic acting does not carry great distances, and some realistic settings are lost on a very wide stage. *Ghosts, The Lower Depths, The Seagull,* and *The Glass Menagerie* are examples of plays which are best suited to production on an ordinary sized stage in a relatively small auditorium. On the other hand, plays which depend a good deal for their effect on spectacle either in scenery or in crowd movements, or plays which require a broad style of acting, may be badly cramped on the small stage. *Jacobowsky and the Colonel* and *The Skin of Our Teeth* are examples of modern plays which may be badly cramped on such a stage. Shakespeare's plays, particularly the histories and tragedies, suffer considerably in a limited space. Molière's farces, on the other hand, are effective in a small theatre and in a large theatre as well, because the broad style of acting they require carries well.

If the play is to be produced not in a conventional theatre, but salon-style in the center of a large room, the choice is limited to plays which require few and simple settings. The settings in this type of theatre are limited to what can be achieved with low furniture and set pieces.

The number and elaborateness of the settings is also a consideration. Can the multiset play be provided with the necessary settings, and can these settings be shifted in reasonable time with the machinery and personnel available? A few plays depend heavily on lighting, particularly on changes in light, so one must ask also: "Can the lighting be executed adequately with the equipment available or procurable?"

Outdoor theatres present different problems in play selection depending on the type of playing space, the nature of the setting available, and on the conditions of production. For the natural outdoor theatre which uses only real trees and shrubbery for

This is the setting for a night production of *The Winter's Tale* in the outdoor theatre at Mills College, Oakland, California. With simple three-
dimensional units, drapes, light, and shadow Arch Lauterer quite transformed the playing space. For the theatre in daylight see the illustrations
on pages 12 and 157.

background, the number of suitable plays is very limited. *As
You Like It* and *A Midsummer Night's Dream,* a large part of
which are set in woods and glades, are well adapted to this type
of outdoor theatre. A number of the Greek plays and a few of
Shakespeare's other plays that do not depend much upon setting
might be adapted to production in such a theatre. The modern
realistic play, unless one can be found with a setting which approximates the natural setting provided by the theatre, is unsuitable.

For the outdoor theatre with a permanent or semipermanent
architectural setting, Greek, Roman, and Elizabethan plays are
especially suitable. Many of Molière's plays, too, are well
adapted for production in a permanent architectural setting.
Modern abstract plays such as Turney's *Daughters of Atreus,*
Anouilh's *Antigone,* and Sartre's *The Flies* might be adapted to
such a theatre, but realistic plays are unsuitable.

The modern realistic play is suitable for production only in the outdoor theatre which has a proscenium arch, or in which the effect of a proscenium frame can be suggested, and a stage which duplicates to a great extent the facilities of the indoor proscenium arch theatre.

Cost. Even though the nonprofessional producer usually does not have to make a profit, he ordinarily aims to make expenses. So he should operate on a budget: the probable cost of production weighed against the probable box-office receipts. Here is a check list of the major items of expense:

Royalty	Tickets
Scripts	Programs
Federal tax	Advertising
Scenery	Direct mail
Costumes	Posters
Properties	Newspapers
Lighting	Handbills
Makeup	
Theatre rental	

Royalty, the playwright's fee, is usually a major item of expense. Few good plays, except the classics, are royalty free. Most good plays published since 1895 are protected by copyright laws and may be performed only on payment of royalty. It is wrong to evade this payment; the playwright surely is entitled to payment for the work without which play production would be impossible. Moreover, evasion is sure to lead to trouble in the long run, because it is against the law. Play publishers look after their interests and the interests of their authors, and a group which fails to pay may have to answer in court. At best it will find that it can no longer get scripts from the publishers.

The royalty fee runs from $10 to as much as $75 or $100 for the first performance of a full-length play, and from $5 to $10 for the first performance of a one-act play. Ordinarily there is a reduction in the rate for additional performances, and a theatre like the Penthouse at the University of Washington, which plays forty-odd performances of each play to very small audiences, can get an unusually low rate. Few good plays are priced at less than $25 for the first performance, but play publishers are free to make adjustments on a good many plays and will sometimes reduce the royalty fee for performance in a theatre with a small seating capacity at a low admission charge. Row, Peterson & Company offers some plays on a sliding royalty scale based on box-office receipts.

Acting copies in paper-backed editions are usually obtainable from the play publisher at $.75 to $1.00 per copy. If no acting edition is available, copies of the regular trade edition will cost $2.00 to $3.00 each.

If *theatre rental* or service charges must be paid, this may constitute a major item, but it too will be known in advance.

Scenery is an extremely variable expense, depending on the requirements of the particular play and on the amount of usable equipment on hand. Even if there is available a stock of scenic units, the multiset play is likely to require some expense for scenery.

Properties, if they can be made or borrowed, will cost little, although trucking is expensive; but if they have to be rented, they may be a major expense.

In the well-equipped theatre, expense for *lighting* will be negligible, but if much lighting equipment must be bought or rented, the director will be faced with another major item.

Costuming is another extremely variable expense. If, as in most modern plays, the costumes can be borrowed, there may be little or no cost. If they have to be made, the cost will be considerable, and if any number have to be rented, a major expense will be incurred.

Makeup is a minor but regular item. Five to ten dollars should be figured for most plays, depending on the size of the cast, the number of character parts, and the number of performances.

The major *nonproduction expenses* are for tickets, programs, and advertising. The cost of printing tickets, programs, posters, handbills, and of mimeographing or otherwise duplicating material for direct-mail advertising varies from community to community, as does the price of newspaper advertising space. However, these all can be ascertained accurately in advance. Together they make up a major item of expense.

Thus we can summarize the problem of choosing a play for a single production: the aim should be to choose a good play which can be performed adequately by the actors available, which can be produced effectively in the available theatre, and which will draw a big enough audience to pay the cost of production.

LONG-RANGE CONSIDERATIONS

When each play can be selected not individually but as a part of a season's program or, even better, of a program which is expected to run through several seasons, the problem is considerably modified.

Variety. All the plays should be good plays, of course, but variety becomes a major consideration. If the program is to consist of two plays, these should be selected for contrast: a serious play and a comedy, a realistic play and a fantasy, or a modern play and a classic. When the program is a large one, it ought to present as wide a variety of plays, modern and classic, as conditions permit. In schools and colleges which present half a dozen or more public productions a year, there is a special responsibility to include one or more classics each year in order that the student audience may have an opportunity to see and appreciate examples of Greek, medieval, and Elizabethan drama and such modern classics as Ibsen, Gorki, and Chekhov.

The program of half a dozen or more plays should also include, whenever possible, one original or unpublished play. The nonprofessional theatre has an obligation not only to its audience, actors, and production personnel, but also to the beginning playwright. If the supply of new plays is not to dry up altogether, beginning playwrights must be encouraged by production. Good new scripts are not easy to find, but the American Educational Theatre Association makes a number available at a low royalty, and the National Theatre Conference has from time to time circulated a few. Once it becomes known that a producing group is interested in producing new plays, scripts will turn up. Although audiences may be inclined to prefer the tested success, they can be led to discover that the pleasure of exercising their critical faculties on entirely fresh material can largely compensate for imperfections in the play. And even if the premiere of a new play does not draw so well as the revival of a tried favorite, a minor loss on one production may be made up by the profit on another.

Audience education. Only through long-range planning can any audience education be achieved. By judiciously mixing sure-fire successes with good plays, which, either because they are classics or because they are less familiar in form or style, are presumed to have less general appeal, the taste of an audience can be gradually broadened. See Chapter 8 for a more detailed discussion of this point.

Actor development. Only through a varied program can the actors develop their abilities to the full. Plays should be selected to permit the experienced actors to play a variety of parts in a variety of styles: character as well as straight parts, comedy as well as tragedy, fantastic as well as realistic parts, in the presentational form as well as the representational form.

Plays should be selected not to fit the talents of a few experienced actors, but to provide roles for as many different actors as possible. Any program should include some plays with a number of small parts in which beginners can gain experience.

Only through a varied program of plays can designers and technicians gain any real facility in their respective departments. The opportunity to display artistry and skill in the revival or the fantastic play usually compensates for the extra work they require of the designers and technicians.

Budgetary freedom. Long-range planning, as has already been suggested, permits a much greater freedom in budgeting. Not only can expenses be spread over a whole season, thus permitting a low-cost popular success to help pay for an expensive revival or for a modern classic or new play with limited box-office appeal, but the cost of special scenery or costumes, with careful planning, can be carried by two or more plays in the course of a season or of several seasons. For instance, if an Elizabethan play is to be produced each season, the costumes for the first one may be made (although the expense might be too great for a single play) because they can go into the wardrobe and serve with some alterations and a few additions for a play next season. Similarly, a set of drops required for a fall production may not be too costly if it will provide essential scenery for a spring production also.

Mixing them up. In planning a season of several plays, Alexander Dean's scheme may prove useful. He recommended beginning with a light or comparatively light play in the fall and working toward the most serious offerings in midwinter and then working back with successively lighter plays until the season ends in late spring on a note of gaiety. The scheme takes account not only of the fact that warm weather and light entertainment seem to belong together but also of the fact that audiences lured into the theatre by lighter offerings will continue to come for the heavier plays. A heavy play is likely not to draw as well at the beginning of the season as it would later, when the theatre-going habit has been established.

ONE-ACT PLAYS

One-act plays are frequently used to give experience to beginning actors, directors, and technicians. By dividing up the responsibilities among a larger number, the bill of short plays does provide a better training ground for beginners than does the ordinary full-length play. And the program of one-act plays, if well produced, can have almost as much audience appeal as the long play. However, if it is used as a training ground for beginners, it cannot be well produced. Therefore such a bill might better be included in a season's program as a laboratory production at a reduced admission charge, or free for an invited audience.

In selecting a program of one-act plays, variety of mood and style is usually a major consideration, but sometimes three short plays by a single author, by O'Neill or Chekhov for instance, or three plays on different aspects of a large theme, say "freedom" or "democracy," may provide a good evening's entertainment. In schools and colleges, one is likely to find more original one-act than full-length plays, and the production of a program composed of the best of them will benefit the authors, as well as the actors and technicians.

Planning the Production
GENERAL CONSIDERATIONS

Once the play has been selected, the producer will begin to analyze it on the basis of a careful study of the script, supple-

mented perhaps by a study of reviews of previous productions
and, in the case of older plays, of some of the dramatic criticism
they have evoked. A knowledge of other plays by the same playwright may be useful also as background to the producer's
analysis.

He will decide first of all what meaning or what general effect the play was intended to have in the theatre, and by what
means the playwright intended this meaning to be expressed.
The producer must decide whether the play is realistic, abstract,
or fantastic, or whether it combines elements in different styles.
He must decide what form of production was intended, representational or presentational. He will decide what is the dominant mood. He will analyze the structure in detail. If the play
has a logically constructed plot, he will note the means used in
the exposition of the initial situation, the pattern of climax,
crisis, and action in each scene, and the part each scene plays in
the larger climax, crisis, and denouement of the whole play. If
the plot is episodic, he will look for some pattern of intensification of emotion or action, and for other unifying elements in
pervading mood or idea, in repetition, and in contrast. He will
discover the structure of each individual scene and what it contributes to the play as a whole.

Out of this analysis of the play should come a grasp of its
rhythmic structure, and an understanding of the place each
character and all the materials of production were intended to
play in its realization in the theatre.

The producer will then consider how best he can achieve the
playwright's purpose for *his* audience, in *his* theatre, and with
the actors, production crew, equipment, and material at *his* disposal.

He may decide that the play is too long. Theatre customs
change. Audiences today expect a play to last about two hours
and a half, including intermissions, and they may grow restless
at a play which runs much more than that, as many of the older
plays uncut will do. Cutting may be justified for other reasons.
The modern hard-boiled swearing in *The Front Page* may alienate some audiences, as may the poetic cursing in *The Playboy of
the Western World*. It may be better to cut or tone down the
oaths than to risk putting the audience off.

In any revival a decision must be made on the theatrical form.
Shall we produce Shakespeare's plays as they were intended to be

produced with direct contact between actor and audience, or shall we produce them in the representational manner of today, or shall we adopt some compromise? If the play is fantastic in style, what character shall the distortion of reality take, and how far shall it go? The answers to these questions depend in part on the nature of the theatre in which the play is to be produced, but even more on the training and experience of the actors and on the sophistication of the audience.

What part is *setting* to play in production? Limitations of space, machinery, or equiment may require a considerable simplification of the settings as described in the stage directions. Some scenes may be omitted, or transferred to another setting, in order to reduce the number of settings or to facilitate changes of setting.

THE PROMPTBOOK

For most plays, the settings cannot be planned without a fairly clear conception of the pattern of movement and the principal groupings of the characters. The director will draw a ground plan of each setting to scale, showing the location of each piece of scenery and furniture on the floor of the stage. If possible, he may wish to add to this elevation drawings, plans of each wall of each setting, in order to specify vertical dimensions, and a perspective sketch to show how the setting is to look.

The director will consider how light can be used to realize the playwright's purpose. He will prepare a general plan of the lighting showing the location of spotlights and floodlights, and the approximate area to be lighted by each, the intensity, and color. He will make tentative notes on the color and intensity of footlights and borders, and suggestions for light changes.

From his analysis of the play and of the individual characters and from his knowledge of available resources, the producer will prepare a description of the costumes required for each character with suggestions about borrowing, making, or renting.

He will make a sound and music cue-sheet indicating what sound effects and music are required, how they are to be created, and how they are to be used in the production.

He will plan the makeup for each character, preparing a chart on which is described as specifically as possible the effect required and the means of achieving it in the makeup of each actor.

Before he goes into rehearsal with the actors, the director will have blocked out the action of the play; that is, he will plan on paper the principal groupings of the characters, and the movements by which one group is broken down and another built up.

All this material gathered in a notebook constitutes a plan of the production, a *promptbook,* invaluable in rehearsals and in other phases of production.

The director may, of course, delegate the planning of one or more of the elements of production to qualified collaborating artists or technicians. In such cases there should be agreement beforehand on the aim of the production as a whole and on the style and theatrical form it is to take, and all plans should be approved by the director before execution is begun.

The time for planning different elements of production will vary. Settings should be definite, at least in ground plan, before groupings and movements are planned, or else the settings should be designed to conform to the blocking-out. In any case, settings should be designed before rehearsals are begun. The general character of the lighting should be planned with the settings and groupings, but since it is one of the last elements added to the production, details may be left until the last week of rehearsal. The general character of the costuming, and tentative general ideas of individual costumes may be formulated before casting, but final detailed plans cannot be made until it is known what actor is to play what part. Detailed plans for makeup, likewise, should wait until the play has been cast, for they too will depend a good deal on the physical appearance of the particular actors.

Although careful analysis and conscientious planning well in advance are not the whole art of play production, without them sensitiveness, flare, and inspiration cannot be fully effective. Inspired extemporization is doubtless better than methodical plodding, but inspiration will function all the better if the way for it has been prepared. Of course, no plans should be regarded as sacred; the discipline of actual execution nearly always requires some changes in them. Nevertheless, planning saves time, energy, temper, and frequently money, and only with planning can the best efforts of all those involved in production come to full fruition in performance.

Questions

1. What are the short-range considerations in play selection?
2. What are the principal items of expense in estimating the cost of production?
3. Name the long-range considerations in play selections.
4. How can the audience be "educated" through play selection?
5. How can actors and production workers be "educated" through play selection?
6. What are some principles for selecting a program of one-act plays?
7. What material makes up the *promptbook?*

Exercises

1. Select a play for production by a particular group, in a particular theatre, at a particular time. Give reasons for your choice.
2. Plan a program of six long plays to be produced by a particular group in a particular theatre. Give reasons for your selections.
3. Formulate a long-term (several-year) policy for selecting plays for production by a particular group in a particular theatre. Give reasons for your proposed policy.
4. Analyze a play for purposes of production.
5. Cut a play for production in a particular theatre. Give reasons for the cuts.
6. Prepare a promptbook for the production of a one-act play in a particular theatre. (Note: This exercise should not be required until the student has covered most of the material in this book.)

Bibliography

Theory

Dolman, John, Jr., *The Art of Play Production,* New York: Harper & Brothers, rev. ed. 1946.

Heffner, Selden, and Sellman, *Modern Theatre Practice,* New York: D. Appleton-Century-Crofts, Inc., 3rd ed. 1946.

Smith, Milton M., *Play Production for Little Theatres, Schools and Colleges,* D. Appleton-Century-Crofts, Inc., 1948.

Plays

Kozlenko, William, *The Best Short Plays of the Social Theatre,* New York: Random House, 1939.

————, *Contemporary One-Act Plays,* New York: Charles Scribner's Sons, 1938.

————, *American Scenes,* New York: The John Day Company, 1941.

Mayorga, Margaret, *Representative One-Act Plays By American Authors,* Boston: Little, Brown & Company, 1937.

One-Act Plays for Stage and Study, New York: Samuel French, nine vols., 1924–1938.

Shay, Frank, and Pierre Loving, *Fifty Contemporary One-Act Plays,* New York: D. Appleton-Century-Crofts, Inc., 1936.

Smith, Milton, M., *A Guide to Play Selection,* New York: D. Appleton-Century-Crofts, Inc., 1934.

Wilde, Percival, *Contemporary One-Act Plays from Nine Countries,* Boston: Little, Brown & Company, 1936.

For full-length plays, see the Bibliography to Chapter 3.

PART TWO

THE CONDITIONS
OF PRODUCTION:
The Audience and
the Theatre

CHAPTER 8.

THE NATURE OF THE AUDIENCE

The play exists for an audience. It is written for an audience, chosen for an audience, and produced for an audience. All that is said and done on the stage in the performance of a play is directed toward an audience, whether it appears to be or not. So important is the audience that some theorists of the theatre have treated it as one of the collaborators in play production along with the actors, the producer, scene designer, and so on. This may perhaps be an exaggeration, but everyone agrees that even a full-dress rehearsal to an empty house is not the same as a performance, so the audience must play more than a merely passive role in this complex art.

The active effect of the audience upon the performance is most obvious in the production of comedy. The actor must adjust his performance to the audience response as it is expressed in laughter. If he is adroit in "holding" the laughs, that is, in holding his next line until the laughter begins to die out, the audience will be encouraged to laugh. If he rides over the laughs, attempting to speak against the competition from the audience, the audience will gradually cease to laugh at all, partly because it misses a good many of the funny lines and partly because it really wants to hear what is being said.

Needless to say the production which gets its full quota of laughs will seem quite different from the production which gets very few. Moreover, no two audiences will react in quite the same way to the same production of the same play, and the actor must be prepared either to hold his line if the audience laughs, or to proceed without pause if no laugh is forthcoming. Thus, although the performance in its general outlines and even in many details remains as it was perfected in rehearsal, it is given its particular form in many of its details by each successive audience.

Audience participation in the performance of serious drama is less obvious but nonetheless real. When the serious play is having its full effect, the audience is silent, absorbed, straining all its faculties to see everything that happens on the stage and to hear every word uttered by the actors. Even the coughers are silent. When the serious play is not holding its audience, this will be apparent in the multiplication of little noises. Coughs will no longer be suppressed. Throats will be cleared, seats will creak, programs will rustle. If the actor is alert, he will be aware of this restlessness, recognize it as a sign that audience attention is weakening, and will increase his efforts to project the play.

Audiences differ—just as individuals differ—in alertness, understanding, and appreciativeness, and there is no doubt that a good audience inspires the actors to do their best, whereas a poor audience may get only a poor performance.

In representational production, which pretends to be unaware of the presence of the audience, the active participation of the audience can go no further. However, in presentational production the audience plays a still more active part. Some speeches are spoken directly to the audience, and the whole performance is affected by its unconcealed recognition of the presence of the audience. The production, instead of being centered on the stage behind the proscenium arch or in a little circle from which the audience is excluded, reaches out beyond the proscenium or beyond the circumference of the arena stage and includes the audience in its world of make-believe. Unhampered by the necessity for maintaining an illusion of separateness, all the materials of production may be used to produce certain effects on the audience, and the actors are free to adjust their performance to different reactions, without having to pretend that no reactions exist.

Since the audience is not only the reason for the production but also plays a part in shaping the particular performance, the producer should know as much as possible about theatre audiences in general and about his own audience in particular.

General Characteristics

The theatre audience is made up of individuals, and the reactions of individuals to the kinds of sensations provided in the theatre are capable of analysis and are important to the producer. But individuals react somewhat differently when they are assembled in a group, and these differences are perhaps even more important.

THE AUDIENCE IS A "CROWD"

The theatre audience, like any other audience, has much in common with the psychological *crowd*. Members of a psychological crowd (a collection of individuals, all of whom are attending to and reacting to some common stimulus or set of stimuli) tend to react as a group rather than as individuals.

Emotional expression. In such group reaction, individual inhibitions are relaxed. Each member of the crowd, aware that the other members are reacting in the same way he is, realizes that he need not hide his feelings. As a result, emotional expression is stronger in the individual when he is a member of an audience than it would be if he were witnessing a play by himself. He laughs and cries more easily and freely in a group than he does when alone.

Actors often feel that they do better in performance than in rehearsal, and better before a full house than they do before a half-empty one. This feeling may very well be due not so much to any difference in their own work as to the difference in the emotional expression of the audience, absent when there are no spectators, weak when there are many vacant seats, and strongest only when every seat is full.

Emotional experience. Moreover there can be little doubt that emotional *experience,* as well as emotional expression, is stronger when one is a member of an audience, perhaps because emotional expression and emotional experience are closely linked. A comedy seems funnier to most people when they see it on the stage than when they read it, a serious play more powerful. No doubt this is due in part to the inability of the reader to fully imagine the effect of the acting, setting, lighting, etc. on the stage, but not altogether. A comedy seems funnier to most people and a serious play more powerful when they see it in performance than when they see it in rehearsal. As a member of an audience the individual's emotional experience is intensified.

Emotional experience is intensified also if the individual is able to identify himself pleasurably with one or another of the characters of the play. At a football game the spectator strains in the direction of the goal line when *his* team is carrying the ball. In the same way the spectator at a play leaps with the hero to thwart the villain or suffers with the persecuted heroine. This sympathetic identification or imitation is not constant—now it is with one character, now with another—but it enables the spectator to feel in a diluted way as if he were performing the movements and uttering the speeches, and especially as if he were experiencing the emotions. Except in the very naïve spectator, identification with the characters is limited by an awareness that he is watching a play performed by actors. A great deal of the pleasure which the spectators gain from the performance of a play depends upon the degree of such identification they experience.[1]

Because this identification contributes materially to the emotional experience of the spectator, plays with a number of sympathetic characters (characters with whom the spectator can take pleasure in identifying himself) are likely to be the most popular, and it is a truism of the theatre that a play with no sympathetic characters is bound to fail. Inexpressive movement and speech by the actors, and any hitches in the performance, such as obvious lapses of memory, mislaid properties, delayed curtains, and so on, interfere with the spectator's response to the play. Extreme realism in the representation of physical suffering and death is likely to make spectator identification unpleasant and so destroy the audience's enjoyment of the play.

Polarization. Since the audience, as long as it remains a collection of individuals, cannot fully experience the effect of the play, it is important that this collection of individuals be *polarized,* that is, be turned into a *crowd,* just as quickly as possible. The audience will remain a collection of individuals just as long as its members are paying attention to a variety of things. It will not become a crowd with the crowd reaction until the attention

[1] The term *empathy* is sometimes applied to this phenomenon, but it had better be reserved for use in its original sense, namely, to designate the unconscious attribution by the spectator of his own feelings to a natural object or to a work of art. When we say a particular landscape is "peaceful," we are attributing to it the feeling of peace which we gain from looking at it. In *empathy* the spectator feels distinct from the object and from the emotion it has aroused; in *sympathetic imitation* he feels one with the object and the emotion.

Audience attention is held by actors in Philip Barry's *Spring Dance* in the University of Washington Penthouse Theatre. Glenn Hughes, director.

of every individual is riveted on the performance. *The first requirement for the effective performance of any play is to capture the attention of its audience.* Because of the contagious character of the crowd reaction, it will be easier to polarize the audience, the more concentrated the audience is. As we have noted, the best crowd reaction comes from an audience which fills every seat. If the auditorium is only half full, polarization is easiest if the audience is spread over two-thirds or three-quarters of the house, and not concentrated in unbroken rows. A small audience in a large auditorium tends to be inhibited by the empty spaces and its members react more as individuals and less as a crowd. If there are no provisions for cutting off parts of the auditorium, it is better from the point of view of the audience to play one performance to a full house than it is to play four performances each to a quarter of a house.

Polarization of the audience means capturing its attention, and since the performance must not only capture the audience's attention at the beginning but also hold that attention for over two hours, the director should understand the general nature of attention and the particular character it assumes in the theatre audience.

WHAT IS ATTENTION?

Attention is a concentration of all the senses upon a particular source of stimulation, combined with an attitude of alertness, of readiness to respond. When one pays attention to the playing of a dance number, one concentrates one's faculties on that particular sequence of sounds, excluding very largely other sounds and often visual sensations as well, and one is ready to respond either by dancing, by humming, or by beating time with a foot or finger. The runner on his mark at the start of a race provides an example of attention in a concentrated form with particular emphasis on the readiness to respond. All his attention is on the starter, and he is ready to leap forward at the crack of the pistol.

When one pays attention to a play, one's senses are concentrated on the sights and sounds presented by the production. The clearing of a throat, the creaking of a seat, the rustling of a program either are not heard at all, or if they are heard these make so little impression that they do not interfere with one's reaction to what is occurring on the stage. A member of a theatre audience, when his attention is strongly held by the performance, strains forward in his seat eager to catch every word and every movement. He is not like the runner ready to respond in practical physical action, but he is ready to respond emotionally, to experience the feeling of a particular character sympathetically or to experience the emotion projected by a situation or by a stage picture. And, as we have noted, when he is part of a *crowd* he is ready to give expression to his emotion by laughing or crying.

However, *attention is not static.* It cannot stand still for more than a second or two. It is essentially mobile and exploratory, requiring constantly new or partially new stimuli if it is to be maintained. If the object or field of attention presents a complex pattern of light, color, form, and sound, attention constantly shifts from one part of the total pattern to another. Most of the time the performance of a play presents an extremely complex pattern of this sort, constantly changing in time as well as in space. On those occasions when for a moment or two there is no movement and no speech, actors and setting present a picture, a complex pattern of appeals to the eye, through which attention moves from one part to another.

Attention is contagious. We tend to pay attention to what obviously holds the attention of others. This is easily verifiable. If you are walking along the street, and the person ahead of you stops and looks up at the roof of a building, you have an almost irresistible impulse to do likewise. The larger the number of people paying attention to something, the stronger is the compulsion for others to do likewise.

In the theatre this characteristic of attention is important at two levels. If in the early moments of performance most of the spectators are in their seats and paying close attention to the play, late-comers will quickly do likewise. If the attention of most of the spectators has not been strongly caught, they will be distracted by the late-comers, who in turn will be much slower to come under the spell. The performance should appeal as strongly as possible to audience attention during these early moments, and distraction should be reduced to a minimum by good house management.

On a second level, the spectators will pay attention to what obviously holds the attention of the actors. If the actors, not merely the one who happens for the moment to be speaking or doing something, but *all* the actors, pay close attention to the play, they almost compel the audience to do likewise. More particularly, since the focus of attention on the stage shifts frequently from character to character and from one part of the stage to another, the actors can do much to insure that audience attention moves from one focus to the next throughout the entire play by shifting their own attention clearly and definitely.

WHAT HOLDS ATTENTION?

Attention is by definition discriminating. It is held by certain appeals or stimuli and in so doing it excludes others. Some stimuli make stronger demands on attention than do others, and it is possible to distinguish certain attention *values*.

Variety. Psychologists agree that variety is the strongest attention value. Attention to a single stimulus is very brief, at most about two seconds, and usually much less, so that variety, in the sense of change of stimulus, appeals strongly to attention. For this reason, a movement in one part of an otherwise static picture captures attention immediately. Both actor and producer should be fully aware of this. Of course, if half a dozen actors are moving at the same time, some other means will have to be found to focus attention on the most important movement.

But variety is essential to the producer in a much more fundamental way. If the production is to hold the attention of an audience, it must present either a succession in time of stimuli sufficiently varied, or else a static field of stimulation so complex that the observer's attention can shift constantly within it from one focus to another. Although variety is important in all departments of production, it is vital in acting. Any good play is a plan for a complex pattern of stimuli. Lack of variety, monotony, indicates a failure to realize this pattern. Scenes which are monotonous in the acting call for a renewed study of the script. Even the effect of monotony itself must be achieved in the theatre not through real lack of variety in the production but through variety within a limited range.

Intensity. The stronger the stimulus, the greater will be its appeal to attention. The louder sound will tend to win attention over the softer sound. The strong, rapid movement will hold attention against the slow, weak movement; the brightest spot on the stage will pull attention from the less brightly lighted areas. A strong red will take attention from a grayed red. The actor will have to speak more loudly than usual to hold attention against incidental music or sound effects. In the visual field the large object has more attention value than the small object, and the nearer it is to the spectator, other conditions being equal, the greater will be its demand on attention. This should be kept in mind in scene design, in selecting and arranging the furniture and other properties, and in planning the grouping and movements of the actors.

In a succession of stimuli following each other in time, however, change is more important than mere increase in intensity. Additional loudness will often secure attention, but a sharp reduction in volume has attention value too. If an actor, who has been speaking loudly, suddenly drops into a whisper, that whisper will have a very strong demand on attention. Thus variety becomes once more the deciding factor.

Repetition. Although variety is such a strong attention value, repetition too has an appeal to attention. It is paradoxical but true that for most people there is appeal both in the novel and in the familiar. However, repetition should be used only sparingly if monotony is to be avoided, and it is most effective when it is combined with variety. In fact, the combination of the novel and the familiar presents perhaps the strongest possible appeal to the attention. In play production, the field of stimulation is always complex, and if part of this is familiar and part of it is new we have the ideal union of repetition and variety. For example, in Thornton Wilder's *The Long Christmas Dinner,* although much of the business and a number of the lines are repeated, they are repeated by different characters, so that the effect is of the old or familiar in a new setting.

Striking quality. Although pink reflects more light, saturated red appeals more strongly to attention. High pitches exercise a stronger appeal to attention than do low pitches of the same loudness. The unusually pleasant or unpleasant quality of voice will command greater attention than the ordinary quality of voice. Striking quality must be a consideration in several departments of play production. The relative attention values of deep and pale colors must be taken into account in scene and costume design. The actor will find uses for high pitch and for unusual voice quality.

Definiteness of form. The more distinct the form of an object the greater will be its appeal to attention. This principle has a direct application to details of scene and costume design and of acting. The clearer and more distinct the form of an element in the setting, or of a costume, the greater its attention value. The clearer and more distinct the actor's movement, the greater will be its appeal to attention.

This principle is important also on the more complex level of the entire stage picture and of the production as a whole. Experiments have shown that most people can attend visually to no more than four or five simple objects at one time. The more complex the objects, the narrower the span or scope of attention. However, we tend to see objects not individually but in groups, and consequently it is possible for us to pay attention to a very large number of objects if they are organized into a group. The picture presented by the stage at any point in the progress of the play should present such an organization of objects, and the stronger this organization, the clearer and more distinct the form of this stage picture, the stronger will be its hold on attention.

The same holds true to an extent of the succession of visual and auditory stimuli in time. The stronger the organization and the clearer the pattern of physical movement and the pattern of sound, the greater will be its appeal to audience attention.

Individual experience. The attention values described above are unlearned. They do not depend on individual experience but appear alike in all human beings. However, the experience of the individual also is a strong factor in determining what will catch and hold his attention. The desires, likes and dislikes, opinions and attitudes of the individual motivate his attention, making it easy for certain types of stimuli to win their way into his consciousness and making it difficult for other stimuli to do so. This leads us to a consideration of the particular experience, attitudes, and likes and dislikes of the theatre audience.

Special Characteristics

Most people come to the theatre because they want to, and they want to come to the theatre, for the most part, because they expect to be entertained. They expect to gain pleasure of some sort from the performance, to be diverted from their cares and worries, to be moved to laughter or tears, or to gain some insight into life and living.

FACTORS FAVORABLE TO ATTENTION

Thus the spectators are fundamentally ready to pay attention to the performance. They have seen and enjoyed plays before, perhaps by the same author, perhaps in the same theatre, perhaps acted by some of the same actors. Most of them know something about the play: its title, whether it is comic or serious, the name of the author, perhaps the names of the principal actors. Some may have read reviews of the play, and so are familiar with the main outline of the plot. A few may even have read the play in printed form.

The specific conditions preceding their arrival in the theatre are likely to be favorable. They have arranged to spend this evening in the theatre, probably bought tickets in advance, dressed for the occasion, and travelled some distance, perhaps at considerable inconvenience, all to see the play.

In the theatre itself, they join others assembled for the same purpose. They are ushered to their seats and handed programs. The program contains information about the play and the production: at least the name of each character and of the actor who is to perform the part, and a synopsis of scenes—an indication of the place and time of the play's action. The program may in addition contain some comment on the play, and some information about the playwright, the actors, and the director.

Overture music or some other signal indicates that the performance is ready to begin: the house lights dim, stage lights come up on the front curtain, and the curtain rises. At this moment, it might seem that the performance has every advantage in its initial bid for audience attention.

DISTRACTING FACTORS

Nevertheless, there are powerful factors working to distract the spectator. For the first ten minutes after the curtain rises, the performance has stronger competition for audience attention than at any other period. Some members of the audience have arrived late, and must get to their seats. With the aid of the ushers they grope their way down the aisles, crowd past those already seated, remove outdoor clothing, settle themselves in their seats, and try to read their programs in the semidarkness. Others, although seated, may not yet have removed their wraps or settled themselves comfortably. There is a medley of whispers, footsteps, bangs, creaks, and rustlings against which the performance must compete. And although most of the spectators are eager to see, hear, and understand what is happening on the stage, everyone of them still has in his mind remains of other matters—business or personal cares, recent irritations, or ideas set stirring by conversation of the last few minutes.

Novelty. Moreover, when the curtain rises each member of the audience is suddenly presented with a complex pattern of sights and sounds, some of which may be familiar to him from previous experience inside and outside the theatre, but many elements of which are entirely novel. He may see the stage well enough and he may hear the actors speak, but he has more or less difficulty in understanding the meaning of what he sees and hears. Usually several minutes, sometimes as many as ten, pass before order comes out of this initial confusion, before (in the language of psychology) there is set up in the spectator a state of attention leading to perception, before he not only sees and hears but *understands*.

Director and actors can by conscious effort reduce this period to the minimum by making sure that the first ten minutes of the performance go unusually slowly and emphatically. This means that even in realistic representational acting, the actors must try harder to project during these opening minutes, and frequently this must be done at the expense of illusion. The first ten minutes of most professional productions, no matter how realistic the play, usually seem highly artificial, mainly for this reason. On the whole, artificiality is preferable to un-intelligibility.

Technique of a somewhat higher order is required to achieve immediate intelligibility without apparent effort or artificiality. The writer recalls seeing William Gillette in one of his last performances of *Sherlock Holmes*. For the first ten or fifteen minutes, only Mr. Gillette was intelligible. One could hear the other actors, but could understand nothing of what they were saying. Every line of Mr. Gillette's was perfectly understandable, and he did not seem to be making any special effort nor to be speaking at all unnaturally.

Similar obstacles are present after each intermission, but they are less serious and yield more quickly to the appeal of the performance. By this time the spectator is familiar with the voices of the actors and with their appearance, and he is familiar enough with the play itself, so that his attention is quickly regained in spite of competing factors.

Fatigue. Although increasing familiarity with the content of the play and with the elements of the production make it increasingly easy for a time to hold audience attention, fatigue eventually sets in and becomes a strong competing factor. Even the most comfortable chair becomes cramping and confining if one must sit in it quietly for half or three-quarters of an hour, and many theatre seats are far from comfortable. Even if they are well designed and well upholstered they are likely to be set too close to the seats in front, so that the occupant's legs are cramped. Often the auditorium floor is not adequately raked or the seats not properly staggered, so that the spectator has to crane his neck

in order to see over or between the heads of the persons sitting
in front of him. Frequently the ventilation is poor, so that the
air becomes hot and stuffy.

If prolonged, all these discomforts end by distracting the
spectator's attention from the play to himself. He shifts his
position in his seat, clears his throat, coughs, and rustles his
program—actions that distract his neighbors' attention from
the play. Such noises, of course, occur intermittently throughout a performance. They constitute, indeed, a pretty reliable
measure of audience attention. Any sudden increase in such
noises of unrest is a sure sign that the performance is losing its
hold on the audience and must either make a stronger bid for
attention or else give the audience a rest.

INTERMISSIONS

It is difficult to say whether human limitations or less fundamental conditions of play production are responsible for the
present-day custom of allowing in the course of a full-length
play two intermissions long enough for people to get up and
stretch and smoke a cigarette. It is probable that in Shakespeare's time plays were performed without any intermission at
all, but this may have been possible because the members of the
audience were not confined to seats but free to move about
pretty much as they wished during the performance. An occasional modern play, Philip Barry's *Hotel Universe* for example, has been written for continuous performance, but this is
exceptional. Most modern plays are written in three acts and
provide for two intermissions.

The custom is thus a strong one, and creates a problem in
the production of Shakespeare or any other play—*The Adding
Machine* for example—which is not written in the three-act
form. Shakespeare's plays undoubtedly lose something of their
full impact if they are broken up for intermissions. However,
they may lose more through fatiguing the audience, if they keep
it sitting two or three times as long as it is accustomed to sit.
Sometimes a compromise is possible. *Macbeth* has one logical
resting place after the murder of Duncan; *Julius Caesar* after
the funeral orations. *The Adding Machine* builds strongly
through the courtroom scene and permits an intermission between Scenes Four and Five.

Mere length is itself a matter of custom and habit. Today's audience is used to a play that lasts two to two and a half hours, including intermissions. Performances which last much longer than that run the risk of wearing the audience out. It is possible that both Maurice Evans' uncut *Hamlet* and Eugene O'Neill's *The Iceman Cometh* might have seemed better if they had been half as long.

SCENE WAITS

Although audience attention seems to require a rest every thirty or forty-five minutes, it is likely to be dissipated entirely by too frequent rests. For this reason the play of many settings raises a particular problem. Even the brief pause necessary to lower the curtain and raise it again makes enough of a break so that if it occurs often audience attention is weakened. If the curtain remains down a minute or two each time to cover a change of setting, the breaks seriously reduce the effectiveness of the production. Consequently, techniques to permit rapid changes of scenery are of the utmost importance, and devices to provide continuity of mood can be very useful.

AUDIENCE EXPECTATIONS

An audience comes to the theatre not only with a will to attend to the play and a capacity for attention limited by the factor of fatigue, but also with a definite, though somewhat generalized notion of what it expects to find in the theatre. This notion is based upon the experience of the individuals of which the audience is composed and necessarily varies from place to place and from time to time. Two hundred years ago no one was disturbed by the sight of characters entering and leaving the stage through the apparently solid walls painted on the wing pieces. Today's audience would find such a sight disturbing or ridiculous. We have become accustomed to seeing actors enter and leave through pretty solid-looking doors. This theatre experience is the strongest factor determining what the audience expects to see in the theatre.

The theatre today, however, is predominantly realistic; most of what we see in the theatre is supposed, outwardly at any rate, to resemble life as we know it. Consequently, the spectator is likely to make judgments in terms of life, saying this performance is "real" and that one "unreal." Actually, most people are too busy living to observe life closely; that is the artist's vocation. For this reason, the audience's notion of life is based largely not on observation of life but on observation of art—in this case the art of the theatre.

Today's audience expects that the actors will look and act like ordinary people, that they will behave as if the audience were not present, and that they will not indulge in asides or long monologues. If the performance conforms to these requirements it will be accepted as "real." The audience will overlook the artificiality of the conventions which are necessary to this realistic style of theatre art: the absence of the fourth wall, the triangular grouping of furniture and actors, and so on. It is used to these conventions and pays no attention to them.

The fantastic play is likely to have to overcome the prejudice of an audience which is accustomed to seeing only characters who talk and act like the man on the street. *Our Town* has been an extremely popular play, but some spectators are always disturbed by the fantasy in the last act. However, if the fantasy is presented in representational form—the play kept behind the proscenium arch with no direct communication between actors and audience—the audience's expectations will be less outraged; and if the audience is prepared beforehand for the fantasy by publicity and through the program, the play's novelty may prove an attraction for most people.

Departures from the representational form are likely to encounter even stronger opposition. Some people found the mingling of narration and action disturbing in *I Remember Mama*. The fact that Kathy sometimes spoke in her person as author and then moved into the action as a character in her story destroyed the illusion for them. And a great many people found the direct presentational form of *The Skin of Our Teeth* so disturbing that they walked out on the Broadway production.

However, in the last twenty years there have been enough experiments in the presentational form so that some audiences may not be outraged by such a radical departure from what they expect to find in the theatre. Plays like *The Adding Machine, Strange Interlude, The Hairy Ape, Our Town,* and *The Skin of Our Teeth* have not broken down the representational form, but they have weakened it to a point where the more sophisticated audience may find the presentational form an attraction.

Some people walked out on *The Skin of Our Teeth,* but a lot of others were wildly enthusiastic about it.

There can be little doubt that plays written for presentational production lose much of their power when they are confined behind the proscenium arch and cut off from direct communication with the audience. It may be that audiences are not ready for Shakespeare produced in the Elizabethan manner or a modern equivalent, but something is gained by breaking down the barrier of the proscenium with an apron built out over the orchestra pit and by permitting the actor to include the auditorium if not the audience in his performance. Molière becomes twice as funny presented in presentational form, and so does Sheridan.

Actually, most audiences will accept unfamiliar conventions in the theatre fairly quickly if their expressive purpose is immediately obvious. As in the case of fantasy, the audience should be prepared in advance for any radical experiment in theatrical form, through newspaper and other forms of advance publicity and through program notes or some form of prologue. If the publicity is handled skillfully, the departure from the familiar conventions may turn out to be an asset rather than a liability. As we have noted, the novel as well as the familiar has its appeal. Some of the success of *Our Town* and of *I Remember Mama* was certainly due to novel elements in their style and form.

What Does the Audience Want?

We have noted that the audience today expects the realistic style of play and the representational form of production, but we must ask also: what does the audience want in play content? A theatre audience wants to be entertained, but entertainment, in the theatre as elsewhere, means different things to different people. Many people will be satisfied with a play that "holds their attention agreeably," distracting their minds for two hours or so from the cares and irritations of life. However, most people are likely to be more enthusiastic about a play which wrings them with suspense, moves them to tears, or shakes them with hearty laughter. And some people seek still more in the theatre: the stimulus to action or to thought, or that deeper emotional experience which great art in any medium can confer.

In selecting plays for production these general audience wants must be considered, if the theatre is to pay for itself at the box office. It is possible, if not to say exactly what a particular audience wants, at any rate to be more specific about audience preferences. On the whole, audiences seem to prefer comedies to serious plays, modern plays to revivals, plays with a love interest to plays without, plays of spectacle and action to plays which depend largely on dialogue, and plays of which they have heard to plays which are entirely unknown to them. Although audiences like to laugh, unadulterated satire, perhaps because it usually presents no sympathetic characters, seems to have the least audience appeal. Because a degree of familiarity always has some appeal, the fact that a particular play has been seen in moving-picture form by many of the potential audience may add to its box-office appeal, especially if the picture has not been shown too recently and if it was popular. The theatre can cash in on some of the moving picture's publicity.

Fortunately, an audience is not homogeneous in its tastes. It is likely to be made up of individuals of various ages, temperaments, and experience. If the younger members prefer the latest Broadway success, the older members may be most enthusiastic about a lively revival of Shakespeare. And it is fairly safe to say that most audiences will like any good play that is well produced, at least well enough to justify the production. It is no good, of course, to produce good plays badly. Shakespeare, the greatest of the English classics, has suffered most from this disservice at the hands both of professionals and non-professionals.

The moral, religious, and political prejudices of the audience cannot safely be ignored. In the community theatre the shocking play will alienate subscribers; in the school theatre it may cost the director his job. Communities vary greatly in what they will accept in the theatre. New York audiences will accept what may bring protests and perhaps censorship in Boston. Audiences will accept from a professional company what they will not accept from amateurs, and from adults what they will not accept from students.

There is no use in rebelling against such prejudices; they are one of the conditions of play production. The director should try to learn beforehand just what things the people who will make up his audience are likely to find objectionable, not so much by asking individuals about particular plays he may have in mind, as by finding out what plays have aroused an unfavorable reaction in the past, and why. Such vicarious experience should prevent serious blunders while the director is acquiring firsthand experience.

This does not mean that the producer must be strictly and forever bound by the prejudices of his audience. Prejudices are not fixed and unalterable. They fade away, they change, and sometimes they yield to careful education. A play may be produced which might be expected on the basis of past experience to shock a few people. If there are no serious repercussions, some ground has been gained.

There is no sense in trying to beat down prejudice, however unreasonable it may appear, by frontal attack. Speech in the theatre probably can never be any freer than the tolerance of the audience will permit.

Questions

1. How does audience reaction affect the particular performance of comedy? Of tragedy?
2. What is a "psychological crowd"?
3. Why is a play usually more effective in performance than it is in rehearsal?
4. What is *sympathetic imitation* and how does it function in the theatre audience?
5. What is meant by "polarizing an audience"?
6. What is *attention?* What are some of the characteristics of a state of attention?
7. What are the universal attention values?
8. What factors favor the theatre audience's attention to the play?
9. What factors tend to distract the theatre audience's attention?
10. How is the number of intermissions related to the problem of holding audience attention?
11. What does the theatre audience expect today?
12. What does the theatre audience want?

Exercises

1. Select a play unfamiliar to your audience in form or style and outline a plan by which the audience may be prepared to give it an understanding reception.

2. Analyze the expectations and wants of a particular audience with which you are familiar.

Bibliography

Eisenson, Jon, *The Psychology of Speech,* New York: D. Appleton-Century-Crofts, Inc., 1938. Contains a good summary of the present scientific knowledge of attention.

Hollingworth, H. L., *The Psychology of the Audience,* New York: American Book Company, c 1935. The audience in general.

Kjerbühl-Peterson, Lorenz, *The Psychology of Acting,* Boston: The Expression Company, 1935. Contains one of the very few analyses of the theatre audience.

Langfeld, Herbert S., *The Aesthetic Attitude,* New York: Harcourt, Brace & Company, 1920. An attempt to apply the concept of empathy to the arts.

CHAPTER 9.

GETTING AND LOOKING AFTER THE AUDIENCE

*M*ost people enjoy the theatre, but many have got out of the habit of seeing plays, because plays are few and far between in many communities, and the moving pictures provide similar entertainment at a relatively low price. However, most people prefer a performance by living actors, and if prices can be kept at or not much above movie prices, they can be lured back to the theatre by a program of good plays well produced. In order to effect this change in their habits however, an intelligent and energetic publicity and ticket-selling campaign may be necessary.

Getting an Audience

PUBLICITY

Material for publicity must come largely from the play itself: its theme, mood, setting, and characters. The author may be a source of material too, if he has written other successful plays or if the play has grown out of particular experiences of his own. Previous productions of the play, particularly professional productions and movie versions, should provide more material: names of stars who appeared in it, reviews, and perhaps pictures. Although the nonprofessional theatre ordinarily does not have stars and in general does not exploit personalities as does the professional theatre, the name of every person who works on the production has publicity value. "Names is news." And if the production makes certain unusual requirements, a set of masks, special light or sound effects, ingenious settings, these and the people who are handling them will provide especially good publicity material.

Direct mail. For publicity by direct mail a mailing list, preferably a selected one, must be secured or compiled. A letter or printed or mimeographed circular sent out about three weeks before the production date (most people don't plan entertainment more than two or three weeks in advance), followed up perhaps by a postcard two weeks later, is likely to be effective.

A circular attractively laid out with the essential information printed so that it is easy to read at a glance is more effective than a form letter. A few of the most striking things about the play and the production, the time and place of performance, the prices of seats and how and where they may be purchased are the essentials. An order form which may be mailed in will appeal to some people who like to have their tickets sent them. Direct-mail publicity will be more effective in many communities, if it also provides for reservations by telephone.

Moreover, the number of mail and telephone orders provides the only check on the effectiveness of this form of publicity.

Posters. Small printed or silk-screen posters which shopkeepers are usually willing to display in their windows can be printed or made relatively cheaply and doubtless do some good. Larger, well-designed, handmade posters, of course, are much more effective, if someone can be found to make them, and if suitable places can be found to display them. The theatre itself often provides such a place, and schools usually have bulletin boards designed for such purposes. Sometimes a large department store can be persuaded to provide space for a good looking poster, and a hotel lobby is another good spot for one. In some communities printed posters in buses or streetcars may not be too expensive.

In some communities it is possible to hang a canvas banner across a main street in the business district. The theatre building itself, if it does not boast a marquee, may be a good location for such a large banner. On a college campus, other good locations may be found for this large-scale outdoor advertising.

Throw-aways. The handbill is useful in small communities where it is possible to cover every house without too much legwork, and in schools where the potential audience is strongly concentrated during certain times of the day. Handbills or circulars are useful, too, in direct contact with clubs and organizations, as will be described below. The same type of circular used for direct-mail publicity may be distributed from house

This is a silk-screen poster for a production of *Ten Nights in a Barroom* given by Brooklyn College Varsity Players. Barnard Hewitt, director.

to house, handed out at the entrances to a campus or to the major buildings, or distributed through the individual classrooms of a high school.

Newspaper publicity. Paid newspaper advertising is expensive and probably most useful for a theatre which produces regularly throughout a season. However, some newspapers will give little or no publicity through their news columns unless some advertising is bought.

Newspapers are likely to limit the amount of news space they will give in any case. If obtainable, five or six stories spread over the three weeks preceding performance are desirable. The series of stories should be planned as a whole, and the available material should be divided up to fit the schedule. Here is an example of publicity divided into six stories:

1. The play, the author, and a description of the play's success elsewhere, with laudatory comments from critics.

2. Cast of the original New York or London production or, in the case of a classic, stars who have appeared in it.

3. The story of the play.

4. The cast, with previous experience of the actors.

5. The production staff with human interest angle on production problems.

6. Rehash of the high points of the previous stories.

This schedule is intended to be suggestive only. Any production may have special features more newsworthy than any of the standard items. If a contest is held, or an exhibit, or if opening night is made a special event, these will provide good material for newspaper stories.

Some newspapers will welcome a well-written story neatly typed, although they may not use all of it. Others may prefer only the facts and do their own writing. If one is dealing with more than one newspaper, each should get the same facts at the same time but the treatment should be different enough so that the stories will not seem identical. Large papers in big cities are more likely to publish good, clear, interesting photographs than they are long news stories.

If the newspaper runs a local gossip column, an effort should be made to find an item or two suitable for that medium. Usually such a column is much more widely read than an ordinary news story.

Radio. Sometimes a radio station is willing to provide free time for a scene from a play, if the scene is skillfully adapted and reasonably well presented. However, copyright restrictions prevent broadcasting of scenes from most modern plays. It may be possible, too, to persuade a merchant who advertises regularly on a local station to include a sentence about the play in his commercial for several days, in return for credit on the play program.

Direct contact. Without doubt, one of the best means of publicity is direct contact with groups and organizations. The college or school theatre that wishes to expand its audience in the town can best do so by working through business and professional clubs, womens clubs, and parent-teacher associations. The community theatre in turn will work through the schools. Clubs and organizations are frequently in need of speakers and of entertainment, and arrangements are ordinarily not hard to make. Of course, the speaker and the entertainment must be good or the publicity will be bad. If possible, circulars advertising the play should be distributed to each member of the club. This direct contact may be extended to include the actual sale of tickets, as described below.

Lobby exhibits. It may be useful in securing the support of an organization, if an exhibit of its work can be held in the lobby of the theatre during the performances. This is not inappropriate in the case of photography clubs, and other art and craft groups.

Contests. A contest staged in connection with the production provides additional publicity material and generally stimulates interest. A poster competition with a prize or prizes for the best entries is appropriate and exploitable. Through it, one may in addition uncover artistic talent useful in costume and scene design. It may be useful, too, to offer a prize or prizes for the best criticisms of the opening performance. One or more of these may be publishable and provide good after-premiere publicity. Any such contest should be planned carefully and well in advance. The rules should be clear, and qualified judges chosen, if possible from among people well known in the community.

Opening night. A good deal of publicity may be gained by building up the opening night as an artistic or social occasion

or both. In the beginning, it may be necessary to distribute
complimentary tickets to prominent and influential people in
the community to insure an audience of this type. First night in
New York is traditionally the critics' night and the night for
fashionable theatre-goers. Publicity can be slanted to give this
tone to the nonprofessional first night also. Some special cere-
mony may be added, such as serving coffee in the lobby during
one of the intermissions or after the performance. Premieres of
million-dollar motion pictures have gone to ridiculous extremes. Nevertheless, within the bounds of good taste, the more
glamorous an occasion the first night can be made, the greater
its publicity value.

Small aids. In schools, a tag designed to attract attention and
to suggest the play, if worn by each of the students connected
with the producing organization, may prove a useful device,
and such tags are not difficult to make.

Restaurants that use typewritten menus can sometimes be
persuaded to include a line or two advertising the play.

TICKET SALE

If the publicity has been good, ticket-selling itself is a simple
matter. The main thing is that it should be easy and pleasant
for people to buy tickets. This means that tickets should be sold
at one or more central points during the hours when people are
most likely to buy, and that the ticket sellers should be courteous
and helpful. A department store may permit a booth to be set up
on its ground floor for selling tickets, if the theatre itself is not
centrally located. In a school the student store may be willing
to handle the ticket sale for a small commission.

In selling tickets, the patrons' seat preferences should, of
course, be respected as far as possible. Nevertheless, the seller
can sometimes judiciously exert pressure to build the house in
a particular way. For instance, unless the auditorium is so large
that only part of the house is likely to be sold, it is better not
to sell in solid blocks but to scatter the early sales, selling some
seats in as many sections as possible. Thus some locations in all
parts of the house are left for later purchasers, or, if the sale is
light, the house will look better filled than it really is.

However, this spreading of the house should not be carried
to such an extreme that the members of the audience lose the

sense of oneness, which, as noted in Chapter 8, is so important to effective play production.

Ticket sellers should try also not to leave too many single seats unsold. Comparatively few people go alone to the theatre. Most sales are in couples, some in threes and fours. Consequently, as one nears a sellout it is more difficult to dispose of the single seats.

Active selling. If the ticket sale lags for some reason, active salesmanship through personal contact will be necessary. This is relatively easy in a school, where the potential audience is strongly concentrated. A squad of energetic salesmen, who will take the tickets direct to fellow students in the halls and lunchroom and to meetings of clubs and organizations, can usually increase sales greatly. A community theatre should arrange to send ticket salesmen to schools, clubs, and other organizations through which a considerable number of possible buyers can be reached at one time.

It is sometimes worth while to make reductions in price to organizations which will guarantee to sell a certain number of tickets. If the reductions are substantial enough, a club may buy out a house or part of a house, sell the tickets at the regular price, and keep the difference for its own treasury.

Late sales. The theatre box office should, if possible, be so placed that on the evenings of performance people waiting to buy tickets do not have to block the entrances to the auditorium. The box office should be open early and staffed so that sales and reservations can be handled efficiently.

Season subscriptions. If a season of several plays is being presented, there is much to be said for selling subscription tickets which admit the purchasers to all of the plays. Such a sale guarantees at least part of the audience for each play, provides cash with which to begin operations, and makes budgeting less of a gamble.

Because subscription sales are income assured in advance, it is possible to offer them at a price which represents a saving over the cost of the same number of individual tickets. This is a strong selling point. Subscribers can also be offered their choice of seats, and the same seats for each play—which is usually some inducement. People who like to come to the theatre are glad to save themselves the trouble of buying seats on each occasion. Subscription sales save time and trouble for the business staff, since each subscriber has to be sold only once a season.

To sell a substantial number of subscriptions, a producing organization must have a reputation for creditable productions, and a definite program of plays, and it must devote several weeks to an intensive sales campaign using as many as possible of the advertising media and sales methods described above. Unless all ticket sales are handled through a single office, subscription sales should be concluded before the sale of ordinary tickets for the first play is begun, or embarrassing duplication of sales is likely to occur.

Taking Care of the Audience

It is not enough to sell plenty of tickets and so secure the necessary audience; the audience must be cared for when it comes to see the play. If patrons find the lobby congested, the ushers inattentive and inefficient, the auditorium too warm or badly ventilated, their enjoyment of the play is reduced and they are less likely to come to the next one. Proper management of the front of the house is simple, but nonetheless important.

HOUSE MANAGEMENT

The care of the front of the house is the responsibility of the house manager, who is in charge of the auditorium and lobby on nights of performance just as the stage manager (see Chapter 15) is in charge of the backstage areas. His job is to see that the audience is able to enter and leave in an orderly fashion and that it is as comfortable as possible at all times during the evening. In addition, he co-ordinates front-of-the-house activities with the backstage schedule to the best of his ability. Under him are the ticket-sellers, doormen, ushers, checkroom attendants, and any other workers who are concerned with the audience.

Before the house is opened to the audience, the house manager should see that it is in good order, with seats and floor clean, and seats turned up. If the front curtain is still up, he will order it lowered before the first patrons are admitted. He will see that doormen and ushers are at their posts and that the ushers are supplied with programs. He will check on the heat and the ventilation.

Thereafter, he will keep a sharp eye on lobby, foyer, and house and see that everything goes smoothly.

As curtain time approaches, he will advise the stage manager of the state of the house. It is desirable to start at the advertised time, or at most ten minutes later, as is the custom of most Broadway theatres, but sometimes a late-arriving audience makes this undesirable. Several minutes before the curtain is scheduled to go up, he will see that people still lingering in the lobby and foyer are warned, and when the curtain does go up he will see that the entrance doors are closed. If the foyer or lobby lights must be dimmed, that is his responsibility also. During the first act or part of it, he should remain most of the time in the lobby to see that late-comers are admitted with as little disturbance as possible.

At the end of the first act the house manager should see that the doors to foyer and lobby are opened so that those who wish to get out to stretch or smoke during the intermission can do so easily. He should see that these people are warned far enough in advance so that they can return to their seats before the second act curtain goes up.

At the end of the play, the house manager should see that all exit doors are open. His responsibilities cease when the last of the audience has left the theatre and all doors to the front of the house are closed and locked.

TICKET-TAKING AND USHERING

The doorman or doormen who take the tickets should be familiar with the seating arrangements so that they can give patrons preliminary directions as they tear off the stubs. If they are dressed in tuxedos, they will be easy to distinguish from members of the audience, and semiformal dress adds dignity to the occasion.

A head usher should be responsible for securing the ushers and for supervising their work. The number of ushers will vary with the size of the house. Unless the house is very small, at least two ushers should be assigned to each aisle, and in a large house four ushers may be required on each aisle. The ushers should be thoroughly familiar with the seating plan, and should be courteous and quick in showing patrons to their seats. The ushers should not be permitted to treat their job as an occasion for sociability either among themselves or with their friends in the audience. Sociability should be confined to the lobby and foyer during the intermissions.

After the curtain goes up, fewer ushers are needed. The head usher should remain near the entrance to be sure late-comers get started in the right direction, and one usher to an aisle should be adequate, unless there is a rush of late-comers. Each usher should be equipped with a small flashlight to guide late-comers down the aisles after the house lights are off.

Late-comers whose seats are easily accessible should be seated, of course, but those who will be forced to push into the center of front rows should be seated temporarily, if possible, in empty side and rear seats. If there are no such seats, it may be desirable to keep them standing in the rear until the first curtain. Of course, if this means a half-hour wait, it may be better to seat them in their own seats, a few at a time, and with special effort to keep them quiet.

One or two ushers should remain on the job in each section of the house until the performance is over.

Ushers should be attractively and, if possible, similarly dressed. Well-dressed ushers add to the pleasantness of the occasion, and if they are similarly dressed they can be easily distinguished from the members of the audience.

Actors in makeup and costume should not be admitted to the house, nor should backstage workers in work clothes. Actors and production workers should be admitted only if they can come in and out without disturbing the audience. In any case, members of the production crew, ushers, and doormen should not be permitted to stand close to the back seats.

CHECKING

A checkroom for hats and coats adds considerably to audience comfort, particularly in cold weather. Of course the checkroom should be adequately staffed and efficiently run.

REFRESHMENTS

In small theatres with the necessary facilities, coffee and cookies served in one of the intermissions add to audience enjoyment, and the additional good will is probably well worth the small cost in money and extra effort.

This discussion of front-of-the-house management has been in terms of the conventional picture-frame indoor theatre, but most of it applies to the audience in the arena type of indoor theatre and to the various types of outdoor theatres. The aim is always to make the audience as comfortable as possible under the prevailing conditions. If that is kept in mind, common sense will dictate any necessary modifications of procedure.

Questions

1. What are the possible sources of publicity material?
2. What are the principal methods of securing publicity?
3. How might opening night be used to secure extra publicity?
4. Formulate some "Tips for the Box-office Man."
5. What are the advantages of selling season subscriptions?
6. What are the duties of the house manager?
7. Formulate some "Tips for Ushers."

Exercises

1. Get up a circular to be used in advertising the production of a particular play by a group with which you are familiar.
2. Lay out a window card or poster, advertising the production of a particular play by the same group.
3. Plan a large poster for the same purpose.
4. Plan a program of newspaper publicity for the same purpose.
5. Write a sample newspaper story as for Exercise 4.
6. Plan a program of direct contact with clubs. Which ones? When? How? What?
7. Plan a contest to be used to publicize a particular production.
8. Lay out a circular to be used in advertising a sale of season subscriptions.
9. Make a chart of the personnel and organization necessary for good front-of-the-house management in a theatre you are familiar with.

Bibliography

Dean, Alexander, *Little Theatre Organization and Management for Community, University, and School,* New York: D. Appleton-Century-Crofts, Inc., 1926.

Hinsdell, Oliver, *Making the Little Theatre Pay,* New York: Samuel
    French, 1925.
McCleery, Albert and Carl Glick, *Curtains Going Up,* New York:
    Pitman Publishing Company, 1939.
Selden, Samuel, ed., *Organizing a Community Theatre,* Cleveland:
    The National Theatre Conference, 1945.
Stanton, Stanford E., *Theatre Management,* D. Appleton-Century-
    Crofts, Inc., 1929.

CHAPTER 10.

THE THEATRE

$\mathcal{P}$lay production is strongly affected by the physical conditions under which the art is practiced. Early plays probably required only a space for the two essentials of production: the actors and the audience. Some plays can still be produced well enough on a level space outdoors with the audience standing around the acting space or seated on a convenient hillside, and some plays can be produced adequately in the center of a room with the spectators seated all around. However, most existing plays were written for a permanent, specially built place of production, for a *theatre,* and most modern plays were written for production in a particular form of theatre, called the *picture-frame theatre.* By far the largest number of theatres today are of the picture-frame type, and most play production takes place under the special conditions which this form of theatre sets up.

The Picture-Frame Theatre

This form of theatre consists fundamentally of two distinct parts, two boxlike shells, abutting each other and opening into each other through the *proscenium arch.* One of these shells, the *auditorium,* is designed to house the spectators and to provide them with seats from which they can see and hear what occurs on the stage behind the frame of the proscenium arch. The second shell, the *stagehouse,* is designed to house the production and all the equipment and machinery it requires.

AUDITORIUM

The auditorium is shaped like a rectangular box, set on its bottom, with a part of one end cut out for the proscenium arch. A good, efficient auditorium of this type (seating about seven hundred) will be about seventy feet long and about sixty feet wide at its widest point. It is not much wider at the stage end

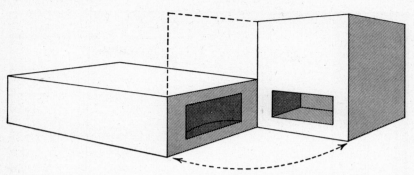

The fundamental shape of the picture-frame theatre is shown by two boxes joined at the prosecenium opening.

than the width of the proscenium opening. The walls curve or slant out as they move away from the stage and reach the full sixty-foot width about two-thirds of the way back.

Beginning at a level about three feet below the stage floor, the auditorium floor, after the space left for the orchestra pit and the first row of seats, is slanted or *raked* upward to the back of the auditorium at a rate of about two inches to the foot.

The seats are arranged in rows facing the stage on a very flat curve and staggered so that one seat is not directly behind another.

Audibility and sight lines. No spectator is seated so far from the stage that he should have difficulty hearing the actors, and every spectator has a good view of the playing space through the frame of the proscenium arch.

Spectators seated in the front left seats will be able to see beyond the playing space into the wing space on stage left, and spectators seated in the front right seats will be able to see into the stage right wing. Those seated in the front rows will be able to see above the stage into the *fly space* behind the top of the proscenium arch. About half the spectators, since they sit only a little above the level of the stage, will have a more or less foreshortened view of the stage floor. These sightlines must be taken into account in planning the production.

Variations. Often, in order to increase the number of seats without placing some of them too far from the stage, a balcony

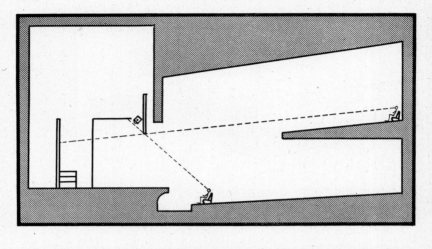

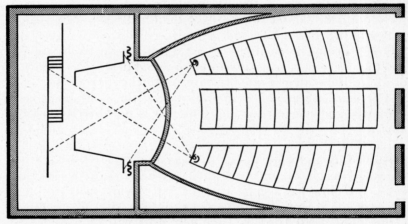

The vertical and horizontal sightlines in the picture-frame theatre are shown here.

or even, in older theatres, two balconies are added above the last half or third of the orchestra seats. Then the vertical sight-lines become of additional importance. Balcony seats provide a good view of the stage floor, but the higher they get the more the view is cut down by the top of the proscenium arch. Care must be taken that the backwalls of settings are not so far upstage as to be invisible and that actors do not play so far upstage that they are out of sight from the rear balcony seats.

If the auditorium is much deeper than seventy feet, a broad style of acting, unsuitable to many representational plays, will be required to carry to the further seats, and in the very large auditorium a public address system may be required to insure audibility.

If the auditorium at the front is much wider than the proscenium arch, the sightlines from a good many side seats will be bad. Such a condition can be partially compensated for by using shallow settings and by keeping the actors center and downstage as much as possible.

If the auditorium floor is raked little or not at all, the spectators will have difficulty in seeing over the heads of those in front. The view for some of them can be improved by incorporating in settings, whenever possible, higher acting levels toward the rear of the acting space.

THE STAGEHOUSE

The stagehouse too is shaped like a rectangular box, but it is set on an end with the proscenium opening cut out of the front face near the bottom.

If the proscenium arch is thirty feet wide and eighteen feet high (good, standard dimensions for the modern picture-frame theatre), the stage floor should be about sixty feet from side wall to side wall (leaving fifteen feet of wing room on either side of the proscenium opening) and about thirty feet from the proscenium wall to the back wall. The stage floor ordinarily extends no more than three feet into the auditorium just enough to hold the footlights. It should be made of soft wood which will take without difficulty the stage screws of the braces by which a good deal of the scenery is supported. It may contain one or two trap doors in the part visible through the proscenium arch. These provide access to and from a storage room beneath, called the *dock*.

Forty-eight to fifty-four feet above the stage floor is a network of steel beams called the *gridiron,* with enough room between it and the roof for a man to walk or crawl. The space between the top of the proscenium arch and the gridiron is called the *fly space* or *flies*.

The part of the back wall of the stage which can be seen through the proscenium arch should be finished in rough plaster

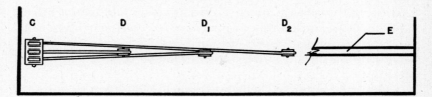

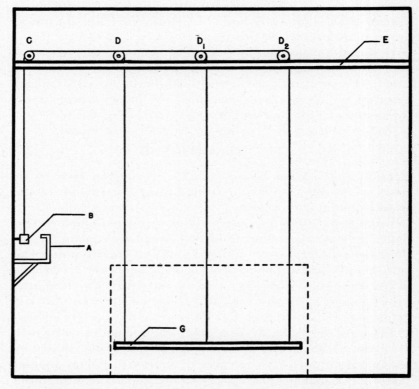

The rigging of one set of lines is shown here. **A**, fly gallery; **B**, pin rail; **C**, three-sheave head-block; **D**, **D**^{1}, **D**^{2}, three one-sheave loft blocks; **E**, gridiron; and **G**, batten.

and kept free of doors, radiators, and so on, so that it may be flooded with blue light and used as a sky backing for exterior settings. One side wall is pierced by a door large enough to admit scenery and large properties from a shop or storage room, and the other side wall is pierced by an ordinary-sized door leading to the actors' dressing rooms. A well-designed stage-house provides access from one side of the stage to the other through a passageway or rooms behind the back wall of the stage or under the stage at the dock level, so that actors and technicians can get to either side without crossing the playing space.

Standard scenic equipment and machinery. To the gridiron are fastened sets of pulleys, or *sheaves,* to permit the raising and lowering of curtains, drops, other scenery, and lights to and from the flies. For every foot of stage depth there should be a set of three pulleys, one stage center, and one on either side just inside the acting area. A rope is passed through each of these three pulleys, and the set of three ropes is drawn over a three-sheave head block near the side wall, down the wall, and is tied off on a pin rail fastened to the wall near the stage floor or on a narrow gallery twenty or more feet above the stage floor. Large sandbags can be fastened to these lines as counterweights to facilitate the lifting of heavy loads.

On the best-equipped modern stages, a *counterweight system* is substituted for the pin rail and sandbag arrangement. With the counterweight system, each set of lines is fastened perma-nently to a metal rack in which metal weights may be placed. This rack is pulled up and down on a vertical track built into the side wall of the stage by means of a a rope running over pulleys at the grid and at the floor. This permits any load to be well enough counterbalanced so that little effort is needed to raise or lower it.

Just upstage of the proscenium arch is hung a decorative border about six feet deep called the *grand drape.* This dresses the top of the picture frame and ordinarily cuts three or four feet from the height. Just upstage of the grand drape, on a steel cable instead of rope, is hung the *asbestos curtain* required for fire protection by the building codes of most cities. Immediately behind this hangs the *front curtain,* of either the drop type on a set of lines or the draw type on a track. Behind the front curtain hangs the *teaser,* a neutral-colored border six or more feet deep, which is used to reduce the height of the proscenium opening still further and to vary the height from play to play or from setting to setting.

On either side of the proscenium arch, just upstage of the

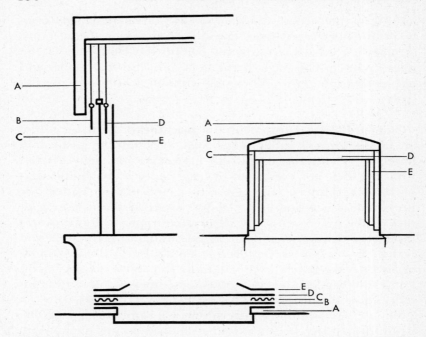

Here the proscenium arch is shown in section, perspective, and ground-plan. **A**, proscenium arch; **B**, grand drape; **C**, front curtain; **D**, teaser border; and **E**, tormentors.

teaser border stands some form of *tormentor*. The tormentors help to mask the wing spaces from view of the audience and to reduce the width of the proscenium opening. They should be the same color as the teaser, and with the teaser they form a flexible frame inside the fixed frame of the proscenium arch.

One form of tormentor consists of a two-fold flat or screen about fifteen feet high. One fold, about five feet wide, stands parallel to the proscenium just upstage of the teaser. The other piece, about eighteen inches wide, is hinged to the onstage side of the first so that it can be set at different angles. The whole tormentor can be slid onstage so that it cuts as much as five feet from the width of the proscenium, or offstage so that the full width of the proscenium can be used. The side wall of the box set is brought down within a foot of the tormentor and then carried offstage with a *return,* a flat the same color as the setting placed parallel to the proscenium. A space is thus left through which it is possible to throw light from behind the tormentor.

A more common type of tormentor is merely a flat painted the same color as the teaser or covered with the same material and placed parallel to the proscenium just upstage of the teaser. It is equipped with hardware for fastening it to the side wall of the setting. Tormentors of this type are useful in masking the wings and in cutting down the width of the proscenium opening, but they leave no opening for tormentor lighting.

The part of the stage floor visible through the proscenium arch is ordinarily covered with a groundcloth of heavy duck canvas neutral in color. This keeps the floor from splintering and deadens footfalls.

The electrical equipment (switchboard, outlets, and permanently installed lights) will be described in the chapter on Lighting.

Using the picture-frame stage. This standard modern stage is well suited to representational production. Behind the proscenium it is relatively easy to create the illusion of an action which is separate from the audience in a place which is distinct from the theatre. The first step in creating this illusion is to define the place of the action by separating it from the offstage area: the wing space off left and right must be *masked* or hidden from view of the audience; the view into the flies above the stage must be cut off, and the back wall of the stage, unless it is to serve as part of the setting, must be concealed.

For a strong illusion of reality an effect of depth on the stage is nearly always essential. The picture-frame theatre, because it places the action behind the proscenium arch and provides a poor view of the stage floor from most of the orchestra seats, presents certain problems in creating effects of depth. From the seats which give a foreshortened view of the stage floor, the empty stage will not seem as deep as it actually is. The spectator's feeling of depth will depend largely on his view of objects above the level of the floor, on the furniture, the units which make up the setting, and on the actors. Care must be taken in designing the settings and the lighting, in arranging the furniture, and in grouping the actors, to use fully the actual depth of the setting, thus giving it reality to the eye of the spectator.

Paradoxically, because most spectators see the floor not at all or sharply foreshortened, illusions of nonexistent depth are easily created. The eye, lacking a dependable plane of reference such as is provided by a good view of the stage floor, is easily fooled into assuming that distances are greater than they are in actuality.

For exterior settings, effects of limitless depth are often required. To achieve such effects in an actual depth of thirty feet, special care is required in the designing of the setting and the lighting, and in the use of the setting by the actors. The specific significance for those departments of production will be discussed in the appropriate chapters.

Another requisite for a strong illusion of reality and for maintaining audience attention in productions of multiscene plays is speed in changing the settings. The modern picture-frame theatre handles changes of scenery fairly well. The system of pulleys, ropes, and counterweights is well adapted to moving comparatively lightweight drops and borders, and occasionally the whole back or side wall of a setting may be fastened to a batten, hung from a set of lines, and, when it is not needed, hauled up into the flies out of sight of the audience. The heavier flats and three-dimensional set pieces, which make up the greater part of representational scenery, are for the most part shifted by hand on the stage floor. Consequently, they must be built in units small enough and light enough so that each unit can be moved easily, preferably by one or two stagehands.

It is possible, on a stage of the dimensions described, to mount one setting on two wagons (low platforms on rollers), each half the width of the proscenium opening, so that it may be quickly split, and one half rolled offstage right, the other half offstage left, and the setting for the next scene, also mounted on a wagon, rolled downstage to fill the space that has been vacated. This is known to stagehands as the *double shuffleboard*.

Better still, two wagons may be used, each as wide as the proscenium opening and as deep as the available wing space, and each pivoted at opposite downstage corners. With this arrangement, the setting which has just finished "playing" may be rolled on its pivot into the wing on one side, and a second wagon carrying another complete setting—actors too, if desired—may be pivoted in from the opposite wing. From this jackknife blade movement, the device is called the *jackknife stage*. Neither the double shuffleboard nor the jackknife stage will accommodate two settings each the full depth of the stage.

Special equipment. A few picture-frame theatres are equipped with a revolving stage which permits a circular area of the floor, most of the part visible behind the proscenium frame, to be rotated by machinery. On this, a number of settings may be set up simultaneously and the shift made simply by turning the stage so that first one and then another setting faces the proscenium opening. The revolving stage has not become standard equipment, partly because it is expensive, and partly because it imposes sharp limitations on the shapes of settings.

A few picture-frame theatres have a plaster dome, a custom-built wall of plaster curving toward the audience at the top and sides, which stands permanently or semipermanently near the back of the stage. Such a dome provides a better illusion of sky than is obtainable with a canvas drop or cyclorama or flat plaster wall, but it is an obstacle to backstage traffic, and all settings must be designed around or in front of it.

A useful piece of equipment found in some theatres is a curtain track, hung about fifteen feet upstage of the proscenium, to which draw curtains may be attached. This provides in effect an inner stage, which may easily be shut off from view or revealed by closing or opening the curtains.

Variations in the picture-frame stage. Some stages have a narrow proscenium opening. If the width of the opening is twenty feet or less, the production of most plays will be badly cramped. Plays should be selected and the settings, groupings, and movement carefully planned with this condition in mind.

A low proscenium opening will not be a handicap unless the auditorium has a balcony. Twelve to fifteen feet of height is about all that is needed for most plays, although more may be required for a play like *Street Scene,* which calls for a three-story setting.

The shallow stage, less than twenty feet deep, makes difficult or impossible any strong illusion of distance in exterior settings, and in interior settings cramps the arrangement of furniture and actors in depth.

The very wide proscenium opening combined with a comparatively shallow stage makes effects of depth very difficult to achieve, and tends to impose a flat style of setting and acting. For some plays on this type of stage, it may be desirable to mask-in the sides of the proscenium opening to make a better

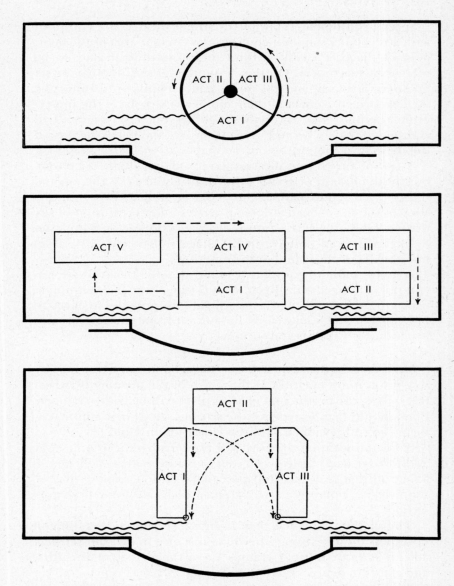

Top. This is the groundplan of a revolving stage divided into three settings and showing method of masking. **Middle.** This is the groundplan of a full wagon stage. The settings, as indicated, are less than full stage width for lack of maximum wing space. **Bottom.** This is the groundplan of a jack-knife arrangement of wagons for quick changes.

proportioned playing space, even if this means cutting off the view entirely from some seats in front on either side of the auditorium. Of course, these seats should not be sold.

On the other hand, the comparatively narrow and very deep stage limits the actors' movement from side to side and forces too many of the scenic units into the sides of the settings. Settings on this type of stage have a tendency to resemble tunnels.

The picture-frame stage with inadequate depth and wing space presents special difficulties for the production of the play of many scenes. There is not enough room to store the scenery and furniture for the settings not occupying the playing space. Under such cramped conditions settings should be planned so that as much of the scenery as possible can be flied, and the changes of setting should be simplified so that they can be achieved with the fewest possible different pieces of scenery and furniture.

When the stage has little or no fly space, the system of pulleys, ropes, and counterweights will be of no use in the shifting of scenery, although still needed for hanging borders, drapes, ceiling pieces, and lights. Settings for this type of stage will have to be planned for shifting by hand or with wagons on the floor level.

The picture-frame stage with a standard proscenium width and unusual wing space and depth (thirty feet of wing space on each side and forty to fifty feet of depth), is suited to the full use of the wagon system of scene-shifting. If necessary, on such a stage, five complete settings can be set up at one time each on its separate wagon: one behind the proscenium arch in view of the audience, two in one wing, one upstage in the other wing, and one upstage behind the first setting. A change can then be made in a few seconds by rolling the first wagon into the space left for it in the wing and rolling the second wagon on from the opposite wing to replace it. While the second scene is being played, the wagons backstage can be moved around so that wagon three is in position for the next change, and a space is left in the opposite wing to receive wagon two. With the back wall so far from the proscenium, a drop or cyclorama will have to be used to represent sky.

Some stages are accessible from one side only. For a stage of this kind it is often desirable to design settings so that most entrances and exits are made on the accessible side of the stage. This is especially true if the setting uses the full depth of the stage and so does not permit actors to pass behind it from one side of the stage to the other without being seen by the audience.

If the back wall of the stage is not clear of doorways, radiators, ventilators, and so on, or if it is finished in brick or wood instead of rough plaster, it cannot be used as part of the scenery for exterior settings. A canvas drop or cyclorama will be needed for effects of sky.

The lack of trap doors in the stage floor is no obstacle to the production of most plays, but it makes difficult the creation of occasional scenic effects, such as Ophelia's grave in *Hamlet,* the entrance to the basement in *Street Scene,* and the entrance from downstairs in *The Medium.*

REPRESENTATIONAL CHARACTER

The picture-frame theatre is admirably suited to the representational form of play production, which aims to create the illusion of life, real or imaginary, going on independent of audience and theatre. The proscenium arch provides at the same time a strong architectural separation between the audience and the play, and a frame which conceals the machinery by which the illusion of life is created on the stage. The separation of audience and play is intensified by the use of the front curtain to cover scene shifts and by the custom of darkening the auditorium when the curtain is open.

On the other hand the picture-frame theatre presents definite obstacles to the presentational form of play production. Even though the actors may direct their performance to the audience, the effect is weakened by the fact that they are separated from the audience by the proscenium arch. Consequently, for presentational production the divisive effect of the proscenium arch is frequently broken down by extending the acting space into the auditorium. In a production of Sartre's *The Flies* by the Dramatic Workshop of the New School, the walls of the auditorium were decorated with temporary murals which expressed the theme of the play in a variety of symbols, and characters entered and exited down the aisles. The presentational effect was not strong, however, because the auditorium was kept most of

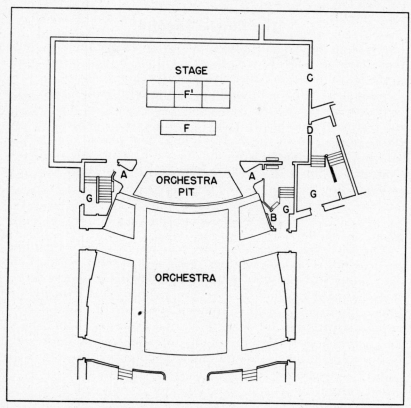

This plan for the Brooklyn College Little Theatre in College Center and Arts Building attempts to make the ordinary picture-frame theatre more adaptable to presentational production. The floor of the orchestra pit can be elevated to provide an apron stage with proscenium doors, **AA**, and with proscenium balconies (not shown) at the second level. The lighting control is located off the right stair hall, **G**, near porthole, **B**, through which the operator has a good view of the stage. The entrance to the shop is **C**; to the dressing rooms **D**. The large trap is **F**. The trapped area usable as a whole or in part is **F**[1]. Chapman and Evans are the architects.

the time in darkness and most of the acting took place behind the proscenium.

The presentational effect can be strengthened by building the stage out temporarily over the orchestra pit so that more of the acting can take place in front of the proscenium arch.

The Plastic Theatre

Although most theatres in use today are of the picture-frame type, there are a few which place part or all of the playing space in the midst of the audience and make little or no use of the proscenium arch. Furthermore, most of the great plays of the past were written for *plastic theatres,* and in producing them today the picture-frame theatre is often temporarily modified to suit the requirements of these older plays. The plastic theatre sets up quite a different relationship between actors and audience from that set up by the picture-frame theatre and poses its own problems for the producer.

THE ARENA THEATRE

The only type of plastic theatre which shows signs of gaining permanence is perhaps best described as the *arena theatre.* Fundamentally its consists of a square, rectangular, or oval acting space set in the midst of the spectators, who are seated on all four sides, either in two or three rows on one level, or in many rows rising sharply from the floor level away from the acting space. The acting area is illuminated by overhead spotlights. Scenery is three-dimensional. Actors and audience use the same entrances and exits, of which there are likely to be two (one at either end of the playing space) or four (evenly spaced around the playing space).

Salon type. The success of Glenn Hughes' Penthouse Theatre at the University of Washington has popularized the small, salon type of arena theatre. He has found it most effective for the production of one-set modern comedies. Serious plays have not fared well in the Penthouse Theatre, nor apparently have the few revivals.

The form of production is representational, and the production methods are designed to maintain an illusion of reality separate from the audience. A blackout at the beginning and end of each act takes the place of a curtain. Actors are discovered in position at the beginning of each act and leave the playing area at the end of the act under cover of darkness. Plays are selected or revised so that the action will not depend on scenic units like doors and windows, and since changes of setting must

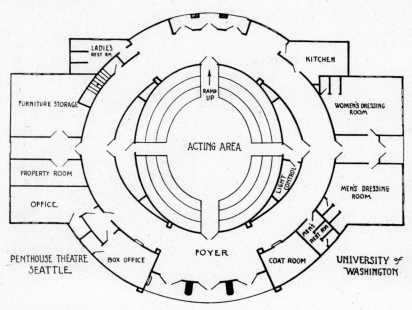

This is a plan of the Penthouse Theatre at the University of Washington, Seattle, Washington.

be made in view of the audience, these are kept as few and as simple as possible. Atmospheric lighting is impossible.

Albert McCleery, formerly Director of the Fordham University Theatre, believes that serious plays, particularly modern serious plays, seem out of place in the salon theatre, because the actors are too close to the audience. He thinks that actors are inhibited when they play intimate emotional scenes, which in life would take place behind closed doors, in the midst of spectators some of whom are close enough to touch. He thinks too that the audience is embarrassed by its proximity to such intimate emotional scenes as modern drama presents. Consequently, he draped the playing area with gauze (leaving entrances for the actors at either end of a long, flat oval), and by lighting that area from above and separately from the audience area he effectively divided them.

The spectators see the actors and elements of the setting through the gauze, somewhat less clearly than if the gauze were not there, but they cannot see the audience seated on the oppo-

This is the auditorium of the Penthouse Theatre, University of Washington, Seattle, Washington. The furniture is set up for performance. Glenn Hughes, director.

ite side of the oval acting space. The audience is invisible to the actors. With this device it is possible to get atmospheric lighting on the acting area. When the audience is lighted, and the acting area dark, the latter is almost invisible behind the gauze, although it is light enough for scene changes to be made and for actors to get into position without having to grope their way in complete darkness. Thus the gauze is made to substitute both for the proscenium arch and for the front curtain of the picture-frame theatre.

Whether the salon theatre is used with or without the gauze between actors and spectators, the closeness of the audience to the spectators and the plastic relation of playing space to audience affect all departments of production. The particular effects on acting, setting, light, and so on will be described in the appropriate chapters.

Considered from one point of view, the salon theatre appears to be the culmination of a tendency, which began in the latter half of the nineteenth century, to reduce the size of the auditorium and bring the spectators closer to the stage in order to strengthen the production's illusion of reality. With the specta-

This salon theatre is shrouded with gauze for Martinez-Sierra's *The Two Shepherds*. The photograph is taken inside the gauze looking from one entrance toward the other, the length of the playing space. The audience is invisible behind the gauze left and right. Note the realistic ceiling treatment. Fordham University Theatre.

tors relatively near, the smaller points of realistic acting and the elaborate and detailed realism of the setting could have something like their full effect. However, until the advent of the salon theatre, the production remained sharply divided from the audience by the proscenium arch, the front curtain, and separate illumination. Specifically, the salon theatre seems to owe its origin to a desire to provide in the live theatre something equivalent to the close-up in the moving picture. The extreme intimacy, in the salon theatre as on the screen, has been used almost exclusively for dramatic expression that is representational in form and realistic in style.

From another point of view, the salon theatre may be regarded as a reaction against the picture-frame form, since it makes possible the revival of an older type of relationship between production and audience—a relationship which is intimate not merely because the actors and the audience are close to each other, but also because the actors communicate directly with the audience. Since a completely representational setting is impossible in the salon theatre (even Mr. McCleery's gauze permits only very limited representation of place), the salon form may prove to be better suited to presentational production. For instance, most of the comedies of Molière and Shakespeare do not require representational settings, and they gain considerably in effectiveness when they are taken from behind the proscenium arch and put back where they were born, in the midst of the audience. Moreover, with the adoption of the presentational form of production most of the clumsiness of the salon theatre disappears: blackouts may be dispensed with; scenery and properties may be changed in view of the audience without apology; and general as well as specific illumination may be used.

Boxing-ring type. A few experiments have been made with an arena theatre, which seats many more people. Many rows of seats are built up at a steep rake on four sides of the central playing space in an arrangement similar to that used for prize fighting. Most of the spectators look down on the playing space. Both actors and audience use some of the same entrances at the corners or sides of the playing space. Scenery must be three dimensional and comparatively low so as not to cut off vision from the lower seats, and it must be moved on and off through the entrances used by the actors and audience or through traps in the floor of the playing space. The lighting must be done with spotlights, largely from overhead.

This form of arena theatre is best suited to the presentational production of abstract or fantastic plays, the simplification and exaggeration of which are necessary to carry to the further seats. It is fairly well suited also to the representational production of fantastic plays, but it is not suited at all to the representational production of realistic plays.

THE GREEK THEATRE

Greek drama was originally produced in the open air, mainly in a large, level, circular space called the *orchestra* surrounded on three sides by tiers of seats rising one above the other. The orchestra in the Theatre of Dionysus at Athens is now believed to have been sixty-five feet in diameter. A building called the *skene*, pierced at the center by a single large door, stood tangent to the orchestra circle on the open side. A space called the *parados* on each side between the ends of the tiers of seats and the skene served as entrance for the spectators and also for the actors.

In the earlier period the altar in the center of the orchestra was the focal point of the performance, but with the development of the *skene* as an element in production, some of the action moved to the segment of the circle before that building. The skene was first a temporary wooden structure and later built permanently of stone. However, it was probably not so inflexible as was once supposed, but was capable of being fitted with temporary fronts in a variety of arrangements of steps, doors, pillars, and so on.

The action of most Greek plays takes place outdoors, but machines were used for revealing the results of action which had passed within the scene building. The actors, on a low platform, (*exostra*) were either pushed or rolled out through a doorway, or else a section of the wall revolved as a butterfly valve (*ekkyklema*) bringing the tableau out and closing the space behind it. A crane or flying machine was almost surely erected on the roof of the scene building for the appearances of gods, and it is probable that an underground opening in the orchestra provided for the entrance of phantoms from the underworld.

The Greek theatre was strongly plastic. The spectators surrounded the playing space and most of them looked down on it, as is shown in the illustration on p. 12. The effect was similar to that of a performance in the modern circus or athletic stadium. The arrangement provided large spaces for the movement of the actors, particularly needed for the chorus. Because the performances were given in daylight, the whole production was presentational and nonillusionistic in the modern sense.

Modern substitutes. There cannot be much doubt that Greek drama is best produced today in outdoor Greek-type theatres. However, this is not always possible, and the problem of producing it in the modern picture-frame theatre arises. In such production, the proscenium arch as a barrier between actors and audience should be de-emphasized. For the production of *Alces-*

This is a picture-frame theatre modified for a Greek play. Note part of the chorus on the orchestra level from which seats have been removed, stage built out over orchestra pit, and reproduction of a Greek *paraskenia*. *Alcestis*, Illini Theatre Guild, University of Illinois. Charles Shattuck, director; Elizabeth Harris, technical director.

tis at the University of Illinois (illustrated above), the stage floor was built out over the orchestra pit and a section of the orchestra from which seats had been removed was used for the maneuvering of the chorus.

If building out into the orchestra is not possible, some of the plastic effect of the Greek acting space can be achieved by building up a setting of many different levels behind the proscenium arch. Such a setting not only makes the performance more plastic but also facilitates the handling of the chorus.

THE ELIZABETHAN THEATRE

The Elizabethan theatre is extinct, but a few permanent reconstructions of the form have been built and are used for revivals of Shakespeare, and temporary reconstructions are sometimes made for a single production.

The Elizabethan theatre was round, hexagonal, or octagonal

This is a cross-section of a model of the Globe Theatre from John C. Adams' specifications made by students in theatre history, University of Illinois. Charles Shattuck, director.

in shape, and was built around an open yard or pit. Three-quarters of the inside wall was taken up with three balconies one above the other, in which sat the more affluent members of the audience. The less affluent stood around the forestage which extended from the fourth quarter of the inner wall almost to the center of the pit. At the back of this forestage, in the center section of the stagehouse, was a shallow, inner stage provided with a set of draw curtains. Above this was a second inner stage, similarly provided with draw curtains, with a very shallow railed balcony across its front. Still above this was a smaller inner room provided with draw curtains and used ordinarily by the musicians.

On the forestage level, in each of the obliquely placed side walls flanking the inner stage, was a large, permanent stage door providing access from the stagehouse to the forestage. Above each of these doors was a large projecting bay window with practical casements.

The floors of the forestage and of the two inner stages were trapped. Movable scenery was probably not used on the forestage, but it may have been used on the two inner stages. Furniture was used on the two inner stages, and on the forestage too, when it was such as could be carried on and off by servants who were characters in the play.

Production took place by sunlight, so that realistic and atmospheric lighting were impossible.

The arrangement of the Elizabethan theatre provided a large number of different playing spaces on a variety of levels: the forestage, the two inner stages, the balcony of the upper stage, the two window stages, and even on occasion the musicians' gallery. The whole constituted a permanent setting that permitted the action to flow without interruption through the play of many settings. If the first scene was laid in a street or public place, it began with the actors' entrance through the permanent doors or through a slit in the curtains of the inner stage, was played on the forestage, and when it was finished the actors exited through the permanent doors. As they were exiting, the curtains parted on one of the inner stages, and the next scene began there with no lapse of time at all. Interior scenes with a large number of characters were begun on the first level inner stage and soon spread out to use the forestage also. Smaller interior scenes were played on the second level inner stage. The balcony could be used for the battlements of a castle, the deck of a ship, the brow of a hill, and so on. Ghosts might have appeared in the musicians' gallery.

There was no separation of stage and audience, no proscenium arch, no front curtain, and no distinction in lighting. The forestage placed the actor in the midst of the audience where his playing was of necessity plastic, and the whole stage arrangement drove the action toward the audience.

The Elizabethan theatre was admirably suited to the presentational production of plays written in many brief scenes instead of in acts. Most Elizabethan plays, and the plays of Lope de Vega and Calderon are of this kind and gain tremendously from production in the Elizabethan form of theatre.

Modern substitute. A modern picture-frame theatre can be turned into a modified Elizabethan theatre by building a temporary apron out over the orchestra pit and constructing behind the proscenium arch the façade of an Elizabethan stage with

This is a reconstruction of the Globe Theatre for Illini Theatre Guild productions, University of Illinois. The apron is built out over the orchestra pit and part of the orchestra. Note inner stages with musician's gallery above and the permanent doors and windows on the sides. This was planned by Wesley Swanson and executed under his direction.

doors and windows on either side of the inner stages. The front curtain will not be needed, although it may be used to indicate the beginning of the play and for intermissions, if intermissions cannot be dispensed with. Artificial illumination will be used and atmospheric lighting possible. This modern equivalent will have most of the fluidity of the Elizabethan theatre but only part of its dynamic, plastic quality. For an approach to the full effect, seats must be removed from the front of the orchestra and a forestage built out at least fifteen feet in front of the proscenium arch.

THE APRON THEATRE

The apron theatre is extinct also, although some existing picture-frame theatres retain a vestige of it in the form of a

Here is shown the use of an upper stage in *Antony and Cleopatra* produced on the reconstruction of the Globe Theatre stage by the Illini Theatre Guild. Charles Shattuck, director.

stage which projects eight or ten feet into the auditorium. In the apron theatre, the principal playing area was a forestage or apron extending twenty to thirty feet into a horseshoe-shaped auditorium and flanked on either side by boxes for spectators. The proscenium arch at the rear of this apron stage framed a space used almost entirely for setting. The arch and the front curtain with which it was equipped separated the actors from the setting. Permanent doors in the walls on either side of the proscenium arch provided access from the stagehouse to the apron. The apron was lighted by one set of lights, the scenic area behind the proscenium arch by another set. Actors either entered directly onto the apron through the proscenium doors or were discovered when the curtain rose to disclose them in front of the setting. They then came forward to play the scene. Although the larger part of his audience was in front of the actor, the occupants of the stage boxes were on either side of him and very close. Scenery was largely painted on wings, drops, and borders, and furniture was confined to the area behind the proscenium

arch. The set-
ting was re-
garded not as
an actual place,
but as an illus-
trative back-
ground for the
action.

The apron
theatre is well
suited to the
production of
certain presen-
tational drama,
particularly
English Resto-
ration and
eighteenth-cen-
tury comedy,
which loses
considerable of
its effect when
confined be-
hind a prosce-
nium frame.

**Modern sub-
stitute.** A pic-
ture-frame the-
atre with ade-
quate front-of-
the-house light-
ing can be
turned into an
apron theatre
by building
out a tempor-
ary apron over
the orchestra
pit and setting
up an inner

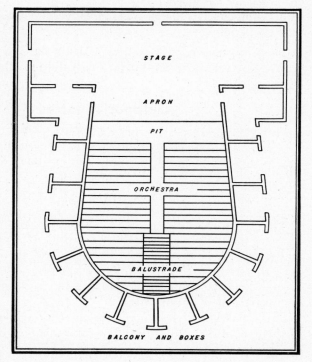

This is a sketch and groundplan of a horseshoe theatre
with an apron stage. Note proscenium doors, proscenium boxes, and the separation of acting area
from scenic area.

This is a modern equivalent of the old apron stage with the apron built out over the orchestra pit and temporary proscenium doors and proscenium arch within the permanent proscenium. *The Rivals,* Illini Theatre Guild. Barnard Hewitt, director; Joseph W. Scott, technical director.

proscenium with a draw or drop curtain flanked by proscenium doors. The regular front curtain will then not be used at all.

Outdoor Theatres

Play production out of doors presents special problems in setting, lighting, and acting, but these differ considerably, depending on the arrangement of acting and audience space.

NATURAL

The natural outdoor theatre which seats the audience on benches or temporary seats on a hillside, or on a lawn roughly facing an open space backed by trees and shrubbery, imposes very sharp limitations on play production. Only plays whose action takes place in a similar setting are really suited to production under these conditions.

Ordinarily, facilities for lighting are not available in this type of theatre, and production must take place in daylight. Consequently properties, any scenery which must be used, costumes, and makeup must all be adapted to sunlight rather than (as is usual in play production) to artificial light. Lacking the attention-compelling aids of a proscenium frame, and a concentration of light, a particular burden falls upon the acting. Some plays may be adapted to this type of theatre by eliminating ac-

Aeschylus' *Choephoroe* as produced by Marian Stebbins in the open-air theatre of Mills College, Oakland, California. Note the formal arrangement of the chorus and the dramatic use of the natural shadow cast by one wing of the scene house.

tion which depends upon setting. If changes of setting must be suggested these will have to be effected by means of properties changed in view of the audience.

In the absence of a front curtain and of lights, a fanfare of trumpets followed by a prologue will be helpful in indicating the beginning of the performance and securing audience attention to the playing space before the play itself begins. Since the setting remains unchanged, a greater effort should be made to create expressive groupings and patterns of movement in the acting.

GREEK TYPE

The Greek type of outdoor theatre with a low platform stage, some equivalent for the *skene,* and with an orchestra playing space from which seats for the audience rise in tiers is suitable for the production of Greek tragedy and comedy, Roman comedy, and a few Elizabethan plays by daylight, and if proper lighting facilities are available, for production at night. This type of

Setting up a scene on an outdoor stage viewed from the stage-right light tower, Cain Park Outdoor Theatre, Cleveland Heights, Ohio. Dina Rees Evans, director; Gerard Gentile, technical director.

theatre provides a greater variety of playing space and background for the performers, but most of what has been said about production in the natural outdoor theatre applies equally well to this type also.

GARDEN TYPE

There exist some outdoor theatres which seat the audience in a garden and make use of a covered courtyard or gallery for the playing space. Such an arrangement at once supplies the chief lacks of the other types of outdoor theatres: a structure which conceals the offstage space and necessary lighting facilities. Many more types of plays can be adequately produced in such a theatre, for the conditions approach those of the indoor picture-frame theatre. However, scenery should be kept at a minimum, for it will have to be changed in view of the audience, and special means must be found for supporting it. Scenery, costumes and makeup will be adapted to artificial light as in the picture-

Real and artificial scenery combined in a spacious production of *Our Town* in the open-air theatre, Cain Park Outdoor Theatre, Cleveland Heights, Ohio. John Hulburt, director; Graham Gloster Bird, designer.

frame theatre. On the whole, abstract plays are better suited than realistic plays to the rigid architectural setting.

STAGE TYPE

Some outdoor theatres are similar to indoor theatres in building up the audience space facing a raised stage on which the production must be presented. They differ from the indoor theatre in having no stagehouse. Instead, there are likely to be two towers, one on either side of the stage, concealing the wing space and providing locations for the principal lights. The back of the stage space may be the wall of a building or, as at Cain Park, the massed foliage of trees. Almost any type of play can be produced in this type of theatre, although the more realistic plays present particular problems. There are no flies and the floor has to be weather resistant, usually concrete. Scenery must be built so that it will stand by itself or else special devices must be used to prop it up. All scenery must be built to withstand the weather, particularly wind and rain. By focusing light on the plane of acting, the lack of a proscenium arch across the top will hardly be felt. For realistic plays requiring the effect of a box set, flats can be set up for the walls and light kept low, or a shallow ceiling border or beam suspended between them.

The sky, trees, and lake provide most of the setting for one scene of Paul Green's pageant drama *The Common Glory* in Matoaka Lake Amphitheatre, Williamsburg, Virginia.

If lighting facilities permit, scene changes can be partially screened from the audience by turning the stage lights onto the audience during intermissions.

In large outdoor theatres, a public address system may be necessary to insure audibility in the further seats.

It should be clear from this chapter that play production is always dependent on the theatre which it has at its disposal, and that different types of theatres raise different problems in play selection and in many of the departments of production. The lesson of this chapter is that the producer should be thoroughly familiar with the particular theatre in which he must work, so that he may make the most of its advantages and may labor intelligently to overcome the disadvantages it is almost sure to present.

Questions

1. What is the fundamental shape of the picture-frame theatre? Name its two parts.
2. Describe the sightlines of the picture-frame theatre.
3. How does the addition of balconies affect the sightlines in the picture-frame theatre?
4. In a picture-frame theatre, what are good standard dimensions for proscenium opening, stage depth, wing space, and height to gridiron?

5. What access is provided to the good picture-frame stage?
6. What is a counterweight system, and how is it used?
7. What is the grand drape? the teaser?
8. What are the tormentors? What are their functions?
9. Why is it necessary to mask the wing and fly space?
10. What problems does the picture-frame stage raise in achieving effects of depth?
11. What is the double shuffleboard?
12. What is the jackknife stage?
13. What are the advantages and disadvantages of the revolving stage?
14. Of what use is a curtain track hung above the playing space?
15. What are the effects on production of a very wide proscenium opening and a very shallow stage?
16. How do inadequate wing space and depth affect production?
17. Why is the picture-frame theatre especially suited to representational production?
18. How is the plastic theatre better suited to presentational production?
19. Describe the salon type of plastic theatre.
20. What are the significant characteristics of the Elizabethan stage?
21. Describe a modern substitute for the Elizabethan stage.
22. Describe the apron stage.
23. Describe a modern substitute for the apron stage.
24. What are some of the special problems of production in outdoor theatres?

Exercise

Make or secure a ground plan to scale of a particular stage and enough of the auditorium to show the horizontal sightlines. Add to it all the essential vertical dimensions. Then point out the particular characteristics which must be taken into account when planning a production in this theatre.

Bibliography

Modern Picture-Frame Theatre

Architectural Forum, *Theatre Reference Number,* September, 1932.
Burris-Meyer, Harold and Edward C. Cole, *Theatres and Auditoriums,* New York: Reinhold Publishing Corporation, 1949. A detailed analysis of the planning, construction and equipment of the common types of theatres today. Many illustrations.
Isaacs, Edith J. R., ed., *Architecture for the New Theatre,* New York: Theatre Arts, Inc., 1935.

Pichell, Irving, *Modern Theatres,* New York: Harcourt, Brace & Company, 1925.

Modern Plastic Theatre

Hughes, Glenn, *The Penthouse Theatre,* New York: Samuel French, 1942.

Older Plastic Theatre

Adams, John C., *The Globe Playhouse,* Cambridge: Harvard University Press, 1943.
Nicoll, Allardyce, *The Development of the Theatre,* New York: Harcourt, Brace & Company, 1927, rev. ed. 1937.

Outdoor Theatre

Cheney, Sheldon, *The Open Air Theatre,* New York: Mitchell Kennerley, 1918.
Curtain Time Sundown, the Story of Cain Park Theatre, City of Cleveland Heights, Ohio, pamphlet, 1945.

PART THREE

THE INANIMATE
MATERIALS:
Setting, Light, and Sound

CHAPTER II.

SCENE DESIGN

The use of material objects to reinforce the action of a play has been a slow development in the theatre. On the other hand, it has never been completely absent. The savage used costumes and properties in his mimic dances, and the Greeks employed a kind of elementary scenery known as *periaktoi*—though what these consisted of we are not quite sure. The Greeks had certainly discovered one thing, though—that the audience could be distracted by being allowed to see too much; that an actor should be kept out of sight until he actually began to figure in a play, and further, that his importance could be considerably built up if he were to reveal himself in a central, elevated position. And so they built an architectural screen behind the dancing space—they called it the *skene*—to *mask* the actors while they were waiting for their entrance cues, and to *emphasize* the appearances of the important characters by providing them with a large central door leading to a platform which raised them above the space occupied by the chorus. A modern reconstruction of such a *skene* is to be seen in the Greek theatre at Mills College (see p. 12).

The playwrights soon made capital of the fact that this *skene,* with its imposing façade, suggested a palace. From it Clytemnestra emerges to welcome her husband, Agamemnon, back from the Trojan War—and to his doom. Around it group the people of Thebes in supplication to Oedipus, their king, to rescue them from the plague that is oppressing the city. The side doors which flanked the central portal door were used to suggest minor entrances to the palace or to other buildings of the town. It is even thought that they were sometimes disguised with painted scenery to make them suggest the caves and grottoes needed for the comedies and satyr plays which usually appeared on the same bill with the tragedies. This was done, no doubt, not only in order to enable them better to *designate* the place of the action, but also because it was found that the quiet dignity

164

of the architectural *skene,* so right for the Greek tragedy, did
not at all suit the *mood* of these lighter works. Perhaps the ancient producers also discovered that the three rigidly placed
entrances were not always located in the right place for a particular play. Perhaps they occasionally wished that the entrances
were closer together, so that a character in hiding could slip
quickly from one door to another, or farther apart, so that such
a character would be forced to traverse the whole stage and
therefore render himself quite conspicuous. Certainly later stag-
ers found the classical *skene* too rigid to motivate stage business
to the fullest advantage.

General Characteristics of Setting and Scenery

We have used the word *scenery* in the preceding paragraph
to refer to *temporary* portions of the actor's background, put
there for a *specific* purpose. The Greeks had no such generic
term; the *skene* (meaning "booth" or "tent"), from which our
own word derives, was applied to the stage-building as a whole.
Indeed, it was not until the Renaissance, when the painter entered the theatre in a big way and the stage receded behind its
picture-frame proscenium, that the word *scenery* took on its
present meaning. Even then the term was inadequate, because it
applied only to the *pictorial* background, leaving out the forestage and proscenium doors, which were still very much a part
of the action.

It took two philosopher-designers—Adolphe Appia and Gordon Craig—to convince us that detail of locale is only one function of the actor's environment (and a highly overemphasized
one, since it had become so elaborate that it was difficult to see
the actor in front of it) and that a play is, after all, an impact on
an audience, in which all the various stimuli of language, voice,
movement, mass, color, and line bombard a spectator from the
stage and must add up and fuse into one single impression. It
therefore became evident that a broader, deeper term than *scenery* was needed to describe the physical environment in which
the play takes place, and which makes it possible for the action to
occur. Such a word has long since been coined in German and
French: *inscenierung* and *mise en scène.* English and American
designers have by now pretty well agreed on *setting* as the
proper way to refer to the whole stage picture (except for the

actor) which, like the setting of a gem, should safely, comfortably, and unobtrusively contain the action of the play, enable it to display to the greatest advantage its inner light, and with it to form a jewel—*a work of art* of greater value than any of its parts could possess alone.

The setting of a play, then, is the total picture with the actor absent. It may be framed within a proscenium, or it may include the audience and the auditorium, as it did when Max Reinhardt rebuilt the Century Theater into a cathedral to house *The Miracle*. It may be composed of *scenery*—that is, of pieces of background designed to figure actively in the expression of the play, or of *neutral backgrounds* like drapes, which by their nature tend to recede from the audience's consciousness, or of a combination of these. It may even be empty space, as in the arena theatre, where actors perform entirely surrounded by the audience. But whatever form it takes it must fulfill four functions: two of these are mechanical, and aim to provide the actor with a physical environment that he can use to best advantage. They are (1) to *mask* or conceal things and people until—and unless— they should be seen and (2) to provide means of *emphasis* for important characters and *motivate* the action by means of strategically located levels and openings. The other two are psychological, and aim to make the audience sense a space where the action of the play would naturally occur. They are (3) to *designate* (or indicate) the time and place and (4) to express the predominant *mood* of the play through line and color.

Basic Requirements

There are certain factors which must be taken into consideration when planning the setting of a play. By far the most important of these is *suitability*. A setting must be "right." It must, as has been pointed out, be a place where the action of the play would naturally occur. This does not mean a literal reproduction of an actual place, complete in every detail, for we have long since learned that art is a matter of selection, and that too many details may be more disturbing than too few. Furthermore, the action itself may not be "real," but quite fantastic, and hence may demand a locale the like of which no man ever saw. Or the producer may decide that a script can better be expressed in some novel way, as when Orson Welles did *Julius*

Caesar on a bare stage and in Nazi uniforms, and *Macbeth* as a study in Haitian voodoo. So the setting must suit not only the *meaning* of a play, but also the *style* chosen for its interpretation.

Running counter to this—though really part of the same problem—is the factor of *plausibility:* Will the particular audience accept this particular set? This goes much deeper than obvious anachronisms like having ancient characters ride in automobiles (in a satire this might seem appropriately funny) or architectural implausibilities (for years people quite readily accepted the fact that stage walls had no thickness). It is a matter of balancing the creative imagination of the designer against a shrewd judgment of how far the expectations of his audience can be disregarded. For the first few minutes of *Our Town,* audiences often had the uncomfortable feeling that they were watching a rehearsal. Some people never were able to accept *The Skin of Our Teeth.* But this problem is really only a matter of suitability; if a designer can make his spectators believe that his setting is "right" for that particular play, they will accept it no matter how daring it may be.

A more tangible consideration which a designer must keep in mind is *visibility:* Can the important details of the setting—and the even more important actors who use it—be seen from all parts of the house? Stage technicians have a name for this: they call it "observing sight lines." Of course, some important detail of the setting might be completely in the audience's line of vision and still not be seen because of its smallness, paleness, or indistinctness of outline. So the carrying power of the setting must also be considered.

An equally important requirement which scenery must meet is that of *practicability.* This means, first, "Can it be built?" Since man has a habit of doing the impossible, perhaps we should add at once, ". . . with available workers and materials?" Any producer who has lived through the period of war-time shortages will appreciate this problem. It is an old story in schools and little theatres where personnel is all voluntary and usually untrained, sources of supply are remote, and budgets are scandalously limited. But this factor should never be allowed to become an alibi, for imagination can overcome handicaps of personnel and budget in the same way that it can solve mechanical problems. Of even more importance is the question, "Will it work on my stage?" This sometimes defeats even professional producers. Some Broadway shows (*Around the World in Eighty Days,* for one) abandon much of their scenery because they find that it will not fit into the theatre. But here again, imagination and skill can work wonders.

Part and parcel of practicability are the qualities of *mobility* and *durability,* which mean, in essence, the ease and speed with which a setting can be mounted, shifted (i.e., the scenes changed), transported, and stored without falling apart. To reconcile these two factors, of course, one must not only combine lightness with strength through the choice of materials, but also employ special techniques of design and construction. These techniques will be discussed later. Of prime importance in this connection is the particular stage involved. *The Eternal Road,* for example, was postponed for six months while the cellar of the Manhattan Opera House was being excavated to accommodate its massive scenery. But spatial limitations, too, should be a challenge to ingenuity. While not many schools have attempted *The Eternal Road,* yet *Men in White,* whose nine scenes involve three bedrooms, a medical library, and an operating room with running water, has been successfully produced on stages with little floor or wing space and no fly loft.

A final factor which the designer of settings must face is *economy.* Many Broadway productions (including the two mentioned above) have been "in the red" before they opened because of the too-heavy production costs. To the designer in the nonprofessional theatre, this problem is doubly acute. He must ask himself not only "How much will this particular set cost?" but also "How much of it will be useful later on in other shows?"

SUMMARY

These are the problems, then, which face the designer of a setting: First, he must see that it fulfills the four basic functions: (1) To mask the offstage space, (2) to provide emphasis—or focus —for important characters and scenes, (3) to designate the locale of the action, and (4) to express the mood of the play. Second, he must make sure that the set built from his designs will meet the seven basic requirements of suitability, practicability, visibility (from all seats), mobility, durability, and economy. To accomplish all this, he must be a man of many parts. In addition to skill as a draftsman and talent as a graphic artist, he should have a wide background in the histories of art, architecture, furniture, and decoration. Like the director referred to in Chapter 1, he should also be familiar with the history of the theatre, and have an understanding of all the crafts involved. On top of this, he must be a mechanic of real skill and ingenuity, especially in the craft of scenery construction, which will be discussed in Chapter 12.

Kinds of Scenery

INTERIORS

The most obvious way to classify scenery is into exteriors and interiors. Since the vast majority of the latter consist of man-made rooms, usually built on square lines, they present a much simpler problem to the stage designer than the former. A convincingly solid-wall texture can easily be achieved with paint on the surface of tightly stretched cloth, and an impression of thickness can be had by building "in the round" those pieces that protrude into the room, like fireplaces, mouldings, etc., or that frame the openings, such as doors and windows. Since the outdoors is never more than glimpsed through a window or the open door, a painted screen (or *backing*) properly illuminated, will provide an adequate impression of sky, especially if portions of familiar objects such as trees, shrubs, and porch railings or posts, are interposed in front of it.

The *box set,* as the conventional interior is called, usually consists of a series of wood frames covered with cloth, set edge to edge to form three walls. A ceiling (also of tightly stretched cloth) adds much to its solidity. The shape, however, need not be rectangular to the point of boredom, for it is possible not only to break up a room with offset corners, alcoves, bay windows, and the like, but also to "skew" the viewpoint so that the spectator looks at it on a slant, or into the angle of one of its corners. This offers the designer not only the use of sharp accents, such as corners present, but opportunities for unusual furniture arrangement as well. This also makes it possible to bring adjacent rooms partially into view through arches or French doors.

EXTERIORS

In exteriors, on the other hand, the general impression desired is not of enclosure but of space. Only on an exceptionally well-equipped stage is the illusion of completely open space possible, as this requires a cyclorama of vast height that completely encircles the playing space and is independently lighted by battery after battery of floodlights, both from above and from below. However, part of an object, protruding from behind a larger, nearer object, is accepted by the spectator as evidence that the whole object is present. Consequently, a designer can quite convincingly achieve the outdoor effect by filling a large portion of the rear of the stage with sky, and letting this disappear at the top, bottom, and sides behind objects that would naturally shut it off from sight. For example, hills often hide the horizon line. These, with the sky, can disappear behind trees or buildings, or even neutral drapes, at the sides. Overhead sight lines can be stopped by the spreading branches of trees, or by *borders* of neutral drapery. The extremities of the foreground objects will, in turn, be hidden by the frame of the proscenium. Note how this is done in the scene from *Brigadoon* illustrated on page 196.

The formula for an exterior set, then, is to frame a central rear area of sky with natural forms, or with a combination of neutral masking pieces. In essence, this corresponds to the eighteenth-century *drop-and-wing set,* which consisted of a large *drop* or "back cloth" with a distant landscape painted on it, hung at the rear of the stage, each side being flanked by a row of freestanding screens set parallel to the footlights. The visible or onstage edges of these *wings* were usually shaped—and the whole screen painted—to represent nearby objects such as trees or buildings. Overhead, joining the tops of corresponding wings, cloth strips (*borders*) were hung. These, too, were shaped and painted to simulate boughs, clouds, or even plain blue sky. As has already been indicated, the middle-distance objects were often disengaged from the back drop and brought slightly forward, painted on profile *ground rows*.

The drop-and-wing method was originally employed for interiors as well as exteriors by shaping and painting the wings to simulate pilasters and panels, and the borders like beams. But

This is the profile set as used for the bunkhouse scene in *Paul and the Blue Ox* by E. P. Conkle at the State University of Iowa. Theodore Viehman, director; Arnold Gillette, designer.

with the rise of realism this practice was abandoned in favor of the more convincing box set. Even in exteriors, the tendency now is to use three-dimensional trees and buildings instead of painted profile wings, especially for nearby objects.

Styles of Scenery

From one point of view, the division of scenery into exteriors and interiors is a rather pointless distinction, since there are many kinds of each. These vary according to the style involved, falling generally (as has been previously noted) into three types: realistic, abstract, and fantastic.

REALISM

When a designer employs the realistic style, he sets out to make the spectator believe he is seeing actual material objects in their familiar forms and relationships. This he can do either by building all essential details (trees, fences, doors, windows, baseboards, mouldings, etc.) in the round, or by painting them on a flat surface so cleverly that the observer will be fooled into thinking that they have depth.

The spot set is shown in two scenes from Shaw's *The Devil's Disciple* as produced at Brooklyn College. Elizabeth Casey, director; J. F. Foster, technical director. **Top,** Mrs. Dudgeon's cottage; **Bottom,** the minister's cottage.

Simplified realism. Under the influence of the modern tendency to eliminate unnecessary details so as to get at the "essence," certain techniques have been evolved which, although they employ too much reality to be properly classed as abstract, still represent attempts to break away from the confinements of too literal interpretation by reducing the amount of scenery and filling in the vacant spaces with *neutral setting*. They deserve special mention not only because of the added scope they give the designer, but because they offer the opportunities to economize on time, space, and budget which the nonprofessional designer often desperately needs.

The most common methods of achieving simplified realism are as follows:

The profile set. In this type of set no attempt is made to carry the edges out of sight. Instead they are either feathered off so as to blend into the surrounding neutral drapes, or terminated by a prominent detail of design or structure which may be silhouetted against sky. Thus, the bunkhouse in *Paul and the Blue Ox* terminates at the eaves, the roof having been left to the audience's imagination.

The spot set. In the two scenes from *The Devil's Disciple*, "spots" of scenery shaped to suggest gables surround each door and window. (See p. 172.) The spaces between are filled by neutral drapes. Since the units are reversible as well as movable, considerable variety is possible with a minimum of scenery.

The spot set is most often seen in revue sketches, where actual scenery is reduced to a small section of the stage, usually the up-center portion, and surrounded either with a sky cyclorama or with neutral drapes. The two scenes from *Call Me Mister* illustrate this. In the "His Old Man" number, the scenery consists of a screen, a crib, and a chest of drawers so arranged as to suggest the corner of a room. In the other, it is reduced merely to a single panel appropriately shaped and provided with the necessary opening: in this case, a shack with a sign "Truck Drivers Wanted." The line of men which, in actual scene, grew so long that it stretched across the empty stage, convinced the audience of the authenticity of the locale without the use of any further atmospheric details.

The drape set. The ultimate in simplification is to use draperies for all three walls of the set, and either to insert door and window frames between individual sections of the curtain or to leave all such architectural details to the imagination. Some effect of realism is achieved by the furniture used with this neutral background.

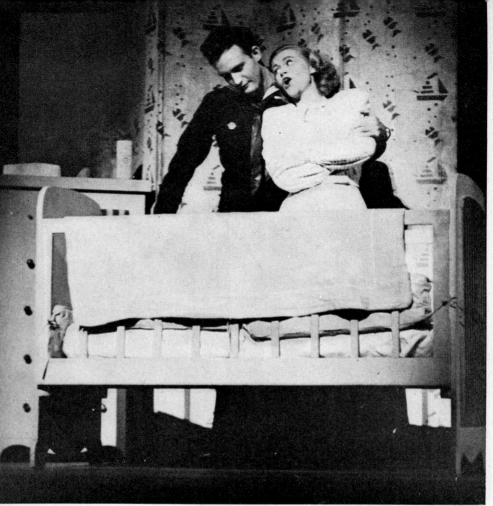

Fred Fehl

This shows a spot set in a scene from the musical revue *Call Me Mister*, designed by Lester Polakav. This is the "His Old Man" number.

ABSTRACTION

One of John Galsworthy's characters, in trying to define expressionism, said that it meant "not caring about the *outside* except insofar as it expressed the *inside*." This is descriptive also of designers who abstract or prune away details by eliminating "unnecessary" items altogether, or by blurring their outlines so that they become inconspicuous and simplifying and often magnifying the more important features.

The borderline between realism and abstraction is not clearcut, as has already been indicated. Indeed, the degree of abstrac-

This is another spot set from *Call Me Mister*. It is the "Red Ball Express" number.

tion in many of the types of scenery already cited depends more on their treatment than on their structural form. There is, however, another scenic method which arrives at simplification—and thereby opens up possibilities for abstraction—by *formalizing* essential details rather than by reducing their number. This is the *unit set* system wherein only part of the scenery is changed, a large portion being so designed that it will blend in with new pieces to form quite different combinations.

The formal unit. The architectural *skene* used by the Greeks (and described above) quite nearly approaches what is now

These illustrations and the two following on page 177 show the formal unit used for *The Tidings Brought to Mary* as produced at the State University of Iowa. Marian Galloway, director; Arnold Gillette, designer. **Top,** the clay model of the kitchen set; and **Bottom,** the actual construction of the barn.

Top, the road in *The Tidings Brought to Mary;* and **Bottom,** the cave scene.

Here and on page 179 is shown the portal unit setting for *Much Ado About Nothing*, Brooklyn College production. Jo Davidson, director; J. F. Foster, technical director. **Top,** before Leonato's house; **Middle,** room in Leonato's house; and **Bottom,** banquet hall.

known as a *formal* set. This same principle is employed by modern designers when, as in Jacques Copeau's well-known Théâtre du Vieux Colombier, they arrange arches, sections of wall, steps, and platforms—sometimes simulating rocks or stone work—in such a manner that these offer a wide variety of playing areas, and back them with either sky or drapes, or with a surrounding wall of the same texture containing formalized openings. Sometimes, as in Arnold Gillette's setting for *The Tidings Brought to Mary,* the whole unit is placed on a turntable so that different aspects may be presented to the audience. In such a set, change of locale may also be suggested, often quite effectively, by changing the properties and by illuminating first one area, then another, and sometimes the whole set. This type is least useful for comedy because of its austerity, but for this very reason it suits tragedy well.

The portal unit. Somewhat similar to the formal set is the popular type of unit frequently used in the late twenties and early thirties, by Woodman Thompson in *The Merchant of Venice* in which George Arliss appeared, by Jo Mielziner in Katherine Cornell's *Romeo and Juliet,* and by Lee Simonson in

Marco Millions, for example. It consists of a portal of some fairly neutral texture, usually simulating stone, which spans most of the stage a short distance back of the proscenium, forming an inner stage, which often contains a platform. This space can either be left open all the way to the cyclorama, closed in at the upstage edge of the platform with scenery which blends in with the portal, or shut off by a drop or curtain just behind the portal allowing the forestage to be used as a shallow set. On either side of this portal is an arch of the same material, joining it to the tormentors. These arches, too, can be left open and backed either by the same sky that backs the portal or by special pieces such as *hallway wings,* or they can be closed off by large flats containing doors or windows to make an interior.

It is not to be wondered at that two of the examples cited are productions of Shakespeare, for its fluidity makes the portal unit especially useful for the Elizabethan play. Indeed, the whole system stems from the Elizabethan theatre, with its side entrances and its inner stage which could be set and used, or closed by an "arras"

Nillog Studios

Continuing the portal unit setting for *Much Ado About Nothing* we have **Top**, prison; **Middle**, Leonato's orchard; and **Bottom**, a chapel.

tapestry. Note the model and reconstruction of Shakespeare's Globe Theatre on pages 151 and 153. Columbia University's production of *The Taming of the Shrew* pictured on pages 182

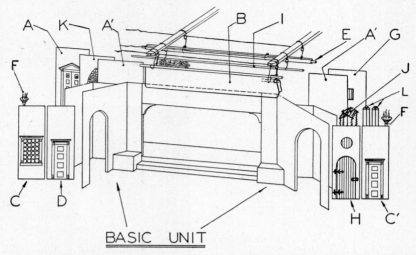

BASIC UNIT

This is a diagram of rig for portal unit set for *Much Ado About Nothing*. **A,** door flat for street scene; **A**^{1}, plain flats to be used with door, chapel window, and prison window; **B,** tapestry tripped for flying in narrow space to be lowered in room scene; **C, C**^{1}, window and door filler flats ready to be lashed into arches for room scene; **D,** door filler replacing window filler in stage right arch for banquet-hall scene; **E,** drop for banquet-hall scene rolled for flying; **F,** torchere for banquet-hall scene; **G,** window flat for prison scene to be set on platform up center with plain flats **A**^{1}; **H,** door filler to be lashed into stage left arch for prison scene; **I,** batten with hanging leaves to be lowered for orchard scene; **J,** arbor for orchard scene to be set on platform up left; **K,** church window flat to be set on platform up center with plain flats **A**^{1} for chapel scene; and in **L,** trifoil columns for chapel scene to be set right and left of church window.

and 183 shows a free adaption of this technique, which offers a comic compromise between the Elizabethan inner stage and the modern portal unit.

The simultaneous setting. In medieval times a large stage was laid out in the cathedral square for the presentation of Mysteries, and pavilions were built around its periphery, with "Heaven" at one end and "Hell" at the other, and those in between used consecutively for whatever earthly locales were needed: the manger of Bethlehem, the carpenter shop at Nazareth, the temple at Jerusalem, Herod's palace, and so on. After one pavilion had been used, the action moved on to the next, and the scenery on the first could be changed to represent another locale required later in the play. Modern designers have used this principle, building scenic houses all around the stage and sometimes out into the auditorium on either side, and then playing from house to house as the scene changed, lifting a panel in the side of the house if necessary. This was done effectively in the Theatre Guild's production of the *School for Husbands*. In large outdoor productions this technique is particularly useful. The *Passion Play* at Oberammergau employs it to a certain extent, flanking its conventional picture-frame stage with built-up streets down which the processions come.

The space stage. Similar to the drape set in its simplicity, but of a quite different feeling, is the *space stage*, which consists of a series of platforms and steps, most of them permanent,[1] providing different acting areas that may be differently lighted and set with properties to form different scenes, as in the formal set. Unlike the formal set, however the space set uses no background except drapes or sky, unless small spot sets or simple architectural details such as columns, arches, or pylons are added. Such a set was used by the Federal Theatre in its production of *Murder in the Cathedral,* and by Norman Bel Geddes for *The Eternal Road.* (See p. 187.) These examples indicate the type of play for which this technique is most suited.

FANTASY

A designer employing the *fantastic* style will aim not merely to get at the "essence" of his subject by stripping away superfluous details; he will go further and ask his audience to accept the patently unreal or abnormal. This he does by distorting familiar forms, by employing them principally for their symbolic meanings, or by discarding them altogether in favor of unearthly shapes.

This is a difficult style in which to work, not only because of the heavy demands it makes on the imagination, but also because it drives so far into the unfamiliar that there is danger of

[1] When the term "permanent" is used in connection with a setting, it means, of course, permanent only for that performance or series of performances. All scenery should come apart so that the production can travel to another theatre or to the storehouse.

Here and on page 183 is shown the Elizabethan stage adapted for use with modern scenery in scenes from *The Taming of the Shrew,* Columbia University production. Milton Smith, director; Victor Jacoby, designer. **Top,** Padua, a public place; and **Bottom,** Petruchio's house.

leaving the audience behind. It is also a difficult style to discuss because, originality being its strongest point, it does not divide neatly into categories.

Constructivism. The *constructivist* skeletonizes his forms, reducing them to the framework which holds them up. This is done most often to achieve unusual playing areas, though some-

Here is shown a third example from *The Taming of the Shrew* of the Elizabethan stage adapted for use with modern scenery. The scene is before Lucentio's house.

times it is done for symbolism. In his setting for *Death of a Salesman*, Jo Mielziner stripped a frame house down to its rafters and studding, exposing the actions of its inhabitants as mercilessly as the playwright, Arthur Miller, had laid bare their souls.

Expediency may also figure in the choice of this style. The taxicabs in *Two on an Island* and *On the Town* were skeletonized no doubt largely because this made the occupants much more visible and because the nonrealistic form made the lack of moving scenery behind them more acceptable. In Piscator's production of Sartre's *The Flies* a constructivist set was used for less obvious reasons but with equal effect.

Expressionism. For want of a better word, the term "expressionism" is used here to refer to that kind of design which, in an attempt to portray the inner state of the characters, relies almost wholly on symbols. This is not completely satisfactory, since it is now considered the duty of the designer, even in the most realistic play, to express the inner state of the characters, and to do so he must employ symbols. Here again, the difference lies more in degree than in kind. This is true even in the most extreme form of expressionism—surrealism—wherein the dream-

Here and on pages 185 and 186 is shown simultaneous setting. This shows the medieval Valenciennes Passion Play.

shapes the designer uses have recognizable details, the oddity lying chiefly in their combination.

Thus the designer for the fantastic play has at his disposal all the known kinds and styles of scenery, plus any new ones he can invent. He is free to recombine or distort his details to the limit of his imagination. He can change their outlines to typify the disturbed state of the characters who use them. He can surround them with looming figures or abstract forms, or even blobs of color. These can be built in the round or painted or projected on the background. Examples of most of these techniques may be seen in the three scenes from Brooklyn College's production of *The Adding Machine* (see p. 190), the scene from *Peer Gynt* (p. 40) and the settings for *The Master Builder* (p. 293).

Design

Having considered the basic functions of stage settings, the possible styles of expression, and the types in which they usually materialize, let us now consider the principles of design under which the creator of settings must work in order to get best results.

AESTHETIC PRINCIPLES

Much has been said in Chapter 1 about unity, rhythm, variety, contrast, balance, and so on. In Chapter 20 will be found a discussion of design principles as they relate to costume. All of this applies directly to the design of settings. For the setting, being a composition, must fulfill the same laws of unity, coherence, and

Vandamm Studio

The simultaneous setting for the seventeenth century adaptation for the
Guiterman-Langner version of Moliere's *A School for Husbands*. Lee Simonson, designer.

emphasis as any other composition. What makes the set designer's problem different from that of other pictorial artists is that
he must compose not only on the vertical plane of the proscenium arch but also on the horizontal plane of the stage floor.
Furthermore, his work is only *part* of a composition, the focal
point of which is the constantly shifting actor.

PHYSICAL PRINCIPLES

The designer's chief media being line and color, he is subject
to—and is implemented by—a special set of physical principles,
or natural laws, that pertain to these media.

What is meant by *line* is, of course, *outline*—the tendency of
the eye to travel over the contours of an object, and to recognize
that object when taken again over that same path, as in a picture,
or even an outline drawing. Such eye movements tell us much
about the position of an object as well as its shape. They are
involved also in the consideration of *perspective,* which has long
been a part of the designer's stock in trade.

Perspective. The function of perspective is to give objects
portrayed on a two-dimensional surface the illusion of three-
dimensional depth by means of the principle that parallel lines

Eileen Darby

The simultaneous setting is here given constructivist treatment by Jo Mielziner for Arthur Miller's *Death of a Salesman*.

(the edges of a square object, for example) when viewed at an angle seem to converge as they recede. In the heyday of the elaborately painted backdrop, this was a major problem for the designer. Now he is more likely either to conventionalize his drawing and thus be not so strictly bound by the laws of perspective, or to break up his picture into three planes (which the landscape painter does, too, by suggestion), building his foreground objects in the round, rendering his distant objects in two-dimensional profile but reducing their size and the intensity of their colors and perhaps blurring their outlines, and backing the whole composition with sky—which is infinite distance. (Incidentally, in a stage picture, heavy foreground objects are usually massed at the sides in order to mask the offstage space.)

Occasionally, the designer is faced with the problem of making a room (or an object) seem deeper than it actually is, or of putting a long piece of furniture into a space too shallow to hold it. In this he is greatly aided in the conventional theatre by the

The space stage setting for *The Eternal Road* by Franz Werfel. Norman Bel Geddes, designer.

fact that, since people usually view the stage from dead ahead and from the surface level, they depend almost entirely upon the muscular sensations involved in eye-focusing to judge upstage and downstage distances—a highly inaccurate method. Therefore, an object can be considerably foreshortened and still appear its usual depth. In cases where foreshortening alone will not serve (as in the setting for *The Gentle People,* where a pier seemed to extend for hundreds of feet away from the audience), false perspective may be employed. That is, the upstage end of an object may be reduced and its sides slanted inward. The billiard table in *Jacobowsky and the Colonel,* for example, was a tilted trapezoid. Two factors render this technique dangerous. First, perspective may look "right" from one point of view (usually the center of the theatre orchestra), but it may seem queer to people sitting in the side seats or in the balcony. Second, to be convincing it must be consistently followed throughout the whole set, as close comparison with a normal object immediately gives it away. For this reason, the billiard table, set in between undistorted bar and piano and surrounded by undistorted human figures, does not seem right. (See p. 194.)

A safer method than perspective for making an object on the stage appear larger than it really is, however, is to allow part of it to disappear behind a nearer and larger object. Let the end of a wagon protrude from behind the corner of a barn and the audience's imagination will supply the whole wagon; let a hill

Alfred J. Balcombe

This picture shows constructivism in a scene from Sartre's *The Flies* as produced by Erwin Piscator for the Dramatic Workshop of the New School, New York. Willis Knighton, designer.

extend out of sight behind a clump of trees (or a black drape, for that matter) and the spectators will accept the whole landscape. On the other hand, once let the edge of a drop become visible and the entire illusion is destroyed.

Color. Color is in reality light. From the physicist's point of view it consists of waves sent out by a vibrating medium. These vary in wave length (i.e., the distance between the peaks) from about .00007 cm., which is almost heat, to .00004 cm., which is getting close to radio. They travel in a straight line unless their course is changed by some obstacle they encounter. Some materials, like glass, pass light freely but slow down its speed and therefore bend its rays. Others reflect it back, either in a regular pattern or in a scattered or diffused manner. (This phenomenon is treated in more detail in Chapter 13.) Still other surfaces reflect only certain wave lengths, absorbing all others. This produces the phenomenon of *hue,* for a substance that absorbs all wave-lengths except the large ones mentioned above (.00007 cm.) will look red; one that reflects only the shortest will look purple. Those in between produce the other hues, green, blue, yellow, and so on.

Of course it has been known since prehistoric times that a surface could be made to reflect any given hue by smearing it over with the proper *pigment*. But primitive painters soon learned that there are three hues that can be mixed in such combinations as to produce all the other hues. When red and blue are mixed in equal proportions, violet (or purple) results; red and yellow produce orange; blue and yellow give green. Hence, red, yellow, and blue

Vandamm Studio

Constructivism as shown by the taxicab designed by Oliver Smith for the musical comedy *On the Town*.

have become known as *primary* pigments; orange, green, and violet as *secondary* or *binary* colors.[1] If one primary predominates, the resulting hue will take on more of its characteristic color, as for instance, yellow-orange, which contains about three parts of yellow to one part of red. All these hues can be diagrammed in the form of a circle (see p. 426). Hues next to each other on such a color wheel are termed *analogous* colors.

Now, if two colors on opposite sides of the circle (for example, red and green, or purple and yellow) are mixed together, they will gray each other, or reduce the *intensity* of the color. An equal mixture of two *complementary* colors (as these opposites are called) will produce neutral gray.

If white (which reflects all colors equally) is added to a color,

[1] Physicists contend that yellow, magenta, and blue-green are the true pigment primaries, since each absorbs one of the light primaries, red, blue or green (see Chapter 13), and therefore, when mixed, any two of them would absorb two of the primaries, reflecting only the third. However, in practice, red, yellow, and blue pigments will combine quite well to produce the secondary hues, especially if the red has a purplish cast and the blue is slightly on the green side. And so these familiar hues (red, yellow, and blue) are cited here as the *pigment primaries*.

Here and on page 192 are shown examples of expressionism in scenes from *The Adding Machine*, Brooklyn College production. Barnard Hewitt, director; J. F. Foster, technical director; Stanley Ferber, designer. **Top**, courtroom; and **Bottom**, graveyard.

it will pale, or become higher in *value;* if black (which absorbs all colors) is added, the value will be lowered. These variations in value are also referred to as *tints* and *shades.*

In theory, then, it should be possible to produce any value or intensity of any hue by means of the three primary colors plus white and black. In actual practice, it is difficult to obtain pigment primaries—even if we were sure what they are—in such a pure form that no chemical change would occur in their colors when they were mixed. It is therefore wise to keep quite a wide variety of hues and shades on hand rather than to depend too heavily on mixing.

PSYCHOLOGICAL PRINCIPLES

Although the single impact of a play reaches the audience through both the ear and the eye, the designer is concerned only with the latter.

The eye has in it two kinds of sense organs, or *receivers,* by which the incoming light waves are detected and transformed into sensory impressions: the *rods,* which are sensitive only to light and shade, and the *cones,* which register color.

The rods enable us to perceive the *outlines* of objects, and thus to judge their sizes, shapes, and relative positions. They also enable us to get some idea of the *mass* and *texture* of an object without touching it. (It is not difficult to tell a statue from a real person, or a snow bank from a cloud, even in a black and white photograph.) But, most important to stagecrafters, the rods make it possible for us to sense *movement,* which is the very essence of theatre art.

Influence of line movement. All these properties carry meaning, both intellectual and emotional, as has been indicated above. To illustrate further in the field of shape—or *line movement,* as the designers call it—we have but to compare the feelings we get when we think of jagged rocks and waving willows; of breaking waves and circling ripples; or, for that matter, of angular men and curvaceous women. Experience has taught us that sharp angles are more likely to hurt than smooth, round objects, and so we have learned to associate angularity with ruggedness, conflict, violence; and flowing curves with grace, ease, sensuousness. This is no doubt why the effete courtiers of

Another example of expressionism from *The Adding Machine*. This shows Elysian Fields.

the late Renaissance decorated their drawing rooms in the baroque style, where one must look hard to find a single straight line, while the castles of the medieval knights were crowned with jagged crenelations and sharp conical towers. These styles in line movement were carried out as faithfully in the clothes of the respective age as in its architecture, and were characteristic of the people who wore them. It would be as hard to imagine a satin-and-lace-clad sycophant of the court of Louis XV going on a crusade as it would be to picture a belted night mincing a minuet.

But this is not the only way in which line movement affects us. At least it would be hard to explain in this way the lift the human soul gets from the very direction "up." To stand in the midst of a forest of giant trees, in the nave of a Gothic cathedral, or in front of the Radio City tower, automatically produces a thrill of awe. And, conversely, many people feel bored, if not downright depressed, when they find themselves in low-ceilinged

False perspective is shown in the pier scene from Irwin Shaw's *The Gentle People*, Group Theatre production. Boris Aronson, designer.

buildings or caves, or even outdoors on a flat plain. Again, when the eye, following a line, is brought up with a jerk and sent sharply off at an angle by encountering a cross line, a jangle of the nerves is much more likely to result than if the gaze were carried gently to the new direction through a curve.

Of course, line movement never acts alone, but always in connection with the object that embodies it. The latter usually has meanings of its own that are far more obvious than those engendered by the general direction of its contours, and may even contradict them, as the busy façade of the cathedral at Pisa contradicts the spaciousness of its interior. Nevertheless, it is generally true that tall vertical lines do induce a feeling of solemnity, long horizontals peace and calm—even to the point of depression, flowing curves romance, and sharp angles conflict.

To see this in action, compare the bridge scene in *Winterset* on page 195, with the pier in *The Gentle People*, pictured above. Both have long, straight lines, and both have sharp angles. But the former towers majestically upward; the latter stretches flatly off. One would hardly have to be familiar with the two

False perspective is shown in the bistro scene from S. N. Beherman's adaptation of Franz Werfel's *Jacobowsky and the Colonel*, as produced by the Theatre Guild. Stewart Cheney, designer.

plays to sense that one is a poetic tragedy of social injustice, the other a homely picture of the struggle of the good against the greedy. Note again that in *Brigadoon,* the romance of a mythical Scottish village, flowing curves predominate by a wide margin, so that the stage picture is given an elusive, shimmering quality.

Influence of mass. Weight and bigness also affect the emotions, as can be seen by comparing the *Winterset* and *Brigadoon* sets. There is something terrifying in the looming mass of the bridge support. The mossy ruin, on the other hand, where little of the masonry is left, may be eerie but it is certainly not terrifying.

Influence of color. The three dimensions of color—hue, value, and intensity—have already been pointed out. Because of associations that have been formed around them, certain hues have taken on degrees of meaning. Red is the color of blood; orange of fire; yellow of gold; green of growing things; blue of the sky, and so on. Also, because purple dye was once rare, that color became known as *royal,* since kings alone could afford it.

It is not difficult to notice that the colors on the red-yellow side of the spectrum have much more violent connotations than

The use of line and mass to express mood is shown in the bridge scene from Maxwell Anderson's poetic tragedy *Winterset*, Playwrights Producing Company production. Jo Mielziner, designer.

those on the green-blue side. (Psychological tests have indicated that they have similar effects on the nerves.) It is for this reason, probably, that we have come to speak of *warm* and *cool* colors. Mae West made use of this when she wore a scarlet dress to portray the seductress "Diamond Lil." No doubt the old masters had the same principle in mind when they pictured her antithesis, the Virgin Mary, in celestial blue.

It should be noted also that cool colors tend to recede, while warm colors seem to advance. An amazing effect of depth can be obtained on a very shallow stage by filling the back wall full of blue sky. On the other hand, a yellow wall will seem to push the actors right out on the apron.

As to value and intensity—or shade, if you prefer—it is a common experience that the brighter a color is, the more powerfully it affects us. And so we have come to think of pale tints in connection with daintiness and dark shades with sombreness; of bright colors with activity, and deep tones with solemnity.

Because of its effects on the emotions, color is extremely use-

The use of line and mass to express mood is shown in the wedding scene from the musical romance *Brigadoon*, produced by Cheryl Crawford. Oliver Smith, designer.

ful to the scene designer in helping him create a setting in which we feel that a certain type of action can take place. Shakespeare did more than provide the designer with a field day when he specified a Venetian courtroom in which Shylock demands his pound of flesh and a moonlit garden for Portia's homecoming. Those who remember the sombrely splendid murals with which Woodman Thompson provided George Arliss for the former scene, and the feathery cypresses with which he surrounded the latter, will fully appreciate this. Or compare the riot of bright hues in which that gay romp, *Oklahoma!*, takes place with the misty shades of *Brigadoon*.

Of course, this sort of planning should never be obvious, especially to the uninitiated. Indeed, the designer himself may not take it consciously into consideration. But if one looks carefully at the plays one sees, one finds it subtly present in the most outstanding productions. And a trial will show that it works.

SUMMARY

In brief, then, the designer has three media in which to embody the spirit of the play: *line movement, mass,* and *color.* Generally speaking, straight lines are to be preferred for tragedy, curves for comedy or fantasy. Tall vertical lines are exalting, long horizontals depressing; long, flowing curves induce a feeling of romance, tight curves and circles gaiety. Sharp angles suggest tension, conflict. Mass is oppressive in proportion to its weight and size. Colors affect us through association. Warm hues are exciting and cool colors soothing. In general, the stronger the intensity of a color, the stronger its effect. Pale values are emotionally lighter, while deep shades are more sober. If used subtly, these principles will prove of considerable value.

Questions

1. Compare a landscape by Van Gogh with one by El Greco. How do they differ in mood? Why?
2. Look at a reproduction of Leonardo da Vinci's "The Last Supper." What has the artist done to emphasize the figure of Christ? Find a picture of a stage set or a scene in a motion picture in which the setting was used in a similar manner to feature a character.
3. Examine some of the pictures of interiors by the Dutch *genre* painters, such as Vermeer. What details are used to indicate the period? The season? The weather? The place?
4. From pictures and advertisements in current magazines, find examples of three different kinds of line movement (i.e., long verticals, crossed lines, and curves). Does the feeling engendered by the line movement fit in with the caption under the picture? With the color scheme? Would the picture serve as the basis for a stage set? What sort of scene could be played in it?
5. Find a picture of a landscape where the sides are masked by some nearby object. What other objects would you have to introduce in order to make the picture serve as a stage set that permitted no spectator to see into the flies and wing space?

Exercises

1. Take a realistic picture of a room and see if you can simplify or distort it into an abstract or fantastic set.
2. Take a picture of a landscape or a city scene and see if you can evolve a space stage or formal set from it.
3. Make a scrapbook or file of interesting stage sets, illustrations, and advertisements that seem to be potential stage sets.
4. Find an advertisement or illustration in which the color combinations are predominantly exciting; find one in which they are restful. Cut out a figure from one and place it in the other, and see what happens.

5. Select a play as a term project. Write out its *theme* in a single declarative sentence, and state how you would express this theme in line and color.

Bibliography

Appia, Adolphe, *Stage Settings,* A Portfolio of Reproductions of Designs. Zurich, 1929.

————, *Theatre Arts Monthly,* August, 1932. An issue devoted to translations from, articles about, and designs of a man who has had great influence on modern scene design.

Cheney, Sheldon, *Stage Decoration,* New York and London: The John Day Company, 1928. Interesting analysis and excellent pictures.

Craig, Edward Gordon, *Scene,* Oxford: Oxford University Press, 1923. Designs by a man who, like Appia, has had a great influence on modern scene design.

————, *Towards a New Theatre,* New York: E. P. Dutton & Company, 1913. Designs and comment.

Friederich, Willard J., and John H. Fraser, *Scenery Design for the Amateur Stage,* New York: The Macmillan Company, 1950. A simple but fairly comprehensive explanation of how to plan stage settings.

Fuerst, Walter René and Samuel Hume, *Twentieth Century Stage Decoration,* London: Alfred A. Knopf, 2 vols., 1928. One volume of interesting text and one volume of excellent illustrations.

Gorelik, Mordecai, *New Theatres For Old,* New York: Samuel French, 1940. The most stimulating recent analysis.

Jones, Robert Edmond, *The Dramatic Imagination,* New York: Duell, Sloan, & Pearce, 1941. The views of America's most eminent designer.

Komisarjevsky, Theodore, and Simonson, Lee, *Settings and Costumes of the Modern Theatre,* London and New York: Studio Publications, 1933. Excellent illustrations and interesting comment.

Simonson, Lee, *The Stage Is Set,* New York: Harcourt, Brace & Company, 1932. An interesting, if opinionated, discussion by a leading American designer.

————, *The Art of Scenic Design,* New York: Harper and Brothers, 1950. An excellent "pictorial history."

CHAPTER 12. ~~~~~~~~~~~~~~~~~~~~~~

SCENE CONSTRUCTION

~~~~~~~~~~~~~~~~~~~~~~~~~~~~~~~~

*B*efore attempting to put the principles of any art into practice, one should know the materials with which he has to work. While it would appear to the scene designer that these are legion, since each play is such a complex problem and since there are so many different kinds of settings, yet on examination it will be seen that all this complexity consists mainly of variations on three basic units: the *drop,* the *flat,* and the *set piece.*

Basic Units of Scenery

To put it another way, there are three kinds of scenery, which are constructed in different ways and used for different purposes: suspended, framed, and plastic.

SUSPENDED SCENERY

Suspended scenery is limp and will not stand by itself. When fastened to a batten (i.e., a long strip of wood or pipe) and hung from fly lines, it presents a flat surface to the audience—and usually only a surface, all the edges except the bottom, and often even that, being masked.

The drop. The principal unit of suspended scenery is the *drop,* which is a large sheet of cloth fastened permanently to two battens, one at the top edge and one at the bottom. When lines are attached to the top batten, the weight of the bottom batten stretches the surface taut and smooth so that a scene may be painted on it, or so that it may be illuminated as a sky. If a drop is extended on curved pipes so as to surround the entire stage (or the greater part of it) it is called a *cyclorama.*

Sometimes a grove of trees is painted on a drop and the spaces between the trunks cut out, or an architectural design used and the appropriate openings (doors and windows) cut through.

199

This is called a *cut drop*. Occasionally a profile frame of foliage or architecture is painted across the top and down the sides of a drop and the entire center section cut out. This is called a *leg drop*. It is used in place of two wings and a border for masking the top and sides of the stage.

A short drop that does not touch the floor and has only one batten (the one on the top edge) is called a *border*. Its main purpose is to mask the overhead area, although it is often integrated into the design by having beams painted on it. A narrow border that does not reach all the way across the stage is called a *tab*. Borders that are cut and painted to look like leaves and branches are termed *foliage borders*. These are the kind most commonly in use today.

Drapes. It will be noted that nothing has been said about drapes. This is because they are nothing more than *neutral* (instead of *representative*) suspended settings. They may be hung in the form of cycloramas, leg drops, borders, and drops, and thus made to serve the same purposes of masking. The one difference is that drapes can be hung so that they can be *drawn aside*, while drops cannot.

FRAMED SCENERY

Framed scenery is so constructed as to stand up by itself, with no other aid than a steadying brace. It presents both its surface and its edges to the audience, and may therefore be called "two-dimensional," in a double sense; that is, it has the dimensions of area and contour, as well as height and width.

The basic unit of framed scenery is the *flat*, a light but strong wooden frame covered with tightly stretched cloth and painted. A flat may be of any height, but the usual height for a small stage is 12 feet. Flats for the professional theatre are usually 14' to 16' high. The standard width for a flat is 5'9"—wider pieces will not easily go through doors. A narrower flat is called a *jog*, because it is used in "jogging" the walls of a set in and out to form alcoves, offsets, etc. A short flat that is used between two flats of full height to form a door opening is referred to as a *header;* one that is used to fill in a fireplace or window opening to make a plain surface is called a *plug*. Sometimes a flat (or pair of flats) is built large enough to cover the top of an entire box set. This is called a *ceiling piece.*

Door flats, window flats, fireplace flats, and *arch flats* may be made by building special framework around the appropriate openings (windows are usually 3′ × 5′; doors 3′ × 7′; fireplaces 2½′ square) and cutting away the canvas in between. A flat whose edge has been shaped into the profile of a tree or building is called a *wing;* one that is laid on its side and has its top edge shaped, usually like distant hills, is called a *ground row.* A short ground row—that is, one which does not extend all the way across the stage—is a *raking piece.*

SET PIECES

Under the term *set (plastic) pieces,* is included all three-dimensional scenery. Some items, such as door and window frames, base boards, mantel pieces, and the like, are made to be *applied,* or fitted on to flats. Others, like rocks, stumps, tree trunks, etc., are *free-standing.*

There is no minimum number of drops, flats, and set pieces which a well-equipped stage should have on hand. They should be built as needed.

Preliminary Planning

Having examined the basic units of scenery, and most of their variations, let us now turn to the problem of making them up into a set. Before attempting to build anything, however, certain preliminary planning should be done so that three basic, and often troublesome, problems may be solved. The first of these is to *fit the requirements of the particular play* (its shape and size, the number of entrances and levels it will require, etc.) *to the limitation of the particular stage* (its width, depth, wing space, height, facilities for cross-overs, accessibility to dressing rooms, etc.). That is usually accomplished by making a *ground plan.* The second problem is *to realize the color and line scheme* (chosen for the play) in the form of a set, as indicated by the ground plan. This is done by making a *color sketch.* (Some designers prefer to work the other way around; that is, to project their visualization first, and then adapt it to the stage.) The third problem is *to reconcile the visualization and the mechanical solution* in such detail that an actual set can be constructed which will fit both the stage and the play. The usual way of achieving this is by a *scale model,* although working drawings and accurately scaled color renderings may be substituted by a competent draftsman.

THE GROUND PLAN

The ground plan is in reality a map of the set. It is a small-scale reduction of what one would get if one took a piece of chalk and outlined the bottom of every piece of scenery as it touched the stage. The scale is usually ½" or ¼" to 1'. Through the ground plan the designer should establish the number, type, and location of all the pieces of scenery needed for the set. From it he should also be able to test his sight lines and devise ways of improving visibility from bad seats. That is, he should decide whether he must "rake" the side walls (i.e., push their downstage ends outward so that they slant offstage instead of meeting the tormentor perpendicularly); or whether he will "jog" (see the side wall of the *Silver Cord* bedroom, page 245). The amount of offstage space available for storing properties and other scenery after the backings are placed should be evident from a ground plan, and any overlooked masking problems should show up. This process can be facilitated if an accurate plan of the stage be printed, so that ground plans of prospective sets may be drawn directly on it. Such a plan, prepared for the stage of Brooklyn College, was used in making the ground plan of *The Silver Cord,* shown on the next page.

THE SKETCH

The sketch not only gives the designer his first opportunity to realize his color and line scheme in terms of an actual scene, but also gives him the chance to work out many decorative details. It should be his idea of what the set should look like—subject, of course, to what it *must* look like (in the way of special arrangements) in order to fit the requirements of the play and the special limitations of the stage. A sketch need not be in scale, although this is advisable; but it must at least follow fairly accurate proportions. As we said before, some designers prefer

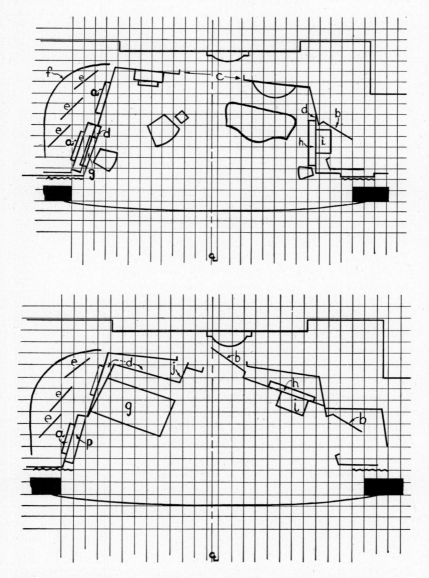

Here are shown the groundplans for *The Silver Cord* pictured on pages 243, 244, and 245. **Top,** living room; and **Bottom,** David's bedroom. **A,** windows; **B,** doors; **C,** arch; **D,** double-faced hinged flats; **E,** trees; **F,** cyclorama; **G,** bed (folded in scene 1 and lowered in scene 2); **H,** fireplace; and **I,** chest of drawers (serves as backing for fireplace).

to make a sketch before attempting a ground plan. Others, who do not draw very well or who have an unusually keen sense of visualization, omit it entirely and proceed directly to the model.

THE MODEL

The scale model, when properly made, should furnish an accurate reproduction in miniature of the complete set. It should show the number, size, and type of scenic units needed, where they will be located, how they will be joined together, where and how they will come apart. (The latter is not actually shown in the model as a rule, but from a well-made model the builder can easily work it out.) In short, an experienced builder should be able to take a model and reproduce it in full scale without difficulty. The scale employed is usually ½" to 1', although ¼" to 1' is sometimes used where storage space for models is limited. So small a scale as the latter is not recommended, since it makes accuracy difficult.

The model is of great value to other people besides the builder. It gives the designer a chance to check his proportions and color harmonies, and it shows up any errors that he has overlooked. (For example, he may have placed a window next to the door leading to another room without indicating a "wing" of the house.) It shows the director just what he may expect in the way of openings, levels, etc. (it may differ radically from what he expected), and often suggests new business for his actors. And it shows the electrician how much space he will have in which to place his lights (he may demand a new design).

Tools needed. To make a model one needs simple drafting tools (drawing board, T-square, 45° triangle, ruler, and pencil), 2-ply (*not* 3-ply) bristol board for the flats and drops, balsa wood for the stair rails, furniture, etc., and heavy cardboard for the mounting base or floor. The proscenium may be made from medium weight cardboard or bristol board. For paints, any water color will do, although tempera most nearly approximates scene paint. Airplane glue is recommended to fasten the parts together.

Step No. 1. Layout. The first step in making a model is to lay out the large pieces. In a box set these would, of course, be the walls. (In this discussion, let us stick to the box set, not only be-

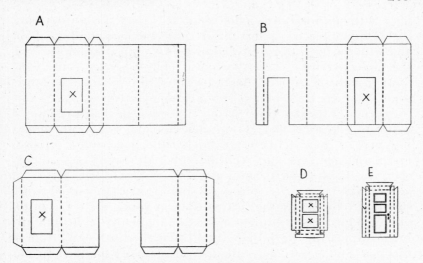

This is the layout of the model for *The Silver Cord* when produced by Brooklyn College. **A,** stage-left bedroom wall with double-faced swinging section; **B,** stage-right bedroom wall with double-faced swinging section; **C,** upstage section of living room; **D,** window to be inserted in D. R. bedroom wall; and **E,** door—two are needed.

cause it is the most frequently used type, but also because most of the techniques involved apply equally well to other types.) After the bristol board sheet has been thumb-tacked to the drawing board (its bottom edge squared against the edge of the T-square), three horizontal lines are ruled all the way across: one line ½" from the bottom (to leave a glueing flap on the bottom of the set), one line 6" above that (if ½" scale is used and the flats are to be 12' high—the customary height for a small stage), and one line ½" above this (for another glueing flap). Then, along one of these lines (preferably the one next to the top) a dot is put where the corner of each flat will come, starting with the right tormentor and proceeding successively around the set to the left tormentor. (In ½" scale each flat will be 2⅞" wide; each 4' jog 2" wide, and so on.) With the vertical edge of a triangle held against the T-square, these same locations can be carried down to the edge of the scenery, and V's marked at the corners where the set will fold.

Step No. 2. Openings. Next, the openings are laid out. If the tops of all the doors and windows will be located 7' above the floor (a usual procedure), a dot is put $3\frac{1}{2}''$ from the bottom line, the T-square placed against this dot, and the tops of all the door and window openings are ruled in lightly, one after another, in the respective flats where they occur. The bottoms of the windows (usually 3' from the floor) are ruled in the same way. Since these openings are generally centered, one measures $1\frac{7}{16}''$ from the corner of the flat, then $\frac{3}{4}''$ on either side of that (to center a 3' opening in a 5'9'' flat). From these dots the sides of the openings may be ruled in, using a triangle held against the T-square. Fireplace openings vary considerably, although $2\frac{1}{2}'$ square ($1\frac{1}{4}''$ in the model) is common.

Step No. 3. Painting. The walls should then be painted, with care not to obliterate the cutting lines. A good "spatter" can be obtained for a final toning coat by stroking with a knife a toothbrush dipped in the proper color. Stencils can be cut from a block of gum eraser, and wallpaper thus rubber-stamped on the set. When dry, the set can be cut out, the flaps scored on the face (as they fold outward), and the corners where the set bends inward scored on the back. The V's that mark these corners should be cut out. When properly folded, this set should exactly fit the outline on the ground plan.

Step No. 4. Set pieces. Door and window pieces should be made separately, like little boxes (see diagram), and slipped into the openings. Or, if preferred, the frames may be made of cardboard strips $\frac{1}{2}''$ wide scored down the middle and bent, so that when they are glued around the edges of the opening to form a facing, the other $\frac{1}{4}''$ will protrude offstage and form a *reveal* or *thickness*. Sashes and doors may be made separately and fastened to the back of the frames with scotch tape.

Steps and platforms may be "laminated" from successive layers of $\frac{1}{4}''$ cardboard, furniture and stair railings may be made from bristol board or balsa wood, and statuary may be carved out of soap.

Interior backings, being merely two-fold flats, are made as described above. So are cycloramas, except that the flaps must be nicked every $\frac{1}{2}''$ so they will curve. (This goes for arch reveals, too.)

Step No. 5. Mounting. After the set has been glued to the base, making sure that the outline of the ground plan has been followed, the *trims* may be installed. (Paper towel does nicely for draperies.) A proscenium may then be made from bristol board

This is the model for *The Silver Cord* mounted on the base before the proscenium and backings have been installed.

(painted black), with the opening cut to the exact width of the set and ½″ to ¾″ lower than its top. The face should extend about 3″ beyond the opening. Flaps should be left for glueing, and a 1″ edge folded at a right angle around the top and sides to give rigidity. (The corners of this should be held together with scotch tape, or a flap left and glued.)

Hints for making models of exteriors. For exterior sets, wings are made like flats, their edges being cut to profile. (A razor blade will do, but curved gouges will be found handy for cutting foliage.) Drops may be mounted on the base (like cycloramas), since bristol board is stiff enough to stand, particularly if an inch strip at each end is bent in at a right angle to give the piece rigidity. Two "beams" of cardboard or thin wood should be inserted at either side of the stage between the corners of the proscenium and the backdrop for hanging borders and drapes. (Paper towel or crepe paper will serve for these better than cloth. Small dowels are useful as battens.) Corrugated paper simulates roof tiling fairly well; dyed turkish towel makes good grass; trees and shrubs may be made by cutting and dyeing sponges.

Construction of Scenery

It has already been indicated that building a full-scale set is merely a process of reproducing certain basic units in various sizes and shapes. For this work, mechanics have developed certain materials and techniques by which a satisfactory combination of strength and lightness may be achieved. Of course, a certain amount of latitude is possible. The professional theatre, for instance, since it is more concerned with strength and better equipped with machines than the nonprofessional theatre, is inclined to do things "the hard way." Still, the traditional methods are uniform enough to be described fairly accurately. Let us consider, then, how each basic unit of scenery is constructed. Where a choice is possible, the method found most serviceable to amateurs in the experience of the writer will be described.

DRAPES

It is not recommended that the nonprofessional technician attempt to make his own drapes; they may be obtained easily, either new or used, from a theatrical dealer, and the quality of the workmanship, combined with the saving in trouble, is worth more than the additional expense. From a dealer, too, one is much more likely to get fireproof material than from a dry-goods store. Professionally made drapes will be sewed to webbing at the top (and usually pleated to about one-third fullness), provided with grommets and ties for hanging, and with a chain run through the bottom hem to keep them in place. The seams will run vertically.

Material. By far the best material for drapes is *velour*. It is also the most expensive, but worth the cost, since it is durable and opaque, takes light beautifully, and hangs in pleasing folds. *Duvetyn* is also fairly durable, opaque, and light-absorbent, but its fuzzy surface is less rich than velour. It is, however, less expensive. *Repp* is semi-opaque and must be lined for a front curtain. Its corded texture takes light well and hangs nicely. It may be had in pleasing colors: navy blue, maroon, taupe, and gray. (A satisfactory black can be had only in velour.) *Monk's cloth*, thought quite pleasing in appearance, is less suitable for the stage because its loose weave passes light too readily and is

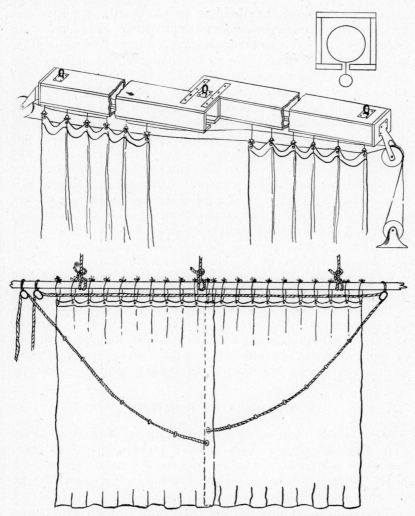

Here are two types of curtain riggings. **Top,** traveller track for laterally opening stage drapes, and cross-section showing ball float; and **Bottom,** "tableau pull" which will open in a "festooned" drape.

subject to snags. *Outing flannel,* a very poor fifth choice, should be used only when time or budget absolutely requires it.

Arrangement. An adequate set of stage drapes will consist of a *rear section* of two pieces, each about six feet wider than half the proscenium opening, to allow for an overlap at the center and for offstage masking; two *side sections* of two pieces each, the width of each piece varying from nine to twelve feet, depending on the depth of stage space to be spanned; and at least two *borders* a few feet longer than the width of the proscenium and about six feet wide, hung from battens at six foot intervals from the teaser to the rear section. The height of the side and rear drapes will vary from fourteen to eighteen feet, according to the height of the proscenium opening. Such a combination will permit the drapes to be hung as a cyclorama, with entrances possible at the corners and in the center of each wall. (An extra section, about one-third as wide as the rear wall, will permit two rear entrances. A few tabs or narrow sections seven feet shorter than the full drapes are useful to hang over doors and windows.) Another possible arrangement is the drop-and-wing style, which may be obtained by hanging the side pieces parallel to the rear wall, so that they form "leg drops" with the borders.

Black is likely to be the most useful color, with taupe probably next best.

It is wise to have the back sections hung on a *traveler* track (see diagram) so that they may be opened to any width desired, or drawn entirely offstage. *Tableau pulls* (see diagram) will also be found useful at the inner edges of the center and side sections, so that they may be drawn up in a festoon to provide entrances.

DROPS AND BORDERS

Materials. A drop consists mainly of a large sheet of cloth. (The English call it a "back cloth.") *Scenery linen* (theatrical canvas) is preferred, but *enameling duck* (cotton canvas) or a heavy grade of *unbleached muslin* will do. The latter may be obtained in 12′ widths.

Netting, a fairly fine fish net dyed blue is often used across the bottom of a foilage border to support jutting twigs and branches, or across the openings in a cut drop to keep the edges from curling.

Gauze, or bobinette (better known as *mosquito netting,* and not to be confused with *scrim,* which is often sold as "theatrical gauze" in department stores) may also be used for this purpose. However, the finer weave of gauze acts also as a diffusing agent, making objects seen behind it seem blurred and more distant,

Whole drops of gauze are sometimes employed in order to make an actor playing a ghost seem more ethereal, or a landscape more distant.

Scrim is a heavy loose-weave material which, when illuminated from the front, seems opaque, but which becomes transparent when lights strike objects behind it. In this manner, walls can be made suddenly to dissolve, trees or rocks to vanish, or pictures to become three-dimensional and animate. "Shark's-tooth scrim," a fairly new development, is much to be preferred to the department store "gauze" variety, as its long, narrow mesh takes paint and reflects light better than the square weave of the latter. (See p. 246 for an illustration of a scrim in use.)

Scrim, gauze, and nettings may be had in 30′ widths.

Construction. To make a drop, sufficient strips of material, cut square to the proper lengths, are sewed together with ordinary lap seams, and one of the outer selvage edges tacked to long strips of 1″ × 3″ or 4″ clear white pine, or better still of special batten stock with rounded edges, which have been laid end to end the length of the drop. The tacks should be zigzagged from one side of the wood to the other, and the material drawn fairly taut. When this is done, a similar set of strips is screwed on top so that the cloth is clamped firmly between the two layers of wood. (The joints between the upper strips should fall at least six feet away from those below, for reasons of strength.)

When the bottom edge of the drop has been similarly treated, the whole should be stretched tight on the floor (or on a paint frame), the battens nailed down and the edges of the cloth temporarily tacked down, and the whole surface given a coat of *size* (a solution of approximately equal parts of whiting and warm water, with about one pint of melted carpenter's glue to every four gallons of water). It may then be painted (this process will be described later).

Borders, of course, are made in a similar manner, except for the omission of the bottom batten. Both borders and drops must be held stretched tight while being painted or sized because scene paint shrinks when drying. Thinner mixtures and lower glue content are used for drops than for flats.

Cut drops and foliage borders follow the same pattern. No cutting should be done until after all the paint has dried. After that, the superfluous parts are cut out, the unit turned over, and netting or gauze glued on the back surface with *Rosene,* a commercial preparation, which should be melted in a double boiler and applied with a paint brush. When large areas are to be covered, the reinforcing material should be held in place temporarily with tacks while it is being glued.

When painting on scrim, extra-thin paint should be used so as not to clog the pores of that material.

FLATS

Materials. All framed scenery should be constructed of *grade A white pine,* which splits less, warps less, and is lighter and stronger than any other readily available wood. In size, $1'' \times 3''$ is recommended for nonprofessional work. (The actual dimensions run slightly less, as these are sizes before planing.) For covering, scenery linen is preferred; enameling duck satisfactory, but muslin is a poor third choice because of its lack of body. All fabric should be bought flameproofed.

Construction. The construction of flats usually requires five major operations, or steps.

Step No. 1. Cutting. To make a flat, two *stiles* (side pieces) should be cut the full length of the flat minus twice the width of the stock. (Experience shows that the end pieces, not the stiles, should run full length, as this reduces the chances of chipping the corners.) For a 12' flat, three *rails* (or stretchers) must be cut, two the full width of the flat (5' 9") and one (the toggle rail) short by twice the width of the stock. (In taller flats, more rails will be needed—one for every 5' of height.) Care must be taken that all cuts are perfectly square.

Step No. 2. Joining. A *butt joint* is recommended for connecting these pieces (the end of one is "butted" against the side of the other), the angle they form being "trued" with a carpenter's framing square, and two 5/8" no. 5 *corrugated fasteners* driven across the joint, at a slight angle to the grain, to hold them together. Then the flat is turned over and one corrugator driven in each joint, a *clinching iron* (about one square foot of 3/16" boiler iron) slipped under it, and a *corner block* (a triangle 8" to a side, made of 1/4" plywood) nailed to the joint with 1 1/4" *clout nails,* which clinch on the iron as soon as they penetrate the wood. These nails should be distributed, five to each piece of wood, in the form of a *W.* The corner block should be placed

1″ from the outer edges of the frame, so as not to interfere with lashing. (If placed at the outer edge of the stile, the edge of another flat meeting this one at a right angle from behind will not fit flush because of the corner block.) Extreme care must be observed to keep the corners square when nailing on corner blocks, because the frame is quite rigid after they are on, and errors are hard to correct. The toggle rail should be placed 5′ from the end of the frame. (In a 12′ flat, if the top of the toggle rail is 5′ from the *bottom* of the flat, it will be exactly 7′ from the other end, which means that, if desired, the flat can later be turned over and a door or window built in without moving the rail.) Rails are held in with corrugators and reinforced with *keystones* (plywood strips 8″ long, tapering from 4″ to 3″), which are nailed on with clout nails spaced in the form of the five spots on dice (a square with a dot in the center). The entire frame should be corrugated together before the corner blocks and keystones are nailed on.

Step No. 3. Covering. The frame should now be turned over, a strip of 72″ cloth, slightly longer than the frame, stretched over it and secured temporarily by a tack in each corner. Then two (or four) people begin to tack the sides, stretching the material fairly tight (leaving little or no sag), starting at the *middle* of the *long* side and placing the tacks six inches apart on the *inside* edge of the frame, so the canvas can later be turned back and glued. (If it is the practice to wash flats, these tacks should be driven all the way in; if the flats are to be re-covered when they have been painted as many times as they will stand, the heads of the tacks should be left slightly protruding so they may be removed when the glue has dried.) Tacking should stop about 18 inches from each corner, and the ends should then be tacked in a similar manner, starting at the middle. Each corner can then be tacked, first from one side and then the other to avoid puckers. The canvas is then folded back and the wood thoroughly painted with *white glue* (equal parts of whiting and ground glue, which has previously been melted in a double boiler), particular care being taken to saturate the edges. (It is wise to protect the floor with newspaper or old canvas during this process.) The cloth is then pressed to the wood with a damp rag, the glue allowed to dry, and the edges trimmed with a razor blade. (If the flat is to be hinged to another flat, a flap of canvas may be left on the hinge side, so as to be glued over the crack.)

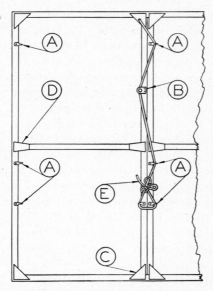

This is the rear of a flat showing the hardware and lashing. **A,** lash cleat; **B,** brace cleat; **C,** corner block; **D,** keystone; and **E,** lash line tied off with stagehand's knot.

Step No. 4. Sizing. When the glue is dry, the flat is sized in the same manner as the drop (see p. 211), the amount of glue in the sizing being dependent on the sag left in the material. (A tightly stretched flat will require no more glue than a drop.) Sizing should be done with a 6″ or 8″ calsomine (soft bristle) brush, the strokes crossed over each other so as to fill all the pores of the cloth.

Step No. 5. Installing hardware. Finally, a *lash line* (a piece of no. 8 sash cord) is run through a hole bored in the upper right-hand corner block (looking from the back), knotted behind the corner, and cut off just short of the floor. *Lash cleats* (iron fingers) are screwed to the frame, protruding inward, 30″ below the upper right corner, 18″ below the upper left corner, and 30″ above the two lower corners (also in between, in a high flat), so that the lash line may be engaged from one to the other on adjoining flats, "tied off" on the two lower cleats, and the two frames thus firmly held together. A *brace cleat* (having a hole) may be substituted for the upper right cleat, or one of the middle ones, so that the "horns" of a *stage brace* (see page 229) may be engaged in it, the "rocker" fastened to the floor with a *stage screw* (or "peg"), and the flat thus made steady.

Flats with openings. Door, window, and fireplace flats are similarly made, except that additional framing must be installed around the opening, and the canvas glued to this. Door flats, having no bottom stretcher, need to have a *sill iron* (or *saddle iron*—a bar of ³⁄₁₆″ × ¾″ strap iron) screwed across the bottom to keep the flat from twisting in two when it is moved. If an opening wider than 5′3″ is needed, two L-shaped flats may be

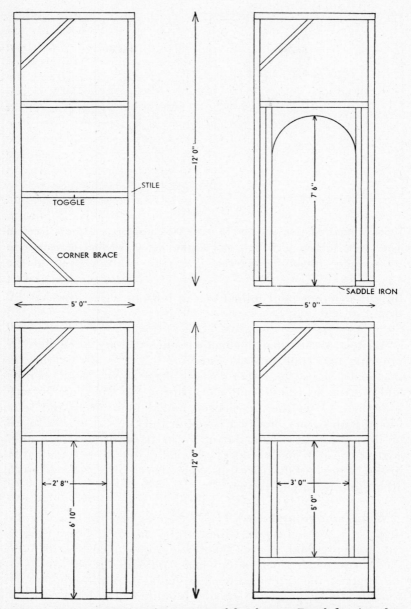

Here and on page 216 we have types of flat frames. **Top left,** plain flat; **Top right,** arch flat; **Bottom left,** door flat; and **Bottom right,** window flat.

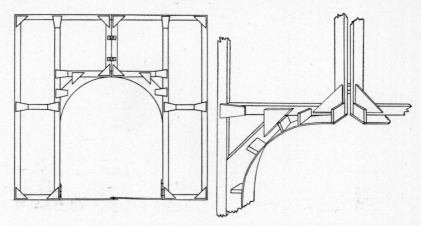

Types of flat frames in addition to those shown on page 215 are pictured here. **Left,** folding arch flat; and **Right,** detail, method of making a "thickness" or "reveal" for an arch.

hinged together, and joined at the bottom with a hinged sill iron.

Arches. Arches may be made from ordinary door flats by mitreing two wide boards (usually $1'' \times 12''$) so that they fit diagonally across the upper corners of the square door opening and meet at its center, and then cutting the curve of the arch into these. After they have been nailed in securely and reinforced with corner blocks, a *reveal* or thickness of beaver board or thin plywood ("bendaboard") can be nailed to the inner edge of the arch and to blocks of wood nailed on perpendicular to the facing and flush with its edge, spaced a foot or two apart all around the arch opening.

Wings and ground rows. Flats with one edge built out in the shape of a profile become wings or ground rows. This profile is cut from plywood, beaver board, or profile board (thin wood sheets with paper glued to each face) and nailed to the appropriate edge of the frame with clout nails. A reinforcing frame, roughly the shape of the profile, is built to the back, and fastened to the flat with corrugators and keystones. Before covering the frame, strips of profile board should be nailed entirely around the face of the frame so as to raise it to the same plane as the profile and thus avoid a ridge in the face of the wing.

Ceilings. Ceiling pieces are of two types, book and rolled. The *book* ceiling is composed of two large flats, as long as the set is wide, made usually of a slightly thicker stock (1¼″ or 1½″) hinged together on the face and hung from three sets of lines attached to the back: one set to the middle, and one set each to the upstage and downstage edges. When the lines are lifted, the ceiling is raised flat, and a set can be mounted under it. When the center set of lines is pulled, the ceiling folds and "flies" in a fairly narrow space.

Because the book ceiling is good only for shallow sets fourteen or fifteen feet deep (since the sections should not be more than six feet wide), the *roll* ceiling is most commonly used. This consists of two long battens (usually of 1½″ × 3″ stock) held apart

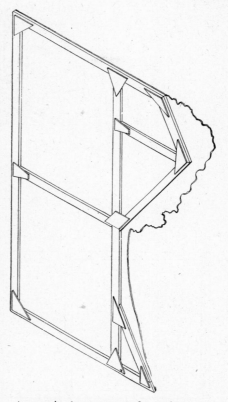

A wood wing as seen from the rear, showing framing.

by five stretchers, which are bolted to the battens by *ceiling irons* (i.e., metal plates with five screw holes in one end to fasten to the stretcher, and a single hole for a bolt in the other). The frame, when bolted together, is covered with a large section of muslin, sewed as for a drop, and glued and tacked to the long battens, but only *temporarily* tacked to the end stretchers. The middle and end ceiling irons should be provided with rings so that fly ropes may be attached and the ceiling raised in order that a set may be mounted under it.

It is possible to fly such a ceiling (if there is sufficient fly space) by detaching the rear lines. When no longer needed, the side tacks may be pulled, the bolts removed, the stretchers taken off, and the ceiling rolled up and stored.

If lumber long enough for the stiles of a ceiling is not obtain-

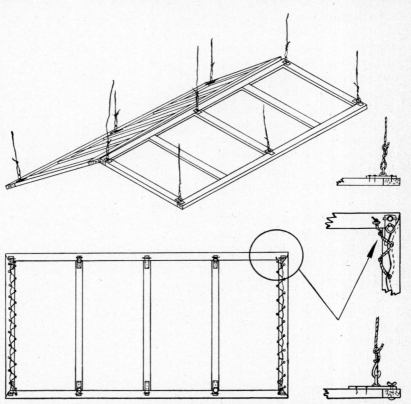

Shown above are two types of ceilings. **Top,** book ceiling; and **Bottom,** roll ceiling, showing method of lashing edges (a better method than temporary tacks), attaching lines for lifting, and bolting stretchers.

able, two pieces may be joined by means of a *scarf splice* (i.e., one end of each may be sawed at a long slant, the two wedges matched, and glued and nailed together).

WINDOW AND DOOR FRAMES

The techniques needed to build applied plastic pieces are quite similar to those of ordinary house carpentry. A *window frame,* for example, like a house window frame, consists of a reveal box, made slightly smaller than the opening in the wall into which it must fit, and having a facing nailed around one edge and sashes fitted snugly into it. At least one of the sashes is loose so that it will move up and down in grooves. (See diagram.)

Materials and construction. For a stage window, the reveal box should be made of $1'' \times 6''$ white pine, the end pieces being $2'10''$ long, and lapped over the sides, which are $4'8''$ long (to allow for the lap and also for a $1''$ margin between the box and the flat, so it will not jam when put in or taken out). The facing may be made of commercial window trim, or of $1'' \times 4''$ or $6''$ white pine with a moulding nailed around the outer edge. The upper corners should be mitred (i.e., cut to a $45°$ angle and fitted together). The lower part of the facing should extend across the bottom to the outer edges of the side facings, and should have a $1'' \times 1''$ strip nailed along the top of its face to simulate the protruding window sill. The sashes are merely frames made of $1'' \times 2''$ white pine, nailed at the corners with $3''$ wire nails and covered at the back with galvanized screen to simulate glass. These frames should be wide enough to fit snugly into the reveal box, and so high that the edge of the lower sash will exactly overlap that of the upper. This upper sash should be nailed into the reveal box, flush with its rear edge. Strips of $1'' \times 1''$ pine should be nailed inside the lower part of the reveal box to continue the plane of the upper sash and act as guides for the lower sash. This is then put in place against these guides, and a long strip of $1'' \times 1''$ pine is nailed to the reveal box in front of it, so as to form grooves in which the sash will slide up and down.

Securing. After the whole window frame is placed in the opening in the flat, small wooden wedges are nailed to the outer sides of the reveal box to hold it snugly in place, and two $6''$ strap hinges screwed to the sides of the box on a slant so that when the upper half is folded downward and outward it binds against the edge of the flat and thus holds the window frame in place.

Doors. Door frames are built in a similar manner, except that they have to be more securely braced, with angle irons at the corners. The door itself, which is hinged to the outer edge of the reveal box, should be made of $1'' \times 6''$ white pine, cut in the shape of panels and backed by plywood or beaverboard. The side opposite the hinges should be provided with a rim lock and knobs. The lock strike should be mounted on the edge of the reveal box. A *door stop* of $1'' \times 1''$ or moulding should be nailed inside the reveal box, following the edges of the door,

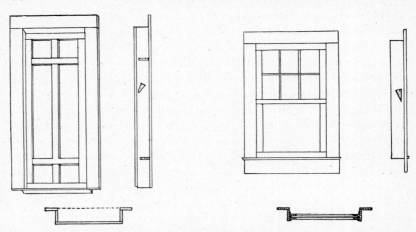

Here are two applied plastic pieces. **Left,** practical door (front view, side view, horizontal view underneath); and **Right,** practical window (front view, side view, horizontal view underneath).

to keep it from swinging too far. Doors are usually mounted to swing offstage and upstage.

Trims. Picture molding, panel molding, baseboards, etc. can be obtained quite easily and cheaply at any lumber yard. In a realistic interior it is worth the trouble and expense to build these trims in, rather than to try to paint them on. Sometimes additional rails have to be put into the wall flats in order to provide something solid to which to nail molding. But these can easily be installed, even with the flat in place, by screwing the keystones on instead of clout-nailing them. Extra rails are often necessary also for hanging pictures. These, incidentally, should never be hung on nails, but on wood screws, driven far in, or on theatrical *picture hangers.* Nails should never be left protruding from the surface of a flat, as they rip other flats to ribbons when they slide past them in storage.

PLASTIC SET PIECES

Rocks, stumps, and logs. All three-dimensional set pieces, except frames like gates and fences, consist of an *armature* or frame of wood and chicken wire, covered with papier-mâché. To make such a piece, the contour of the base is first sawed out of 1″ × 12″ pine, or 1″ × 6″ pieces joined into a trapezoidal frame. (A keyhole saw or a jig saw is needed for this purpose, that is, to saw curves.) A contour of the top is made in the same way. The two are then joined by "fins" of 1″ × 4″ to 6″ pine, one edge of which has also been shaped to the outline of the object. The whole is then covered with chicken wire, which is moulded to follow the contours of the surface desired. Over this sheets of newspaper, dipped in wallpaper paste or glue, are applied, layer on layer, until a strong surface is obtained; then the whole object is covered with muslin dipped in glue. The surface can be wrinkled while wet to simulate bark, etc.

This shows the construction of a man-built tree. **A**, curved blocks to break straight lines of the edges; **B**, contour bases; **B**[1], contour sections to be placed here also and joined to others with fins; **C**, connecting fins with shaped edges; **D**, chicken wire; **E**, papier mâché; and **F**, muslin.

Trees. For a tree trunk an irregularly-shaped flat is built, like a cubist outline of the tree, and its edges curved with a hatchet so as to get rid of all straight lines. Then the base and top are cut out and nailed on, also similar cross sections wherever the tree changes shape or forks, and these are joined by shaped fins. From here on, the process is the same as above.

Columns. Columns are merely regularly shaped tree trunks that need no chicken wire, since their sides are composed of wooden laths.

Suspended tree trunks. Quite impressive tree trunks may be made with much less labor and expense by tacking a length of

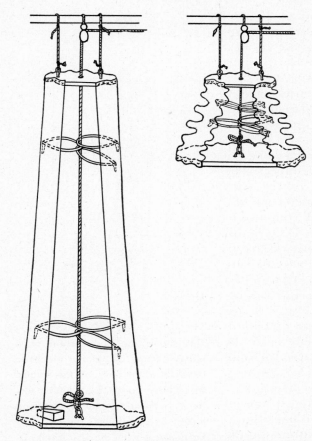

muslin (some four or five yards of 36″ or 42″ stuff will do) to a base and a top, cut out as above. If the bottom is weighted with bricks and the top hauled up taut on a line, the muslin will take the shape of a tree trunk quite realistically, and may be painted appropriately. If the top is *tight-tied* (i.e., tied permanently) and a line run over a pulley, down through a hole in the top, through loops made of muslin strips sewed to the sides every

Suspended tree trunks, rigged for "accordion" flying, are shown here.

four feet, and attached to the base, the whole tree trunk may be folded up like an accordion and flied in a few feet of fly space. (The bricks, of course, having been removed first.) Actors should never be allowed to go near such trees, as they sway easily and give away their flimsy construction.

PLATFORMS AND STEPS

The problem of attaining both mobility and strength is more acute in the making of platforms than any other article of scenery, for platforms have to support people—sometimes many people—often doing strenuous things. But properly placed trusses, held in place by glue in addition to nails, will make very light frames amazingly sturdy.

The parallel. The secret of mobility in platforms is the device known as the *parallel,* which is nothing more than a collection of small flats (uncovered), hinged together in such a way that they will fold up flat or open up and form a cube on which a platform floor may be placed.

The two frames that form the sides differ from ordinary flat frames in four respects: (1) The corner blocks and keystones are glued on as well as nailed. (2) Stretchers are much more closely spaced (every three feet or so). (3) The end stretchers are extended three inches beyond the stile to form legs, and 3″ blocks are fastened under each inner rail for a similar purpose. (These are held in place by using corrugators and by bringing the keystone down to overlap them. An extra-long keystone, or a corner block, should be used.) (4) Trusses (or cross braces) are mitred-in from corner to corner between each pair of stretchers. The size of these frames depends upon the size of the unit needed. For an ordinary stair landing, 3′ × 6′ is ample.

Smaller frames (3′ × 2′6″ for a stair landing) are needed for the ends and the cross sections, of which there should be as many as there are stretchers in the side frames. The corner blocks on these cross-section frames should be placed on alternate sides of the frame, so as to make way for the hinges, which have to be so bolted on (a pair on one side and a pair on the other) as to allow the parallel to fold. This is illustrated in the diagram on page 224. Great care must be exercised to space the hinges accurately, as one pair of hinges a fraction of an inch too close to the next cross section will prevent the parallel from folding.

The *platform,* or top, which is to rest on this parallel, is made from tongue-and-groove flooring, cut the length of the side frames, and held together by 1″ × 3″ cleats screwed across the bottom side. These should be just long enough to fit snugly between the two side frames when the parallel is extended, and placed so that they butt against the sides of the cross-section frames, to hold the parallel steady.

Steps. Although steps are sometimes made in independent units, it is usually more convenient to build them to work in

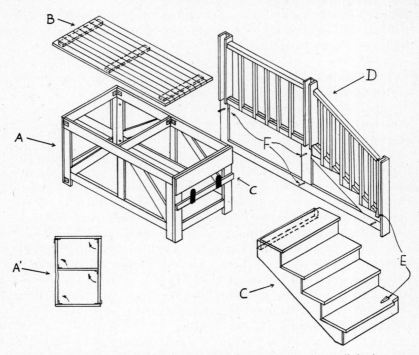

This is a set of demountable stage stairs. **A**, top view of parallel, showing placement of hinges; **B**, platform; **C**, hook-on steps and bar with cleat to hold steps; **D**, bannister piece; **E**, loose-pin hinge to secure newell post; and **F**, bolts to secure bannister piece to steps and parallel.

conjunction with a parallel and platform. This may be done in the following manner:

First, a *stringer* must be laid out on a piece of 1″ × 12″ white pine by holding a framing square against the face in such a position that *1″ less than* the width of a tread on one branch of the square, and the width of a riser on the other, will lie on the wood. (This allows for a protruding step edge.) That is, if we are to use 1″ × 10″ boards for treads and 1″ × 6″ for risers (the actual planed dimensions of these being about 8¾″ and 5¾″) we would place the square on the board, point inward, with the 9¾″ mark on one branch and the 5¾″ mark on the other exactly even with the edge of the board. We would then draw the angle thus described with a pencil, move the square over and draw a similar angle from the point where the first one left the board, and repeat for the number of steps required —which will be one less than the number of times the riser goes into the height of the parallel, since the edge of the parallel and platform will provide the last step. (In the case of a platform 3′ high, there would be five steps.) This board may then be nailed to another (making sure that the top edges are flush) and both stringers sawed from the same pattern. (If the steps are to be wider than three feet, extra stringers will be needed for strength.) At a right angle to the bottom riser and the top tread, the board is sawed off.

Next, the *risers* and *treads,* cut to the width of the parallel, are nailed on, the risers first, since the treads butt against them and protrude slightly at their outer edges. For added strength the risers should be nailed to the treads from the back; 6d or 8d wire nails are suitable. Then a 1″ × 4″ bar is set in flush with the edge of the top riser and the ends of the stringers, and nailed securely. This will rest on a 1″ × 3″ bar just long enough to fit snugly between the stringers, bolted to one end of the parallel 10″ below the top. Two brace cleats, screwed to the face of this bar and protruding upward, will keep the step unit from slipping off, but allow it to be lifted off with ease. The exposed section of the parallel will, of course, have to be covered. A solid sheet of plywood will serve for this purpose. It will serve also for reinforcing the joints, instead of the corner blocks which customarily perform this function.

Stair rails, banisters, and newel posts. The entire visible side of a stair unit should be covered by a separate, shallow piece which fits against one side of the steps and parallel, and bolts on. This will require a stringer which fits the profile of the steps (with the risers and treads in place), and a newel post fastened securely to each end. (For a square post, use a 4′ strip of 1″ × 4″ pine screwed on perpendicular to the tread and protruding beyond the edge of the step just enough to allow a 1″ × 3″ *thickness* to be nailed to its outer edge. A similar 1″ × 3″, cut to fit over the bottom step, must be nailed to the other edge. The top newel, of course, should rest on the platform.) A section of stair rail joins these posts, running parallel to the slant of the steps. Banister rungs (¾″ dowel will serve) must be set into holes bored into the rail and bolted to the stringer, two to each step. The spaces between the rungs and the edges of the risers are filled in with strips of 1″ × 1″, glued and nailed, and a strip of 1″ × 1″ applied to the edge of each tread, mitred at the corner and carried around the end to meet the protruding edge of the step.

A triangular flat is then built to fill in the space between the steps and the parallel, and bolted or screwed securely to the stringer and the two newel posts. The whole unit is then placed against the parallel and steps, and bolted (with ¼″ carriage bolts) at the three corners. Loose pin hinges (1½″ back flaps) are screwed to the newel posts and the faces of the bottom step and platform, in such a manner that the pins may easily be drawn when the unit is to be disassembled.

If a *stair landing* is needed, the whole unit is built out across as much of the parallel as will show, and a third newel post added. (Usually this extension runs to about the middle of the parallel, the rest being used as an offstage landing.)

Assembling

When a set is built and sized, it is a good plan to set it up on the stage to see how it fits together. Sometimes much of the painting can be done best with the set in place. But *at no time* should a set be so securely joined together that it cannot be *struck*, for often a section must be moved slightly, or taken down for painting or remodeling. Often, too, the set must be opened to permit a large piece of furniture or a plastic section to be carried in or out.

JOINING

As has been pointed out, flats may be joined together either by lashing or by hinges. The former is good only for corners, where cracks do not show. When lashing corners, one should be careful to butt the up-and-downstage flat to the flat which faces the audience, so that the crack will be less obvious and will not leak light. When the flats form an acute angle onstage, the lash line, if enough lash cleats are used, will keep the two edges fairly true. When the acute angle is offstage, however, *chock blocks* (small 1″ × 2″ strips) must be screwed to the back of the flat that faces the audience, about ¾″ in from its edge, so that the edge of the other flat will be drawn against these by the tension of the lash line to form a tight, firm joint.

The Stagehand's Knot. When lashing two flats, the following procedure is advised: Throw the lash line over the upper lash cleat of the right flat, then over that of the left flat (this may be a brace cleat). Then place it over the tie-off cleat on the right flat and, with the heel of the left hand, bear down on the line to take out all the slack, snubbing the line quickly against the cleat so it will not slip back. Holding it in place with the right thumb,

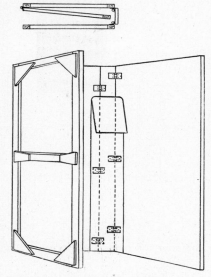

Three-fold "Dutchman" with canvas "Dutchman" glued over cracks.

loop the remainder around the left tie-off cleat (from above), bring it up and around the section of line coming down, and pull the end through the triangle thus made. Any remaining slack can now be taken out by pulling back (down and to the left) on the end of the line. Finally, take a loop of this end around the vertical (taut) line and pull it through to form a half-hitch. (Do not pull the end of the line all the way through, but merely the loop.) This forms a knot which keeps the lash very tight, but which can be undone merely by giving the protruding end of the line a tug. This is illustrated on page 214.

The "Dutchman." When two flats join to form a continuous wall, they should be hinged together and a canvas strip glued over the crack. When more than two flats are hinged together, they will not fold unless a strip of $1'' \times 3''$ is inserted between two of them (the middle two of a four-fold group), and each adjacent flat hinged to this strip. This forms a pocket when folded, with space enough to accommodate the end flats. When in use as a wall, such a folding section must be kept rigid by a *stiffener*—a wooden bar ($1'' \times 3''$) the length of the entire sec-

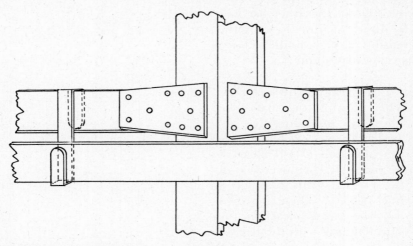

Stiffener rail held in place by keeper hooks.

tion, fastened to the stiles of each flat by 1½″ screws or by loose pin hinges, or dropped into *keeper hooks* hung on the toggle rails.

BRACING

A long section of wall, or one containing a door, should be *braced* to keep it steady. The usual tool for this purpose is the *stage brace,* which consists of two wooden rods about 1″ square, clamped together so that they may be overlapped and made rigid by a thumb screw to form a prop of variable length. The extreme end of one of these rods is provided with a pair of *horns* which may be hooked into a brace cleat on the back of a flat. The other carries a *rocker,* a curved iron strip into which holes have been bored so that a *stage screw* or *peg* may be inserted and the rocker screwed firmly to the floor. The brace should be hooked to the brace cleat "backwards" (i.e., with the horns facing the flat), and then twisted around so that the end is drawn tight against the stile. The rocker is then pegged down, the thumb screw loosened, and the brace extended or shortened until the flat is made to stand straight. Then the clamp is tightened again. If one is not allowed to peg into the stage floor, a sandbag thrown across the rocker will provide a fair anchorage.

In locations where exceptionally rigid bracing is needed,

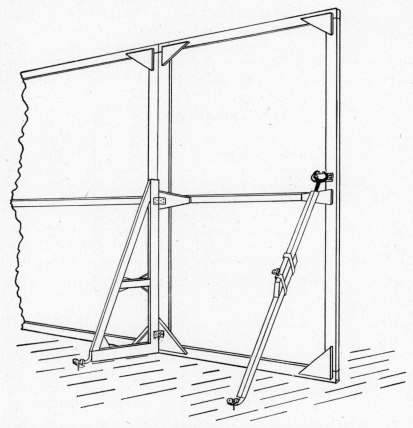

This shows methods of bracing. **Right**, stage brace; and **Left**, jack.

(as behind gate posts) *jacks* are hinged to the piece to be supported. These are triangular wooden frames reinforced with
corner blocks and having a *foot iron* (a piece of strap steel with
a large hole to accommodate a stage screw) bolted or screwed
to the outer corner.

TRIMS

Trims such as baseboards and chair rails should be attached
with bolts and wing nuts if they are to be removed and rein-
stalled (as in a travelling production). Otherwise, they may be
nailed on. (The corners, of course, should be mitred.) Shelves,

and even mantel pieces, may be hung with *picture hangers,* purchasable from any theatrical hardware dealer. In some cases, it may be found necessary to give added strength with 1½″ screws driven in from behind, or with loose pin hinges. Often, such additional reinforcing is needed for heavy door frames.

Painting

In the theatre, *water color* paints are used almost exclusively, the only exceptions being that *dyes* are preferred for drops or curtains that must fold up; *oil stains* are sometimes applied to woodwork that requires much handling; and *shellac* is sometimes used over water color to give it gloss.

Water colors are so universally used because they are (*a*) noninflammable, (*b*) nonglossy (i.e., they will not reflect light), (*c*) inexpensive, (*d*) easily mixed and applied, (*e*) rapid-drying, and (*f*) soluble in water, and therefore easily removed from brushes, pails, or old flats. (To wash an old flat from which the paint has begun to flake, one merely turns a hose on it and rubs it with a scrubbing brush.)

Though some technicians prefer commercially prepared paints of the cold-water or casein-base variety, most scene painters adhere to the traditional method of mixing their own paints from dry pigment, melted glue, and water. This is because the commercial colors are more expensive, available hues are more limited, and the binders are not too well suited to canvas.

Scene paint is mixed in the same manner as sizing, and with about the same proportions of water, melted glue, and *dry pigment.* These pigments are obtainable from most paint stores, though the more unusual colors may have to be ordered from a theatrical paint dealer. A suggested *palette of useful colors* is given below, together with the amount which should be kept on hand.

Recommended Palette

	Suggested Amount (Pounds)
Whiting	50
Drop black (very light and fluffy)	20
Ultramarine blue (all-purpose blue, slightly on purple side)	20

Italian blue (for skies; light and bright; slightly on green side)	10
Royal purple (not quite so brilliant as purple lake, but less fugitive and expensive, excellent for toning spatter)	10
Turkey red (almost as bright as permanent red; less expensive)	5
American vermilion (very heavy and strong; toward orange)	2
Light chrome-yellow (very heavy; fairly intense)	5
Hanover green (bright "spring" green; on yellow side)	2
Medium chrome-green (good all-purpose green, not too intense)	10
Yellow ochre (useful for oak graining; with whiting makes excellent cream)	20
Burnt umber (rich, warm brown; goes gray with whiting)	20
Van Dycke brown (rich, warm, dilutes well)	10
Burnt sienna (brick-red brown)	15

MIXING SCENE PAINTS

The first step in mixing scene paints is to provide a *binder,* because dry pigment, although it apparently disolves in water, will become powder again, as soon as the water evaporates. This binder is made by thoroughly dissolving about two teacups of melted carpenter's glue in a pail of warm water. The glue may be either *ground* or *flake,* but must have been previously melted in a *double boiler* (a 1-gal. vegetable can, resting on a brick inside a pail of water and heated on an electric stove, will serve nicely) because, if set directly on the stove, the glue will burn, and therefore will not only become unusable but will render the whole shop uninhabitable. If a can of glue has been filled with water and allowed to soak overnight, it will melt much more readily.

Pigment should be added to this glue-water a little at a time and stirred thoroughly, as it has a tendency to clot at the bottom of the pail. Different hues may be mixed in the wet batch until the proper shade is reached—which will be several shades *darker* than the final shade desired, since scene paint always lightens as it dries. A sample, therefore, should be allowed to dry before the paint is applied to the scenery, to test whether the proper color has been obtained. Some technicians prefer to mix their dry pigments manually before adding them to the glue-water, on the theory that the final color may thus be arrived at more accurately. The writer has not found this satisfactory, because an even mix is difficult to obtain and also because chemical changes which affect the final color sometimes occur in solution. In any case, care should be taken to get an even mix *in solution,* especially if such heavy pigments as yellow and vermilion are used; these have a tendency to sink to the bottom of the pail and must be stirred constantly, even while the paint is being applied, or the color will change noticeably as the lighter paint on top is used up.

The proportions of pigment and glue to water vary. Drops should be painted with fairly thin paint containing the minimum of glue. On the other hand, when one is trying to obliterate a previous paint job, sometimes a heavier mix will work best. Too much pigment will not spread evenly; too little will not cover. Too much glue will so shrink the canvas as to warp the frame of a flat; too little will cause the paint to rub off when dry. The best test is a manual one: When a finger is dipped into the mix and withdrawn, an even cap of paint should cling to the portion that has been immersed. If this makes a thick layer, like heavy cream, there is too much pigment in the mix and water should be added; if it clots and does not evenly cover the skin, there is too little pigment. When this finger-sample begins to dry, one should feel a slight stickiness—and not until then; if stickiness is evident right away, there is too much glue in the mix, and it should be thinned. If the paint becomes powdered as it dries on the finger, more glue should be added. For paint that is to be used on wood, the amount of glue should be doubled.

Since mixes are very difficult to match, especially after the paint has dried, it is well to make up more than seems to be needed. Batches of paint will keep for several days, even in hot weather, if a few drops of household disinfectant (Lysol or CN) are added to the mix. (Anyone who has smelled "spoiled" paint will want to take precautions against fermentation.) Also, since it is easier to darken a light color than to lighten a dark shade, it is best to add the lighter hues first. Some pigments, notably black and red, are so dry that they do not dissolve readily. A little alcohol added to the mix will hasten the process.

BRUSHES

The scene painter, since his work varies from fine lining to gross daubing, requires a considerable assortment of brushes.

Not only in order to use two or three colors at a time, but also to enable several people to work simultaneously, he should provide himself with several brushes of each type. The following is suggested as a minimum set:

2   6″ or 8″ calcimine brushes for surface covering and spattering.
2   3″ or 4″ flat brushes for smaller surface covering.
3   2″ flat brushes for smaller surface covering and woodwork.
4   1″ flat brushes for lining.
4   ½″ flat brushes for lining.
2   1½″ sash brushes for foliage.
2   scrubbing brushes for brush stippling.

The test of a good brush is in the resilience of its bristles, which should spring back to their normal position even when wet. Therefore, pure-bristle brushes should be selected in every case except the last.

APPLYING SCENE PAINT:
GENERAL SURFACE COVERING

There may be said to be two kinds of painting: general and specific; or, to put it another way, *surface covering* and *detail work*. The former type —in which the scene painter is engaged most of the time—also may be divided into two general types: *flat painting* and *broken color*. The former is used to give a surface a general tone; the latter to give texture.

Flat painting. Flat painting, used mostly to give scenery its first coat or *ground tone,* is done in the same manner as sizing, and with the same sort of brush (a calcimine brush with soft, resilient bristles; a 6″ or 8″ size is best for large surfaces, a 3″ or 4″ flat brush for smaller areas). Indeed, pigment is sometimes mixed in the sizing, and two operations accomplished at once. The danger here is that the canvas will not be opaqued, and, if a strong light strikes it from behind, it may show through and require painting on the back to make it light-proof. A wrist motion, not an arm-swing, should be used; the brush should be dipped frequently, wiped to prevent dripping (a wire stretched across the top of the pail will help), and the painted area should be gradually enlarged, its edge never being allowed to dry. If an old flat is being painted over, great care must be taken not to scrub over a wet surface, as this will pull the old color through the new paint. If this happens, wet surfaces should never be retouched, but allowed to dry thoroughly first.

Puddling. A varied surface, suitable as a background for stonework, for example, may be obtained by dipping the brush successively in different shades of paint (say, blue-gray, tan-gray, and pearl-gray). *Puddling* is another name for this technique for getting a mottled background. It is best done by laying the scenery flat, pouring on different colors in successive pools, and pulling the edges together with a sizing brush. "Puddles" of green, blue, and yellow make an excellent background for foliage; brown, tan, gray, and purple for rocks; and browns and purples for tree trunks. A little aluminum powder in the paint will add a glint to earth or stone surfaces.

Stippling. Texture is suggested by means of *broken color,* of which puddling is an example. But the usual method is by *stippling;* that is, by putting the paint on in small dots or lines.

Sponge stippling is a common and useful technique. It is done with a large sponge with a smooth, even surface, which is dipped in the desired color, wrung out, and dabbed lightly to the surface so that only the points touch. If the sponge is turned continually (in the air, of course, not on the canvas) to avoid a regular pattern, an over-all texture very much like some wallpapers is the result.

Cloth rolling produces a "crackle" pattern of small, irregular, interlaced lines, also seen in wallpapers. When combined with the sponge stipple (say, a tan sponge and a brown cloth roll on a cream surface) a good "oatmeal" texture will result. This is done by dipping two or three square feet of cloth (a scrap left over from the flats) into the paint, wringing it out, and lightly rolling the still-twisted string across the surface with the palms of the hands.

Whipping will produce a pattern of lines similar to the veins in marble. A whip, made of several two-foot lengths of small cotton cord (such as that used for venetian blinds), attached to a short handle, and dipped in black or green paint is lashed against a white surface. To vein a black surface, green and white paint are whipped on.

Spattering, or throwing small drops of paint on a surface by tapping a not-too-wet calcimine brush (6″ or 8″) against the wrist, is a technique used freely by scene painters, not only to simulate a rough plaster surface, but as a final, finish coat to tone in painting of all kinds. The brush should be turned a bit between strokes so as to avoid a pattern. It should never be swung, as this produces lines.

A finer texture may be obtained, in much less time and with half the effort, by means of a *spray*. An air brush, of course, gives best results, but an ordinary garden tank-spray will do. In either case, thinner paint should be used, and carefully strained into the container, as the least obstruction causes a spray nozzle to clog. The tank spray should always be kept up to a good pressure, and always started on the ground, otherwise blobs of paint instead of a fine spray will be thrown on the canvas. Spray nozzles should be constantly moved, usually in a small circle, to avoid overwetting an area and causing drips. If properly used, a final coat of spray or spatter will give an interesting texture to flat surfaces, "tie-in" designs, "take down" obtrusive patterns, and enable the painter to center interest by shading off the corners.

Errors such as too-dark or too-thin spots of spatter can often be corrected by dipping a scrubbing brush into the paint (for a too-heavy spot, use the ground color), holding it close to the surface, upside down, and drawing the blade of a case knife toward you, across its bristles.

Pointillage. Through this method of applying paint to a surface in small dots, primary colors may be put onto a surface in various proportions—which may be varied still more by the use of different-colored lighting—and the desired hue obtained through the mixing that goes on in the spectator's eye. This is the method used by such landscape painters as Seurat, who called themselves *pointillistes*.

Although this method may hardly be relied on for a general paint job, it may be borrowed for special effects. For instance, a very light spatter of red or yellow will brighten a dull set without materially changing its color. Also, sets whose toning spatters contain the primaries—even in pastel tints—can be made to change materially under different lighting. The technique is therefore particularly useful for unit sets. The writer once spattered a gray set with pastel primaries. Under cold light it served well as the chapel in a cathedral; under warm, it became a pink stucco roof-garden.

PICTORIAL PAINTING

Details which must be painted into a set are of two types: *pictorial* and *architectural*. The latter require mechanical aids; the former are usually done freehand.

Pictorial painting is too involved a matter to be treated here, except for a few hints. Let it be said at the outset, however, that humility regarding one's talent and skill should not be allowed to deter one from making a stab at pictorial work if the occasion demands it. Courage means much; simple books on water-color sketching are a considerable aid; and pictures from which to copy directly are easily obtainable. (While originality is a virtue, no designer should hesitate to borrow a detail here and there. Most stage drops are copied from sketches anyway.)

Enlarging a sketch. To reproduce a life-size design on a drop or flat, the surface to be painted must first be ruled off into one-foot squares. This is done by marking the one-foot intervals across the top, bottom, and sides, holding a *snap line* (a heavy cotton cord that has been rubbed with chalk) taut between equivalent points, and snapping the line. The sketch is then ruled into an equal number of squares, and the design can be copied from square to square.

Laying in. After the design has been sketched in with charcoal or chalk, the main areas are flat-coated in, and finally the details are painted, as nearly like those in the sketch as possible.

The following hints may prove helpful:

Colors in *distant* objects tend to lose intensity (i.e., they become gray). Those surfaces of an irregularly shaped object which are nearest the source of light will appear *highlighted;* those that recede—especially those that turn away from the light—will appear *shadowed.* (If you don't know the source of light, assume that it comes from 45° above and to the left.) Some painters recommend making highlights by intensifying the base color, and the shadows by mixing the base color with its complement. A simpler method is merely to heighten the *value* (by adding whiting) for a highlight and, conversely, adding black to the base color for a shadow.

A rounded surface can be suggested by washing-in a spot (or line) of highlight at the point nearest the light source (i.e., blending the edges of the two colors while both are still wet) and washing-in shadows from the surfaces farthest from the light. If the base color is already dry, the highlight and shadow may be feathered off by *dry-brushing* (i.e., allowing the brush to become so dry and the strokes so light that only light lines are made instead of a solid surface).

A pleasing *foliage* effect may be obtained by daubing a puddled surface with light green, dark green, ultramarine and yellow, in successive and slightly overlapping splotches, using a 2" sash brush, and painting in an occasional twig here and there in brown and purple with a 1" flat brush. The area around the twig can later be cut away so as to silhouette it against the sky. For hedges, one should sponge-stipple a "puddled" background (see description, p. 234) with light green, dark green, and yellow.

The effect of *steel* may be obtained by painting first with aluminum powder mixed with glue-water, then over this (when dry) with black. While still wet, the black may be rubbed slightly with a cloth. *Wrought iron* may be simulated to an amazing degree by painting with a mixture of shellac and graphite and rubbing the dry surface with the ball of a hammer.

ARCHITECTURAL PAINTING

One of the chief characteristics of any normal building is regularity. Therefore, unless distortion is his deliberate aim, the scene painter should draw architectural details with the same precision as a mechanical draftsman. Incidentally, he should use the same tools, but on a larger scale: the straightedge (or ruler), square, and compass. (Of course, a string-and-pencil radius will serve for the latter.) A plumb line is useful for drawing perpendiculars.

Bricks. The chief characteristics of bricks are their geometric placement and their slight irregularities in color and form. Therefore, to paint a wall a dull red and rule it with white does *not* produce convincing bricks. What is necessary, given a good ground color (burnt sienna plus a little whiting and a little red), is, first, to put in all the horizontals with a snap line, 2½" apart, then to divide these into 9" sections, staggering every other row, since bricks overlap each other. (That is, if the top row starts with a full brick 9" from the edge, the next row will start with a half brick, and the first vertical line will be 4½" from the edge.) The mortar lines should then be painted in with light gray paint, using a ½" flat brush and a straight edge. Next, two or three shades of the base color should be made, by adding a little whiting to one, some black to another batch, some blue to a third, and scattered bricks should be *dry-brushed* (i.e., stroked with a scrubbing brush that has been dipped lightly) with these colors. Varying the directions of the brush strokes from brick to brick is also wise. Finally, the whole surface should be given a spatter or spray of gray or purple.

Stonework. Stonework is done in a similar manner, except that the colors are different and the mortar lines more irregular. Rough stones should be highlighted and shadowed for depth.

Wood graining. Although nothing is so convincing as natural grain, which can be brought out beautifully by rubbing wood with a cloth saturated with dye such as Bismark brown, artificial graining is sometimes necessary, especially when the surface to be painted is not wood. There are two general methods for doing this: (1) By what might be termed the *positive* process, the surface is painted its basic color, and the grain dry-brushed on. By proper manipulation of the brush, knotholes and sworls may be suggested. (For example, for golden oak, paint with ochre and dry-brush with cream and a darker brown.) (2) By the *negative* process, the *grain color* is painted on, allowed to dry, and the base wood color painted over it. While this is still wet, it is scraped off in lines, ribbons, and circles, with a small piece of wood or the finger nail (patented "grainers" won't work on canvas), in the patterns that wood graining naturally takes.

A combination of these two methods (if one has time) will probably give best results.

Molding. Representing molding in paint is a matter of *lining* with highlights and shadows (see page 236).

For lining, a ½" thin bristle brush is best. If a very thin line is desired, a strip of tin may be folded around the bristles, about half an inch or less from the ends, and hammered flat. This will hold them so that they will paint a line with knife-edge precision. A straightedge should always be used, preferably one with a beveled edge, which will make the line more visible, permit tilting the brush, and prevent seepage of paint under the straightedge.

Examine a real piece of molding for highlights and shadows. If you can't find one, here is a formula:

For a common base-molding:
    Paint basic color (say, cream)
    Rule in $\frac{1}{8}$″ highlight about $\frac{1}{8}$″ from top (whiting added to base color)
    Rule in $\frac{1}{8}$″ shadow below that (black added to base color)
    Rule in $\frac{1}{4}$″ highlight below that
    Rule in $\frac{1}{4}$″ shadow below that

The stencil. The most mechanical means of detail painting is the *stencil*. This device is useful for any definite over-all design, but chiefly (to the scene painter) for wallpaper. (Real wallpaper is never used on the professional stage because it is both too fragile and too inflammable to be safe.) An exactly repeating design can best be obtained by means of a stencil, and when several colors are used (often from the same stencil), and blended slightly by hand, a very convincing wallpaper results.

The main requirements of a stencil design are that it be large enough to "carry," and that the design really repeat. For example, one element in the upper right corner—say a vine—may lead into a similar element in the lower left corner.

The design should be drawn either directly on a stencil paper or on tracing paper which is then thumbtacked across a sheet of stencil paper, and the *positive* sections (the parts where the paint is to take effect) cut out with a very sharp knife or razor blade. Care must be taken to leave no unattached sections, like the center of a ring, or unsupported curves. Small strips should be left at intervals to hold such parts of the stencil together and prevent curling. A coat of shellac over both surfaces will make cleaning easier, and if the paper is tacked to a light wooden frame, it will require fewer hands to hold it in place.

It is wise to make vertical lines with a snap line on the set to guide the placing of the pattern. A chalk mark should also be made at the top of the frame, or at the point where the stencil repeats, to indicate the next position where the frame will be placed. Thick scene paint should be daubed on with a stencil brush or a large sash brush with short, stubby bristles. It should not be rubbed, as this will tend to drag the paint under the stencil. But periodic cleaning of the back of the stencil is advisable anyway.

Stencil patterns are nearly always too definite for comfort on the stage, and should be sprayed down with a good toning color (gray, cream, black, purple, etc., depending on the color harmonies used).

PAINTING WITH DYES

There are some occasions when the need for extreme flexibility precludes the use of scene paint. Some drapes—and even some drops—have to be taken off their battens and folded up. This would cause scene paint to crease and crack. In such cases, it is best to use special dyes, which are made especially for the purpose of painting on fabrics and which are readily obtainable from the larger paint dealers.

Translucencies. Dyes are necessary also in the making of stained glass or blister glass windows. Here *lamp dip* (the dyes used for coloring electric bulbs) will be found most satisfactory, as it has a brilliance next to none. Since this is a very quick-spreading dye, precautions must be taken to keep it in bounds. Fortunately, it is a characteristic of stained glass that each detail —excepting only faces and hands—is surrounded by lead. Hence, if the lead cartoon is first painted in with thick black scene paint, each section may easily be colored without fear of the dye spreading into other areas.

The best medium on which to paint a stained glass effect is *cel-o-glass* or *lumarith,* a galvanized screen whose pores have been filled with translucent plastic film. Not nearly so durable, but equally scintillating, when painted with lamp dye and lit from behind, is *eggshell pongee.*

The window in the church scene in the production of *Much Ado About Nothing,* illustrated in Chapter 11, was made in this manner.

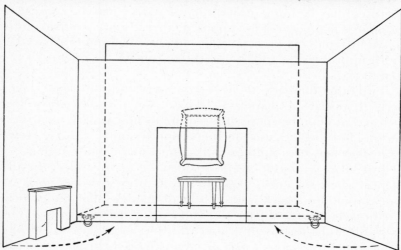

This is a "jackknife" set mounted on a small wagon as used for Farquhar's *The Beaux Stratagem*, produced by Milton Smith for the Columbia Theatre Associates of Columbia University. William Steinel, designer. **Top.** This picture shows Restoration proscenium and inner scene. **Bottom.** This is a diagram of inner set, showing wagon and folding side walls.

Methods of Scene Change

All through this chapter the admonition has been made that scenery should be kept flexible so that it may be *struck*. This, of course, is one method of changing scenery; to strike one set, stack it, bring another on, and set it up. This takes much time and effort. It may be simplified by designing the second set so it will fit *inside* the first—or better still, *vice versa*—so that the larger set may be left standing throughout. This is even more desirable if the larger set has heavy doors, stairways, etc. which are not easily moved. (The larger set must, of course, be constructed so that a section of its wall can be removed to provide access to the smaller set.)

If time is of the essence, however, a more ingenious device must be used. One such device, the *portal unit* set, has been described above, on pages 177 and 178. The principle of the *portal unit*, which amounts to disguising neutral walls by changing the nature and shape of the openings as well as the decorative details, may be adapted to the ordinary box set. Tapestries, or even pictures, may be hung over windows; a door may be concealed by a large mantelpiece or cupboard; a terrace may be made into a hall by removing French doors and setting an interior backing in front of the sky; and so on, to the limit of the designer's ingenuity.

Two other methods, the *revolving stage* and the *wagon stage*, were discussed in Chapter 10. These two machines are so expensive and cumbersome, and require so much space, that they are not very widely used in the nonprofessional theatre. However, they may be simplified and adapted to the small stage.

Instead of a *double shuffleboard* or *jackknife stage*, for instance, where the entire stage floor rolls away with the set on it, one can mount a back wall on a small, narrow platform (which might well provide the floor of an alcove or hallway), hinge the two side walls to this unit, and roll the whole set on and off, folded up. Or, a spot set may be mounted on the front of a small platform and rolled on and off, thus eliminating both a bracing job and a heavy "carry." The former method was employed in the Columbia Theatre Associates' production of *The Beaux' Stratagem* (pictured on page 241) in which the inner set was carried on a wagon and its side walls jackknifed.

As a variation on the revolving stage, one can hinge several side walls, covered on both sides, to posts at the corners of the set, so that, when swung from an up-and-downstage position, two side walls join and become one back wall, while others are waiting to be similarly turned, like the leaves of a book.

Similarly, a double-faced two-fold unit may be hinged to the

Here and on pages 244 and 245 are shown settings for Sidney Howard's *The Silver Cord* as produced at Brooklyn College. Catherine N. Myers, director; J. F. Foster, technical director. The above scene is the living room. A double-faced flat, hinged just below the window, conceals the bedroom window and window seat and carries the bed folded up on its inner face. A similar flat, which carries the mantel piece on one side and a dummy chest of drawers (which serves also as a fireplace backing) on the other, is hinged at the midpoint of the stage-left wall. To the lower edges of each of these flats a similar flat is hinged. These now extend offstage between the tormentors and the proscenium. Their rear surfaces, painted black, act as temporary tormentors.

middle of each side wall, so that it may be swung upstage or downstage through an arc of 180°. When these units are in their downstage position, they cover the lower halves of the side walls (the extra flat of the two-fold, painted black on the back, sliding off between the tormentor and the proscenium). When swung upstage into the corners of the set, they reveal the permanent lower side walls and form a new upstage wall section. An extra piece (a door or jog) may be inserted between them if necessary. (Since the frames of these flats are now completely covered, *lash hooks* must be used instead of lash cleats.) This device not only permits a radical change in color scheme, since the two faces of the double-faced flats and their companion pieces may be painted quite differently, but it also allows considerable variation in shape. For instance, the swinging sections may be pushed all the way into the corners and joined by a header to form a window, doorway, or arch. (A curtained valance might even serve.) Or they may be extended straight out to form a shallow set, or one up and one out to form a *V*, and so on. Also, the concealed sections of wall may contain openings which are revealed

This is a scene in *The Silver Cord* in the process of being shifted. The right hinged section has been swung into position, and now conceals the living-room window and part of the back wall. A stagehand is letting down the bed. Another is pulling the stage-left swinging section out across the stage to join the right section, and thus conceal the entire back wall. The fireplace section is now out of sight behind the section of wall carrying the chest of drawers, and the door down left has been revealed. The center door is being swung into position up center. A third stagehand will bring in a jog to be lashed between the two swinging sections, perpendicular to each, so as to make the back wall more rigid and conceal the cracks where the two sections join.

as the double-faced section moves away. A scheme of this kind was used in the production of *The Silver Cord,* referred to on page 203.

The permanent architectural or *formal unit* has also been mentioned (see page 178). A startling and not very difficult variation on the system may be obtained by combining it with the *scrim disappearance,* described above on page 211. Thus, if the walls of a perfectly solid-looking house are made of scrim, they can be made suddenly to disappear, revealing the interiors of its rooms, merely by lowering the front lights and turning on those inside. In order to achieve adequate opaqueness, it is advisable to keep direct light off the surface of the scrim, and it may be necessary to use two layers stretched a few inches apart. This method was used by Milton Smith in his production of *The Alchemist,* illustrated on page 246.

Abstract and Fantastic Scenery

The basic units described above—the drape, the drop, the flat, and the set piece—are the foundations of all scenery. Al-

This illustration shows the scene in *The Silver Cord* as complete. The entire former set is now concealed, including its furniture, which has been stacked in the hallway. This is David's bedroom.

though they have been described predominantly from the realistic point of view, they merely require modification in shape and variation in placement to adapt themselves to the abstract or fantastic style. For example, flats may be built in odd shapes and the openings in them distorted; set pieces may be made in the form of abstractions, or hung in the air from wires instead of set on the floor; and so on, to the limit of the designer's imagination. The difference lies in the *treatment,* rather than in the *kind,* of the materials.

Settings for the Arena Theatre

In the arena theatre, where visibility is four-directional and audience-contact paramount, scenery should be reduced to a minimum. Low set pieces that can be used in the center of the floor, like bushes, stumps, hillocks, well-heads, or platforms, may be useful. But peripheral objects like doors, windows, cupboards —in fact, most of the stock items in the conventional theatre— must be made transparent or eliminated. Very low fireplaces might conceivably be used, and, in plays that absolutely require doors and windows, these might be indicated in constructivist outline. But since any barrier, however slight, detracts just that much from the intimacy that is the main aim of this form, it is better to leave all peripheral items to the imagination, or to choose a play in which none are needed.

The same principle applies to furniture. Secretaries, high cabinets, wall mirrors, even high-backed chairs are *out.* All furniture must be low and should be centrally placed—nothing used

These illustrations show the scrim disappearance in the setting for Ben Jonson's *The Alchemist* as produced by Milton Smith for the Columbia Theatre Associates, Columbia University. J. F. Foster, technical director. **Top,** the house lighted from the front, its scrim walls appear solid; and **Bottom,** the same setting with the upper room lighted from within, causing its outer wall to vanish.

that would present an obstacle between the actors and the audience. Low modern furniture lends itself well to the requirements of the arena theatre, as can be seen from the illustrations of Glen Hughes' Penthouse Theatre on pages 145 and 146.

Settings for the Outdoor Theatre

In outdoor productions the problem of scenery is complicated by two factors: the weather and the surroundings. Although the same basic units may be used, since the conventional placement of audience-facing stage is generally employed, they cannot be built or mounted in the same way. One heavy rain would take all the paint off a conventional set. So if a production is to run longer than a performance or two, oil paints, or at least casein-base colors, should be used.

Similarly, a wind of even mild intensity will exert tremendous pressure against the large surfaces presented by flats. Hence, "movie set" construction of wood and wall board is preferable to frame and canvas. Even for one-night stands, while heavy timbers may be placed in strategic spots to provide an anchorage for stage braces, it will be found safer to anchor the edges of the flats as well, to keep the wind from taking them off their feet. This, of course, interferes with scene change, so some sort of a unit set is advisable.

The wind also makes the use of a front curtain difficult, and it should be avoided wherever possible in outdoor productions. Various substitutes have been tried, such as the *water curtain,* in which a row of closely-spaced jets separates the stage and audience. When these are turned on with considerable force and volume they block vision very well, especially if illuminated from their bases. Needless to add, they are decidedly decorative —as well as quite expensive. The *light curtain* is another device. This consists of a row of fairly powerful lights across the apron, aimed directly at the audience. Their blinding effect makes it difficult to see what is going on behind them, if that area is kept dark. But the easiest, cheapest, and often most effective way to avoid using a front curtain is to plan a production that doesn't need one. This can be done with the simultaneous setting, the formal unit, the space stage—in fact, most of the less realistic styles.

This brings us from practical problems to aesthetic considerations. Before choosing a type of production for outdoor performance, the designer should first know in what type of outdoor theatre he is being asked to produce: a sylvan glade, a carnival platform, a Greek theatre, or a conventional stage with no roof, like the Cain Park Theatre pictured on page 158. If the

This is the setting for *Mañana Is Another Day* as produced by the Cain Park Outdoor Theatre, Cleveland Heights, Ohio. John Hulbert and Gerard Gentile designers.

sylvan glade is to be the location, the less scenery the better. Of course, the producer can take care of that by choosing a play, such as *As You Like It*, that requires little or no scenery. (For the palace scenes, a canopied chair flanked by plenty of "spear carriers" is really all that is needed.) If he has not been so thoughtful, there are ways of at least getting rid of a proscenium and gridiron, which are most difficult to achieve outdoors. For instance, Raymond Sovey's variation on the *spot set* technique for Jane Cowl's production of *Twelfth Night* may be adapted admirably to the outdoor production of any romance. Here, all the scenes were mounted like illustrations in a big book, the Fool turning the "pages" to show a different "picture" when a change was required. The profile set also lends itself well to outdoor staging, since it needs no ceiling. Such a set is seen being assembled on the Cain Park stage in the illustration on page 158.

For more stark stories, the formal unit and the space stage serve well. But the most satisfactory setting for a large outdoor production is the simultaneous setting—which, indeed, was invented for just such a purpose. With all possible locations spread out at once before the audience, like houses on a street, the action can move from place to place with no break, or fill the whole area if necessary.

An ideal outdoor realistic set is pictured in the hacienda designed by Gerard Gentile for the Cain Park production of *Mañana Is Another Day*. Here the buildings are all topped by their own roofs, and are so arranged as to mask the rear stage and wing space. The rambling galleries and steps offer a wide variety of acting areas. The night sky itself serves as a cyclorama.

Conclusion

With the setting, as in all the other departments of the theatre, the past feeds the future. Forms change, old ones wear out, spectacular new ones appear—and suddenly we find that we are merely using old forms in new ways. The modern formal unit, as has been seen, derives from the Greek *skene*. The portal unit, hailed a few years back as a miraculous innovation because of the way in which it speeded up scene change, springs straight from the Elizabethan stage. The simultaneous setting was invented in medieval times. Thus the designer who knows theatre history has a vast storehouse from which his imagination can draw.

Exercises

1. Make a list of the mechanical requirements of the play you have chosen for a project. (How many doors are needed? Where must they lead to? How many windows are necessary? What do they look out on? How many steps and stairs are required?) Add to this list all features of structure or arrangement that you think you can use to motivate the action or emphasize the characters.
2. Make a ground plan of a setting for your project play, embodying the details listed above, using a stage familiar to you as a basis.
3. Make ground plans for three interiors, differing radically in their contours.
4. Make ground plans for a multiset play, using one of the *unit set* methods to achieve economy of time, space, and materials.
5. Make a sketch for your project play, showing the color scheme and the arrangement of such details.
6. Make a model, combining the layout of your ground plan with the visual details of your sketch.
7. Design a set for a play, using mostly drapes.
8. Redesign your project play (or some other play) for presentation in an arena theatre or in an outdoor theatre.

Bibliography

Barber, Philip, *The Scene Technician's Handbook,* New Haven: Whitlock's Bookstore, Inc., mimeographed, 1928. Now incorporated in John Gassner's *Producing the Play* (see Bibliography, Chapter 3). An excellent practical manual.

Burris-Meyer, Harold and Cole, Edward C., *Scenery for the Theatre,*

Boston: Little, Brown & Company, 1938. A compendium with many illustrations.

Hake, Herbert V., *Here's How*, Evanston, Ill.: Row, Peterson & Company, 1942. Clear and useful manual.

Helvensten, Harold, *Scenery*, California: Stanford University Press, 1931. Theory and practice.

Selden, Samuel, and Sellman, Hunton D., *Stage Scenery and Lighting*, New York: F. S. Crofts & Company, 1930, rev. ed. 1936. An excellent section on the construction and painting of scenery, much of which appears also in *Modern Theatre Practice*, by Heffner, Selden, and Sellman (see Bibliography to Chapter 19).

Smith, Milton, *Play Production for Little Theatres, Schools, and Colleges*, New York: D. Appleton-Century-Crofts, Inc., 1948. A very practical book by one of the best technicians in the non-professional theatre.

Southern, Richard, *Stage Settings for Amateurs and Professionals*, London: Faber & Faber, Ltd., 1937. Particularly good on the uses of drapes.

CHAPTER 13. ~~~~~~~~~~~~~~~~~~~~~~~~

LIGHTING

~~~~~~~~~~~~~~~~~~~~~~~~~~~~~~~~~~~~~~

*L*ighting is by far the newest branch of theatre art. Not until the last three centuries of the theatre's three thousand years of recorded history does it seem to have figured at all. For example, the most famous playhouse of antiquity, the Theatre of Dionysus at Athens, was built facing south, which means that the sun—the only source of light—was behind the stage and therefore at least partially in the audience's eyes most of the time.

Functions of Stage Lighting

After the theatre went indoors, in late Elizabethan times, light became a major problem, for without artificial light the actors could not be seen. A few venturesome souls were tempted to experiment with spectacular lighting. Inigo Jones is said to have used scrim disappearances, lights to dazzle the audience while scenes were being changed, "fairies bearing lights," etc. in various court masques during the early part of the seventeenth century. In medieval times, too, spectacular lighting was employed, at least to the extent of flares and squibs to make the "Hell" scenes more impressive. But few producers dared use the inefficient and dangerous apparatus available (mostly candles) for anything beyond the primary function of *visibility*.

It was not until gas was introduced, well into the nineteenth century, that lighting units became compact enough to permit colored screens to be used in front of them, and so to make possible a second important function of light: to add *color* to the stage picture and to enhance the colors already there.

It began now to be dimly apparent that people feel differently under different colors—relaxed under blue lights and excited under red—and that lines like "How sweet the moonlight sleeps upon this bank" not only go over better under blue lights than in the glare of an afternoon sun, but that lights alone can often

INTERIOR OF THE JOHN-STREET THEATRE, DURING THE REVOLUTION.
Copied from an Old Woodcut.

This is New York's first theatre, illuminated by candles.

put over lines of much lower poetic value. Also it was found that
"Is this a dagger that I see before me . . . ?" is twice as hair-
raising if spoken in gloom, which was now possible merely by
turning down the valve. And so a still deeper function of light
—and of its partner, shadow—was being groped toward: its influence on *mood*.

Thus far, stage lighting had been of only one type: *general
lighting*. The invention of the limelight (a small piece of lime
heated to incandescence by an oxyacetylene flame) opened another field: *specific lighting*. For stage folk soon found that by
placing a lens in front of this gleaming point they could concentrate a powerful beam of light upon the star, and so *accentuate*
him. (People of unusual prominence are still referred to as being "in the limelight.")

But this very innovation pointed up the need for a fourth
function of light; it was found that when this beam struck the
actor straight in the face it eliminated most of his natural shad-

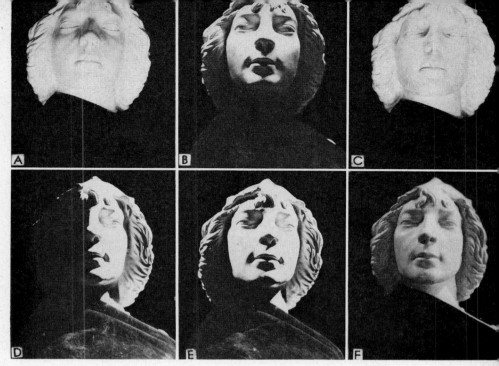

Here is shown the effect on a plaster bust of six different lightings. **A**, general light from below (footlights only); **B**, general light from above (border lights only); **C**, strong general lighting from above and below (footlights and border lights); **D**, side lighting (spotlight from stage left); **E**, balanced sharp contrast (two spotlights, the stronger from stage left); and **F**, balanced "plastic" lighting (footlights dim, borders medium, two spotlights, the stronger from stage left).

ows and so flattened him out. Not until he turned partly sideways did he again assume any real degree of *plasticity*. We know now that by the proper placement of lights we can make an object appear as flat or as rugged as we please. (The plaster cast pictured above demonstrates this.)

At about this same time another *point-source* of light was being experimented with in the theatre, one even more compact and convenient than the limelight: the *electric arc*. This new device was soon turned toward a problem which heretofore had pretty well baffled theatre technicians: *imitation of the effects of nature*. Change of brilliancy had already been achieved. With projection possible and the laws of reflection and refraction pretty well understood, technicians could now begin to let themselves go. So by 1860 we find the Paris Opera, which fourteen years previously had startled the theatre world by making the sun rise, now "wowing" audiences with rainbows and lightning.

Thus by the end of the nineteenth century five of the six functions of stage lighting—to *make visible* the actors and setting, to help *color* the stage picture, to *establish mood,* to *focus attention,* and to *imitate natural phenomena*—were well understood. It took the development of the incandescent lamp, and of its control unit, the dimmer, to bring them all, including the sixth—to give forms *plasticity*—to full realization.

Color in Light

One has only to send a beam of white light through a glass prism to discover that it is really made up of a mixture of all colors, from red to violet. Any one of these colors may be obtained by placing a filter in front of a light that will strain out all the colors except the one desired. (Dyed gelatin sheets are usually used for this purpose. Although subject to fading and buckling, they are much less expensive than glass, and are obtainable in a far greater variety of shades and tints. Cellophane is not recommended, since it is not fireproof. Individual "bulbs," up to 60 watts, may be colored by being dipped into a special lamp dye, but they are not very useful for stage lighting because they will not stand heat.)

Since white light can be refracted by a prism into its component colors, it should be possible to mix these colors and produce white. This can be done. In fact, it has been proved that only three colors—the primaries—are needed, and that if these are mixed in various combinations, any hue may be obtained. (The mixing, of course, must be done by throwing different colors on a common reflecting surface, and not by superimposing several gelatins in the same light.)

THE PRIMARY COLORS

Light primaries are red, blue, and green. These, when combined in *equal proportions,* produce white light.[1] When two light primaries are combined the result is a secondary or binary

[1] Only pure primaries, of course, will produce white light when mixed. These are almost impossible to obtain in gelatins, but Century Lighting Company's no. 36 blue, no. 49 green, and no. 67 red approximate the pure primaries closely enough to produce a pinkish white when mixed.

hue. (Red and green together produce yellow; if red is in predominance, orange will result. Red and blue, as in pigment primaries, give various degrees of purple.) Adding a third primary to any of these combinations will pale the color, as will the addition of white light.

For this reason, some theatre technicians advocate equipping their border lights and footlights with glass roundels in red, green, blue, and white, so that general illumination of any hue or value may be achieved by color mixing. For reasons best known to themselves, some lighting equipment manufacturers substitute amber for white or green. The present writer does not recommend this, as amber is a very harsh color that is extremely unflattering to faces and to other colors, especially yellow, blue, and violet.

Other technicians prefer to achieve the desired tint directly at the light source by using a gelatin medium of that tint, and thereby producing an already mixed color. This is what is nearly always done with *specific lights* which are directed toward particular areas of the stage, and which, in the modern theatre, furnish most of the light in which the actors move. (*General lights* are now used mostly for toning the stage picture.)

The professional lighting technician ordinarily employs a compromise between the two systems of mixing light colors at the unit or on the object illuminated, by using gelatins of three pastel tints in the borders and footlights. Usually, pale tints of the pigment primaries are used, such as light scarlet, lemon, and medium blue (which combine a very pale red, a greenish yellow, and a blue somewhat on the purplish side); or surprise pink, (which has purplish tints), straw (a brownish yellow) and moonlight blue which contains much green). This system is recommended as much more foolproof than the one mentioned above. It is almost impossible to achieve a stage light from pastel gelatins that will kill other colors, whereas unskillfully mixed pure primaries are often extremely harsh.

Sometimes the director may wish to use notes of difficult colors, as when he brings in shafts of late afternoon (amber) sunlight or follows an actor playing a ghost with a green spotlight. Any costume of rich or diluted colors that gets into the range of such a light will "go dead." Unless this is desired, it behooves the director either to demand another costume or to keep the wearer out of these particular lights.

EFFECTS OF COLORED LIGHT ON PIGMENT

Some lights are *difficult* since a colored light tends to gray its complementary hues. Amber, being a very strong reddish-yellow, containing no blue at all, will turn any purple, lavender, turquoise, or blue object that comes within its field into the color of mud. Browns, on the other hand, are not hurt, and gold is enhanced by amber. This, of course, is the other side of the picture: A light of a given hue will tend to enhance its analogous colors, provided there is a contrasting background. Drench the stage in red, and a red dress will look pale; place the dress in front of a blue backdrop and turn a red spot on it, and it will fairly glow. The use of this principle on the stage is obvious. But again, caution should be observed. A pastel tint of red, such as light scarlet, will accomplish much the same pickup in the red field, while at the same time passing all the other hues in such quantities that other colors are but slightly affected.

Optical Principles

Mention has been made of the importance of the *point-source* in stage lighting. Without this point-source it is impossible to take full advantage of the laws of reflection and refraction. Light, as is well known, travels in a straight line, except when it passes from a lighter to a denser transmitting medium, as, for example, from air to glass, or when it strikes a surface that will neither pass it nor absorb it, say a piece of burnished metal. In the first instance, the rays are bent from their original path, or *refracted*. Should the refractor be in the form of a *lens* (a glass disc with at least one curved surface) placed near the light source, the rays that strike it will be focused into a concentrated beam. At a point determined by the curvature of the lens (the *focal point*) an exact image of the source will be projected. If the lamp is moved forward the rays will fan out; the nearer it approaches the lens, the wider will be the spread. This is the principle of the *spotlight,* the basic unit for all *specific* lighting (see the diagram on page 266).

In the second case, when light rays fall upon a nonabsorbent surface, they bounce off. If the surface is completely smooth, they will be *reflected* in a *regular* pattern, and at the same angle (in the opposite direction) as that in which they struck the re-

flector. That is why mirrors on
the stage sometimes have to be
soaped: to keep them from reflecting things that should not
be seen, like fly ropes and spotlights. This is true, of course,
only of a flat mirror, which
will reflect a light source just
as it does an object, but will
not concentrate its rays. Place
a light source in front of a
curved reflector, however, and
its rays will be *focused* either
into a point or a beam, depending on the nature of the
curve. A spherical reflector
will send a light from a source
at its center straight back
through the source, and thus
double the amount of light
coming from the other side of
the lamp. Such reflectors are
often mounted behind the
lamps in spotlights to increase
the amount of light striking
the lens without changing its
source. A reflector in the form
of a *parabola,* on the other
hand, will send out light rays
from a source at its focus in
parallel lines to form a concentrated beam, as in the automobile headlight. This principle
is employed in some stage
units because of its high efficiency in collecting and re-

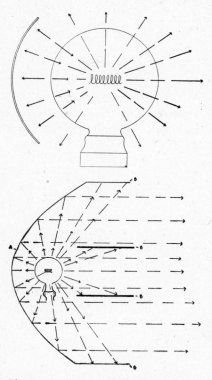

These two line drawings show different types of reflection. **Top,**
spherical reflection. All the light
caught from a source at the center
of the arc is sent back through the
source. **Bottom,** parabolic reflection. Light coming from a source at
the focus of a parabolic reflector,
A, is sent out in a parallel beam,
spill rings, **B,** stop stray rays coming
from the front of the lamp.

turning light; but it has not replaced the lens for spotlighting
for two reasons. First, part of the light (that coming from the
side of the lamp opposite the reflector) cannot be focused, but
is radiated in all directions. This can be at least partially coun-
teracted, in places where such a *spill* is undesirable, by using

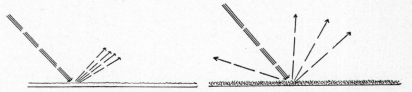

These drawings show the effect of light striking an irregular reflecting surface. **Left**, spread reflection; and **Right**, diffusion.

spill rings (concentric metal cylinders painted black, placed
around the entire opening of the unit) or a *blinder* (a black
metal disc or cup placed in front of the lamp), but these cut
down the efficiency without quite curing the spill, for not even
black is completely light-absorbent. Second, since the light
source is not a point but a closely-packed grid of white-hot wire
coils, the rays reflected into the beam are not evenly spaced but
come together in some places and separate in others. Consequently, the area illuminated has the appearance of a mottled
splotch instead of an evenly illuminated circle, such as one can
·get from a lens spotlight.

But by far the commonest type of reflection—and a very useful one in the theatre—is not the regular type just referred to,
but *diffusion,* which occurs when light rays strike a surface of irregular texture. If the irregularities are only slight, as in the case
of enamel or etched aluminum, the rays may only be spread; but
if the surface is quite irregular, as in a piece of cloth, diffusion
will take place in all directions. Reflectors made of the former
material can be constructed so as to pool the light, with greatest
concentration at the center and with gradual diminution toward
the edges. For this reason they are often employed in the basic
unit on which theatre technicians depend for *general* illumination: the *floodlight*. Attempts have been made to light the stage
indirectly by diffusion from silk or silver screens, but, largely
because of the heavy light loss involved, they have never been
adopted generally.

Lighting Units in General Use

Before considering in detail the variations on these two basic
units, the *floodlight* and the *spotlight,* by which the two kinds
of stage lighting, *general* and *specific,* are accomplished, it might
be well to point out that most lighting technicians add two more

categories: *special effects,* or lights designed for decorative or representational purposes (such as color organs, cloud projectors, burning fires, etc.), and *strip lights,* or batteries of individual lights arranged in single rows, whose function is to contribute to general illumination.

STRIP LIGHTS

Strips were once the only source of illumination on the stage, and are still commonly seen in three positions: as footlights, border lights, and backing lights.

Footlights. Footlights have been such a prominent type of stage light for so long that they have been identified in the public mind with the very term "theatre." They were made necessary by the large apron of the Renaissance stage, which brought the actors out of range of the lights placed behind the proscenium arch. (Notice the row of footlights in New York's first theatre, the John Street, illustrated on page 252.) They were always a poor makeshift because of the inverted shadows they cast. But since the introduction of *beam spots* in the auditorium, footlights are no longer needed to light the forestage. In fact, they should never be used as a primary source of illumination, but only as toning lights to bring out certain colors in the costumes or scenery, or at most to soften the shadows cast by strong overhead lights.

Footlights are mounted on the apron, near its front edge, and should be sunk into the floor just enough to bring the filament of the lamp even with the surface of the stage. They should be angled in such a manner that most of the light is thrown *up* and not against the back wall. In some instances the lamps are kept entirely below the stage level, the light being reflected back to the stage by a curved metal shield placed in the usual position. Footlights are ordinarily made in sections of from nine to twelve lights each, wired in three or four circuits. The latter is preferred by advocates of the "light primaries" since white light is necessary to dilute the hues derived from mixing the primary colors: red, green, and blue. If possible, it is wise to have each circuit of each section connected to a separate switch. This makes it possible, for example, to use the amber circuit in one of the end sections to augment a fireside scene, without going to

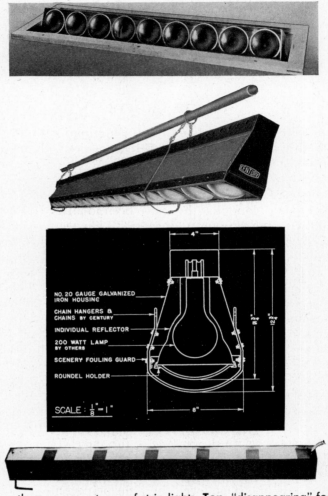

Here are three common types of strip lights. **Top,** "disappearing" footlights —a compartment strip with glass roundels made to fold under the floor when not in use; **Next to top,** reflector-type compartment border; **Next to bottom,** cross section of the reflector-type compartment border; and **Bottom,** exposed lamp backing strip.

the trouble of *backing out* (unscrewing) all the other amber lamps.

These sections are made in three types: (*a*) In the *exposed lamp* variety, the lamps (not larger than a 60-watt P.S., or "pear-shaped" type) are set in a continuous row inside one common reflector trough and depend upon *lamp dip* (alcohol dye which colors the surface of the bulb) or upon natural-colored lamps for color. Since the latter are expensive and the color range limited, and since lamp dip is impermanent, this type of unit is rapidly becoming obsolete. (*b*) The *compartment* type of footlight strip has each lamp mounted in a separate light-tight compartment which accommodates a gelatin frame. This makes possible not only a considerably wider variety of tints, but also the use of frosted gelatin, which softens and diffuses the light. It means, however, that the lamps cannot be placed less than six inches apart (the narrowest compartment that will accommodate a 100-watt P.S. lamp), and so the hazard of shadows is considerable, each color unit in a four-circuit strip being two feet from its nearest neighbor. The answer to this is, "Use frosted gelatins and keep the dimmers low." (*c*) The type of footlight strip most favored by the lighting experts is the *reflector* type, in which a fairly large lamp (usually a 100-watt P.S.) is fitted into a burnished reflector, and covered by a glass roundel that acts both as a color medium and as a diffusing agent. These are usually wired in four circuits, to accommodate the primaries and either white or amber.

Border lights. Strip lights hung on battens above the stage and parallel to the front curtain are called *border lights*. They constitute the modern stage's chief source of general illumination. In earlier days, when exposed lamp borders were the only type available, it was customary to hang row after row of them every six feet or so from the proscenium to the back wall. But when the development of larger and brighter lamps made the compartment strip possible, and especially after the development of reflectors, border lights were gradually abandoned until now it is customary to use only one or two high-powered sections (200- to 500-watt lamps) on the first pipe (i.e., directly back of the teaser) to light the whole acting area, with the rest of the space on the pipe filled with spotlights. This gives a nicely graduated light, with a bright pool at center stage, tapering off at the outer edges.

The type of unit most commonly used today for border lights is the six- or eight-compartment strip in three or four circuits with mogul (large sized) sockets to take 300- to 500-watt P.S.

lamps, and equipped with etched aluminum reflectors and gelatin frames. Such units, especially when in use on the first pipe, are commonly referred to as "X-rays," because the earlier type used glass reflectors manufactured by the X-Ray Reflector Company. Because of their fragility, glass reflectors soon disappeared in favor of the more durable aluminum type. But the name remains.

Some of the more science-minded lighting technicians prefer longer sections of the glass roundel type, which takes 200-watt lamps. But in the opinion of this writer these are not very satisfactory, since the colors obtained from the deep primaries in which the glass roundels are made are quite harsh and unflattering to faces and costumes.

Some border strips are provided at each end with swivels for pipe clamp hangers, which make it easy to adjust the unit to the proper angle (that is, at such a tilt that no light touches the ceiling) and to keep it there. Others have only hanging chains, which make tilting difficult. Often it will be found necessary to bolt two links together just below the pipe in order to keep the border from slipping into a horizontal position.

In box-set interiors where a ceiling is used, the first pipe is, of course, the only one available. But even in exteriors, unless the set is unusually deep, one border is usually ample. A sky drop or cyclorama, of course, will require a special set of lights so placed as to illuminate it alone. A set of powerful compartment strips serves fairly well for this purpose.

Cyclorama lights. The chief requirements of cyclorama lights, or sky borders, are intensity and evenness of illumination. While any good compartment border will serve, a special type, using lamps with built-in reflectors and diffusing lenses, similar to "sealed-beam" automobile headlights, is now available. This unit will evenly and brilliantly illuminate a large vertical area from a distance of only two feet.

Backing strips. The exposed lamp is still used for general illumination only in the backing strips. These are small open-faced troughs with the lamps (usually three to six) mounted end-to-end instead of side-by-side, eight inches between centers, and wired in a single circuit. They are often hung outside of doors that apparently lead to other rooms and often over archways opening into halls in order to shed a soft glow that somewhat counteracts the shadows cast by the more intense stage lights. They keep the actors from entering the stage from seeming darkness. Although such units will accommodate lamps up to 75 watts, this strength is seldom used because of glare. A very satisfactory G-type globular lamp of 25–30 watts is generally available in soft tints (ivory, light yellow, flesh pink, green, and light blue) and at quite low prices. These are generally preferable to dyed lamps or natural-colored lamps, which are too harsh for general use.

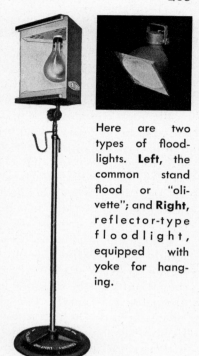

Here are two types of floodlights. **Left,** the common stand flood or "olivette"; and **Right,** reflector-type floodlight, equipped with yoke for hanging.

The brilliancy of backing strips is usually regulated by the number of lamps rather than by dimming. They should be hung high enough to avoid casting shadows when actors pass by.

Floor strips. In addition to those already mentioned, short sections of three- or four-circuit compartment strip lights are often used on the floor for lighting backings or the lower part of the sky (e.g., for sunset glow effects). These will be found more convenient to handle if mounted on casters so they may be easily rolled into position.

FLOODLIGHTS

The floodlight might be termed a semidirectional general-illumination unit. Essentially, it is nothing more than a large lamp (a 500- or 1000-watt P.S. is generally used) mounted in an open-faced box painted black on the outside, to render it inconspicuous, and white on the inside to reflect and diffuse the light. It must be provided with means for ventilation as large lamps get very hot. It also has a pair of grooves along the open edges to hold gelatin frames. (Glass is not often used for color media in floodlights because the size and the heat involved make breakage heavy.)

In the days when only small lamps were available, clusters of these were bunched inside a box to form a floodlight, giving rise to the term *bunch light*. But the development of the high-powered lamp has made this type obsolete.

The most common type of floodlight, sometimes referred to as the *olivette,* is provided with a swivel at its trapezoidal base so that it may be mounted on a stand. Some also have hooks on the sides for chains so they may be hung from a batten, but a special type, the *pendant flood,* whose face opens at a slant so as to direct the light back as well as downward, is more suitable for over-head work. Either type may be obtained with etched aluminum reflectors, which increase the efficiency of the lamp.

Floodlights are chiefly useful for scenery illumination. They should not be turned on the actors unless very sharp, harsh effects with heavy shadows are desired, as in fantastic scenes, and they should not be depended on for long throws, as their light dissipates very rapidly. They are not suitable for direct sunlight effects, because their rays fan out and cast magnified shadows. If, however, looming shadows are desired (as in the wake scene in *Porgy,* for instance), a compact flood made from a spotlight by removing the lens, and mounted in the floodlight trough or in a fireplace will give the desired effect.

SPOT FLOODS

Somewhere between the spotlight and the floodlight is a type of unit with a parabolic mirror that collects the rays of light thrown backward from the lamp and redirects them forward in a parallel beam. The rays from the front of the lamp are either allowed to flood, or are cut off by means of *spill rings.* This principle is employed in the *birdseye lamp,* a 300-watt unit with the reflector moulded into its stem, which, because of its efficiency and compactness, is often used in window display work, on television stages, and many other settings where a powerful, concentrated, short-throw area of light is needed. (The birdseye lamp, of course, cannot be focused.) Handy mounting fixtures and caps for gelatin filters or glass roundels may be obtained for this unit.

Another useful unit is the *beam projector,* a large, well-venti-

lated cylindri-
cal hood with
a parabolic
reflector in
the rear and
a 1000-watt
G-type spot-
light lamp
mounted on a
sliding base,
with a spill-

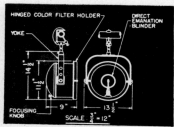

This is a beam projector type
of parabolic spot floodlight.

shield before it. Slots are provided to accommodate gelatin
frames. This light, because it throws an intense beam of parallel
rays (which may be spread somewhat by moving the lamp), is
most useful for outdoor lighting and for simulating direct sunlight.

Both these units, however, give a splotchy, uneven light area,
and they are not to be compared with the lens spotlight for act-
ing-area lighting.

SPOTLIGHTS

As has already been mentioned, the spotlight was first used in
the theatre as a *follow-spot:* a powerful unit placed in the rear
of the house (usually in a special booth at the back of the balcony) which was centered on a prominent character and moved
around to follow him from place to place. This is still done
sometimes in musical comedy to feature a song or dance number. But with the coming of the concentrated-filament incandescent lamps, which did not need an operator and so permitted
spotlights to be mounted anywhere, area lighting became possible, and since then the spotlight has furnished practically all
of the acting light on the stage.

All spotlights contain three basic parts: (1) the lamp, which
generates the light, (2) the lens, which focuses the rays, and (3)
the housing, which keeps superfluous light in but permits air to
flow around the lamp in order to cool it. Some of the more powerful lamps get so hot that the glass bulb blisters.

Good spotlights also contain reflectors. They may be divided
into three general types, whose characteristics differ because of
the type of lens, lamp, and mirror employed.

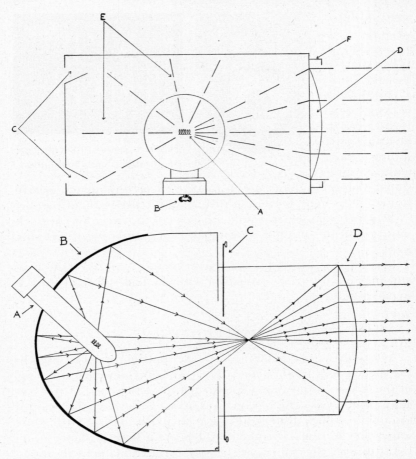

Here are two types of spotlights. **Top,** a plano-convex lens—**A,** lamp; **B,** sliding base for focusing; **C,** air vents; **D,** lens; **E,** light-absorbent hood; **F,** flanges to hold frame for color medium; and **Bottom,** ellipsoidal reflector —**A,** lamp placed at one of the foci; **B,** reflector collects light and concentrates it on other focus; **C,** metal shutters shape beam; **D,** lens bends light rays into beam.

The plano-convex lens or hood spotlight. As its name implies, the plano-convex spotlight, often referred to as a hood spot, depends for its focusing on a glass lens that is flat on the inner face and convex on the outer, which catches the light from a G-type spotlight lamp mounted on a sliding base inside a ventilated

metal hood of
roughly rec-
tangular, oc-
tagonal, or cy-
l i n d r i c a l
shape. Flanges

These are framing shutters for spotlights. **Left to right,**
are mounted   shallow four-way cutoff to shape beam; funnel or "high
in front of the   hat" to prevent spill; four-way cutoff with blinders; and
lens to hold   effect cutoff for special shapes.
g e l a t i n
frames, and either a yoke or a swivel provided so that the unit
may be aimed in any direction when mounted on a telescope
stand or hung from a batten by means of a C-clamp.

This type of unit gives an evenly illuminated circle of light,
which may be spread or narrowed by adjusting the lamp in relation to the lens. In size, it varies from the 100-watt mite-lite,
which is sometimes concealed in the footlight trough or behind
a beam on the stage, to the 2000-watt *follow spot* with an 8″
lens. The 250- to 400-watt *baby* spot with a 4″ or 5″ lens is useful for small stages where a throw of not more than ten or fifteen
feet is required. The 500- and 1000-watt varieties, with 6″ lenses,
are in general use for longer throws.

The sharp edges of the light area cast by this lamp may be
softened by using a frosted gelatin with the center torn out or
with a spot of oil rubbed on. The shape of the beam may also
be regulated to some extent by the use of *cut-offs,* or *framing
shutters,* which may be slid into the gelatin frame guides. No
really sharp-edged framing is possible, however, with this type
of spotlight.

But the plano-convex spotlight's most serious defect lies in
the inefficiency of its light output. Owing to the fact that, for
optical reasons, a fairly small lens must be used, only a small
portion of light given off by the lamp can be utilized (see the
diagrams on page 266). Even if this is augmented by a spherical
mirror behind the lamp (as indicated in the upper diagram on
page 257), some 80 per cent of the light is still absorbed by the
hood.

The Fresnel spotlight. Within the last few decades a new type
of lamp was developed, the T-20, a pre-focus base lamp that
locks into its socket, with its compact filament always in line

with the lens. This lamp has a tubular bulb of considerably smaller diameter than the G-type, which means that the filament can be moved closer to the lens, thus considerably increasing the amount of light collected. At the same time an old type of lens (the type invented for lighthouses by the French physicist Fresnel) was adapted so as to provide a heat-resistant lens of large diameter but very short focal length. In accomplishing this, some sharpness of focus had to be sacrificed—which meant the achievement of another long-sought-after ideal: the soft edge spotlight.

The result is the *Fresnel spotlight,* a unit almost ideally suited for lighting acting areas. The most common size is a 500-watt unit with a 6″ lens. (They range up to a 10,000-watt size with an 8″ lens.) It gives a soft, even pool of light, shading off to darkness at the edges and casting no sharp shadows. It can be focused almost to a point or spread to flood proportions, at twice the intensity of a hood spot of the same wattage. The unit is equipped with a yoke that permits a wide range of aiming either from a C-clamp or a telescope stand. The common sizes occupy less than a cubic foot of space.

Although its heat and intense light bleach gelatin somewhat more rapidly than the old hood spot, the Fresnel has almost completely taken over the function of acting area lighting. It also does very well for direct sunlight effects, on a short throw. It is not so useful on the ceiling beams in the auditorium because of its spill. A *funnel* or *high hat* (a metal cylinder placed in front of the lens) will stop this to some extent, but the Fresnel spot really belongs back of the proscenium.

The ellipsoidal reflector spotlight, or Leko. The type of unit most suited to "out front" illumination is the *Leko*—to use a name coined by one of its earlier manufacturers. This unit was made possible by the development of a T-type lamp with a very narrow bulb. By placing this lamp at the focus of a large reflector in the form of an ellipse, *all* the light from the lamp, except that coming forward, is collected and concentrated into a cone, which can then be focused by a lens into a beam of intense power and completely even distribution. By placing shutters inside the lens barrel, the shape of the beam can be regulated with knife-edge precision. Thus, the light can be framed to the

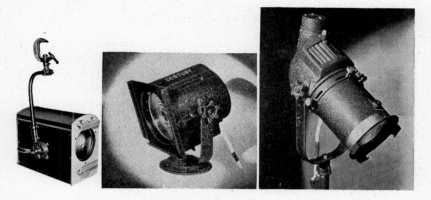

Shown here are three common types of spotlights. **Left,** a "Hood spot" with a plano-convex lens; **Middle,** the Fresnel spot; and **Right,** the ellipsoidal spot or "Leko."

proscenium without a bit of spill onto the teaser, and the inside of an arch can be illuminated without touching the sides. The edges of the beam may be softened a bit by moving the lens forward. This does not change the spread. Because the beam can be shaped, it is possible to use this unit to project patterns of sunlight on a wall.

When lighting the forestage with Leko spotlights, care should be taken that they do not cast sharp shadows on the back wall or sky drop.

These units are bulky and heavy, though not much more so than a 2000-watt hood spot, whose intensity a 500-watt Leko will equal. They are also critical of adjustment, since a lamp a fraction of an inch off-center will cause a "ghost" in the beam. The reflector, which must be kept free of dust, should be removed with care for fear of scratching the highly burnished surface. Also, the long barrel and protruding lamp socket sometimes interfere with aiming.[1] But for front-of-the-house lights where a long throw, a powerful, even illumination, and an adjustable-shaped beam all count, the Leko is unsurpassed.

[1] All spotlight lamps are designed to burn *base down,* with the exception of those used in the Leko, which should always burn *base up.* Using a spotlight upside down will shorten the life of its lamp.

SPECIAL EFFECTS

Perhaps the term "miscellaneous" would be appropriate for that class of equipment known as *special effects,* for everything not primarily concerned with illumination is pigeonholed under that heading. In general, though, they divide pretty well into two sorts: picture projectors and obvious light sources (lamps, fires, torches, etc.).

Projectors. Lighting units that project an image on a curtain or wall are themselves of two kinds: those which depend on lenses to enlarge and focus the image; and *shadowgraphs,* wherein a transparent or cutout design is placed before a point-source of light enclosed in a lightproof hood painted black inside, thus casting a shadow of the design on the wall.

This latter device, called the *Linnebach lantern,* is useful for short-throw projection where sharpness of detail is not essential. A T-type lamp is best for this purpose, as its filament most nearly approaches a point-source. The hood must always be well ventilated. The design can be painted on a sheet of glass with transparent, quick-drying, heat-resistant lacquers. (Lamp dip will serve.) If the plane of the slide is kept parallel to the plane of the wall (or drop) and placed opposite its center, not much distortion will be necessary in the drawing; if the lantern is tilted, the image will be thrown askew and the design then will have to be warped in a counterdirection. If backstage space permits, the projection may be done from behind a transparent backdrop so that actors can move in front of it without walking through the image. Of course, acting lights must never be allowed to strike this drop.

The *optical projector,* or "magic lantern," consists of two sets of lenses: a pair of condensers to concentrate light from the lamp and a set of objectives to focus the image of the transparency (which is placed in the beam of light between the two sets of lenses) on the drop or wall. A unit of this kind can be made out of a 1000-watt hood spot by adding a *dutchman* (an extra plano-convex lens mounted in a frame that fits into the gelatin guides), a slide carrier to hold the transparency (which fits onto the dutchman), and an objective lens in a mounting which slips into grooves on the front of the slide carrier. The design in this case should be photographed on a standard stereopticon slide

and then colored—if color is
desired—since these slides are
so small as to make direct
painting difficult. The objective lenses may be had in various focal lengths, for long or
short throws.

Quite impressive *stars* may
be made with a projector of
this kind by drilling minute
holes in a tin slide.

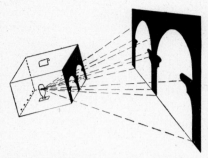

The Linnebach lantern or projecting "shadowgraph."

Moving objects, such as
flames, clouds, rain, snow, pass-
ing landscapes, waving flags, etc., may be projected in this manner by means of a special slide carrier called a *sciopticon,* which
consists of a mica disc appropriately painted and rotated by
clockwork. Such effects can be rented from a stage-lighting supply house.

Obvious light sources. The objects that produce light are so
many and so varied that little can be said of them as a class. Consequently, those most frequently needed on the stage will be
described individually.

Burning logs: Sets of real logs may be nailed together in a
natural pile, the edges blackened, the large logs hollowed out
to accommodate an amber light, above which a small tin wind-
mill spinner rotates on a wire spike. The spinner is driven by
the hot air rising from the lamp, giving the effect of flickering
flames.

Burning coals: Place an amber lamp in a coal grate and cover
with broken beer bottles and pieces of spotlight lenses dyed
amber.

Explosion flash: A 1000-watt flood, flashed on and off, serves
well for the effect of an explosion flash.

Flames: Bits of colored silk tied to the guard of an electric
fan and lighted from below by an amber spotlight make quite
realistic flames.

Lightning: A *lightning flasher* may be rented from a stage-
lighting equipment dealer. It consists of a carbon pencil (from
an arc light) held in a clamp hinged so that it may be pressed
down by a push button to strike a metal plate and brought back

immediately by a spring. The carbon and plate must be connected in series with a rheostat (a dimmer will do) and the whole mechanism should be shielded. (Note: Flashing the borders on and off will *not* serve, since the filaments of the lamps cool off so gradually that a flare is the result instead of a flash.)

Moon: (disc): Cut a 10″ hole in a tin box; conceal small lights in the corners; hang behind the back drop. (That is, if there *must* be a visible moon. In general, moonlight is more impressive if the *light only* is seen.)

Rainbow: Cut an arched slit in a cardboard or tin slide and place in an optical projector (see above). Remove the objective lens and replace with two large glass prisms. (These may be held in clamps on stands borrowed from any physics laboratory.)

Smoke: Although *smoke machines* may be rented, realistic and harmless smoke may be made easily by heating sal ammoniac (ammonium chloride) on an electric stove.

SUMMARY

We have seen, then, that *general illumination* on the stage is mainly the function of the first border strip, the footlights being used for toning only, with the sky drop lighted by strips or closely-spaced floodlights above and below. Floodlights are used to light exterior backings, and small strips to light interior backings.

Specific illumination is the function of spotlights. The Fresnel is best suited to the lighting of acting areas from behind the teaser, and the Leko to front-of-the-house lighting for the forestage.

Direct sunlight is best simulated in a long-range throw by a beam projector, though a powerful spotlight will serve at short range.

Special effects may be projected by the *Linnebach lantern* (*shadograph*) or by the sciopticon or slide projector (through the optical method). Real light sources may be used directly when noninflammable, or simulated if the real thing is dangerous.

Principles of Electricity

The term *watts* has quite frequently appeared in this chapter so far, and some references have been made to *circuits*. These terms must be understood—at least in elementary fashion—along with a few others equally basic, before a stage electrician can "rig his lights" and "set up his board" without blowing a fuse or burning out a dimmer. (The simplified account which follows, however, is strictly for the layman; physicists will kindly pass it by.)

Electricity, like water, is always trying to get somewhere if given a chance, either back to its source or into the ground. (*Warning No. 1: Never touch a live wire. This is always dangerous, but especially so while one is standing on the ground, or while touching metal or concrete connected with the ground.*) Unlike water, it will not travel through the air (at least the kind a stage electrician handles won't) but only through metal, flesh, and other conductors. Rubber, dry wood, and glass are nonconductors.

UNITS OF MEASUREMENT

Like water, electricity can be measured. A *watt* is a unit of volume, corresponding roughly to the gallon. The wattage per hour consumed by a given circuit can be found by adding up the individual ratings of the lamps attached to that circuit. A 100-watt lamp will burn 100 watts per hour; a circuit of ten 100-watt lamps will consume 1000 watts per hour. *Volts* are units of pressure—like pounds per square inch. The current furnished to most houses, and most stages, is kept fairly constant at 110 volts. (*Warning No. 2: If your switchboard has three bus bars running through it, don't connect anything—yourself included —to the outside bars; they are probably carrying 220 volts.*)

The rate at which a current is flowing is measured in *amperes,* and these are always equal to the total wattage carried by a circuit divided by the voltage. In other words: $A = \dfrac{W}{V}$ or $W = VA$

(This is referred to popularly as the "West Virginia rule.") This is important because wires, like pipes, will only take a certain amount of flow. Number 14 *stage cable,* the kind most commonly used in the theatre (it consists of two insulated, flexible wires enclosed in an armor of hemp and braid), will carry 20 amperes, or 2000 watts with safety. Number 16 extension cord, the kind usually found in homes, will not take more than 10 amperes. It should never be used in place of stage cable, not only because of its inadequate capacity, but because it is subject to damage from moving scenery. If too much electricity is pushed through too small a wire, the wire will get hot. This is what happens inside a lamp; only there the wire is surrounded by inert gases and can't burn. Outside, where it can get oxygen, a wire will flare up if too heavily overloaded. This will occur, naturally, at the weakest point in the wire.

PROTECTIVE DEVICES

Knowing this—and knowing also that as soon as a wire burns in two the flow of current is stopped as effectively as if a switch were thrown—it has become a practice deliberately to put a weak piece of wire, having a low melting point, into the circuit, and to inclose this wire in a fireproof container so that when it burns out it can't do any damage. This device is called a *fuse*. A *circuit breaker,* which automatically throws a switch when the load gets too heavy, may be used instead. Fuses and circuit breakers are rated according to the maximum number of amperes they will carry before blowing out: 10, 20, 30, 60, and so on. Homes are usually equipped with plug fuses that screw in like a lamp; theatre switchboards usually have cartridge fuses that snap into two clips.

The worst type of overload is the *short circuit,* where two wires come together and permit current to flow back to the dynamo without spending its energy in any useful way. (*Warning No. 3: A blown fuse is a sign of trouble. Find the fault and correct it before you put in another fuse.*)

CIRCUITS

It has already been hinted that electricity does not flow off into oblivion like water, but goes around in a circle, from the generator out over a wire, past obstacles which require work for it to get by (like a filament of a lamp or the coils of a motor) and back through another wire to the generator again. (The ground will serve as the return wire.) That is, *direct current,* or D.C., behaves in this fashion; *alternating current,* A.C.,—the usual kind—turns around 120 times a second and flows the other way. This has no effect on lamps, which burn equally well on A.C. or D.C., but it does affect some dimmers.

Since every current-consuming unit must be connected to two wires, it has two "leads." This means that there are two ways of connecting electrical apparatus together: stringing them together like people holding hands to form a ring, or connecting each unit to *both* feed wires like people holding on to the rails of a narrow bridge.

Two types of electrical hookups are shown here. **Top,** series circuit, voltage divided among lamps; and **Bottom,** parallel circuit, voltage remains constant.

The parallel circuit. The latter type is called a *parallel* circuit, and is the one most often employed in connecting several stage units to the same pair of feed wires. In it the voltage remains constant throughout the circuit, and every light burns at its full brilliancy.

The series circuit. In the first instance, the chain circuit, the units are said to be connected in *series*. In such a case the current must pass through each unit, one at a time, in order to get back to the dynamo, and if one unit burns out or is disconnected, the whole flow stops. But something else occurs in a series circuit: *the voltage is divided between the units.* Practically speaking, that means one can *reduce the brilliancy* of lights by connecting them in series. For example, if there is a two-light candle bracket that is too bright for comfort, the two lights can be connected in series (that is, one lead is connected from the left candle to a feed wire, one lead from the right candle to the other feed wire, and the other two leads joined together). Both the lamps will now burn at only half their normal brilliancy.

Dimmers. But let us go further: Suppose we have a set of small current-consuming wire coils, so protected (by being baked into porcelain) that they will not readily burn out, all connected in series. This set of coils may be connected in series with a set of lamps (themselves connected in parallel) whose total wattage

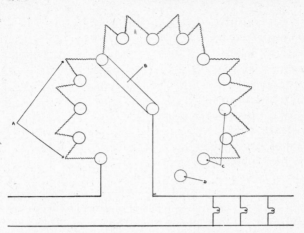

This is a resistance dimmer. **A**, coils of high-resistance wire; **B**, rotating contact arm; **C**, contact buttons; and **D**, "dead" button (not connected).

equals the wattage consumed by the set of coils; the lamps will go out, since not enough voltage will reach them to heat their filaments to incandescence. Suppose, however, that between each coil a brass contact button is placed and that the line feeder, instead of being attached to the other end of the series of coils, is connected to a movable arm that passes across this line of contact buttons, so that one coil, then two, three, and so on are connected in series with the lamps. Then, as the number of coils in series with the circuit increases, the voltage reaching the lamps will gradually decrease, and the lamps will become less and less bright until finally, when the two resistances balance, they will emit no light at all. This is the principle of the *resistance dimmer* or rheostat—the one in most common use, since it works on both A.C. and D.C. In this type, the wattage of the load *must* be balanced within 25 per cent of that of the dimmer. A 1000-watt dimmer, for example, will blow up if with it one attempts to dim a 2000-watt load. On the other hand, it will not take a 400-watt spotlight down far enough to do any good. The solution to this is to connect another baby spot to the same circuit, even if it is not to be used on the stage. Or, if there are no more baby spots available, an electric iron will do. Wattage added to a circuit merely in order to balance the dimmer is called a "phantom load."

There are other types of dimmers which operate only on A.C., but which have much greater flexibility than the resistance type. These are the *reactance dimmer,* which dims any wattage up to its capacity merely by rotating a coil; the *auto-transformer,* which permits one circuit to be dimmed down and another up at the same time by means of the same unit; and the *electronic dimmer,* which is operated by a vacuum tube and can be regulated by a tiny potentiometer, which in turn can be placed some distance away from the actual dimmer, thus making remote control possible. But from the light-man's point of view, they all work the same way: when he pushes a handle up, certain lights get brighter; when he pushes it down, they dim.

(*Warning No. 4: Don't leave lights "down" on a dimmer; cut them off with a switch when the dimmer reaches the bottom.* Unless your dimmer is equipped with a "dead button" as its final contact, current is still flowing, even though you can't see it, and the heat it generates may cause trouble.)

CONTROL OF LIGHTING

In stage lighting, one cardinal principle must constantly be kept in mind when selecting equipment, planning installations and hook-ups, setting up a particular production—in fact, in every step the stage electrician takes. That principle is *flexibility.* This means that he must have the choice of using or discarding every unit in his possession; of using that unit in a given place, or of moving it somewhere else; of using it alone or in combination with other units; and of controlling its brilliancy, either alone or with other units. Since every light must be *installed* or fastened to some means of support, *connected* to the source of supply, and the amount of current it receives *regulated,* the stage electrician must carefully plan for the greatest amount of flexibility in each of these three processes.

Installation. Fortunately, all stage lighting units (with the exception of disappearing footlights) are designed with flexibility in mind. This has already been discussed in connection with individual units. Suffice it to add here that the C-clamp is a most convenient hanger, and most units should be equipped to take it. Also, pipes should be installed on movable lines, if possible, wherever it is likely that a unit might be hung.

Connection. On the stage, no electrical connections should be permanent, but always achieved by a device which makes it easy to disconnect a given unit and plug in another one. There are two such devices in general use: pin connectors and plug-pockets. Ordinary household attachment plugs are suitable only for very light loads.

Pin connectors are used to attach individual units to their feed lines. They may be had in various sizes, but the 5-ampere and the 15-ampere sizes are most common. It is advisable—if one can afford it—to use only the 15-ampere size, for then any unit can be plugged in anywhere. The *female* half of the pair (the section in which each wire is connected by a screw binding post to a brass sleeve whose opening is flush with the front of the connector and into which the pins of the other part fit snugly) is always attached to the line or "live" side. It is usually built to take "cable"—i.e., a large hole enters the bottom end and branches toward each of the two lugs so that the armored part of the cable may be pulled well into the connector and clamped tight by the cover. The *male* half (the one with exposed pins) is always attached to the load, or unit. It is usually built to take "asbestos"—i.e., single holes are channeled from each lug straight out the back end of the connector, so as to keep the wires apart. The reason for this is that asbestos insulation (which is necessary on wires going into hot lighting units) is inclined to slip, exposing the wire and causing a short circuit. (*Warning No. 5: When connecting wires, peel off the insulation to expose just enough of the wire to go around the lug—usually ½" or* ¾". Scrape the exposed part bright, and twist it around the lug *clockwise* so that the screw, when tightened, will pull the wire toward its shank instead of pushing it away, and thus draw the insulated part of the wire up against the lug.)

(*Warning No. 6: Whenever you take a connector apart, put* all *the parts back together immediately so they won't get lost.*)

Every lighting unit should be equipped with a male connector for each circuit it contains. Striplights often have connectors at both ends so that additional units may be linked together. Every feed line (whether permanent or cable) should terminate in a female connector. Often it is well to use a *multiple connector* into which three units can be plugged at once.

If a cable is used for a feeder, its stage end may terminate either in another male connector or in a *stage plug,* a square fibre handle with a clamp at the top to secure the armored part of the cable, and a heavy copper plate on each side, to which the wires are attached. This plug in turn fits into a *porcelain recep-*

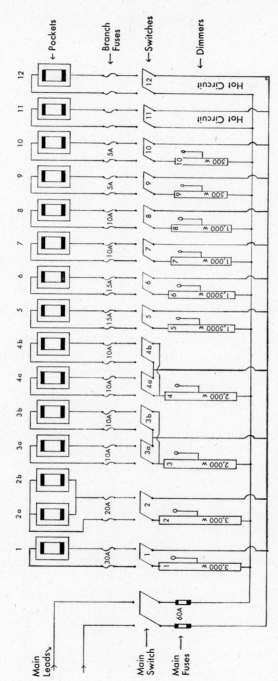

This is a diagram of a switchboard with 15 outlets, 14 switches, 10 dimmers, and a main switch.

tacle or *pocket* which may be mounted either on the switch-board itself or in an iron box set into the floor or wall at strategic points about the stage. These stage plugs carry a load of 60 amperes. (*Split plugs* that fit two to a pocket carry 30 amperes each.) But female connectors may be mounted in plugging boxes or on switchboards in the same way as pockets and are preferred by some technicians because they take less space and make for more uniformity of equipment.

All feeders that must be brought down in conduit should terminate either in a short *pigtail* of cable with a connector or plug on the end, or in a *cross-connection panel*. This is a lattice-work of bus bars, a slight distance apart, mounted in a cabinet. The horizontal bars are connected to the feeders from various lighting units; the vertical bars are attached to the switches and dimmers of the switchboard. By pushing a pin through holes drilled in the bars where they cross, any unit or combination of units may be connected to any switch-and-dimmer circuit. This system, of course, is much to be preferred for school installations.

Regulation. The switchboard is the brain of the stage lighting system. It is the terminus of all the circuits of the stage and in it are concentrated all the switches, dimmers, and fuses that control and protect those circuits.

The first thing that any good board should have (and which many school switchboards lack) is a *master-switch*, so that the whole system may be killed at one throw. This is necessary, not only for safety during repairs, but for blackouts. This switch is usually protected by a set of main fuses. From it bus bars extend across the board, and are tapped periodically for branch circuits, each consisting of a smaller fuse, a dimmer, a switch, and an outlet (either a pocket, a female connector, or a vertical bar in the cross-connection panel). Often two pockets are connected to one switch to provide more plugging space. Sometimes a circuit may branch again into several switches and outlets after it leaves the dimmer, as in stages where one dimmer controls all the floor pockets, but each pocket is on a separate switch. A few hot (i.e., undimmed) circuits are sometimes useful.

As to the number of dimmers, switches, and outlets, there is no set rule; one has as many as one can afford. Ten dimmers and fourteen or fifteen outlets would seem to be an irreducible mini-

mum, although many shows
are doubtless worked with less.
Footlights, if they are to be
used at all, require two to four
dimmers;   borders   another
three or four. Three 1000-watt
dimmers can carry two beam
spots each, and three others
two border spots each. Backing
lights and cyclorama lights,
unless they must dim, can be
plugged in hot. The dimmers
should range in size from 500
to 2000 watts. It is also useful
to have one or two of heavier
capacity—say 3000 to 5000
watts—especially if a sky cyclorama is used.

This is a portable switchboard, manufactured by Century Lighting Co.
in use for a professional production.

The best arrangement is to
mount the switches and outlets
directly above the dimmer that controls them. In any case, they
should be numbered and the wattage clearly marked. For example, "Dimmer 1 (1000 watts), switch 1, outlet 1; dimmer 2 (2000
watts), switch 2, outlets 2a and 2b; dimmer 3 (2000 watts),
switches 3a and 3b, outlets 3a and 3b." And so on. (See the diagram on page 279.)

Dimmers may be equipped with an *interlocking system,* so
that each handle, when set in a certain manner, locks to a bar
and the entire system may be raised or lowered by operating one
master-handle. Since all of the dimmers must be at the same setting before they will interlock, the stage lights cannot be
dimmed out by this system without changing their relative
values. The bright lights, in other words, must dim to the setting of the dim lights before the latter begin to go down at all. A
much more satisfactory method of over-all dimming is to wire a
very large dimmer (one as heavy as the combined wattage of all
the other dimmers) in series with the master-switch. When this
dimmer is lowered, all the lights will come down with it. When
it is raised the lights will go back to their original settings—provided, of course, that their individual dimmers have not been

This is the Century-Izenour control board, a new electronic switchboard to be used in connection with Thyratron tube dimmers. Note the row of potentiometers at the top of the console, each no bigger than a large watch but capable of dimming a stage circuit carrying thousands of watts. Note also the pre-set panel at the left, consisting of ten rows of similar dimming units, each bank capable of controlling any or all of the lights on the stage, and each connectible by a push button to either side of a motor-driven fader, so that one combination of lights may be dimmed, from whatever brightness the setting of the individual potentiometers permit to out, while another bank is simultaneously coming on. To illustrate this: Pre-set Bank #1 may contain a light-blue sky strip, with its potentiometer set at full, a low sun spot at half, and appropriate acting area spots. Bank #2 may contain an azure sky strip, a pink afterglow strip at half, and a different set of acting area spots. If Bank #1 is connected (by a push button) to the left side of the fader and #2 to the right side, and the handle gradually moved down, the sunset lights of #1 will dissolve into the twilight effect of #2, each unit reaching the brilliancy indicated by the setting of its individual potentiometer. Then a bank of moonlight lights on pre-set #3 may be substituted for #1 on the right side of the fader, and the handle moved up, which will produce another dissolve. There is no limit to the number of such consecutive changes possible.

moved—and each light will take the same amount of time to reach its setting. This is called *proportional dimming*.

In remote control boards, where the dimmers are controlled by small potentiometers, a master-potentiometer is often provided for each color, with a *grand master* to regulate all the color masters at once. Such boards often have two potentiometers for each circuit with a master *fader* between the two banks, so that while one scene is playing the electrician may set the lights for a subsequent scene, and change from Scene 1 to Scene 2, even if it involves some of the same lights, by the flick of a dial. Such boards, of course, are costly, but they are worth the investment.

Setting the Lights

Let us now consider the steps which the lighting technician can take in order to bring the six functions of stage lighting—visibility, mood, plasticity, focus, the enhancement of color, and the suggestion of natural phenomena—to realization on the stage in terms of available equipment.

PRELIMINARY STUDY OF THE PLAY

The first step, of course, is to become familiar with the play. From a reading of the script, by examining the designer's layouts, and by consulting with the director, the lighting technician should gather the following information on which to work out each scene of the play:

(*a*) The *time* of day, the season, and the state of the weather.
(*b*) The *place* where the action occurs (the general, as well as the particular locale).
(*c*) The number and location of *openings* in the scenery (especially those through which light must come or be seen).
(*d*) The principal *source* (or sources) of light.
(*e*) The light *cues* (such as turning on lights, carrying in candles, etc.).
(*f*) The *special items* needed (lamps, brackets, chandeliers, fireplace logs, automobile headlights, candles, explosions, etc.).
(*g*) The principal *acting areas* (determined usually by pieces of furniture).
(*h*) The *color scheme* employed in the scenery and costumes.
(*i*) The general *mood* of the scene.

With this information (he might tabulate it in the form of a scene-by-scene chart) the lighting technician can begin to lay out his plans and assemble his material.

LIGHT PLAN

Some technicians prefer to plan their setup in advance by diagraming, on a ground plan of the set, the location of each instrument to be used, the area it will illuminate, and the color of gelatin to be used in it.

The system which governs the choice and placement of instruments and the selection of gelatins varies from technician to technician. The one that seems to be most in favor at present might be termed "area lighting with luminous shadows from an obvious source."

FORMULA

A simple formula (by no means to be taken as absolute) by which this system may be applied to the lighting of a realistic play, and which, since it is based on symbolism as well as simulation, may be modified to suit abstract or fantastic productions, is as follows:

Specific illumination. Cover each acting area with two spotlights aimed from 45° above and 45° to each side, using a brighter, warmer gelatin in the spotlight on the side of the stage where the obvious source of light lies, and a less intense, cooler gelatin in the other. This will give *plasticity* and *visibility* by casting natural highlights, such as a strong, direct beam of light would produce, and luminous shadows, such as would result from reflected light.

Care should be taken to keep these lights off the scenery, so as to avoid casting distracting or ugly shadows and to center attention on the actors and not on the walls. The corners and top edges of the set should by all means be kept dim, so that the picture will shade off as it reaches its frame (the proscenium).

Keep the gelatins cool for morning (for example, straw and daylight blue), warmer for noon (medium straw and light sky blue), quite warm for late afternoon (light amber and light blue-green), and rosy for artificial light (light scarlet and special lavender). Keep intensities lower (more diffused) for daylight, sharper for lamp light.

After the lights have been set, have someone walk around the stage to make sure that faces are properly illuminated at all times and that places where important business occurs are prominently lighted.

General illumination. Bring the borders up slowly until proper balance with the spotlights is reached as determined by the mood. (In general, the more intense the emotion, the sharper the contrasts, and consequently the dimmer the borders.)

Pastel pigment primaries (light lemon, light scarlet, and medium blue) are recommended as most flattering to scenery and costumes, but these may be intensified to suit the mood.

Use a cool combination for morning (blue alone or blue and lemon), bright for noon (all three colors), warm for afternoon (lemon and light scarlet), and purplish for artificial light (light scarlet and blue or light scarlet alone).

If a color needs to be brightened in the scenery or costumes, intensify that particular color in the borders or bring it in from the footlights, remembering the principle that light of a certain color enhances its analogous hues and grays its complementaries. (Stronger colors—red, blue, green—may be tried here if the forestage is adequately lighted by beam spots.) *Reduce the intensity the minute shadows begin to appear on the back wall.*

Blue in the footlights and borders may also help to make the set look deeper, since cool colors seem to recede.

Backing strips just bright enough to soften the shadows cast by the borders, but not so strong as to attract attention, should be installed above archways and doors leading to other rooms.

Sky. Set floodlights or striplights on the sky cyclorama and on exterior backings in such a concentration that the sky seems brighter than the stage proper. (Objects in the acting areas will, of course, actually have a greater intensity.)

Use very light blue (light sky-blue) gelatins for daylight, green blue for twilight, dark blue (navy) for a moonlit evening sky. For night interiors, the sky need not be lighted at all, as the light is so much more intense inside than outside that the sky does not show. For a cloudy day, use a gray (smoke) gelatin. For sunset afterglow, use a pink strip on the floor near the drop.

Bring shafts of sunlight or moonlight into the set whenever possible and logical. (Remember that the afternoon sun never shines from the same direction as the morning sun or the rising moon, and that a change of time may be indicated by a change in the direction of the light.) Use beam projectors or powerful spotlights so the shadows will fall naturally and not spread.

No gelatin is needed for morning sunlight. Straw or light lemon is good for early afternoon, and light amber for late afternoon, since sunlight gets warmer as the day progresses. For moonlight, a clear, almost white blue (daylight or light sky-blue)—*not* green—is best. Trick effects, like moving clouds, visible moon, and even stars, are distracting and should be avoided unless they figure directly in the action.

Special Effects. Finally, whatever lights are needed in the action (such as lamps, chandeliers, fires, etc.) should be provided. Small-wattage lamps that give no real illumination should be used in such units, the pools of light they apparently cast being provided by spotlights from the border pipe, in the footlights, or inside the fireplace.

Any light that is turned on by an actor should be so wired as to be controlled *only* by the electrician in combination with its specific "booster" lights. Otherwise, a lamp will be turned on, and several seconds later the area around it will get brighter. When such a cue has to be taken, the actor should keep his hand on the switch that apparently controls that particular light until the light comes on. This is the only way in which the action and the result can be smoothly co-ordinated.

CUE SHEET

After the lights in a scene have been set, a *complete record* of the setup should be made *immediately*. This should show in a clear and concise manner the *units* used, their *location*, the *switches* that control them, and the *settings* of their dimmers, so that the electrician can quickly reproduce the setup. Light changes and cues should be written-in below as they are set.

Large index cards are good for the purpose. They may be mimeographed to correspond to the particular switchboard, with the outlets listed in order, a space left above for listing the lights attached to each outlet, and a box below for a check mark

LIGHT CUE-SHEET FOR *The Silver Cord* — Act I Scene 1

OUTLETS	1	2a	2b	3a	3b	4	5	6	7	8	9	10	11	12
Units	Border (2 circuits)	Flood #1	Border Spots #3 & 6	Flood #2	Border	Border Spots #2 & 5	Border Spots #1 & 4	Beam Spots #9 & 12	Beam Spots #8 & 11	Beam Spots #7 & 10			Brackets and Backing strip	Logs
Colors	Pink & Str.	Lt. Blue	B & S	Dark Blue	Blue	B & S	Lav. & LSc.	B & Lt. Scar.	L & St.	B & Lt. Scar.				
Switches	x	x	x	x	x	x	x	x	x	x			x	x
Dimmers	½	¾	Out	Full	Full	¾	½	¾	¾	½			Out	
Cue 1: Slow fade from Rise to	¼					½	¼	½	¼	¼				
Cue 2: Mrs. P. turns on lts.: snap to						Full	Full	Full	Full	Full			Full	
Cue 3:														

Electrician's Cue Card for *The Silver Cord*, planned for the switchboard illustrated on page 279.

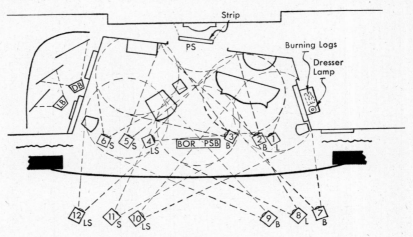

This is the light diagram for *The Silver Cord*, Act I.

to show that the switch should be on. Boxes immediately below these, bracketing the outlets that are *ganged* on a single dimmer, should be provided for entering the dimmer settings. (Such a card, set up for a production of *The Silver Cord*, is shown on page 287.)

After a scene has been set and recorded, it should immediately be rehearsed until the electrician can make all the moves involved smoothly and accurately. Then—and not till then—the next scene may be set, following the same general outline as in the first. Any lights that have been set must not, of course, be changed (with the exception of those readily accessible from backstage, such as stand spots and floods which can be moved or have their gelatins changed by the floor electrician). It is real economy, however, to use as many of the previously set lights in the new scene as will fit in with the changes in light source, time, mood, and so on. Sometimes pairs or gangs of lights can be broken up and regrouped at the switchboard. (The units, of course, should have been so ganged to begin with as to put lights that work together on the same dimmer.) Sometimes the necessary change can be achieved merely by dimming. For example, a light-scarlet spot that, with a lavender spot, covers a table lamp in a night scene, may be dimmed slightly and used again in a daylight scene—after disconnecting the table lamp—particularly if it is re-ganged with a light-blue spot.

This is the Matoaka Lake Amphitheatre, Williamsburg, Virginia, showing light towers right and left of auditorium.

In brief, to set up subsequent scenes the electrician uses what he can, and adds what he doesn't have.

Outdoor Lighting

In outdoor productions, three factors play a part to make the lighting problem different from that of indoor stages. First, there are usually no overhead battens on which to hang the lighting units, which means that borders, border spots, and beam spots are out. These can be compensated for to a considerable degree by the use of light towers built at the sides of the auditorium, well in front of the stage, so that spotlights can be aimed at the stage from an angle of approximately 45°. The Matoaka Lake Theatre at Williamsburg, Virginia, pictured above, uses such towers. *Light tormentors* (i.e., spotlights hung on a vertical pipe behind a screen flanking the sides of the apron, a device which is sometimes used in indoor stages) can illuminate the upstage acting areas. This at least takes care of specific lighting. General illumination can be had from footlights and—if it is deemed really necessary—from batteries of powerful floodlights set on poles above the audience near the stage.

Second, since it is manifestly impossible outdoors to control the light on the sky, the chief means for showing the time and the weather is gone. It is therefore better not to attempt realistic lighting at all, but to strive mainly for visibility and mood.

Third, since distances are usually greater outdoors and there are fewer reflecting surfaces (such as backdrops, ceilings, and even side walls) to contain the light within the stage area, more powerful units must be employed. The beam projector, the Leko, and the Fresnel spotlight are particularly useful because of their high efficiency.

As to the setting of the units, the same general formula of cross-lighting-with-luminous-shadows still holds, as long as the conventional arrangement of audience-facing-stage is observed. If the arena stage is used, the method must, of course, be different.

Lighting the Arena Stage

In the arena theatre general illumination units are even more difficult to use than on the outdoor stage, since it is well-nigh impossible to place them so that they light the actors and not the audience, and, worse still, so that a part of the encircling audience will not get their glare straight in the eye. The general practice is to illuminate acting areas with spotlights directed from quite a high angle (usually from holes in the ceiling), and to depend on spill reflected from the floor and on diffusion from frosted gelatins for general illumination. If enough units are employed so that their areas overlap, quite adequate visibility may be achieved without drenching the audience.

Plasticity, of course, cannot be achieved by two-spot cross-lighting, as in the proscenium theatre, since this would have the characters silhouetted to one-third of the audience. A second shadow spotlight coming from the unlighted direction would of course, eliminate this dead area; but this would mean three units per area instead of two.

Using light to suggest the effects of nature is considerably hampered in the arena theatre by the absence of the sky, where most of the visible signs of changes in time and weather appear.

Alfred J. Balcombe

Projected effects are shown in "Day of the Dead" scene from Sartre's *The Flies* as produced by Erwin Piscator at the Dramatic Workshop of the New School, New York. Willis Knighton, designer.

Low-angle sunbeams, too, are nearly impossible. But through a skillful use of color and dimming, the atmosphere of a rose-and-turquoise evening fading into lavender twilight can be captured satisfactorily. Moonlight presents an easier problem, since the moon is always fairly high in the sky before it gives any appreciable illumination, and therefore a "moon" spot need not be placed so low as to strike the audience in the eye. The effect of lamplight is also easy to simulate, as lamps are usually placed fairly near the center of the stage. A trio of spotlights mounted directly over the lamp and angling outward in all directions, or even a single wide-angle spot pointed straight down, will cover a considerable area around the lamp. If necessary, the "dead" areas at the periphery can be caught from the far corners of the stage with diffused lavender spots.

As to lighting units, the more compact the better. Fresnels serve admirably, especially if they can be concealed in the ceiling. "Birdseyes" (reflector spot and flood lamps) will be found most useful for the arena stage, since they weigh little, occupy small space, and are not so unsightly as the hoods of some lens spots. Aluminum fixtures are now being manufactured to accommodate this type of lamp; these are quite decorative, easily adjustable, and highly efficient. When planning a new building, or extensively remodeling an old one for arena theatre work, it is well to consider the installation of such equipment. But the average arena producer, lacking such fancy gadgets, will continue to hang what lights he can assemble quite frankly in view of the audience. And audiences seldom seem to mind.

Lights in the arena theatre are controlled from some concealed vantage point, usually behind the outer ring of seats. In the Penthouse Theatre at the University of Washington, the switchboard and sound system are mounted in a corner of the building between the two converging outer walls and the curving inner wall that surrounds the audience. One-way-vision windows in this inner wall permit the electrician to view the stage without being seen by the audience. All cables, of course, pass either above the ceiling or under the floor. Ample outlets are provided in the floor and peripheral ring of the stage to take care of incidental lights and special effects.

Abstract and Fantastic Lighting

Lighting for abstract or fantastic productions is not so different from realistic lighting as might be supposed. The same units are used; the same principles of plasticity, focusing, and color augmentation still hold; and, while natural phenomena are less slavishly imitated, the same effects of color and brilliancy on mood (which realists induce by means of weather and the time of day) still occur. The real difference lies in the scope which the lighting technician can allow his imagination in simplifying and exaggerating color, intensity, and form. For example, a voodoo priest may be made more grotesquely horrible by crosslighting him with red and green instead of with pastels, and from the sides or below rather than from above, so that he will cast looming shadows. It is not uncommon for a tragic scene to be played in one single stabbing spotlight, with no cross-lighting at all. Again, the lighting may be made to follow the mood more obviously than usual, as in *Happy Birthday*, where the scene became more rosy as the central character mellowed under the effects of alcohol. Much can be done, too, with projected effects, as in the New School's production of *The Flies* and the University of Colorado's *The Master Builder*, pictured on pages 291

Here we see projected effects in *The Master Builder* as produced at the University of Colorado. J. H. Crouch, director and designer.

and 293, and in Brooklyn College's production of *The Adding Machine*, illustrated in Chapter 11.

But imagination is necessary in all stage lighting—realistic, abstract, or fantastic—if it is to make the theatre "a vista into the unknown, into boundless space," as Adolph Appia, prophet of modern lighting, hoped it would be. With imagination and our present-day tools, "Light, like music, can express . . . the inner nature of all appearance."

Exercises

1. Stand in front of a mirror in a darkened room and hold a light directly above your head; in front of your chest; at one side of your face; at a 45° angle above you, in front of you, and at one side. Notice what happens to your features. Balance this light with a smaller light placed in a similar position on the other side. Try this experiment again, holding a handkerchief over one light; over both lights. Turn on the lights in the room and see what happens to the accents cast by these special lights.
2. Equip three spotlights with gelatins in the primary colors (Cen-

tury No. 67 red, No. 36 blue, and No. 49 green) and aim them at an object—preferably a suspended cube—so that shadows will be cast on a screen or white wall. Note what happens as the colors blend.

3. Hold various colored objects in the beams of these spotlights and note the effect of color on color.

4. Focus the red spotlight on a white background and place a red object in its rays. Replace this with a blue object. Then focus a blue spotlight directly on the blue object, while the red spot illuminates the background. Note the effects on the objects.

5. Make a *light plan* for a play (the one you have chosen for a project), describing each instrument to be used, the color of its gelatin, and the area it illuminates.

6. Make a *light cue-sheet* for your project play, similar to the one illustrated in Chapter 13, based on a switchboard with which you are familiar.

Bibliography

Fuchs, Theodore, *Stage Lighting,* Boston: Little, Brown & Company, 1929. A comprehensive book.

McCandless, Stanley, *A Method of Lighting the Stage,* New York: Theatre Arts, Inc., 1932, rev. ed. 1939. An excellent practical guide.

Ridge, C. Harold, and Aldred, F. S., *Stage Lighting,* New York and London: Pitman Publishing Company, 1935. An excellent book, based on lighting in the English theatre.

See also books by Selden and Sellman, and by Milton Smith listed in Bibliography to Chapter 12.

CHAPTER 14.

SOUND EFFECTS AND MUSIC

In the picture-frame theatre, with its predominantly representational form of production and its predominantly realistic repertoire, we are likely to think of sound effects and music as an unimportant element of production, useful occasionally in imitating sounds and music as they occur in life. Actually, even in the realistic play nonvocal sound can sometimes be of use in creating the required mood, and music can always be of use before the curtain goes up, between the scenes, and after the final curtain, to reinforce the mood of the play.

The chief value of nonvocal sound in play production lies in the immediacy and strength of the emotional effect it has on the hearer. The crash of colliding automobiles, the shriek of an air-raid warning siren, the clanging of the gong on a patrol wagon, the roll of distant thunder, the howling of a gale, and many other common sounds of life arouse emotion in the hearer. When sound is organized into musical forms, especially simple musical forms, the emotional effect on most people is likewise strong. The appeal of a good rousing march or a gay dance melody is almost irresistible.

The emotional effect of nonvocal sound, therefore, should not be neglected, even in the realistic representational play, and the producer should be aware of its possibilities for expression in the freer styles and in the presentational form. If planned with taste and executed with skill, nonvocal sound can play a useful part in the production of most plays.

No matter what the play, about three minutes of overture music will help to quiet the audience, and if the music is carefully selected it can begin to establish the mood of the opening scene. Two to three minutes of entr'acte music at the end of each intermission can perform the same functions, and three to five minutes of exit music, starting when the house lights come up at the end of the play and lasting until the spectators have filed out, can serve to reinforce the mood on which the play

295

ends and to send the audience away with a feeling that the theatre experience has been complete.

In the play of many scenes, no matter what its style or theatrical form, music can be especially useful as continuity to cover brief scene waits. In a number of modern plays, there are more changes of setting than can be covered by the customary two intermissions. Unless a simultaneous setting is used, the curtain must be closed to cover these changes. Even if the interval is no more than a few seconds, the continuity of the play is likely to be broken; and if each interval is as much as a minute or two, the audience will begin to grow restless. Music can fill these gaps, providing a focus for audience attention, and either helping to maintain the mood from scene to scene or preparing the audience for a change of mood. Irwin Shaw's *The Assassin* is an example of a realistic play which might benefit from such musical continuity, and Elmer Rice's *The Adding Machine,* which is constructed in scenes instead of in acts, is an example from expressionistic drama.

Style and Theatrical Form

Like all the other elements of production the use of nonvocal sound varies, depending on the style of the play and the theatrical form used in its production.

REPRESENTATION

In representational plays, sound effects and music must help to create an illusion of life going on independent of the audience and of the theatre. This means that sound effects and music must be motivated, that they must have their logical place in the life of the play.

In the realistic representational play, the motivation must be realistic. Music must be played by the characters, come from a phonograph or radio, or perhaps from a nearby dance hall. The problem in sound effects is not motivation but the realistic reproduction of natural sounds and the proper integration of these with the rest of the elements of production. Natural sounds like wind, rain, and surf can sometimes do more to suggest the place of the action than can any amount of scenery and dialogue. In Martin Flavin's *Children of the Moon,* the sound of surf and later on of the foghorn create a vivid illusion of nearness to the sea. In Elmer Rice's *Street Scene,* the flow of big city noises which accompanies the whole action does almost as much as the setting to create the illusion that the play takes place in the heart of New York City.

However, even in the realistic play nonvocal sound should do more than help to create the illusion of place. We have noted the strong emotional effect of sound and music. They should help to express the mood or pattern of moods, and thus assist in presenting the play's dramatic action. The sound effects in *Children of the Moon* perform this function also. The steady pounding of the surf reinforces the mood of the tragic conflict, and the melancholy warning of the foghorn heralds the catastrophe. By careful selection and arrangement the big-city sounds in *Street Scene* can be made into a kind of cacophony that expresses the changing moods of love, hate, joy, sorrow, disillusionment, hope, and fear which make up the pattern of the play.

Chekhov has indicated such use of nonvocal sound in *The Cherry Orchard.* So important is this element that the play ends with a minimum of words: "One hears all the doors being locked and the carriages driving away. All is quiet. Amid the silence the thud of axes on the trees echoes sad and lonely. The sound of footsteps." Firs enters, delivers his final speech, and lies down. "He lies motionless. A distant sound is heard, as if from the sky, the sound of a string breaking, dying away, melancholy. Silence ensues, broken only by the stroke of the axe on the trees far away in the cherry orchard. *Curtain.*" Chekhov depends very largely on the pattern of sound and silence to create the final effect of his play, and in so doing he has set a problem for the producer. How is the thud of the axes to "echo sad and lonely"? And what about that unexplained sound as if of a string breaking in the sky? Much will depend upon the timing, much upon the volume and quality of the sounds, and a good effect is likely to be achieved only after considerable experiment.

Sound effects in the realistic play must not be obtrusive. When *The Cherry Orchard* was first produced by the Moscow Art Theatre some of the effects, birds singing in the garden for instance, aroused unfavorable comment. Apparently these effects were distracting. Perhaps because of their novelty the effects drew attention to themselves, instead of being accepted as an inevitable part of the life of the stage.

The abstract representational play permits greater freedom in the use of sound effects and particularly of music. The element of nonvocal sound must still be a logical part of the life of the play, but the abstract representational play has lost a close connection with everyday life and established a logic of its own. Thus Saroyan's *My Heart's in the Highlands* was produced to the accompaniment of a complete musical score. The same might be done with Saroyan's somewhat less abstract *The Time of Your Life* or with Sartre's *The Flies*. Although there is no realistic motivation for this musical accompaniment, if it is appropriate to the pattern of the play it will not seem out of place because the life of the play itself is strange and unlike ordinary life.

In the fantastic representational play this becomes perfectly obvious. The life going on on the stage is clearly an imaginary life, different from everyday life, and with its own logic and laws. Plays like *Alice in Wonderland, and Pelleas and Melisande* seem to call for a musical accompaniment which will help to express their pattern of moods.

When musical accompaniment is used, special care must be taken to keep it from drowning out the dialogue. In the revival of Eva Le Gallienne's *Alice in Wonderland* by the American Repertory Company, most of the dialogue of the opening scene was lost because the music was too loud. A really close co-ordination of the music with the dialogue and the action is not easy to achieve.

PRESENTATION

Presentational plays, because they are not concerned with creating an illusion of life independent of audience and theatre, use or permit the use of nonvocal sound with the single aim of dramatic expression. Greek tragedy because of its lyric-dramatic character and its strong emotional unity seems to need musical accompaniment, and the choruses of Greek comedy may gain from such accompaniment.

Shakespeare's plays abound in realistically motivated sounds used to create strong dramatic effects. Lady Macbeth strikes on a bell to summon Macbeth to the murder of Duncan. The dead king's followers knock on the gate. There is the alarum bell in *Othello* and the storm on the heath in *King Lear*. In Shakespeare's own day musicians sat above the stage and were called upon frequently to accompany the group entrances and exits, and the colorful processions across the stage which are to be found in some of the tragedies and particularly in the histories. Margaret Webster in her production of *Richard II* showed the value of reviving such use of music. Incidental songs and dances contribute greatly to expressing the spirit of Shakespeare's comedies. This is true of Molière's comedies also, and of course his ballet-comedies depend heavily on music.

The older melodrama owes its name to the fact that, in order to circumvent the theatre monopoly, cheap plays were presented to musical accompaniment. In reviving them today, musical accompaniment is needed to underline the scenes of suspense, pathos, and great excitement, if not for the entire play. The most obvious type of theatre music is just right for this: the kind which used to be played to accompany silent movies.

The expressionistic drama, which seeks to attack all the senses of the audience as strongly as possible, quite naturally makes extensive use of music and sound effects with little attempt to motivate them. *Processional* uses a variety of music, most of it played by a grotesque band made up of characters in the play. *Beggar on Horseback* uses jazz music, the Lohengrin "Wedding March," Sousa's "Stars and Stripes," "The Soldier's Song" from *Faust,* "Tammany," the clicking of a typewriter, and the sound of machinery. The opposing elements in the play are expressed by opposing musical themes played by the dance orchestra. In its early scenes, *From Morn to Midnight* uses wind, thunder, the ticking of a clock, the "Overture" to *Tannhaüser,* and dance music; in the last scene, hymns sung to organ accompaniment, jubilant music on the organ, a fanfare, rolls on a drum, and the final explosion are indispensable to building up the peak of excitement on which the play ends.

Similarly, sound plays an important part in *The Hairy Ape:* police whistles and the patrol-wagon gong in the scene on Fifth Avenue, the chattering and screeching of the monkeys in the last scene, and particularly in the scene in the stokehold. Throughout that scene the rhythm is set and the mood provided by the engineer's whistle, the scrape of shovels, the clang of the furnace doors, and the roar of the fires.

In *The Adding Machine,* the yowling of a cat, the croaking of frogs, and assorted night sounds are used to help create the atmosphere of the graveyard scene, and the scene in the Elysian Fields is accompanied by faint, sweet music. These are relatively conventional uses of nonvocal sound, but in the office scene after Zero is fired, sound and light combine to express directly the fit of madness in which he murders the Boss. In a realistic play, Mr. Zero would have been made to mime with appropriate dialogue and action the madness and the murder. In this presentational play, the actors stand still, the platform revolves, lights flash on and off, and all the sound effects in the theatre repertory—wind, thunder, horses hooves, breaking glass, and explosions—are built up rapidly in a crescendo on which the curtain falls. Direct auditory and visual stimuli are substituted for an imitation of real-life action. More can be done with sound effects in a play like *The Adding Machine* than is indicated in the author's stage directions. The characteristic sound of an adding machine might be used throughout the office scene, for instance, very faint to begin with but growing gradually louder until it is merged with the medley of sounds at the end. Other possibilities will occur to anyone who studies the play with a view to exploiting sound and music for dramatic expression.

Rehearsal and Performance

A single person should be in charge of all sound effects and of all recorded music to be used in a particular production. In the professional theatre this is ordinarily the property man. In the nonprofessional theatre it may be desirable, especially if the effects are many, to make them the responsibility of a special-effects manager. In consultation with the director he will prepare a cue-sheet with *warning, start,* and *stop* cues for each effect, and he will collect or make the necessary equipment to produce each sound effect needed. Frequently, sound effects must be produced out of sight and hearing of the performance, so that arrangements must be made for cueing them from the prompter's desk.

Live incidental music, if at all elaborate, should be in charge of a musical director, who is provided with cue-sheets and with arrangements for cueing.

Incidental music and sound effects should be rehearsed early and *with* the acting, not only to insure proper cueing, but also to insure a proper relation to the voices. Even in professional productions important lines are too often drowned out by accompanying music, wind, rain, or rolls of thunder.

Before each performance all equipment should be tested to be sure that it is in good working order. During the performance, the effects manager and the musical director, like the rest of the production department heads, are responsible to the stage manager.

Means of Production

There are several means of producing sound effects and music, and none of them is easy to handle well in the nonprofessional theatre. Commercial recordings are in some ways the simplest means. They serve well for overture and entr'acte, as well as for continuity music between scenes, though care must be taken in their selection. If the audience is at all a musical one, it may be well to avoid familiar music. Many sound effects, such as wind, rain, airplanes, crowd and traffic noises, have been recorded on disks which can be purchased without much trouble. Occasionally one of these can be used to good effect with no more equipment than a good phonograph. For complex effects, two phonographs, or one with two turntables, will be needed to fade out one effect and fade in another. The difficulty with these commercially recorded effects is that they seldom fit exactly the requirements of the particular play.

It is possible to record one's own sound effects to suit the requirements of the particular play either on disks or on tape. Disk recording is capable of higher fidelity, but it is more expensive and less flexible than tape recording because the tape can be spliced to shift quickly from one effect to another and accurately marked to make exact cueing easy. Even a suitable tape recorder, however, is comparatively expensive, and recording must be done under studio conditions.

Another method combines the simple playing of phonograph records with the electrical transmission of live sound. This method requires a small sound studio on or near the stage, equipped with a microphone and two turntables connected to a small portable loudspeaker, which may be set up at any point in the flies or wings or behind the back wall of the setting. With this equipment, records may be used on the turntables and special handmade effects may be utilized through the microphone. Not much space is required but it must be relatively soundproof, and a signal system is necessary to cue the effects operator.

If the proper equipment is not available for the use of recorded sound or of electrically transmitted live sound, effects will have to be produced on stage by hand. In any case, certain common effects such as bells and shots are best produced by hand on the spot; the quality is likely to be better and exact timing is more easily achieved.

Offstage incidental music can be handled very well by records as long as it is background music only. Accompaniment for dancing and particularly for singing had better be played by musicians in the orchestra pit or wings, because of the close co-ordination required.

SPECIFIC LIVE SOUND EFFECTS

Described below are some of the standard methods of producing the sound effects most commonly required on the stage. Anyone with ingenuity, imagination, and a little mechanical aptitude should be able to devise methods for producing unusual effects not described here, and to work out improvements on some of these traditional methods of sound production.

Airplanes. Good airplane-effect records are available in considerable variety, but it may be desirable to augment a record with the following device: Six-inch leather thongs with the ends knotted are attached to the pulley of a small electric motor and are allowed to strike the head of a snare drum. An electric fan can be adapted to the production of this and other motor noises by removing the guard and blades and fastening different types of strikers to the revolving shaft.

The striker of a small electric bell (door or telephone type) connected to two dry cells and allowed to strike against the top of a bass drum is a simple substitute for the specially prepared striker.

Automobiles. Good recordings are available for a variety of automobile noises, and there are several methods of creating

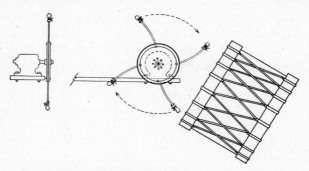

The electric striker is used for airplane, automobile, and a variety of factory machine noises.

different live effects. Automobiles passing can be suggested by using the electric bell striker against a snare drum with the snares released. Or the electric fan shaft (*see* "Airplanes") may be equipped with a piece of wire cable holding a wooden ball on the end and this allowed to strike against a drumhead. Somewhat different effects can be achieved with different striking surfaces: wooden box, cardboard box, tin, plywood, and so on.

A fair effect of a modern automobile driving off can be achieved by starting an electric mixer and carrying it rapidly away from the stage.

A comic auto effect can be done with a wooden rattle for the starter, marbles shaken in tin cans of various sizes with an occasional clank of can against can for the motor, a string rubbed with resin (*see* "Creaking door"), a pop gun and various kinds of whistles for misfiring, stalling, and stopping.

Automobile horns. When an automobile horn is required, use an actual horn of the appropriate type for serious effects, and the resined string and tin can (*see* "Creaking door") for comedy.

Bells and chimes. Plays require a great variety of bell sounds: church bells, school bells, fire gongs, clock chimes, etc. The musician's triangle provides a high-pitched thin tone which may do for the striking of some clocks. An actual set of chimes, such as is used today in some homes for a doorbell, will sometimes be useful.

An iron pipe hung free on a rope and struck with a hammer or stick will give a bell-like note. The diameter and length of the pipe and the type of striker determine volume, pitch, and quality. An automobile cam shaft, hung up and struck in the same manner, gives good tones which vary considerably in pitch depending on the point at which it is struck. The blade of a circular saw, suspended by a rope and struck on the edge, produces beautifully resonant bell-like sounds.

Carriage over cobbles. An irregularly surfaced barrel, containing a loose weight to make its movement somewhat eccentric, rolled along the floor gives the effect of a carriage traveling on a cobblestone street. This should be augmented with the sound of hoofbeats (see p. 308).

Clock strike. For an old clock, the most realistic effect will be achieved with an actual spiral clock strike, obtainable from a clock repair store, mounted on a board for amplification, and struck lightly with a large nail. For other types of clocks see "Bells and chimes" on page 303.

Crashes. A glass crash is best imitated either by dropping a box containing broken glass or by pouring broken glass from one box into another.

A wood crash can be achieved by fastening a number of thin boards on cords knotted to keep the boards apart like Venetian blinds; this is illustrated on page 305. The whole is suspended some distance above the stage and released, so that the boards fall to the floor with a rattling crash. A splintering crash, more prolonged than that just described and capable of some variation, can be produced by crushing an orange crate between a "scissors" made of two lengths of $2'' \times 4''$ bolted together at one end.

For effects of greater duration, a crash machine may be constructed. Such a machine is pictured on page 306. It consists of a sturdy framework about six feet high on which is mounted a slatted drum, which can be turned by a crank, and two sets of hardwood slats sprung to the roller under pressure. Considerable variety in effect can be achieved by varying the rate at which the drum is turned. The thunder drum or sheet operated simultaneously with the crash machine will give another quality and greater volume.

Creaking door. A good device for producing creaks, squeaks, and groans consists of a section of $2'' \times 4''$ with a slot about eight inches long sawed from one end down the middle. A hole to accommodate a large wooden dowel is bored about six inches from the same end. The dowel, equipped with a handle and rubbed with resin, is inserted and is held tight by means of a bolt and wing nut near the end, which draws the jaws of the instrument together. The dowel is twisted to produce the desired sounds. The *bull-roarer* is a simpler but less effective device for the same purpose. It is made by punching a hole in a large tin can or pan, passing through it a cord or wire, and knotting it on the inside so that it may be drawn taut. The can is then fastened bottom up to a board. If the cord is held taut and rubbed with a resined cloth, it will produce low-pitched

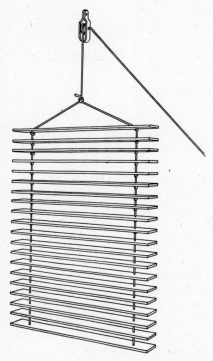

This is a single wood-crash machine.

sounds similar to those made by a creaking door. By varying the size of the can, the size and type of cord or wire, and the tautness, a great variety of pitch and quality can be achieved. This device is used also for animal sounds such as bull or lion roars.

Door and telephone bells. For doorbells, an electric bell, switch, and two dry-cell batteries are connected in a small wooden box which can be carried easily to any point on the stage where the sound is required.

The characteristic sound of a telephone is that of two bells struck simultaneously. This can be achieved by adding a second electric bell to the portable box and connecting it in parallel with the other with a cutout switch, so that it can be rung simultaneously with the other for telephone or singly for doorbell. Or the two bells may be mounted side by side close enough so that the clapper of the right-hand bell strikes the gong of the

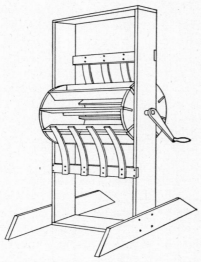

This is a crash machine used for crashes of long duration. It can be modified for machine-gun fire by substituting for the lateral fins a spiral of pegs designed to trip the striking slats one after another, instead of all at once.

left-hand bell on the rebound. They can then be wired separately, the left-hand bell serving for the doorbell, the right-hand for the telephone.

Door slams. The best door slam is made by an actual door. If those on the stage are not close enough or for some other reason unsatisfactory, a short rope may be attached to one end of a heavy wooden plank. Hold down one end with the foot and pull up the other end with the rope, then let go the rope so that the plank slams on the floor. This device omits the click of the latch.

A more realistic effect can be produced by taking two 1″ × 6″ boards two or three feet long, hinging them together at one end, and mounting a lock strike on the other end of the bottom board and a rim lock on the other end of the top board so that they will click together as the boards slam. Mounted on a wall or on an empty box, this device produces a combination click and reverberating bang.

Explosions. If a sheet of thin copper or galvanized screen about two feet square has a small-gauge wire soldered to it and connected to a phonograph pickup in place of the needle, and the amplifier is turned on, a touch on the copper will produce a deafening roar. Volume can be regulated by setting the amplifier. A microphone placed close to the vibrating copper or screen gives a similar effect.

The traditional method is to fire a shot into a metal ash can or oil drum. A .22 revolver, blank cartridge, gives a small explosion, a shotgun a good explosion. Both barrels of a twelve gauge gun fired simultaneously gives maximum loudness. If the fire laws permit, a dynamite cap may be exploded electrically in a heavy ash can by throwing a switch. This method is especially useful when a number of separate explosions are required in rapid succession. Several caps may be set up ahead of time and fired from a distance by the stage manager or effects man. A simultaneous or slightly delayed use of the crash machine (*see* "Crashes") will add to the realism for certain kinds of explosions. For safety, barriers should be erected to keep everyone at least ten feet away from the ash cans.

Factory noises. Rhythmic sounds imitating different types of machine noises can be made by striking a wooden box with a mallet or drumstick. The quality of sound can be varied by different sizes and types of boxes, and by using cans or sheets of metal and by varying the striker: hammer, wire brush, etc. The automatic striker described under "Airplanes" can be adapted to produce factory machine noises. A piece of cardboard or lath held against the spokes of a revolving wheel will give a vibration noise. Real machines like the vacuum cleaner, hand sewing machine, and electric drill are often useful.

The sound of escaping steam can be reproduced by rubbing together two pieces of sandpaper or glass, by shaking shot in a pan, with compressed air, or by a wind machine (*see* "Wind") with a shrill canvas or with strips of sandpaper in place of the canvas.

Fire engines. A hand-driven siren combined with the rumble cart (*see* "Trucks") and a clanging bell (and perhaps another bell of higher pitch for the chief's car) render fairly realistically the sound of a fire engine.

Foghorns and boat whistles. One of the low-pitched wooden pipes used for sound demonstration in school physics laboratories is good for foghorn and boat whistle sounds. If no such pipe is available, blowing into the mouths of bottles and jugs of various sizes and shapes should result in the discovery of the desired pitch and resonance.

A triple-note horn such as is often used on tugboats can be imitated by mounting three different-sized bottles (giving the desired harmony of notes) with their mouths at the same level and each adjacent to a slot in an airtight wind-chest fitted with a mouthpiece. Air forced through the mouthpiece by the lungs

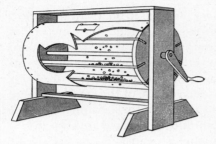

This is a rain machine.

or by a small bellows will be guided into the bottles and the desired three-toned sound will be produced.

Hail. (*See* "Rain.")

Hoofbeats. Two halves of a coconut shell or two blocks of wood with straps for the hands, beaten on a large book, a carpeted surface, or in a box of gravel, provide for different effects of distance and ground surface. The operator should practice the different rhythms of the various gaits.

Machine gun. The machine gun effect may be produced by beating a cushion, a sheet of leather, or a slab of plywood rhythmically with bamboo canes. It may also be done with a modification of the crash machine (*see* "Crashes") with lighter striking slats and instead of the series of lateral fins on the rotor, a spiral of pegs which will engage and trip the striking slats one after another in quick succession. The electric bell striker (*see* "Airplanes") hitting a tin dish pan is another machine gun device.

Motorboat and motorcycle. The effect of a motorboat or motorcycle is best produced with an actual outboard motor or motorcycle, but may be imitated moderately well with the automatic striker (*see* "Airplanes").

Rain. The simplest method of reproducing rain is to roll a handful of buckshot gently from side to side in a tin tray. Another method is to make a long, narrow box crossed with partitions which form a tortuous passage from one end to the other. The box is stood on end and dried peas poured in at the top and allowed to run down the passage to the bottom. Then the box is reversed and the peas allowed to run down again. By varying the angle, the effect of light or heavy rain can be produced.

The effect of a very heavy rain can be produced by rolling a

keg two-thirds full of nails
over a heavily padded floor.

A simple rain-box can be
made with the side of a circular cheesebox, fitted with strips
of lath at intervals on the inside, and mounted on a simple
dowel axle. The ends are covered with heavy wrapping paper. A pint of dried peas is

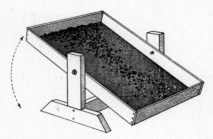

This is a surf box.

poured in this drum through the axle hole, then it is fitted with
the axle, and revolved. There is an illustration of this box on
page 308.

Sea noises. The sound of heavy surf rolling on a beach can be
simulated with a long wooden frame covered top and bottom
with window screen, filled with dried peas, and balanced on a
wooden support so that when it is tilted to one end the peas will
slide down. Tilting back and forth at suitable intervals will give
the desired effect.

For the breaking of wave crests in the open sea, dried beans
or small shot manipulated on a small drumhead or on canvas
stretched on a small circular frame gives good effects. First the
shot is tipped to one side and then swirled around with a
circular sweep until it comes to rest. Surf on a sandy shore can be
simulated with this also. The effect of heavy surf on a rocky
shore can be achieved with small steel balls on a bass drumhead.
Shot should not be used because it blackens the skin of the
drumhead.

Shots. Single shots offstage are usually produced with a .22
revolver firing blank cartridges. Rifle fire may be simulated by
irregular operation of the machine gun apparatus (*see* p. 308).

Slapstick. The noisy, comic beatings in old farces are performed with a *slapstick,* which consists of a piece of thin wood
about 28 inches long and 3 inches wide, shaped to the hand at
one end, with a similar piece of wood about 22 inches long
hinged to it six inches from the handle end, so that when the
slapstick is drawn back for a blow the hinged piece will swing
away from the other and when the stick is brought down, as if

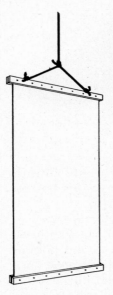

Here is a thunder sheet.

on someone's back, it will swing back against it with a resounding noise. Because of its strength, plywood is the best material. To keep the hinged piece from swinging too far away from the other, the two pieces should be joined by strips of canvas, just long enough to allow the desired amount of separation, tacked on either side near the striking end.

Telephone bell. (*See* "Doorbell.")

Ticking of a clock. A metronome is the best means of achieving the clear, distinct, and monotonously regular ticking of a clock.

Trains. A train effect requires the co-ordination of a number of different sounds. For the whistle, a trap-drummer's whistle mouth-blown or attached to a hand-operated bellows or to a tank of compressed air may be used. For the rhythmic puffing of the engine the trap-drummer's wire brushes may be beaten on a sheet of perforated galvanized iron, or buckshot may be shaken in a large dishpan. The effect of a train passing over the rails may be imitated with muffled drumsticks on a large drum, or better by means of a rumble cart (*see* "Trucks") with metal rollers moved over a few metal strips or corrugated iron. The effect of escaping steam when the engine is halted may be suggested by brushing the wire beaters across the perforated iron or by one of the methods described above under "Factory noises."

Thunder. A bassdrum or kettledrum may be used for making thunder. A special thunder drum is made by stretching a wet cowhide or calfskin on a heavy frame three to five feet square.

A thunder sheet (see the illustration above), a sheet of 20-gauge metal or ³⁄₁₆" plywood three feet wide and six to twelve feet long, suspended by ropes so that the bottom hangs about three feet from the stage floor where it can be grasped and shaken, is standard equipment. The plywood gives a better quality sound and can be used also for distant explosions. A

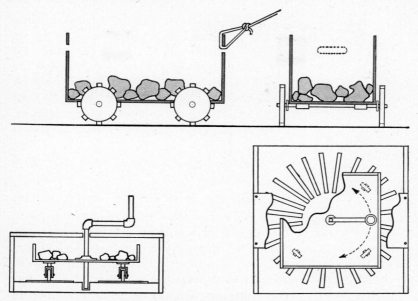

Top, the traditional rumble cart; and **Bottom,** an improved model of the traditional rumble cart.

wooden keg, three-fourths full of sand, rolled slowly across the stage floor will sometimes give the desired effect.

The effect of a lightning crash or bolt close at hand can be simulated by dropping a length of heavy chain from a height of ten or twelve feet on a sheet of corrugated iron laid over the top of an empty ash can. This can be supplemented by thunder sheet and drums.

Trucks. The rumbling and reverberations of heavy traffic such as trucks and buses, if not done with recordings, may be simulated with a rumble cart, types of which are illustrated above. The traditional rumble cart is a small wooden wagon with a box two feet by four feet. The wooden wheels, about one foot in diameter, are irregularly shaped or have wooden lugs nailed to them. The cart is filled with old iron, stones, or bricks and pulled across the stage floor.

A modification requiring less space is a circular platform about four feet in diameter made to revolve on heavy iron casters or rollers by means of a vertical axle and handle. If the floor

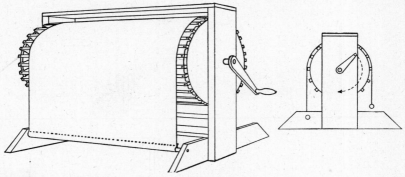

This is a wind machine.

under the platform is made irregular with strips of wood or strap iron, the revolving platform will produce irregular rumblings. The volume can be increased by loading the platform with iron or stones.

Less effective but easier to throw together is this device: Rest two big sheets (about four feet square) of galvanized iron on horses on which lie three or four turns (about three feet in diameter) of heavy iron wire (say No. 10). Jiggling the iron sheets gives pretty good rumbles, especially for train effects.

Wind. A wind machine similar to the hand-operated air raid warning sirens is purchasable, but an effective one is not hard to make. It consists of a cylinder or drum with slats fastened to the outside surface, mounted on an axle and frame so that it will revolve easily when the axle is turned by a crank. A strip of canvas or silk is fastened to the frame on one side, hung over the drum, and weighted on the other side. As the drum is revolved against the cloth, it produces a rustling or whistling sound—depending on the speed. If the volume needed is not great, wind effects can be simulated by drawing a smooth piece of wood along the surface of a two-foot length of wide silk ribbon stretched tightly between two boards. A small siren whistle or a trap-drummer's whistle may be added to get certain wind effects.

Questions

1. What is the chief value of nonvocal sound in a play production?
2. How can music be used to advantage in the multiset play?

3. What are the specific functions of nonvocal sound in the realistic representational play?

4. How can sound effects and music be used in the fantastic representational play?

5. Why has nonvocal sound been used so much in expressionistic plays?

6. What are the different general methods of handling nonvocal sound in a play production? What are the advantages of each?

Exercises

1. Prepare a cue-sheet for the sound in a realistic representational play and indicate how particular effects are to be achieved.

2. Prepare a cue-sheet for the sound in an expressionistic play, adding if you can to the effects indicated by the playwright, and indicate how particular effects are to be achieved.

3. Choose overture, entr'acte, and exit music for a particular production of a particular play. Give reasons for your choices.

4. Construct a wind machine, a rain-maker, a bull-roarer, or a thunder sheet.

5. Get up an automobile effect; an effect of a busy factory.

Bibliography

Gassner, John, *Producing the Play,* together with *The Scene-Technician's Handbook,* New York: The Dryden Press, 1941.

Hake, Herbert V., *Here's How,* Evanston: Row, Peterson & Company, 1942. The more common effects and effect machines.

Halstead, William Perdue, *Stage Management for the Amateur Theatre,* New York: F. S. Crofts & Company, 1937. Some common effects are described, and a valuable index to effects described in other books is included.

Napier, Frank, *Noises Off: A Handbook of Sound Effects,* London: Frederick Miller, Ltd., 1936. The best book on the subject.

Rose, A., *Stage Effects: How to Make and Work Them,* New York: E. P. Dutton & Company, n.d. Stage effects from English pantomime, many of them suitable for ordinary productions.

Whorf, Richard B. and Roger Wheeler, *Runnin' the Show,* Boston: Walter H. Baker Company, 1930. A simple discussion of effects most commonly used.

CHAPTER 15.

BACKSTAGE ORGANIZATION

$\mathcal{I}$t has been told of a famous actor of an earlier day that when at a social function he happened to mention something about rehearsals, one of the nontheatrical guests looked at him in amazement and said, "You mean you go over it beforehand?" This seems ludicrous now, even to the layman, for everyone has become familiar with the long and grueling rehearsals needed to achieve the "illusion of the first time" in a performance. Most people are also aware—some from sad experience—that much advance planning and promotion must be done if one expects to draw an audience. But many would-be theatre practitioners are still just as surprised as the naïve lady mentioned above when confronted with the idea that the stagehands as well as the actors have to rehearse; that to achieve a smooth, fast-moving performance a competent, trained staff is required, whose every movement has been just as carefully thought out and just as thoroughly learned as those of the actors.

Personnel

The unseen corps without whom no theatrical production can function is divided by the curtain into two parts: the front-of-the-house staff and the stage crew. The duties of the former have been outlined in Chapter 9. The backstage workers are sorted by their duties into three "departments": carpenters, electricians, and property men. Their captain is the stage manager.

THE STAGE MANAGER

Next to the director, the stage manager is the most powerful person connected with a production. During rehearsals he is the former's first assistant. He keeps the addresses and telephone numbers of all the members of the cast, and sees that they are notified as to when they will be needed. He sees that the stage

314

(or floor space) is properly set up before a rehearsal begins. That is, he designates the entrances, stairs, fireplaces, and other salient features of the set, either by drawing a plan on the floor or by placing odd chairs to flank doors, and so on. He also places a usable substitute for every piece of furniture in its proper place, such as a row of chairs for a couch, a small table for a desk, a stepladder for a fireplace, a box for a coffee table, and so on. Later, he will see that the property man replaces these with the actual articles that are to be used in the show. When the rehearsal starts, he (or his assistant) will "hold the book" of the play and record every move that the actors make. He will also "throw lines" to uncertain actors, put in all sound cues at the proper times (verbally at first, later the real thing), and make any alterations in the script that the director orders.

On the night of the performance he (or his assistant) will call the "half hour" at every dressing room about thirty-five minutes before curtain time, and will make another call fifteen minutes later, at which time he will check to be sure that all members of the cast are on hand. About five minutes before curtain time, he will call "Overture!" or "First act!" His calls notify all the actors that the play is about to begin, and that they must be on hand in time for their entrance cues. (This is the last notice they will get until the second act call. The American theatre does not employ a "call boy," but holds every actor responsible for his own entrance cues.)

The stage manager will not actually "ring up," however, without first checking with the house manager out front. (In the professional theatre this is the company manager, who is the finance officer and the liaison man between the producer, the treasurer or box-office man, and the company.) When such clearance comes, the stage manager will call "Places!" to his actors and check to see that they *are* in place and that the stage is properly set. He then orders the electrician to bring his "foots" (or house spots) on, and—after receiving an appropriate signal —to "take his house out." (One never leaves an audience in total darkness unless the play requires it.) Then he gives the order: "Curtain!"

While the act is running, the stage manager (or his assistant) keeps an eye on the book to be ready to "throw a line" in case an actor "goes dry" or "jumps a cue," and also in order to take care of all sound effects. These are usually carried out by the property man or a special sound technician, but the stage manager or his assistant, standing next to the tormentor where he can watch the action, gives the cue either by hand (raising his arm for a warning, and dropping it for action), or by switching on an electric light for a warning and snapping it off for action. A general warning is needed about half a page before the end of an act to alert the electrician, curtain man, and clearers. No one will displace any part of the setting, however, until the stage manager orders "Strike!"

It is important that the stage manager write down the time the curtain rises and falls, so that he will know how his show is running, and also when to call "Second act!" and when to flash the house manager to bring the audience back in.

For the remaining acts this process is repeated, until the final curtain, when the stage manager must get his actors onstage immediately in order to get in a curtain call before the applause begins to die down. (If the cast has rehearsed curtain calls, this will be a simple matter.) He will continue to raise the curtain as long as the applause continues strong. When he is sure that it has begun to fade, he will leave the curtain down and order his house lights on, *and not until then*. Once his house lights are on, he will under no circumstances raise the curtain again.

The stage manager's job ends when the show closes its run and he hands the promptbook, containing a complete and detailed record of the performance, back to the producer.

THE STAGE CARPENTER

The setting, *except* for the properties, is under the jurisdiction of the master carpenter, who keeps it in repair and, with the assistance of his crew of "flymen" and "grips" (as scene shifters are called), sets it up, changes scenes, and dismantles it for storage when the play has finished its run. The *flymen*, of course, do the hoisting and lowering of suspended pieces; the *grips* move, set, lash, and brace the pieces that stand on the floor.

THE STAGE ELECTRICIAN

The electrician is responsible for the maintenance and use of all electrical equipment. He rigs and sets the stage lights when the production is being set up, under the orders of the director or designer; replaces lamps and gelatins when needed; and operates the switchboard during the performance. The details of these duties have been covered in Chapter 13 and in the preceding section of this chapter.

THE PROPERTY MAN

According to the stagehands' definition, a "property" is something that is used by the actors. In actual practice, the term includes such decorative pieces as pictures and bric-a-brac, whether used or not, and excludes such electrically wired items as torches and lamps, which have come into the province of the electrician.

It is the job of the master of properties to provide during the rehearsals a usable substitute for everything that is used by the actors as soon as they have learned their parts and can rehearse without "sides" in their hands. This includes filling vessels that are supposed to contain liquids (water will do, of course, until the dress rehearsal) and serving bits or slices of bread or apple when food has to be consumed, so that the process of eating may be co-ordinated with the lines.

Meanwhile he will be hunting for the real furniture, dishes, bric-a-brac, pictures, draperies, etc. that will be used in the actual production. Having brought these to the theatre, he will store them in a safe place until the dress rehearsal period. To be able to find just the right thing, he (or she—for women make excellent mistresses of properties) should be a combination of interior decorator, inventor, and detective. He should know periods well enough to recognize a modern reproduction that is "right" or see possibilities for making an impossible piece suitable by slight alterations. If necessary, he should be able to make a presentable facsimile. And he should have a photographic mind which registers the contents of every room he enters which might provide a source for borrowing.

"Hanging" a Production

Stemming from the time when most scenery was suspended, the process of moving a production into a theatre and rigging it for a performance is still referred to as "hanging a show." Although the amount of hanging has been materially reduced in modern times, it is still the *first consideration* of the master carpenter. For everything that is to be stored in the flies should be sent up out of the way before the standing pieces are brought in. The usual procedure is to start with the back wall and work downstage. If an interior set is to be used, the ceiling piece is hung horizontally (from two or three sets of lines) and raised high enough to permit flats to pass under it.

Next, the ground cloth—if one is used—is laid and stretched tightly. If this has been properly folded, it will automatically center itself if placed at the *pivot point* (the center point of the curtain line). That is, the upstage corners of the outstretched ground cloth should have been brought to the downstage corners, and this repeated until a strip about three feet wide is left, and this strip rolled up simultaneously from the ends toward the center.

During this time, the electrician has been rigging his lights on the "first pipe," which is hauled up as soon as the units have been installed and the cables run.

After this, the flats are brought in, the folded pieces unfolded, "floated" face down, and stiffeners attached. (When a flat is allowed to fall free it will form an air cushion and will float down gently without any assistance if there are no obstructions on the floor. Consequently, when a stagehand wants to lay a flat down, he merely clears the space in front of it and lets it go.) These stiffened walls are then raised, with part of the crew "footing" the bottom edge to prevent slipping and other members pushing against the *wood frame*, not the canvas, and are set up in place on locations previously marked on the ground cloth. If no ground cloth is used, marks should be plainly made on the floor at each corner of the set, with paint or tin strips, using different colors or designs for each scene. When all the flats are in place, the applied plastic pieces (windows, doors, stairs, mantels, etc.) are set in place and fastened securely with bolts, screws, and pin hinges.

All heavy furniture is brought in before the walls of the set are finally lashed together. After the furniture has been placed, the trims (draperies, pictures, etc.) hung, the backings set, and the ceiling lowered on top of the set, the electrician can aim his lights, the carpenter can adjust the teaser to the proper height, and the property man can set up his offstage props on a convenient table.

The set—if there are more than one—is then struck and stacked, and the process repeated for the next scene.

Scene Shifts

To achieve rapid and silent scene changes—so often vital to a play—three things are needed: (1) an ample staff, (2) proper planning and clear assignment of individual duties, and (3) adequate rehearsal. In elaborate productions with many scenes, special *technical rehearsals* are often necessary. In these the stagehands meet at a time when the actors are absent, set up the stage for the first scene, and then make all the subsequent scene changes in order, slowly at first and later as quickly and quietly as possible. The stage manager usually times these changes. When a shift runs too long, he confers with the crew to see how the moves can be replanned so as to speed things up.

SIZE OF THE STAGE CREW

The number of stage hands needed depends on the number and complexity of the changes, and the time allotted for the shifts. A one-set show with simple properties and few effects can easily be operated by the three department heads alone. In a three-set play when full intermissions are allowed for each shift, the size of the crew will depend on the number of men needed to carry the heaviest section of scenery—probably two or three grips in addition to the master carpenter. A flyman may also be needed to raise and lower the ceiling, and the property master may require a clearer or two for heavy furniture. (In a nonprofessional show, the flyman can help out here.) If the changes are complicated and fast, the crew should be increased so that no one man has to make more than two moves per shift.

ASSIGNMENT OF DUTIES

Since no two sets are exactly alike, no ironclad rules can be laid down as to scene change. However, there are certain general principles which a master carpenter or a stage manager can apply so as to get the most work done with the least expenditure of time and effort.

(1) The set should be allocated in sections so that each man

will be working in one limited area and not waste time running all over the stage. A popular plan is to split the crew into three teams, working, respectively, right, left, and center. These may be further subdivided into a striking team, which will unlash and unbrace a section of scenery and carry it to the "dead" stack, and a setting team which will bring a section of the new set from the "live" stack, place it on its marks, and secure it in position.

(2) Duties should be so planned that every step counts. If it is necessary for a stagehand to return to the stage after stacking a piece of scenery, he should not do so empty handed, but carrying a new piece of scenery or furniture.

(3) Storage places for scenery should be so planned as to save steps and time. If possible, all scenery that will not be needed again should be placed in a separate stack instead of on top of flats that will later have to be used. If space permits, there should be such a pair of live and dead stacks on each side of the stage. In cramped quarters the live stack may be placed on one side, the dead stack on the other, so that the old scenery moves out of the way of the oncoming set. In any case, the scenery needed next should always be on top of the pile, even if this takes re-arranging the stack while an act is playing.

(4) Moves should be planned in logical sequence so that no bottlenecks will occur. Often a wall cannot be moved until the furniture is out of the way, or *vice versa*. Similarly, furniture is difficult to move when it is full of small props; and so on. So it behooves the property crew to clear *all* movable small props *immediately,* using a tray or basket to speed up their collection. (If the butler has left a tray on the set, everything movable may be piled on that tray and taken out at once.) It is often advisable to move large furniture down center until the walls are opened and it can be carried off. But any unnecessary moves should be avoided.

(5) Stagehands should learn the easy way to do things. One man can move a single flat without any trouble by gripping it at about shoulder level with one hand and waist level with the other (so that it can't tip over), lifting the near corner and letting the other trail. Two people can carry off most of the furniture if it is properly piled: a small table upside down on a large table; chairs nested (seat to seat) on their sides on a sofa or desk; and so on.

(6) Every member of the crew should have his duties explained to him so carefully (in a complicated shift they should be written down) and should be so thoroughly rehearsed that he performs those duties quickly, smoothly, quietly (he should wear sneakers), and does not attempt to do anything else except in an extreme emergency.

Below is a sample chart outlining the duties of the stage crew at Brooklyn College for the fast change from the living room to the bedroom in *The Silver Cord* (the sets for which are described on pages 243 and 244), a change which was made in 45 seconds.

The Silver Cord, II–1 to II–2

FLYMAN: a. Raise ceiling (on II–1 curtain)
           b. Lower ceiling (on signal from head carpenter)

PROPS: *Right Team:*   *Left Team:*

a. Nest st. chair and arm chair and carry off through arch.	a. Clear small props; place end table on sofa.
b. Set night table and L. C. chair.	b. Carry off sofa through door D. L., after wall swings.

GRIPS: *Right Team: (1 man)*   *Left Team: (1 man)*

a. Swing R. wall.	a. Swing L. wall.
b. Let down bed.	b. Help prop team.

Center Team: (2 men)

a. Strike secretary through arch.
b. Bring on jog and lash to R. and L. wall sections.

ELECTRICIAN: a. Disconnect fire.
                  b. Connect dresser light.

SCENE SHIFTING IN THE ARENA THEATRE

In the arena theatre, where there is no curtain to conceal the stagehands when they go into action, it is probably the best course to adhere to one-set shows so that all their work may be done before the audience is admitted. Wanting this, there are

322   PLAY PRODUCTION: THEORY AND PRACTICE

three possible courses open. The first is to have the clearers work openly and frankly in full view of the audience. There will be few if any grips, since there can be no scenery other than small set pieces. This is the method employed in the Penthouse Theatre at the University of Washington. When a change must be made, it is made in view of the audience, and Professor Hughes reports that the audience enjoys watching the comparatively simple shifts.

Another method is to have the crew costumed as characters in the play and to integrate their actions with the play's sequence of events, as when servants rearrange a room. This can be done without too much difficulty in some Elizabethan plays; in fact this was probably the method employed in the Elizabethan theatre for moving furniture on and off the apron or forestage.

The third method is to make all scene changes in the dark. For many reasons, this is a highly treacherous process. Unless the crew has been highly trained and thoroughly rehearsed, even down to the exact number of steps they will take for each move, bad collisions may occur, furniture is likely to turn up in the wrong place, and stage hands can get lost and remain on stage when the lights come up. A few "markers" in luminous paint, to designate exits and furniture spotting, will prove helpful. But even so, the changes are likely to consume so much time that the audience will get restless.

Whatever method is used, the same requirements hold good as on the picture-frame stage. If a smooth, fast shift is to be achieved, careful and co-ordinated planning, definite assignment of duties, and adequate rehearsal are essential.

Properties

Properties are usually thought of under four categories: (1) *Trim props* are hung on the scenery or stood on shelves or furniture to decorate the set. These include pictures, draperies, books, bric-a-brac, etc. (2) *Set props* are useful articles which stand on the floor or on other properties. They include telephones, furniture, books (if used), etc. (3) *Hand props* are small articles that are transported by the actor, such as cards, knives, cigarette cases and lighters, money, letters, etc. (4) *Mechanical* (not electrical) *effects,* such as rain, snow, mechanical sound effects, etc., are also under the jurisdiction of the property man.

Since every play is a problem unto itself, it is impossible to treat the subject of properties exhaustively, or to lay down any rigid rules. Bounds are set mainly by the inventiveness and re- sourcefulness of the property man, but a few general hints might be useful.

TRIM PROPS

Let us first consider those articles which, although they are seldom used by the actors, also come under the aegis of the property man.

Books. In large quantities, books are too heavy to permit much handling, so if a book case must be struck it is wise to fill it with *prop books*. These are made by gluing the backs from real books to strips of wood the proper size (usually 1″ to 2″ width and 6″ to 10″ long) whose edges have been beveled with a plane to give them an oval shape. (If real book-backs are not available, a clever painter can simulate them directly on the wood.) When nailed side by side to a board the length of the bookcase shelf, a whole section can be filled with "books" whose weight is negligible. If they are packed so tight that the sides cannot be seen, the audience will not be conscious of the fact that they have none.

Tapestries. A most realistic tapestry can be painted on burlap with thin scene paint. Chinese embroidered panels may be simu- lated with paint on sateen or velour.

Draperies. Window curtains and side drapes should be chosen and hung with care, and never skimped, since at least 50 per cent fullness is required to achieve pleasing folds. Expensive bro- cades may be imitated by stenciling or painting cheap materials with dye. For ease in striking, an entire drapery rig may be built into a valance box and hung to a window casing by picture hangers so that it may be quickly removed and replaced with other draperies. (It may not be necessary to remove draperies during a scene shift, as walls are often stacked with the draperies in place, particularly if they are not in danger of damage from other stacked pieces of scenery.)

Bric-a-brac. Small decorative articles such as vases, statuettes, clocks, etc. are usually breakable, so unless they are to be picked up during the action they should be wired down securely to screws or tacks driven into the surface on which the article is to stand. If this surface is highly polished and would be marred by screws or tacks, the object can usually be filled with sand to make it steady. If an object is required to fall by itself, it can be pushed over with a dowel stick from backstage through a small hole in the scenery.

Ash trays should be plentiful and large enough to accommodate a maximum of butts. A little water in each will prevent distracting curls of smoke from discarded cigarettes.

SET PROPS

Furniture is the most prominent item in the category of set props, but most pieces needed in the average production can usually be rented, borrowed, or bought from a property studio, a storage warehouse, or an auction room. When just the right thing cannot be found, however, or turns out to be too expensive, it is surprising how easily even a period piece can be simulated (using dowels, plywood, and papier-mâché), accurately enough to fool an audience across the footlights. A mixture of newspaper bits and wallpaper paste can be appliquéd on a surface and modeled with a spoon handle into quite presentable carving. (It is well to drive tacks where the papier-mâché is to be applied, so as to hold it more securely.) A piece of small rope tacked on makes a good armature on which a running design may be modeled. Spindles can be turned out of dowels, or sections of half-round nailed together, by means of a wood rasp. Boxlike articles such as dressers and desks are easily constructed of light framing ($1'' \times 2''$ or $3''$ white pine) covered with plywood rubbed with stain, or with beaver board which is then grained and shellacked. Slabs of the same material, equipped with handles and tacked on the face make convincing drawers. The boy's bureau which acted as a backing for the fireplace in Act I of *The Silver Cord* (seen on page 245) was made in this manner.

Most producing groups will do well to accumulate stock pieces of furniture. When the audience grows tired of seeing a couch or a chair too often, it may be effectively disguised by lightly tacking new upholstery material over the old. A coat of water-color paint will change the appearance of the frame without seriously damaging the finish. These processes are not recommended for borrowed furniture, however.

HAND PROPS

Torches. Live flames, of course, are very dangerous on the stage. A fairly convincing torch, however, may be simulated by mounting a pen flashlight in a hole bored in the heavy end of a tapered piece of wood (a 2″ × 2″ piece, shaped with a hatchet, will do), with "flames," cut out of amber, straw, and red gelatin wired in a bunch around the bulb.

Weapons. Small arms are a frequent concern of the property man. As with most properties, the real thing is usually to be preferred to a dummy. However, some most convincing replicas of army rifles, cowboy revolvers, etc. are to be had from toy stores or war surplus outlets. Wanting these, any good whittler with a supply of white pine scraps and dowels can turn out a replica of a pistol or rifle that, when painted with a mixture of shellac and flake graphite and rubbed (when dry) with the head of a hammer, can hardly be distinguished from the genuine article at twenty paces.

Swords and daggers also can be simulated easily. Rapiers—if they are merely worn and not drawn—can be made from two strips of oval molding nailed together, covered with velvet and tipped with heavy metal foil. (These may be glued on with rubber cement or Rosene.) The hilt may be built out by wrapping it with strips of cloth dipped in glue. The guard, made of twisted wire, may be similarly wrapped. The short, comparatively thick blades of Greek and Roman swords can be planed out of a piece of lath, the hilt built out with wood blocks and whittled or rasped to shape. A practical scabbard can be made from panels of beaverboard for the sides, separated by two thin strips of plywood for the edges. These edges should be spaced so that the blade of the sword fits snugly between them. Helmets and breastplates may be molded from papier-mâché in the same manner as masks, painted with shellac and graphite, and burnished by rubbing with the head of a hammer.

Masks. Masks may either be built up directly on a clay model, by laying on, and molding in, successive strips of paper towel dipped in paste (wallpaper paste will do), or molded indirectly, in the same manner, in a plaster mold that has been made of the model. If many duplicate masks are made, this latter process is to be preferred. In either case, the mask will be stronger if covered with a piece of cheesecloth also dipped in paste and molded to fit the features.

Letters and documents. Letters are often important items in a play. It is usually best not to have them contain legible writing, as there is too much chance for substitution, either through carelessness or through malice aforethought on the part of a practical joker. If the actor has not memorized the contents of the letter he is supposed to read, the whole scene may be wrecked. If he has, and sees something else there instead, he may "blow up." So an unintelligible scrawl or meaningless gibberish is safest. The outward appearance of the letter is the thing that counts, anyway: the size of the envelope, the shape of the fold, the kind of paper. Parchment may be simulated by rubbing spots of oil into a heavy grade of cream-colored wrapping paper.

Food. Probably the most frequently occurring item on the prop list is *food*. It should be simply simulated rather than provided in full, for sufficient time is almost never allowed in a play for the consumption of a full meal, and the actor is too busy with talk to be able to eat much anyway. On the other hand, nothing is more disillusioning than to see an actor drink out of an empty glass, or a butler bring in one small saucer when a steak dinner has been ordered. Simple, easily-handled, nonfilling (and particularly nonchoking), easily chewed items should be substituted for heavy food, taking care that they somewhat resemble the original in color and shape. Bits of apple serve well for potatoes, cauliflower, or any white vegetable. Lettuce takes up much space and looks right to the audience. Slices of bread cut to shape, will often pass for meat, especially if covered with gravy. For hams, roast legs of lamb, and tongues, that must be carved on the table, a papier-mâché prop can be made on a wood and chicken-wire armature, the end made flat to resemble a sliced surface and duly painted and shellacked. Real slices of meat may be laid against this surface, to be carved off by the actor.

Dishes, kettles, teapots, etc. may be made to steam by partially filling them with water and dropping in a piece of dry ice.

For a convincing stage meal, the proper dish is more important than accuracy in the food it is supposed to contain, since it is considerably more visible to the audience. Hence, any "prop girl" who is confronted with an elaborate stage menu to simulate should consult an experienced hostess in order to guard against such glaring errors as serving soufflé on a platter, or bouillon in a soup plate.

Drinks. Beverages offer much the same problem. A liquid of the proper color, poured from the right bottle into the right glass will be accepted by the audience without question. Yet it is not uncommon in "home talent" plays to see champagne poured from whiskey bottles into cocktail glasses, or even into tumblers. Nor is it unheard of for an inexperienced drinker to pour out a tall glass of "straight whiskey" and gulp it down as though it were tea—which indeed, it might well be, as tea is fairly close to rye whiskey in color, although caramel sirup is the most common substitute for amber-colored alcoholic drinks. This soda-fountain staple can be diluted to the color of rye, scotch, sherry, or even sauterne merely by adding water. Grape juice, of course, does well for red wines. For beer, nothing is so believable as beer, although root beer will do for bock or porter.

Real alcoholic beverages, with the possible exception of beer, should never be served on the stage, as they are likely to cause the actor to choke. Any practical joker who substitutes real whiskey for its prop imitation during a performance should be severely disciplined, since this is inviting disaster, especially if the actor involved is not aware of the substitution.

It might be mentioned at this point that at the dress rehearsal of any play containing food the director should impress upon the cast and crew in no uncertain terms the necessity of keeping hands off all properties. Otherwise, everything edible (or smokable) is likely to disappear before the curtain goes up.

MECHANICAL EFFECTS

Most of the mechanical effects for which the property man is responsible have been described in Chapter 14. Those described below depend on sight rather than sound.

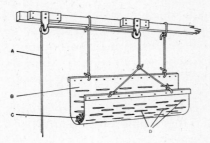

This illustration shows a snow cradle. When rope, **A**, is alternately released and pulled, movable batten, **B**, is lowered and raised, causing chopped "snow," **C**, to sift out through slits, **D**, in canvas cradle.

Snow and falling leaves. Prop snow consists of chopped paper that has been flame-proofed. It can be bought from a theatrical supply house. (Inflammable paper should never be used.) Soap flakes will also serve. The flakes are stored in a *snow cradle*, hung above the space where the flurry is to be seen. This consists of a sheet of canvas about six feet wide and as long as necessary, tacked to two battens, one of which is "tight-tied," or suspended in a rigid position, the other being moved up and down by means of a pair of lines run over a pulley. The pocket thus formed is packed with "snow." Slashes are cut in the third of the canvas nearest the movable batten, about six inches apart, so that when this batten is lowered the pack of snow rolls toward it, and sifts through the slits. By practiced manipulation a continuous fall, light or heavy, can be achieved. A canvas or muslin sheet should be spread on the floor under the snow cradle, so that the snow can be kept clean, gathered up, and used again. *Falling leaves* are imitated in a similar manner.

Rain. Sciopticon projections (see Chapter 13) or the noise of dripping water offstage will convince most spectators of rain, particularly if entering actors are provided with drenched umbrellas and well-spattered coats and hats. A large brush or feather duster dipped in a pail of water and swung at the "victim" in the same manner as one spatters scenery will do the trick.

Occasionally, however, a half-inch pipe with a row of small holes drilled in its under side is run along the eaves of a stage building, or even across the entire first border, and connected to a garden hose. Of course, a trough of tin or waterproofed canvas must be provided to catch and hold the fallen water. If the flow is heavy and continued it will be necessary to connect this trough to a drain.

Marching soldiers. A startlingly realistic effect of a passing army can be obtained by seating a row of property men on the floor (offstage) under a window and having them pass bayonets or short spear shafts from one to the other, so that the tips are seen to pass the window. The result is even more convincing if the rhythm is co-ordinated with the beat of a "marching machine." (See Chapter 14.)

Exercises

1. Plan a shift for an intricate, multiscene play. Use a Samuel French acting edition of a Broadway play if you have no fully designed script readily available.
2. Make *cue cards* for each stage hand on your hypothetical crew, listing in sequence all the moves that each will have to make.
3. List in order the pieces of scenery that will have to be placed in the "live stack" so as to be readily available during the shift. Locate this stack on a plan of your stage.
4. Plan a layout of your *prop* table so that all hand props will be readily available when needed.
5. Make a list of the sources (shops, storehouses, homes, rooms, and offices in your school, etc.) where you think the properties for your project production could be obtained. Go on a spotting tour if necessary.
6. Make an estimate of the expense involved in collecting your properties. Do not overlook haulage.
7. If a professional company or little theatre group is playing in your neighborhood, arrange to go back stage and talk shop with the stage manager and department heads (chief carpenter, electrician, and property man). Make a list of the new ideas you pick up.
8. Make a list of the properties used in the next motion picture you see.

Bibliography

For an exhaustive treatment and a copious index to other books, see Halstead, listed in bibliography to Chapter 14. Useful material will also be found in books by Selden and Sellman, Burris-Meyer and Cole, Milton Smith, and others listed in bibliography to Chapter 12.

PART FOUR

THE ACTOR AND HIS ACCESSORIES

CHAPTER 16.

THE ACTOR'S TASK AND TOOLS

*A*cting is pretending, and apparently pretending is entirely natural to human beings. Pretending makes up a large part of children's play. They pretend because pretending is fun; but it is useful as well as enjoyable because much of it is imitation of adults and consequently educational. Adults do a good deal of pretending also, but so much is it a part of everyday life that we are not likely to be strongly aware of it. Of course we are aware of pretense when it is used for criminal or unethical purposes with the intent to profit from deception, but ordinary life is filled with pretending of various kinds which harms no one. Indeed it oils the wheels of society; highly organized life in large groups is hardly possible without it.

Acting as an art requires the conscious cultivation of this ability to pretend, which nearly everyone has to some degree, and the systematic application of the ability to the particular requirements of play production.

The Actor's Task

The actor, on the basis of the dialogue and stage directions of the written play, must imagine a character, a being who has existed hitherto only in the mind of the playwright. He must imagine this character complete in physical appearance, posture, walk, gesture, voice, and speech, and in mental and emotional makeup. It is not enough that he imagine this individual alone and in a single moment, as the painter or sculptor might imagine the character. The actor must realize him in relation to other characters and as a participant in a more or less complex action or series of actions taking place sometimes in a variety of places and over a considerable period of time. Moreover, this series of actions is unified and expresses something about life.

When he has imagined this character, the actor must create

it or re-create it through the medium of his own body, and he must project his creation in the theatre under the conditions of production in such a way that it will live for an audience. Unlike the painter or sculptor, who does his work only once, or at any rate finishes his sculpture or his painting and is done with it, the actor usually has to repeat his creation in several performances, at set times, and before an audience which may differ considerably from performance to performance.

Medium and Training

Like any other art, acting requires the cultivation of certain faculties and the development of certain physical skills.

FACULTIES

Imagination. Obviously the actor needs a vivid imagination, and although individuals seem to differ considerably in imagination, there is no doubt that this faculty can be expanded and developed. The beginning actor should read as many plays as he can, consciously trying to imagine each of the characters as completely as possible. Novels and short stories also, which present characters through narration as well as through dialogue, should stimulate his imagination. Representational painting and sculpture, too, provide examples of characters as they appear directly to the eye, not built up through the indirect medium of words.

He should observe real people, including himself, and attempt to see them as characters in a meaningful action, with intelligible motives and objectives which are expressed in their movement and their speech.

The actor should see as many plays in the theatre as he can—if plays are largely unavailable, moving pictures have some of the same values—not in order to imitate the acting of others, but in order to experience characters projected on the stage.

Memory. All of these methods of stimulating the imagination in the field of acting require keen observation and the ability to recall what has been observed. Conscious cultivation of the actor's memory for what he has read and seen in the other arts, and for his own life experience and his observation of others should provide his imagination with a storehouse of material from which it can draw.

THE MEDIUM

No matter how well the actor may be able to imagine the character he must play, this will avail him nothing if he cannot re-create the product of his imagination through the medium of his own body, if he cannot make the character live through his movement, voice, and speech.

Body. The actor must have a flexible body under complete control—a body capable of performing at his will any movement, no matter how large or how small, which may be necessary to project a character in the theatre. The primary aim in training the body for acting should be not obvious beauty or grace, but complete control and economy. Graceful and conventionally beautiful movement should be in the actor's repertoire, and so should deliberately awkward and ugly movement. A sure command of all the muscles, including the muscles of the face, and the ability to use them without strain should be the actor's goal.

Fencing, dancing, gymnastics, and most athletic games develop such command over the larger muscles. The athlete has a head start over the unathletic in the field of acting. However, control established in athletics is useless unless it is adapted from the conventionalized patterns of sports and gymnastics to the realistic requirements of pantomime. The dance, since it is concerned with expression, although in a much more abstract field than acting, is likely to be better training for the actor than fencing or gymnastics. But the beginning actor will work particularly on exercises in pantomime, attempting to express through posture and movement alone different emotions, ages, temperaments, mentalities, occupations, and social levels. Still more specific exercises, in which the actor aims to express through pantomime only particular characters from life or from plays, will bring him close to the actual problem of bodily expression in play production.

Care should be taken that in such exercises movement is not

Alfred J. Balcombe

The actor needs a flexible body as shown by the High Priest in Sartre's *The Flies*, Dramatic Workshop of the New School, New York. Erwin Piscator, director.

used *in place of speech*. Pantomime of this kind has a whole set of special conventions, which are out of place in acting as it is generally understood.

Voice. Just as the actor needs a flexible and controllable body, he needs a flexible and controllable voice capable of fulfilling any demand a role may make upon it. Vocal sound, like any other sound, has four variables: duration, volume, pitch, and quality. The actor needs as wide a range as possible in each of these variables of voice and complete control of them.

Since singing and speaking are similar, exercises of the type used by singers may help the actor to increase his speaking range and improve his control of his voice. However, proficiency in singing does not necessarily carry over into speaking. Most exercises for the singer are designed to improve the quality of voice, to increase the richness and fullness of tone in a wide range of pitch. The actor also should be able to command richness and fullness of tone in a wide range of pitch, and these exercises may help him achieve this, but in addition he should command qualities of voice which are hard or constricted or nasal. The technique of the more conventional art of singing must be adapted to the needs of the more realistic art of acting.

Exercises based upon observation of the voices of real people should help increase the actor's vocal repertory. The reading aloud of poetry, particularly narrative and dramatic poetry, with special attention to vocal expression of emotion may also be useful in this respect. And the whole of dramatic literature provides material for practice in vocal expression especially adapted to the theatre.

Range and control, rather than beauty, as the word is usually understood, should be the actor's aim.

Speech. The actor is concerned with voice primarily as it manifests itself in speech. Consequently, he should be able to form correctly all the common sounds of American speech, and he should have enough control over his articulators so that when necessary he can learn quickly to use the less common sounds, not only of American speech, but also of other languages.

There was a time when the actor had to know *stage speech,* a modification of South British speech once in general use on our stage. This type of speech is appropriate to some plays, to seventeenth- and eighteenth-century English comedy, to Oscar Wilde and Noel Coward, and so it should be in the versatile actor's speech repertory.

However, *stage speech* has no place in most contemporary drama, which presents largely characters with a wide variety of background, education, and economic level. In order to be able to suggest the Brooklyn taxi driver, the London clerk, the Kentucky mountaineer, and the Texas ranch hand, the actor requires command over a much greater number of speech sounds. And if in addition he is to use individual modifications of speech as part of his characterization in particular roles—modifications which express temperament—then his speech repertory must be wide indeed.

Relaxation. Movement and speech are physical activities dependent on the functioning of nerves and muscles. If they are to be performed with full effectiveness, the actor must be free from unnecessary tensions which interfere with the proper functioning of his body. No matter how well his body functions under other circumstances, his physical gifts will be useless if, when he steps on the stage to move and speak as a character in a play, nervous tensions constrict his limbs and muffle his voice. He must learn to relax.

There are, of course, different degrees and kinds of relaxation. The most complete relaxation comes in sleep, and conscious states close to sleep are characterized by the relaxation of most muscle tensions. Of course, such complete relaxation is not desirable in acting.

Any physical activity performed effectively—throwing a ball, jumping, swimming—is performed without strain. This does not mean that it is performed without effort, but without *unnecessary* effort. Acting is a physical activity also, and to be done effectively must be done without strain, without unnecessary muscle tensions.

Self-consciousness produces such unnecessary muscle tensions, but these should disappear with experience in rehearsal and performance. Unnecessary muscle tensions may arise too from trying too hard. Trying too hard in golf or tennis produces an erratic swing. In acting it produces stiff, awkward, uncontrolled movements, and unexpected vocal effects which are almost sure to be bad. Like hitting a golf ball, kicking a football, or throwing a baseball, acting requires for best results a relaxation of the muscles not actually needed for the performance of the action, and a tonicity, a readiness to respond, in those muscles which *are* needed.

Most people are unduly tense only when they try to perform an unfamiliar physical activity which requires a high degree of muscular control. Acting for the beginner is such an activity. Practice and experience in acting will go far to banish the undesirable tension. However, some actors and most teachers of acting advise exercise in relaxation and the development of a technique of conscious relaxation.

Concentration as shown in Dan James' *Winter Soldiers*, Dramatic Workshop of the New School, New York. Erwin Piscator, director.

Concentration. If the actor must be able to relax properly, it is equally important that he be able to concentrate correctly and completely. Indeed, bad muscle tensions may be due in part to improper concentration. The actor who tries too hard is probably concentrating on producing an effect instead of concentrating on himself as the character in the play.

Almost everyone who has written on acting has said or implied that throughout his time on the stage the actor must imagine that he is the character he is playing and that he is in the situations of the play. In order to *act* the character he must actively imagine that he *is* the character. It is not enough for him to have done this in rehearsal, nor for him to do it from time to time while he is on the stage; he must do it every minute he is before the audience.

Any relaxation of his attention in this respect produces undesirable results. The apparently unaccountable lapses of memory which most actors experience occasionally are due to such relaxation of attention. Secure in the knowledge that he knows his lines and business perfectly, the actor's mind wanders to other matters. He ceases to concentrate on himself as the character in the action of the play. For a time all goes smoothly, but suddenly he realizes that his cue has been spoken and that he hasn't the slightest idea what his next line is.

Such lapses, fortunately, are infrequent, but they are a symptom of a much more serious weakness. If the actor, relying on a pattern of speech and movement thoroughly learned, relaxes his attention to the play, he may continue to move and speak without obvious lapses, but the life will have gone out of his performance. It will have lost a large part of its expressiveness. To the critical observer, the learned and automatic character of his speech and movement will have become apparent.

No matter how well lines are learned, they will not be uttered expressively unless they are informed with content by an imagination functioning *at the time of utterance*. Movement, too, loses its expressiveness if it is performed merely through muscular memory and not in response to the inner stimulus provided by an actively functioning imagination.

Such concentration is not easy. It requires effort and it requires constant vigilance.

Energy. Some actors project better than others. They somehow seem to get across the footlights in a way that others do not. When such an actor enters, the audience sits up and takes notice. It does not matter much what he does, his mere presence seems to inject life into the production; he makes the scene "stand up." In the professional theatre such actors are likely to be stars, and one might suppose that their superior projection is due to superior artistry. However, actors with this quality of projection are found in the nonprofessional theatre also. They may make appalling mistakes in characterization and commit all kinds of technical blunders, but they are never dull and uninteresting. This quality has sometimes been laid to "personality" or "magnetism."

The writer is inclined to think that the source of this power of projection is sheer energy. The fact is, acting is work. These actors who hold our attention so strongly do what they have to do on the stage with energy, to the hilt. Even if they are expressing the lack of energy, indolence, feebleness, apathy, they express it energetically, with their whole being.

Relaxation and concentration will help to insure that the actor's energy is made the most of, that it is expended economically, but there is no substitute for energy itself.

GENERAL CULTURE

In addition to a lively imagination and a store of experience to feed it, a flexible body and voice capable of energetic expression, the actor needs knowledge of the art of the theatre as this can be gained from a study of books and pictures. The written drama, its theory and criticism, aesthetic theory as it is applied to play production, theatre architecture, scenery, costuming, lighting, and makeup should be his special field of study.

However he should not neglect fields of knowledge less closely related to acting. Play production is an artistic interpretation of life, so that no field of human knowledge can be wholly alien to the art of acting. The more the actor knows about history, philosophy, science, and the arts, the greater his chance of being a creative artist.

Questions

1. Cite instances of necessary pretending in life.
2. What is the actor's medium?
3. How does the actor's task differ from that of the painter?
4. How can the actor develop or stimulate his imagination?
5. What should be the aim of developing the body for acting?
6. Why is the dance better training for acting than is gymnastics?
7. What should be the aim of developing the voice for acting?
8. What should be the aim of developing speech for acting?

9. What is *stage speech?* In what kinds of plays is it suitable?
10. Describe the kind of relaxation necessary in acting.
11. What studies will be particularly useful to the actor?
12. Why should the actor acquire, in addition to specific skills, a general culture?

Exercises

1. Write a careful description of a character in a novel or short story. Try moving and speaking as you think the character would move and speak.
2. Observe carefully a character in a painting. Try moving and speaking as you think the character would move and speak.
3. Observe carefully the movement and speech of an actual person. Do a brief imitation of the person.
4. Invent and perform a brief pantomime expressing (*a*) a particular age, (*b*) a particular emotion, (*c*) a particular occupation, and (*d*) a particular type of personality or temperament.
5. Recall yourself as definitely as possible in some past situation. Try to re-create the recollection in movement and speech.
6. Read aloud a dramatic monologue, using your voice and speech to express the character of the speaker.
7. Read a brief speech (half a dozen or so sentences) in two different varieties of American speech.
8. Read the same speech in *stage speech.*

Bibliography

Theory

Albright, H. D., *Working Up A Part,* Boston: Houghton Mifflin Company, 1947.

Anderson, Virgil A., *Training the Speaking Voice,* New York: Oxford University Press, 1942.

Boleslavski, Richard, *Acting: The First Six Lessons,* New York: Theatre Arts, Inc., 1933. The need for imagination, observation, and concentration presented in the form of literary dialogues.

Dolman, John, Jr., *The Art of Acting,* New York: Harper & Brothers, 1949. Emphasis on external technique.

Lees, C. Lowell, *A Primer of Acting,* New York: Prentice-Hall, Inc., 1940.

Rosenstein, Sophie; Larrae A. Haydon; and Wilbur Sparrow, *Modern Acting: A Manual,* New York: Samuel French, 1936. Exercises in observation, relaxation, concentration.

Selden, Samuel, *First Steps in Acting*, New York: D. Appleton-Century-Crofts, Inc., 1947.

Also Gassner's *Producing the Play*, for which see Bibliography to Chapter 3.

Material

In the above books, Albright and Selden reprint scenes from plays and other practice material.

For dramatic monologues look in the writings of Cornelia Otis Skinner, Dorothy Parker, Ring Lardner, John O'Hara, and Robert Browning. Most of those printed in collections labeled "dramatic monologues" are so poor as not to be worth working on. Collections of selections for oral interpretation usually contain some good dramatic monologues.

CHAPTER 17.

FOUNDATIONS OF ACTING: THE PLAY AND THE ROLE

The Play

Since the actor is an interpretative artist, his first concern is with the written play, the foundation on which his performance must be built. The assumption of this book is that the aim of the production is to realize the written play in the theatre as fully and as truthfully as possible. But even if the actor uses the play only as an excuse for some independent creation of his own, he must know what kind of a springboard he has chosen. By careful reading and analysis—if necessary with the help of reviews and criticisms—the actor should seek to understand fully the playwright's aim. He will ask: What does this play mean? Why was it written? What effect was it intended to have upon an audience? And in what style has the playwright chosen to express what he thinks and feels about life? What is the dominant mood? And what theatrical form has the playwright imagined for his play? How did he expect it to be presented in the theatre? What is the structure of the play? And what is its rhythm?

When the actor has answered these questions satisfactorily, he is ready to analyze his own role, to discover what its place should be in the production as a whole.

IDEA

Idea, as such, is in many plays not strongly evident. Many tragedies express not an idea which can be adequately stated in a sentence, but a *feeling* about the essential value of life and the greatness of the human spirit. Many comedies express only the idea that men and women behave foolishly. Melodrama may have no idea but to harrow an audience, farce no idea but to make an audience laugh.

On the other hand, tragedy may be informed with a specific

342

Realistic acting is shown by Manders and Mrs. Alving in *Ghosts*, University of Chicago Theatre, staged by Caroline Rose and Christian Rohlfing. George Blair, supervising director.

idea. Maxwell Anderson's *Winterset* seems to have been designed to show that the desire for revenge is sterile and destructive. Comedy and farce frequently ridicule particular follies, and melodrama is often used to focus attention on specific social injustice. Moreover, in a large number of modern plays idea and ideas are of major importance; for example, Ibsen's *Ghosts*, Shaw's *Man and Superman*, Gorki's *The Lower Depths*, and Howard's *Yellow Jack*. The idea and ideas must be projected, or the play, no matter how entertaining it may be or how strongly it may hold the audience, fails of its purpose.

With the idea, aim, or purpose of the play firmly in mind, the actor should consider the means by which the playwright has chosen to express it.

STYLE

We have seen in our analysis of the written play, that plays vary considerably in the style with which they treat the materials drawn from life, and that it is possible to distinguish three styles different enough to warrant separate analysis: realism, abstraction, and fantasy. These different styles of writing call for different styles of acting.

Realism. Realistic acting is usually the easiest style for the actor today because he is most familiar with this style in the written play and on the stage. He must express the meaning and achieve the purpose of the play by creating the illusion that he is a real person involved in lifelike situations and actions taking place under conditions which give an effect of ordinary life. He will draw the material for his creation from his observation of life, selecting and fitting to his particular role the experience he has gained either directly or from realistic literature, the social sciences, and psychology. He must take care that all of his movement and all of his speech has the stamp of surface reality, but he must also be sure that it fits the requirements of the particular play and of the particular character. One of the major pitfalls of the realistic style in all arts is the temptation to include details just because they are lifelike. They must be lifelike, but they must be more than that. They must be necessary to express the meaning of the play.

The second major danger in realistic acting is the tendency to *underproject*. It makes no difference how lifelike his acting is, if it is not projected to the audience. The actor must be seen, and he must be heard and understood.

Abstract acting is used for satirical comedy. Papa Peachum brings Tiger Brown some advice about law and order in *Three-Penny Opera*, Illini Theatre Guild, University of Illinois. Charles Shattuck, director.

Abstraction. Just as the writer of abstract drama selects, and rearranges to a much greater degree than the writer of realistic drama, the actor too must select and rearrange to a much greater degree. He may find that his direct experience of life does not provide the material he needs and that he must look to abstraction in other arts—literature, the dance, sculpture, and painting for the kind of experience which will help him create the characters of Sophocles, of Shakespeare, or of Saroyan. These playwrights are less interested in creating an illusion of life than they are in expressing their interpretation of life, and although their characters are not obvious distortions of characters to be found in real life, they are presented so much more clearly that lifelikeness or surface resemblance is no longer of primary importance. In the Broadway production of *The Beautiful People,* Owen Webster, the fourteen-year-old boy, was played by Eugene Loring, a dancer. Loring did not look fourteen years old, but he gave a performance which, in the movement particularly, expressed a kind of essence of fourteen-year-old boy. Incidentally, it made the rest of the acting seem inept or stereotyped.

The nature of the selection and rearrangement will differ greatly from play to play. Saroyan bears no outward resemblance to Shakespeare. A study of the particular play with the realization that resemblance to ordinary life is no longer a major aim should help the actor to find appropriate patterns of speech and movement.

Fantasy. If the characters of abstract drama are somewhat larger and clearer than life, the characters of fantastic drama are obviously extreme exaggerations or distortions of life. The characters of abstract drama might be accepted as lifelike by the unthinking, but the characters of fantasy will never be so mistaken. The dialogue is far removed from the speech of ordinary life, and it is inconceivable that these obviously imaginary creations should move like ordinary mortals.

Observation of ordinary life may provide the actor some material useful in the acting of fantasy, but he is more likely to find help in the play itself. The playwright may have given hints in the stage directions, but if not, the actor must find them in the meaning of the play as a whole—in the mood, the action, the language, the motive and action of the character, and in the rhythm. Clues to the patterns of speech and movement necessary to the acting in *From Morn to Midnight* may be found in the violence and nervousness of the action and in the staccato rhythm of the dialogue, to the acting of *Alice in Wonderland* in the topsy-turvydom which is Lewis Carroll's principal satirical device. The illustration from *Peer Gynt* on page 40 affords an example of fantastic acting.

If the actor feels the need for assistance outside the play and his own imagination, he is most likely to find it in fantasy in other arts: painting, sculpture, and music.

THEATRICAL FORM

Representation. Actors today are accustomed to representational drama and particularly to representational production, and the representational form of acting presents only familiar problems. Since its aim is to express by means of the creation of an illusion of life going on independent of theatre and audience, the actor must pretend to be unaware of the presence of the audience and must play *in* whatever setting has been provided for him. He must seem to *be* the character in the play and an integral part of the life of the play. The chief danger, particularly in the representational acting of realistic plays, is that he may actually ignore the audience, becoming so completely a part of the life of the play that he fails to project his speech and his movement.

Presentation. Presentational plays present a real problem. There are those who say there is no such thing as presentational acting. It is true that presentational acting is hardly ever seen today in the legitimate theatre, but it flourishes on the musical-comedy stage. When a comedian like Bobby Clark appears in *The Would-Be Gentleman,* the character of presentational acting becomes clear. Representational acting is concentrated on the stage or playing space; presentational acting takes the audience into the circle of the play. It does not pretend that the actor is a real person in a real world separate from the audience. It is frankly acting—acting which reaches out and takes the audience into its confidence. Instead of allowing the audience to eavesdrop on the play, presentational acting takes the play to the audience.

This attitude on the part of the actor inevitably affects the whole of his acting, although the effect is most obvious in his handling of so-called *soliloquies* and *asides.* In presentational acting, these are not mumbled in an attempt to make them sound like thinking aloud, nor are they spoken out over the heads of the audience as in poor public speaking, but they are delivered directly to the audience as a good public speaker addresses his audience.

Because presentational acting is so seldom seen on our legitimate stage, the actor will be forced to study it where it still exists, in musical comedy, vaudeville, and the circus. Much of it, of course, is bad, stereotyped, and dull; its techniques must be modified, particularly for serious drama, but the essential form is there.

Much of the older presentational drama is written in verse. Greek tragedy is usually translated in verse, and so are the choral odes of Greek comedy. Shakespeare's tragedies and parts of his comedies are largely in blank verse. Molière's verse plays have been variously translated.

The reading of dialogue written in verse form presents a particular problem to the modern actor, who is accustomed not merely to prose dialogue but to prose dialogue which in language and sentence structure is very close to the dialogue of life. Even the most irregular of blank verse departs very far from the language and sentence structure of most speech in life.

The modern actor, required to use this unfamiliar form of dialogue, is likely to fall into one of two errors. He will deliver the lines as if they contained nothing but sonorous sound; he will sing or rant. Such delivery is usually unintelligible and expressive of nothing except a generalized state of emotion, perhaps only the actor's own sense of strain. This style, we are led to believe, was characteristic of much acting in the eighteenth and nineteenth centuries. Or, in an effort to avoid rant, he may go to the opposite extreme and make the verse sound like prose. This style is somewhat more bearable because it does convey some meaning, but it fails entirely to convey the effect intended by the playwright.

The meaning of any good verse is inseparable from the verse structure: the length of line, the complicated pattern of stress, the arrangement of the sounds, and the rhyme, if it is rhymed. Any delivery which ignores the verse structure inevitably presents only a ghost of the playwright's meaning.

Dramatic dialogue in verse should be read as dramatic dialogue in prose should be read, for its full meaning, but the actor should be guided in his decision as to the meaning of a speech by the verse form in which it is cast. This does not mean that the verse should be scanned, read as a pattern of strong and weak syllables. Scansion is only a rough generalization, indicating to the student of metrics the number of relatively weak syllables and the number of relatively strong syllables to the line. Actually, any line of verse contains many more degrees of emphasis than scansion indicates. In a regular iambic line of ten syllables, five strong and five weak, there will probably be five different degrees of strength among the strong syllables and as many more among the weak syllables. Vocal expression of this far more complex pattern is necessary if the meaning is to be conveyed. A word placed at the end of a line of verse, almost regardless of its place in the sentence, acquires more prominence, and if rhymed it is more prominent still. These departures from the normal prose patterns are not arbitrary or for puposes of decoration, but are essential to the expression of the thought and feeling.

The inexperienced actor had better attack verse dialogue from the point of view of meaning, and then correct his analysis by the formal structure of the verse. The actor more experienced in the speaking of verse may be able to work directly from the verse form, being sure, however, that he does not obscure the sentence structure. Dramatic verse should sound like verse, but it should be just as full of meaning and as highly communicative as the best prose dialogue.

Some presentational plays have passages which are markedly different in other ways from the realistic dialogue to which we are all accustomed. In Shakespeare's earlier plays there are passages of dialogue which have the character of formal debate. Richard persuades Lady Anne to marry him by sheer argument (*Richard III*, Act I, scene ii) in a scene which seems as artificial as recitative in opera; but the argument is impassioned and it is dramatic, for it does not stand still. The actor must breathe life into this (to our ears) artificial dialogue by realizing the strong emotions of the characters and expressing the drive and dramatic progress of the scene. *Wings Over Europe* is one of the few modern plays which depends heavily upon impassioned argument, although the dialogue is much less obviously artificial.

Greek drama contains choral odes, passages which may be chanted or sung and are clearly lyric in character like the arias of opera. Elizabethan drama contains no such formal lyric passages, but it does use language to build up emotional tension in a way modern drama seldom does. We find, particularly in the

Tragic acting is shown by Tiresias and Oedipus in *Oedipus Rex* as produced by the Old Vic Company of London.

earlier Elizabethan plays, long speeches which are dramatic in the sense that a stirring public speech is dramatic. Lear's "Blow winds and crack your cheeks!" and Macbeth's "Tomorrow, and tomorrow, and tomorrow," are examples from Shakespeare's mature playwriting. These speeches do not advance the action; they give powerful expression to deep emotion. In order to speak them well, the actor must be able to grasp the emotion imaginatively and possess unusual range and control of voice.

Lyric in lighter moods are Lorenzo's "How sweet the moonlight sleeps upon this bank" and Mercutio's Queen Mab speech. These speeches evoke a mood, and in their play of fancy they have movement, though movement of a kind seldom found in our theatre. The actor must learn to appreciate and to express the dramatic values in these unfamiliar forms.

MOOD

All drama is expression through emotion. Even the advocates of epic drama and theatre, who would like to banish emotion from the theatre that the light of truth may shine there unobscured, burn with the *passion* to enlighten. And, as we have seen, plays differ greatly in their emotional content. What does this mean for the actor?

Tragedy. Tragedy is likely to require of the actor great range and control of the voice, boldness and strength in movement, and unusual poise and stillness in repose. Simplicity and grandeur are terms frequently used to describe good tragic acting. These qualities are necessary to express the profound emotions of tragedy.

Big emotional scenes must be worked up to gradually and played with apparent abandon but with actual restraint. Controlled power is needed for the acting of the major tragic roles. The suggestive method of modern realistic acting is useless in the older tragedies. This was apparent in Walter Huston's performance as Othello. In the earlier scenes he appeared adequate, but when he reached the latter part of the play he seemed to make no effort to express the tremendous emotions of the character. His acting appeared to be merely an intelligent and polite reading of the lines.

Serious drama. Most serious plays do not make such heavy demands upon the actor as does tragedy. The emotions are likely to be less deep and less powerful. However, scenes of strong emotion must be carefully built up, and restraint must be exercised in their culmination if the effect is not to be comic or grotesque. Characterization is fundamental. The actor must be certain that everything he does and says is firmly grounded in the character he is playing.

Melodrama. A fully rounded characterization is not essential to melodrama. The actor, therefore, should present a character adequate for the purposes of the plot and concentrate on the action with the purpose of wringing from *it* the maximum of suspense, surprise, and shock. Melodrama requires an expression of nervous energy rather than of deep emotion, and the big emotional scenes are ordinarily not built up to, as in serious drama and in tragedy, but are the result of surprise twists in the plot.

If there are scenes of farce comedy interspersed between scenes of suspense and violent serious action, the actors will need to take care that the changes in mood are made sharply. After a scene of comic relief, the audience is likely to continue to laugh, and a special effort by the actors may be needed to re-establish the serious mood quickly and firmly.

Comedy. It is difficult to generalize about the acting of comedy because comedies differ greatly in their attitude toward the faults, weaknesses, and vices of human beings. One can say that all comedy is rooted in character, and that good comic acting presents a strong characterization. The pattern of movement and speech should spring inevitably out of the character. There should be no irrelevant gagging.

In what has been called "pure" comedy the characters are likely to be close to those of real life, but they accentuate certain follies and weaknesses which bring minor calamities upon themselves. The acting requires a good deal of the effect of a high-spirited romp, and the suffering of the characters must be presented in the spirit of play if it is to arouse laughter and so prove pleasurable rather than painful.

In humorous comedy there is a greater balance between the follies and the good qualities of the character, so that he arouses not only laughter but a warm feeling of sympathy.

In satirical comedy, on the other hand, the sympathetic characteristics are entirely omitted and the faults so greatly exaggerated that there is danger that the character will no longer

Comic acting is shown in *Androcles and the Lion* as produced by the American Repertory Theatre.

arouse laughter. This will almost surely be true unless the exaggeration of the playwright finds a counterpart in the acting. Satirical comedy such as Jonson's *Volpone* requires grotesque acting.

All comedy depends very largely on incongruity, on an implied or stated contrast between what a man is and what he should be, or between what he is and what he thinks himself to be. The actor must discover the incongruity or incongruities established by the character he is to play, and he must make these the guide to his speech and action.

The carefully built up effect of inevitability is characteristic of tragedy, but surprise, the unexpected, is characteristic of comedy. Sometimes the surprise is for the audience, sometimes only for the character. The actor should be strongly aware of the series of shocks and surprises which are the result of the character's faults and weaknesses in order to convey the effect of blindness which leads to them and the effect of pained surprise which is their end product. The audience is often permitted to anticipate the character's disillusionment, but the character must never appear to do so.

Some comedies, such as those of Congreve and Wilde, are characterized by verbal wit. Many of the lines are displays of the comic spirit on the plane of language. They require of the actor unusual clarity of utterance and considerable lightness and dexterity in the use of the voice. If the witty lines can be given some sort of roots in the character of the speaker and in the situation and action of the play, they will be funnier than if they are treated as something existing independently.

The actor of comedy must learn how to produce and to handle audience laughter. Incongruities of movement and speech growing out of incongruities in character are the main means of arousing laughter. However, there are some technical devices which, if they are used properly, not for themselves, but because they express the character and the situation, are useful in building up or creating laughter. Contradiction between the line and the accompanying action, contradiction between the words and the way they are uttered will produce laughter. In line-reading, frequently, the comic point is driven home with a single word. If that word is given extra emphasis (by one or more of the methods described in Chapter 20) the line is more likely to get a laugh.

Sometimes the actor will have a speech of several lines each one of which is mildly funny. If he permits the audience to laugh at each one, the effect will not be nearly so satisfactory as if he consciously builds the speech to the end, when the accumulated amusement will explode in a *roar* of laughter. Something of the same technique is useful in passages of fast-moving dialogue, such as scenes of argument or insult. The actor should "top" the preceding line; that is, by some kind of vocal change he should appear to build on what has gone immediately before, so that the comic tension is increased until the scene reaches its peak.

When he has inspired laughter, the actor must handle it properly. Because the audience must be allowed to laugh, the actor must delay delivering his next line; but he must continue to act with his body so that the play does not stop and so that when the laughter begins to die out he can speak the next line strongly and firmly. If he "rides over the laughs," the audience will soon stop laughing, because it wants to hear what he says.

Farce. In farce, as in melodrama, character is superficial and the emphasis is on plot or action. Farce depends for its laughs on more or less contrived surprises, rather than on the disclosure

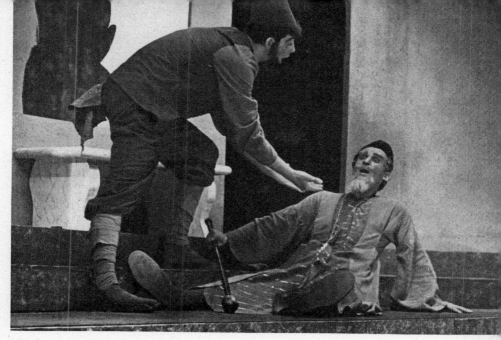

Here is seen energy in farce. Lucas has floored Geronte in *The Doctor In Spite of Himself,* Brooklyn College Varsity Players. Barnard Hewitt, director.

of more and more ridiculous difficulties growing out of a consistent character. The actor should make use of what comic characteristics the playwright has given to his role to give a semblance of logic to his actions, but he should concentrate on re-acting to the difficulties and dilemmas into which the playwright has plunged the character. He will need to be capable of quick changes in voice and speech, and of equally quick changes in the tempo and character of his movement.

Farce frequently requires the expenditure of a great deal of energy in speech and movement. *You Can't Take It with You* depends very largely for its effect upon the frenzied activity of a crew of zany characters, each pursuing his own hobby with the utmost seriousness and the greatest concentration.

High spirits, mentioned above in connection with the acting of comedy, are essential to farce also. Slapstick action with the physical suffering characteristic of farce will be highly unpleasant if it is not presented in the spirit of play.

The techniques of creating and handling audience laughter described under *"Comedy"* are equally useful in the acting of farce.

PLAY STRUCTURE

Play structure should be as much the concern of the actor as it is of the playwright. Through its structure, the play holds the attention of the audience and conveys its meaning. Unless the actor understands how the play is put together, he cannot be sure of contributing his share to the realization of the play in production.

Logical structure. The actor should recognize the plot development through cause and effect in the logically constructed play. He should be aware of the importance of the opening exposition—whether it is in the form of direct address, dialogue, or action—in order that he may drive home each element in the initial situation. He can do this to an extent through his attitudes and actions, but he should look for key words in the lines —the words which convey indispensable information. The particular words will vary from play to play, but names are always important. The audience wants to get the characters straight. Particular emphasis should be given to words which reveal the character's relation to other characters, to the environment, to the situation, and words which indicate the conditions out of which the play's action will develop. The opening exposition is the foundation of the logically constructed play. If it is not laid down solidly, the structure erected on it will be rickety.

The actor should be aware also of the sequence of situation-crisis-action as the play progresses to its major crisis and denouement. He should note particularly the words, phrases, clauses, and sentences that contribute to or express this progress. He must be sure that he gives them their full value when he speaks them. He should analyze the play into scenes on the basis of his entrances and exits and discover the place and function of each scene in the logical development of the plot. On each entrance, he should be strongly aware of *why* the character enters. Then he should consciously build the scene to its peak and exit with just as strong a purpose as motivated his entrance. If the actor makes a good entrance, one which brings him immediately to the attention of the audience, with the new direction or fresh impetus which the character is intended to give to the play, the scene will be off to a good start. If he makes a good emphatic exit, one which allows him to act until he is near the place of exit, deliver his last line with energy, and get promptly off, the scene has been brought to a good conclusion.

If, in addition, the actor is strongly aware of the place of each scene in the development of the action of the play as a whole and if he concentrates strongly on the main line of the action, he will be able to do his part properly in making the play stand up on the stage.

There is a natural tendency for inexperienced actors to reverse the climactic order which is the backbone of the logically constructed play: to start the play strongly and become less effective as the play goes on, to start each scene strongly and let it taper off. Through concentration on the steps by which each scene, each act, and the entire play are built up, the actor should combat this tendency.

On the other hand, an actor is sometimes carried away by an emotional scene early in the play, and gives it all he has, only to discover that there is still another act or so to go and he is out of ammunition. He has hit his peak too early, and the balance of his part, if not of the whole play, has been destroyed. Again a strong awareness of the structure of the play as a whole will save him from such errors.

Episodic structure. Without the line of a logically constructed plot to follow, the actor must seek to understand the play as a whole and to see how every episode in which he appears contributes to the expression of the play's meaning. He should ask: Is the episode like the one it follows in mood, in action, in lines, in tempo, and in intensity? Or is it different? Does it build through repetition or through contrast? And how can the role which I am playing contribute to the particular value of the episode as determined by its place in the play as a whole?

Rhythm. The actor's analysis of the play structure, his visualization of the action, and his study of the dialogue should give him a feeling for the rhythm of the play as a whole, for the rhythm of the individual scene, and finally for the rhythm of his own role. His chief concern, of course, is with the one character he is to play, but in order to be sure that this character is really the character of the play and not some interesting but irrelevant creation of his own, he must at every point be aware of the character's place in the entire pattern, of its relation to the other characters, and of its value in the play as a whole.

The Role

As the actor reads and rereads the play with more and more attention to the character he is to portray, an imagined picture of the character will begin to form in his mind. This picture will move and speak, and the actor will begin to move and speak in imitation of the mental picture. Or the process may be even more direct: without the intervention of any clear mental picture, study of the play with special attention to one character will cause the actor to begin to move and speak like that character. This embodiment will be fragmentary at first, but it will gradually be filled out and completed through study and rehearsal.

MOTIVATION

One method of speeding up the process of imagination and embodiment is to analyze the part in terms of motivation. In each scene, what does the character want? The answer should be in terms of action: he wants to win the hand of the heroine, to protect his wife, to be admired by his children, to rest, to keep his job, to live. The correct answers will come by considering not only the character and the particular scene but also the action, mood, and meaning of the play as a whole.

LIFE

If the play alone fails to give the actor a full understanding of the character, he may find it helpful to relate consciously the character or situation of the play to something in his own life experience, to recall a similar situation from his own life. Or if the play is not a modern play, he may find help in the histories and biographies of the period. Material from these sources can seldom be more than a stimulus; it cannot be used unchanged.

ART

Even more helpful, especially in abstract and fantastic plays, may be the expression of similar ideas and emotions in other arts—in literature, painting, sculpture, and even in music.

Through other artistic media the actor may be helped to understanding and sometimes to inspiration.

EMOTION

Is it necessary for the actor to experience the emotion of his part? This question has always concerned actors and writers on the art of acting, but it has not been answered satisfactorily and probably never will be. The Stanislavski system for actors consciously cultivates sense impressions, memory of emotions, and imagination with the avowed purpose of helping the actor to feel the emotions of his part completely in every performance.

On the other hand, some actors and directors after sifting experience and testimony have concluded that the actor not only does not feel, but cannot feel, the emotions of his part for more than a few moments at a time, and these moments usually in rehearsal.

Yet everyone who has acted knows that emotion of some kind is necessary to acting; without it the performance will be lifeless. It has been suggested that this necessary emotion is the general excitement produced by the actor's work. When this excitement is present, the actor is alert; his attention is fully concentrated on the play, and his body and voice respond easily to the demands made upon them. When it is absent, the actor is sluggish; his attention wanders, and his body and voice fail to respond adequately.

Leo Stein, in his *A-B-C of Aesthetics,* has advanced the theory that distinct emotions do not exist separate from their bodily expression; that is, one can feel *general* emotion while sitting or standing still, but one cannot feel such *specific* emotions as joy, sorrow, and anger without giving expression to them in movement and speech. If this theory is true, it explains further why the actor needs the excitement of performance to give vitality to his work. The generalized *emotion* aroused by the conditions of performance, by the stage, the scenery, the lights, the costumes, and above all by the audience, is poured into the expressive pattern of movement and speech developed during rehearsals, and is thus transformed into the specific *feelings* of the part, giving to the pattern of expression a content which makes it ring true.

The chief difficulty with accepting the theory that the actor must feel the specific emotions of his part, such as hate, love, or fear, arises from the assumption that these imagined emotions are of the same intensity as the emotions of real life. The effects of strong emotions in life are well known; they destroy conscious control of the body. Rage may render one speechless or make one's voice crack in a ridiculous manner. Terror may induce flight or cause one to faint. Horror may induce nausea. Grief may produce uncontrollable sobs and tears that make speech unintelligible. Such effects are no good on the stage; the actor must have absolute control of himself. If the actor feels, he must keep the expression of his emotions within the bounds of art.

However, it is quite possible that imagined emotions are less intense than real emotions although similar to them in quality. If this is true, we have another possible explanation of the paradox of acting: emotions are necessary, but they are imagined rather than real and consequently lacking in the effects which prevent the actor from controlling his speech and movement.

Fortunately, the question of emotion does not need to be answered categorically one way or the other. Everyone agrees that the actor must in performance *imagine* himself to *be* the character he is acting in the situations of the play, but that at the same time he must not forget that he is an actor acting a part for an audience. Whether or not he experiences the emotions of the character fully, to some degree, from time to time, or not at all does not matter as long as he makes the character live for the audience. Whether the Stanislavski method succeeds in creating real emotion, imagined emotion, a generalized excitement, or no emotion at all, it remains useful, for it reduces to a system the processes which the actor must use unconsciously if not consciously. The actor must observe clearly and accurately life and art as he perceives them through his senses, storing these impressions in his memory. When he sets out to study a play, it will stimulate him to draw from his memory impressions that his imagination can reshape into patterns expressive of his role.

IMPERSONATION

The actor seeks to develop a pattern of movement and speech for his own body which will project the character in the play. This means that the actor *impersonates;* he does not play himself. On the other hand, he does not necessarily obliterate himself. He does not really try to deceive the audience into believing that the character and not the actor is living on the stage. Without makeup so elaborate that it is likely to be a hindrance to expression, such deception is really impossible except for the first few minutes. Moreover, it is probably not so satisfying to the audience, which gains an added pleasure from an appreciation of the skill with which the actor projects a character different from himself. Such pleasure is strongest of course when the actor's personality is not concealed. This does not mean that the actor should impose his own traits of movement and speech, or his habitual tricks of acting, upon every character, but rather that the actor should use his command over his own flexible body and voice to suggest or express a character different from himself and from every other character he may have played.

Questions

1. What should the actor know about the play before studying the role he is to play in it?
2. What is the aim of the actor in the realistic play? What are the pitfalls to be avoided in realistic acting?
3. What is the best source of material (outside the play) for the acting of fantasy?
4. What is the actor's relation to the audience in representational acting? In presentational acting?
5. How should verse dialogue be read?
6. What are the vocal and physical requirements for the acting of tragedy?
7. How should big emotional scenes be acted in serious drama?
8. What should be the actor's focus in acting in melodrama?
9. What problem does a scene of comic relief present to the actor?
10. Distinguish between several varieties of comic acting.
11. What does witty dialogue require of the actor?
12. What is meant by "holding the laugh?"
13. What particular requirements does farce make of the actor?
14. Formulate some tips on the handling of exposition.
15. What is meant by a good entrance? A good exit?
16. What are the conflicting theories of emotion in acting?
17. What is Leo Stein's theory of the emotions, and how does it seem to apply to acting?
18. In what sense does the actor impersonate?

Exercises

1. Analyze a one-act play preparatory to studying your part in it.
2. Work out a pattern of voice and movement for a realistic character. For a fantastic character.

3. Play a scene from Molière or from Shakespeare first in the representational form, then in the presentational form.
4. Work up and present a lyric-dramatic speech from Shakespeare, complete with movement.
5. Act a scene from tragedy or serious drama, concentrating on the mood.
6. Do the same for a scene from melodrama, from comedy, from farce.
7. Practice the various means of controlling audience laughter in a scene from comedy or farce.
8. Play a scene concentrating on the motivation of the character.
9. Play a strongly dramatic scene, building carefully and slowly to the crisis.
10. Work up a part in a scene from any good play, applying as much as you can of the material in this chapter.

Bibliography

Theory

Cole, Toby and Helen Krich Chinoy, *Actors On Acting,* New York: Crown Publishers, 1949. Theories, techniques, and practices of the world's great actors told in their own words.

Downs, Harold, ed., *Theatre and Stage,* London: Sir Isaac Pitman Co., 2 vols., 1934. A variety of essays on various aspects and problems of acting, as well as other departments of production.

Gassner, John, *Producing the Play,* New York: The Dryden Press, 1941, Section on the "Actor and Actor-Training."

Nichols, Wallace B., *The Speaking of Poetry,* Boston: Expression Company, 1937.

Stanislavski, Constantin, *Building a Character,* New York: Theatre Arts Books, 1949.

See books by Albright, Dolman, Lees, and Selden listed in bibliography to Chapter 16, and by Leo Stein, mentioned in Chapter 1 bibliography.

Material

Cosgrove, Frances, ed., *Scenes for Student Actors,* New York: Samuel French, 9 vols., 1924–1938.

Lowther, James B., *Dramatic Scenes From Athens To Broadway,* New York: Longmans, Green & Company, 1937.

And anthologies of plays listed in Bibliographies to Chapters 3 and 7.

CHAPTER 18. ~~~~~~~~~~~~~~~

THE CONDITIONS OF ACTING

$\mathcal{T}$he art of acting is not performed alone in the privacy of a studio. It is strongly affected by the special conditions of its performance: by the presence of an audience, by the size and arrangement of the theatre building, and by the other actors. To a lesser degree it is influenced by the lighting, and by the costume and makeup which are usually worn in acting.

The Actor and the Audience

All acting is directed to an audience, whether it appears to be or not. The actor must hold the attention of an audience; he must be continually interesting. He must present to the eyes and ears of the audience a continually changing sequence of visual and auditory stimuli designed to express the character and the play.

MOVEMENT

In movement the actor must achieve a continually changing pattern designed to express the character and through it the play. Monotony must be avoided. A meaningful variety should be the aim.

Variety. Beginning actors frequently move scarcely at all, but remain stiffly planted in one spot for long periods, like lamp-posts. They must relax, and seek motivation for movement in the situation and particularly in the lines. Tension often results, on the other hand, in the unconscious repetition of movements: nodding the head when speaking, shifting the weight from one foot to another, or pump-handle movements of the hands. The actor must find a proper release for his tension in movements carefully designed to express the character as he reacts to a particular situation.

Meaning. *Every movement must be meaningful.* Any lack of control of the body that produces unintentional and unnecessary movements is therefore the foe of expression. Many such movements unrelated to the character and the play may be the result of the tension noted above, but some are likely to spring from the actor's own offstage habits. The actor should not be limited to his own natural walk, for example, but should be able to adapt it to the particular characterization. The same is true of movements of the head, arms, hands, and so on. Straight parts traditionally require ease and unobtrusive grace in movement. The straight character should ordinarily walk easily erect, with legs swinging freely and apparently effortlessly from the hips. He should sit without first ducking his head and shoulders, and he should rise easily to his feet without first heaving forward the whole upper part of his body or pushing himself up with the help of furniture. Such awkwardnesses should appear only when they are required to express old age, illness, weakness, and so on.

Economy. Any lack of economy in movement results in awkwardness which carries connotations of timidity, physical or mental weakness, or uncertainty and is to be avoided unless the character and situation require such expression.

The general rule that the actor should step off first with the foot nearest his destination and gesture with the hand nearest the object of his gesture springs from the need for *economy*. It is uneconomical to side-step from one position to another, to back up (except at the point of a gun), and to move in any but the shortest path from point to point. This means that the actor will ordinarily move in straight lines. However, if furniture or other actors stand in his way, the shortest path will be a flat curve skirting the obstacles. The most economical means of reversing direction while walking is to pivot on the ball of the foot. The pivot is in general use by active people off the stage, but the inexperienced actor is likely to walk painfully around, suggesting that the character is crippled or very old.

Clarity. Each movement of the actor should be necessary to the progress of the play, but if it is to be fully expressive it must be clear. If the actor attempts to do several things at one time, the spectator's attention is diffused or lost. The magician directs audience attention to irrelevant movements in order to conceal the movements vital to the performance of his tricks. The actor's aim is not to conceal but to reveal. Consequently, the rule in movement is *one thing at a time*.

Effect of spontaneity. We are accustomed on the stage to movement which appears spontaneous and unlearned. Learned movement which is executed mechanically from kinaesthetic memory will not have this effect. In order for his learned movement to appear fresh and spontaneous, the actor must think his way around the stage in every performance.

The actor should be aware, too, of the characteristics of movement in life. Ordinarily the eyes lead; that is, they are first focused on the end point of the movement. Then the rest of the body follows in organic sequence: head, shoulders, trunk, and finally legs. Failure in acting to reproduce this natural sequence produces an unnatural effect which may be distracting to the audience.

There are exceptions, of course. When movement is performed unwillingly or uncertainly the eyes often do not lead and the organic sequence is broken up. A small boy ordered out of the room in which he wishes to remain is unlikely to look where he is going. The young man after quarreling with his fiancée, uncertain whether to go or stay, will not look steadily in the direction of his exit. Without proper motivation, walking in one direction and looking in another is very bad, indeed, but properly motivated it will produce awkward and grotesque effects which may be useful, especially in comedy. A character may be so fascinated by something on the stage that in exiting he falls over a piece of furniture or blunders into the side of a door. Similarly, in *The Doctor In Spite of Himself,* Valère, unwilling to beat the famous doctor who is being so unreasonable, may cover his eyes with one hand in order that he may not see the infamous act which he must perform.

Another kind of exception is the movement which is so habitual or so simple that it is ordinarily performed with one's attention completely or almost completely on something else. (This is an exception to the *one thing at a time rule* also.) Thus when one enters one's own room reading an important letter, one may very well hang up one's hat, walk to a chair, and sit down, without once taking one's eyes from the letter. As soon as the secondary action requires more than this very limited attention

—if the chair is not in its usual place, for instance—the eyes are again called on to assist.

When the hand is involved in a movement of the whole body —for example, if one must cross to the door and open it, or move to the table and pick up a letter—the hand anticipates the performance of its part. One does not cross to the door or to the table and then lift the hand to turn the knob or pick up the letter, one starts to raise the hand as one approaches, so that when one is near enough the hand is in position to perform its part of the movement. Failure to reproduce this natural organic sequence produces a mechanical, robot-like effect, which might be utilized on occasion but which is obviously undesirable for most roles.

MOVEMENT AND SPEECH

Nearly always, movement and speech are related in acting. Consequently, the actor must be aware of the nature of this relationship, if he is to use them effectively.

Unity. Ordinarily, when movement and speech occur at about the same time, both spring from the same inner source of thought and feeling and both express the same thing. If one says "No!" with conviction, the body expresses the negative as clearly as the voice, perhaps by a shaking of the head, perhaps by retreating, perhaps by less marked but nonetheless negative movements. Observation of people in life shows that ordinarily the expression in movement slightly precedes or else accompanies the vocal expression with which it is correlated. The body begins to express the negative an instant before, or at the latest simultaneously with the voicing of the "No!"

Reversal of this order, the movement beginning slightly later than the vocal expression, however slight the lapse, will produce an unnatural effect. Hence the general rule: *Move before you speak.*

Effects of disunity. Certain special expressive effects can be achieved by violating this customary unity. Movement which comes just slightly late will suggest the mentally or emotionally abnormal person. More marked separation in time is comic, and extreme separation burlesques acting itself, as when Thisbe says loudly: "Come, blade, my breast imbrue!" And after a good long pause in which nothing happens, she suddenly stabs herself. Indecision and conflict are expressed by a contradiction between speech and movement. Subtle contradictions of this kind can be used in serious drama to create effects of pathos. Crass contradictions can be used for comic effects, as when Bob Hope declares loudly that he is not afraid, while his knees are knocking together or while he is backing away from the source of danger.

Union in dialogue. Movement on a small scale is essential to an effect of spontaneity in dialogue. Except in extremely conventionalized acting, the actor, even though he has memorized his lines and rehearsed them over and over, must deliver them in every performance as if he were uttering them for the first time. In spontaneous conversation between two alert people, one speaks, and at a point somewhat before he has finished, the second grasps the meaning of what is being said. The listener thinks what he will say in reply, gets ready to speak, and when his friend stops, he says what he has been thinking.

If the actor is to create the same effect of spontaneity, he must reproduce the same process. He must listen to what the other actor is saying and *show* that he is listening, he must grasp the meaning of the other's words and *show* that he has grasped it, he must *obviously* seek for words with which to reply, and he must *show* that he is going to speak—all before he utters a word. All these movements are likely to be slight and of brief duration, hardly distinguishable one from the other. If the actor will really put himself imaginatively in the place of the character he is playing, they should come of themselves, but they are essential to *the illusion of the first time*.

If the actor omits this process, the lines he utters will appear memorized and unrelated to what has gone before. If the actor waits until he hears his cue, the last word in the preceding line, and then starts to react as described above, he will appear to be stopping the play in order to act.

VOICE

Although movement and voice frequently express the same thing and are closely connected, voice can be considered separately from movement as a second instrument for holding audience attention and conveying the meaning of the play. The actor's voice must have easily controlled variety in loudness, pitch, rate, and quality if it is to hold audience attention and be adequately expressive. In theory, if the actor has a normally good voice, imagines his character fully, and in performance concentrates completely on himself as the character in the play, his voice as well as his body will display the variety necessary to expression. Nevertheless, the common vocal faults can be combatted objectively to some extent, and are therefore worth noting.

Voice production. Voice is produced by breath forced out of the lungs and through a narrow opening made by the tensed vocal cords in the larynx. Overtones produced by resonation in the enclosed spaces of the larynx, pharynx, mouth, and nose amplify the original voice, which is finally shaped into the sounds of speech by the articulators: the soft palate, tongue, teeth, lower jaw, and lips. Of the variables in voice, *duration* depends upon the amount of breath available and on control of exhalation, *loudness* on the amount of breath forced over the vocal cords and on the number and kind of overtones set up in the resonators, *pitch* on the tension of the vocal cords, and *quality* on the number and kind of overtones.

Volume. Since breath is the motive power of voice, the actor needs an adequate breath supply or capacity. Most people have adequate breath capacity, if not for Lear or Othello, at any rate for the demands of most roles. Many people, however, do not have adequate control over their breath, especially under the conditions of acting. Instead of exhaling slowly and steadily, thus providing a smooth firm support for speech, they exhale jerkily in puffs. The voice is likely to be too loud on the first few words and to trail off until it is inaudible on the last words. It may be useful to the actor to practice maintaining a firm support for his voice through long sentences.

Inadequate volume is more likely to be due to inhibition of vocalization than to inadequate breath capacity. Plenty of air is forced over the vocal cords, but their vibration is inhibited by muscular tensions in the larynx. Such tensions can be set up consciously; if marked, they produce the whisper. General nervousness may set up such tensions without our being aware of them. Some people, either out of timidity or a false notion of good manners, have acquired a voice which is habitually breathy. Before they can be effective as actors, they must learn consciously to relax these inhibiting tensions. Temporary tension arising from the acting situation can usually be dispelled by experience and by conscious relaxation.

Adequate volume will depend not only upon breath control and full vocalization but also upon the production of overtones through the use of the resonators. Volume increased by forcing more breath over the vocal cords requires the expenditure of more energy, but volume may be increased without added effort through fuller resonation. Indeed, fuller resonation is the result not of greater effort but of greater relaxation. The fullest resonance is the result of speaking with the "open throat," with greatest relaxation of the muscles of the throat. It is useful to sing or intone individual sounds in order to get the feeling of full resonance and then to try to carry over the same feeling into speaking. It is sometimes helpful also to try to feel that the voice is flowing out of its own accord, or that the sounds are being made in the front of the mouth instead of in the throat.

The actor should be able to control the volume of his voice through its whole audible range; he should be able to whisper, to speak softly, loudly, or to shout, each with certainty of the result.

Pitch. The actor needs control of about two octaves for adequate vocal variety. Pitch responds best to thought and feeling and is difficult to control directly, yet if the actor's habitual range is not wide enough for the stage, he can do something consciously to widen it. Practice in running a sentence up and down the scale, and a deliberate attempt in speech to lift the peaks of pitch and drop the cellars should help. The tension which acting produces in the inexperienced often temporarily reduces the pitch range. Conscious relaxation and concentration on the play will widen the range again. Very high pitches are expressive of uncontrolled emotion, of hysteria; low pitches express controlled emotion. However, variety is the major requirement.

Quality. The actor needs good, full resonance not only in order that his voice may carry without undue effort but also in order that it may be capable of emotional expression. Other vocal variables enter into emotional expression, but voice quality is the most important. We can tell from the sound of a person's voice, even if we can not understand the words, whether he is sad or happy, serene or angry. The thin, unresonant voice suggests the absence of emotion; full resonance gives the voice warmth and emotional coloring. The harsh voice suggests bad temper. The actor should be able to command as many different qualities of voice as possible: the cold, hard, bad-tempered qualities as well as the warm, soft, good-humored qualities.

Fuller resonance can be cultivated as suggested above in the discussion of resonance as a factor in loudness. A command over various qualities needed for the expression of different characters and different emotions can be cultivated by reading poetry and emotional prose aloud, with every effort to make the sounds express the various feelings. Something can be done also by consciously imitating voice qualities one hears in oneself and others.

Common defects in resonance, besides a relative lack of it, are habitual nasal quality and glottal quality. Nasal quality is caused by the failure of the soft palate to shut off the nasal passages during the utterance of the nonnasal sounds. It is easy to diagnose, because the operation of the soft palate can be observed in a mirror, and it is therefore relatively easy to cure. Glottal quality, which is caused by unnecessary muscle tensions in the throat, must be attacked through sensation. Its cure is complete relaxation of the throat during vocalization.

Articulation. The formation of voice into the sounds of connected speech is the easiest phase of voice to modify because the articulators are fairly easy to see and feel in operation. Faults in articulation, in the formation of individual sounds, are many, and they vary with the background of the speaker. In general a clear articulation of the consonants and a full resonant sounding of the vowels should be the actor's aim. The stop consonants *t, d, k, g, p, b* can give an edge to speech, but the vowels and the continuant consonants, particularly *m, n, ng,* and *l* give body, carrying power, and by far the greatest expressiveness to speech. The actor should become aware of the expressive power of the different sounds and learn to exploit them. In addition, he should be capable of modifying his articulation of particular sounds according to the variations of different dialects of English speech.

SPEECH

However, speech does not consist of separate sounds, nor of separate words, but rather of groups of sounds uttered in sequence with no perceptible pauses between the members of a group. These groups of sounds may be represented in print by words separated into a phrase, a clause, a sentence, or a paragraph. The actor should remember that speech, on the contrary, is a relatively uninterrupted flow of sound. If he gives too much attention to the articulation of individual sounds or to the pronunciation of individual words, his speech is almost sure to strike the hearer as unnatural and therefore distracting.

Phrasing. Therefore *phrasing,* the grouping of words according to their sense, is fundamental to expression in speech. The pause is the punctuation of vocal expression, but printed punctuation, though often helpful as a guide to phrasing, cannot be taken as a direct indication of where to pause. Much that is expressed to the eye by printed punctuation is expressed vocally by changes in volume, pitch, and quality; so the printed punctuation should be used to get the meaning from the page, and the meaning should dictate where to pause.

Centering. The actor must be able also to give more attention value to some parts of the phrase than to others. Some of the sounds need greater emphasis than others if the proper meaning is to be conveyed. The process of focusing attention on some parts and subordinating others is known as *centering.*

The most obvious method of emphasizing certain sounds is to utter them more loudly, but the possible range of loudness is comparatively limited, and the necessary variation so wide that this method soon grows monotonous. The actor should not forget that change is more emphatic than increase, and therefore a sharp reduction of volume is emphatic also.

Emphasis may be gained too by reducing the rate of utterance on the sounds which carry most of the meaning, by taking more time to articulate them. This method too is limited, and if used very much results in a tiresome, drawling delivery.

A pause before a group of sounds will draw extra attention to them, and it is invaluable within the phrase to italicize an occasional word. However, it too is limited in possible variety and easily abused.

Change in quality, although effective, is very difficult to achieve unless combined with the pause.

The most natural method of gaining emphasis and the most useful because it is capable of the widest range of variation is through the *intonation pattern,* the sliding of the voice up and down in pitch. And of course movement of the body helps to emphasize vocalization. The actor should not depend on one or two of these methods of centering but should strive to make full use of them all.

In any printed sentence some words are obviously more important than others in conveying the meaning. It is even possible to classify the parts of speech according to their relative importance. Ordinarily, nouns and verbs are most important, adjectives and adverbs next, then pronouns, then prepositions and conjunctions, and finally articles. Such an analysis of the actor's lines may be useful in correcting overemphasis on unimportant words, but it is dangerous because it suggests that speech consists of separate words rather than a sequence of sounds. The actor had better regard as the unit of speech all the words between any two pauses. His pattern of emphasis within such a unit would be represented graphically not by a series of dashes of different length or thickness, but by an unbroken line rising and falling to indicate different degrees of emphasis.

Rate. When one is concerned with speech rather than with voice or with individual sounds, *tempo,* or *rate* of utterance, becomes an expressive variable. The actor should be able to command a range of tempo from the very slow to the very fast. Two elements contribute to the rate of utterance, *duration,* the length of time taken to utter the individual sounds, and *pause.* One may cut short the vowel sounds and continuant consonants or prolong them considerably; one may take many and long pauses or few and short ones.

Although occasionally an actor may speak too slowly, it is a much more common fault to speak too rapidly, pouring out the

words so quickly that much of their meaning is lost. Most inexperienced actors can afford to speak much more slowly, and if
by so doing they are able to get more meaning out of their lines,
they will *appear* to be speaking more rapidly. It may be useful
to the actor to think of each line as being full of meaning as an
orange is full of juice. His job is to squeeze every last drop of
meaning out of it.

The same conditions which produce awkward and irrelevant
movements also cause monotonous or unexpected vocal effects.
In his endeavor to be heard, especially in a large theatre, the
actor may mistake loudness for intelligibility; he may shout instead of making use of all the vocal variables to project his meaning. Under the tension of performance, his speech may acceler-
ate to such a degree that it can convey little meaning; his
intonation patterns may flatten out, and his voice may become
breathy or harsh. He must consciously combat these tendencies.

Variety. Acting, even in the professional theatre, tends to
repetition of vocal pattern from line to line. The commonest
type of pattern is the downhill slide; the actor attacks each line
vigorously but allows it to trail off toward the end. Any repeated
pattern is monotonous and inexpressive, but this one has the
further disadvantage of being contrary to the general pattern of
American speech. In nine out of ten sentences in American
speech the meaning is not complete until the last word, and in
normal speech the point in the sentence where the meaning is
complete is the point of highest emphasis. The downhill pattern
therefore emphasizes the less important part of the sentence and
obscures by comparison the more important part. One might,
of course, deliberately adopt such a pattern to express a timid
or indecisive character, but then one should take special care
that meaning is not lost, despite the downhill pattern, and that
other factors counterbalance this vocal monotony.

There is a strong tendency among nonprofessional actors to
imitate each other unconsciously; that is, two actors playing a
scene together tend to speak at the same rate, with the same
loudness, and within the same range of pitch. Even their personal differences in voice quality sometimes become obscured
in this mutual imitation. The vitality of almost any dramatic
scene lies in the *differences* between characters. The actor should
be strongly aware of these differences and of the *new* element he

adds with each of his lines, and he should consciously strive to express these differences and to move the scene forward vocally by changes in rate, loudness, pitch, and quality.

The need for vocal variety becomes most evident in the delivery of a long speech. Actors may do reasonably well under the stimulus of the give and take of dialogue but find that the long speech is difficult to bring to life. Here too a consciousness of the *new*, of the forward progress of thought and feeling through the speech, is essential. If the actor analyzes the long speech as a unit which begins, develops, and reaches a conclusion, and if he consciously uses all the variables of his voice to express this structure, the speech may become a triumph instead of a thankless chore.

In general, if audience attention is to be held and the forward movement of the dramatic action to be expressed—not only within the scene but from scene to scene through the whole play—the vocal characteristics of loudness, pitch, quality, and rate must be constantly varied.

The Actor and the Theatre

The actor's task is to express the meaning of the play for an audience, and the methods he uses to perform this task are necessarily determined in part by the place of production: by the nature of the theatre, by its size, and by the relation of the acting space to the audience space.

THEATRE SIZE

In a small theatre, where the actor is close to all the spectators, he will be able to speak with little or no attention to the carrying power of his voice and with little or no effort to make himself understood. His movements, likewise, can be of ordinary scale and without the danger that they will not be clearly seen by everyone.

However, if the theatre is large enough so that some spectators are seated as far as twenty-five feet from the acting space, some extra effort will be needed to project the voice and the meaning of speech, and some heightening of the pattern of movement will be necessary.

As the size of the auditorium increases, greater and greater exaggeration in speech and movement are necessary to project the play to the farthest spectators. In very large theatres it may be impossible to project realistic acting adequately.

THE ACTOR'S RELATION TO THE AUDIENCE

The picture-frame theatre. We have observed how the picture-frame theatre separates acting space and audience space by means of the proscenium arch, and how it sets actor and audience face to face. As a result of this arrangement, the actor's best position (leaving out of account all considerations except individual visual and auditory effectiveness) is downstage center, as close to the audience as he can get. The farther he moves upstage away from the audience, the less easily can he be seen and heard. Moreover, the sightlines of the theatre and the proscenium frame itself tend to focus audience attention at center stage, so that the actor is more effective in that area. The weakest positions for the actor are upstage left and right, on the fringes of the playing space. Here he is least easily heard and seen. From some side seats he may perhaps be seen only with considerable difficulty. Upstage center is more effective, and when the actor is on the stage alone, downstage center is his most effective position.

The actor is most effective also in a front position, giving the audience a full view of his face and of the rest of his body. In such a position his voice is best heard, his facial expression best seen, his whole body most easily expressive. Three-quarters front is less effective, profile still less, and full back least effective.

Movements which pull the actor into downstage and front positions are stronger on the same grounds. Entrances from the side are best made with the upstage foot entering first; turns made downstage keep the face visible to the audience. Perhaps most important of all, crosses made downstage of the furniture and of the other actors are far more effective than crosses made behind furniture and other actors. If a cross is important, expressing something essential to the play, it should always be made downstage. If it is intended as background—for example, the cross of a servant while other characters are carrying on essential dialogue and action—it should be made upstage.

Since the audience must see clearly every expressive movement, the actor will not gesture upstage of his own body or upstage of other actors.

The actor must speak his lines more or less toward the audience, not away from the audience. Voice projection is easier when he faces downstage, but this is not the only reason why such delivery is preferable. Facial expression is a considerable aid to vocal expression, and of course this is lost if the actor turns away from the audience. The inexperienced actor usually has a strong feeling that he must look at the person to whom he is speaking. If he happens to be upstage of that person, this is satisfactory from the point of view of projection, but if he is downstage, it will swing him around with his back to most of the audience. Even if realism is one of the aims, truth to life does not require that the speaker always look at the person to whom he is speaking. Often one does not, because one is ashamed, or timid, or lying, or merely because what one is saying is not especially important, and one knows that the other person is there and will hear.

On the other hand, in representational acting there will be occasions when, all things considered, the actor will be most effective if he speaks with his back to the audience. Such occasions are likely to be infrequent, should not be prolonged, and require special care in voice projection.

Representational acting is aided by the picture frame; presentational acting is made more difficult by the sharp separation of acting and audience space.

The plastic theatre. In the plastic theatre the actor is not face to face with his audience, but in the midst of his audience. Spectators are all around him. The more of his audience he faces the more effective he will be both in movement and speech. If entrances make breaks in the surrounding audience, as is usual in the salon type of plastic theatre, the actor will have his back to fewer people when he stands with his back to one of these entrances, and crosses made on the axis of two of the entrances will be more effective than crosses made without reference to them.

At best, however, the actor will always have his back to a number of spectators, so frequent changes of position which give a front view now to one portion of the audience, now to another, are essential.

Since even though he may play a good deal on the entrance axis and shift his position frequently, the actor will still be presenting a back or partially back view to a part of the audience, he must work to make his body always expressive from those angles, in a way that is required only occasionally in the picture-frame theatre.

Representational acting in the salon type of plastic theatre will require care in maintaining the illusion that the actor is unaware of the presence of the audience. Presentational acting will be made easy by the closeness to the audience.

In the large arena type of plastic theatre the actor has the same general problem of enlarging his pattern of voice and movement as is presented by the large picture-frame theatre modified by the different relation to the audience.

The outdoor theatre. The special problem of acting in outdoor theatres is to hold audience attention against the competition of greater distractions. Even at night, when the acting area can be picked out by light from all that surrounds it, there is still more to distract the audience from the acting than in an indoor theatre. And in the daytime it is extremely easy for the spectator's attention to wander to passing clouds, to distant landscape, or to his immediate neighbors in the auditorium. The actor will have to devote even more attention to the task of holding his audience.

The Actor and the Setting

The proper relation of the actor to the setting is essential to play production. In the first place the actor must seem at home on the stage. He must feel the stage floor solidly under his feet and tread it firmly, unless the situation requires an expression of uncertainty, timidity, or fear.

REPRESENTATION

In the representational play, the actor's positions and movements go far to defining the boundaries of the setting. He must not in the plastic theatre overstep the imaginary circumference separating setting from the audience. He must not in the picture-frame theatre come downstage beyond the line of the setting.

Expressive use of furniture is shown in a scene from *Claudia* as produced at the University of Illinois by the Illini Theatre Guild. Charles Shattuck, director.

The actor can help create the illusion of place by using all parts of the playing area. In the picture-frame theatre this means the upstage as well as the downstage part, and the sides as well as the center.

Interior setting. In the representational interior setting, he will play as much as possible among the furniture and will use the different practical parts of the setting such as doors, windows, fireplaces, stairways, and the furniture to full advantage. These should suggest to him patterns of movement and positions expressive of his role. He will not circle the tables and chairs as if they were dangerous, but will use them naturally, laying a hand on the back of a chair or the top of a table or the jamb of a door when he is near it. By his use of the furniture and the practical parts of the setting, the actor gives them substance and reality. If he does not use them, the effect is one of strangeness. In the picture-frame theatre, if the actor plays constantly downstage in front of the furniture, which the desire to be effective may

For the complete illusion of depth, actors will have to keep their distance from the backdrop in a setting like this for Dorothy Sayers' *The Devil To Pay,* Fordham University Little Theatre. Albert McClerry, director.

lead him to do, the furniture loses reality. It becomes background only and in effect like furniture painted on a backdrop. Moreover, unless the actor uses the full depth of the interior setting at different times, the setting will appear shallower than it actually is.

Exterior setting. On the other hand, in the representational exterior setting, which must give an illusion of *great* depth, the actor must keep out of the background zone, so that his own unalterable dimensions will not reveal the actual nearness of the "distant" landscape and sky.

Formal setting. In the setting which consists largely of architectural units such as steps, platforms, columns, and arches (the plastic setting frequently used for abstract and fantastic plays), the actor by his use of the different levels emphasizes the plastic reality of the setting, just as by his use of the furniture in the realistic interior setting he emphasizes its reality. The different levels are there for him to walk, stand, sit, and lie on. When near a step, he will put a foot up; he will lean on a parapet or a column. He will find that the different levels suggest to him an

This shows the expressive use of levels in a scene from Lope de Vega's *The Sheep Well*, Dramatic Workshop of the New School, New York. Erwin Piscator, director.

expressive pattern of movement infinitely richer than any possible on a single level. They should suggest to him positions and movements which express his state of mind and emotion, and they should provide support or opposition for these expressive positions and movements.

Pictorial setting. The actor's relation to the pictorial setting is quite different; it is pictorial rather than spatial or plastic. Any attempt to create a plastic relationship between the actor and a setting painted on wings and backdrop will be comic. The ancient vaudeville gag of hanging a hat on the hatrack painted on the backdrop illustrates this point. The pictorial setting includes the actor in its design, but on a single plane only. If we think of the stage as a picture composed on a single plane behind the proscenium frame, the painted setting will draw attention more strongly to some parts of that plane than to others, and the actor will need to take this into account in discovering his pattern of movement, and particularly in choosing his positions. For examples of the pictorial settings, see the photograph of *Aaron Slick* on page 44.

In the picture-frame theatre the actor must remember that he is one element in a complex and constantly changing picture composed on the plane of the proscenium arch. He must constantly relate himself pictorially to the design of the setting, which is fixed, and to the arrangement of the other actors, which is constantly changing. The actor can do a good deal to insure pictorial unity if he will "fill the stage," that is, use all the space from left to right. When he is alone on the stage and preparation for another actor's entrance does not demand that the picture be deliberately unbalanced, a position near center, either upstage or downstage will fill the stage or focus the picture. When two actors are on the stage the space will best be filled if they do not remain too close together but if each fills, in a pictorial sense, roughly half the stage. Obviously this is only a generalization to which there are many exceptions; intense conflict may bring them face-to-face, or the picture may be deliberately unbalanced to prepare for the entrance of a third character. Similarly, a number of actors should not ordinarily bunch at center, left, or right, but should spread out at irregular intervals, dictated by the relations between the characters, over the full width of the stage. Usually the focus of such a large group is roughly center, although there are exceptions to this also.

Except on the extremely shallow picture-frame stage, the actor is also a part of a plastic unity composed on the plane of the stage floor as seen somewhat from above. His fellow actors and the setting, unless the latter is purely pictorial, are elements in this second type of unity. The actor can take his proper place in this plastic composition by maintaining a depth relationship with the setting and the other actors. When a number of actors are on the stage, each (with occasional exceptions) will use a different degree of stage depth. Failure to do this results in a line across the stage, not quite straight enough to be interesting and expressive as a line and without the variety necessary to expression through composition in depth.

In the plastic theatre, the actor need not worry about pictorial unity, but he must be even more strongly aware of his place in a plastic unity. Along with the other actors and the elements of the setting, he must contribute to a unified and expressive composition on the stage floor as viewed from above.

PRESENTATION

All that has been said about pictorial and plastic unity in representational acting applies to presentational acting also. The actor must always be concerned with an expressive use of the space and of the setting, but in presentational acting he is free to use the acting space and the setting without concern for creating an illusion of real life. If he is playing in the conventional modern theatre, he will make use of the proscenium arch. If he is playing in the salon theatre he will use all the available playing space. Without the need to maintain an illusion of real life, he is free to use the theatre space for direct expression.

SPACE AND MOVEMENT

Setting provides the actor with a certain space in which to move, and it prescribes the boundaries of his movements. The distance from door to chair, from chair to table, from table to window, etc. is fixed; it cannot be expanded or contracted. The actor's pattern of movement must be developed in relation to these fixed dimensions; whatever he can express in movement must be expressed within these dimensions. Sometimes the space is very large and the distances so great that the problem may be to get from one position to another without apparent haste and without slowing up the lines. More often the space is smaller than one might wish and the distances less, and the actor, especially the inexperienced actor who tends to be prodigal with

Here is shown listening with back to audience in a scene from *Shadow and Substance*, University of Delaware E52 Players. C. R. Kase, director.

movement, must learn to economize, must learn to make every inch count. He may need to make a half step do the work of two or three, or even of five full steps. In any case the actor should learn to think of space on the stage as something to be used, a raw material which with his movement he can turn into drama.

Certain elements of setting are dynamic; they imply movement on the part of the actor. Doors imply movement in and out. Stairs imply movement up and down. Chairs and sofas imply

Arnold Morrison

Listening front is shown in this scene from *The Inspector General*, Dramatic Workshop of the New School, New York. Erwin Piscator, director.

sitting down and standing up. The actor should be aware of such elements in the setting so that they will stimulate him to expressive movement.

The Actor and His Fellows

We have been discussing the work of the actor very largely as if it were performed alone, but actually the actor seldom

Triangular grouping, natural, is shown in a scene from André Obey's *Noah,*
Brooklyn College Varsity Players. Elizabeth Casey, director.

works by himself. Nearly always his performance must be co-
ordinated with one or more other actors.

It is essential to such co-ordination that the actors listen to
each other. The simplest way for the actor to appear to be listening is to look intently at the speaker. In the picture-frame
theatre, if the actor is downstage of the speaker, this means he
must look, or appear to look, upstage; but if he actually turns
his back on the audience a good deal of his reaction will be lost.
If the focus is strongly on the speaker, this may not matter, but
if, as often happens, the focus is on speaker and listener as a
unit, the speaker's effectiveness will depend to a great extent on
the series of reactions in the listener. The actor then has two
alternatives: he may turn his head slightly and his eyes further
in the direction of the speaker and thus give the impression that
he is looking at the speaker without hiding his own facial expression from the audience, or if the situation permits (if he is
being reprimanded, for instance), he may turn frankly away
from the speaker toward the audience and depend on his bodily
reactions to show that he is listening. If the actor is upstage of
the speaker, he can of course look at the speaker and be wholly
visible to the audience without special effort.

When two or more actors are on the stage together, the upstage
position belongs to the one on whom the major interest falls.
This focus varies with the development of the play, and the
actor should be alert for opportunities to move into an upstage
center position when the focus shifts to him and for opportuni-

Triangular grouping, abstract, is shown in a scene from *Mourning Becomes Electra,* Dramatic Workshop of the New School, New York. Erwin Piscator, director.

ties to move out into a downstage left or right position when the focus shifts away from him. Remembering that the most effective group is a relatively flat triangle with its open base toward the audience and the center of attention at its apex, he should try to keep his proper place in each of the succession of these groups.

A scene which begins with a roughly triangular grouping often tends to flatten out as it approaches its crisis. Conflict between two characters nearly always is expressed by confrontation, and in the picture-frame theatre this tends to take place downstage toward the audience. When the crisis is past and the tension is relaxed, the actors should look for opportunities to form a new triangular group similar to the one that has broken down, but ordinarily with a new focus of attention.

In the plastic theatre, the groups tend to be circular with the focus in the center of the acting space. As the focus shifts, one actor should move out of the center to the periphery and another from the periphery to the center. A scene which begins with a grouping spread over most of the acting area will concentrate the actors toward the center as tension increases. When the

Here is seen the choral use of orchestra space in a plastic theatre in *Hippolytus* as produced in the outdoor theatre at Mills College, Oakland, California. Marian Stebbins, director.

crisis is past, actors should help form a new group with most of them near the periphery. Confrontations resulting from strong conflict between two characters are better played on an axis of the entrances or, if the audience is not seated in the corners, on the diagonals. In such a position their backs are to fewer spectators. However, confrontation *across* the axis of the entrances seems to express conflict more strongly.

In discussing the actor as an individual we considered means by which he holds audience attention to himself, but when we consider him as a member of a group, we are concerned with ways in which he may shift attention from himself to another in response to the shifting focus of the play. He may of course sometimes efface himself from the scene by turning away into an upstage corner and remaining completely motionless. Any movement is likely to draw attention to him. Hence the rule that the actor should move on his own not on another actor's line unless the movement is in direct reaction to the other's line.

On the positive side, he can direct attention to another actor by looking at him and reacting to him. When the actor is himself the focus of attention he may look toward the audience on his own eye level, but when the focus is on someone else he can do much to insure proper audience attention if he will look where the audience should be looking. The tendency of inexperienced actors to look at the floor, the footlights, up into the flies, or off into the wings is undesirable because it directs audience attention away from the play.

The actor should consider his positions on the stage as parts of a series of groupings or tableaux designed to focus audience attention now on one actor, now on another. And he should consider each of his major movements as one of a series of movements by means of which one such expressive tableau or grouping is broken down and another built up.

The Actor and Other Elements

LIGHT

Good lighting is designed to make the actor visible as well as to contribute more directly to the production, but ordinarily it is not designed to make him equally visible in all parts of the playing space. It is said that one can tell a professional actor from an amateur by his apparently instinctive ability to get into the spotlight. Of course, no actor should always be in full light, but any actor will do well to note the locations of spotlights, the direction or directions from which the acting area is lighted, and what parts of it are more brightly lighted than others. He will not be able to do this until late in the rehearsal period, perhaps not until the final dress rehearsal.

The adjustments in position which he may then need to make will be slight but very important. A half step up or down or left or right may make the difference between playing an important scene with his face in half and in full light. Sometimes he will find that when he is playing close to another actor his shadow is thrown across the other's face, or he may note that the other actor is shadowing him. A slight change in position, perhaps no more than can be achieved by shifting the weight, will very likely get rid of the shadow.

COSTUME AND MAKEUP

When the actor imagines the character he is to play, he should imagine the character complete with appropriate costume and makeup. If the costume is similar to the clothes he habitually wears, this may not be important; but if it is different, failure to do so may be disastrous. Clothing, particularly footwear and leg coverings, affects the way the wearer moves. A woman walks

A strongly rhythmic grouping, but fully effective only from the balcony, is shown in *Oedipus Rex* as produced by the Old Vic Company of London.

differently in a long skirt from the way she does in a short skirt and differently in a full skirt, than she does in a tight skirt. Bare feet, flat heels, clogs, and high heels all produce different types of walks. The variety for men is not so great, but doublet and hose, medieval long gowns, the Roman toga, and the Greek hymation all require patterns of movement more or less unfamiliar to the trousered man of today.

Some adjustment can be made if the actor fully understands the character of his unfamiliar costume, and he will do well to bolster that understanding with study of the painting and sculpture of the particular period. But he should try to approximate in rehearsal such elements of the costume as he can. No one should rehearse a Greek character in high heels. If a sword is part of a man's costume, the actor should wear it or a dummy early in rehearsals. Of course, as soon as the actual costume is ready it should be worn in rehearsal as often as possible.

Makeup seldom affects the actor's work so directly, but if the role calls for a beard or mustache, the actor should have this clearly in mind. A beard and even a mustache may interfere with some of his movements. More important, it may suggest to him movements appropriate to the character.

Questions

1. What are some of the causes of visual monotony in acting?
2. Why should the actor ordinarily move in straight lines?
3. Why "one thing at a time" in acting?
4. How can learned movement be made to appear spontaneous?
5. In a large bodily movement, what is the normal organic sequence of movement in the different parts of the body?
6. Describe an exception to this general rule. What does it express?
7. When and how does the hand "lead"?
8. What is the normal relation of movement and speech?
9. Describe an exception to the above, and give an example of how it may be used in acting.
10. What is meant by "the illusion of the first time" in dialogue? How may it be achieved?
11. What is meant by *phrasing?* By *centering?*
12. To what extent is printed punctuation a guide to *phrasing?*
13. Why is realistic acting difficult in a very large theatre?
14. In the picture-frame theatre what is the actor's most effective position when he is alone on the stage? When there are others on stage with him?
15. In the plastic theatre, what are the actor's most effective positions?
16. What major difference is there between the actor's movement in the picture-frame and in the plastic theatre?
17. What is the special problem of acting outdoors?
18. What is the difference between the actor's relation to the plastic setting, and his relation to the pictorial setting?
19. What is meant by "filling the stage"?
20. Describe the different ways an actor can show he is "listening" on the stage.
21. Contrast the tableaux that develop in the picture-frame theatre with those that develop in the plastic theatre.
22. Why must the actor be aware of the stage lighting?
23. How can costume affect the actor's work?

Exercises

1. Present a brief pantomime which you have memorized, but "think" your way around the stage.
2. Demonstrate in pantomime an exception to the "one thing at a time" rule.
3. Present a brief scene, first with the normal co-ordination of movement and speech, then with a slight disunity, and finally with complete separation.
4. Present a brief scene of dialogue concentrating on creating "the illusion of the first time."
5. Demonstrate "filling" the picture-frame stage with one actor; two actors; half a dozen actors.
6. Demonstrate filling the arena stage in the same way.
7. Present a brief scene from Shakespeare, first acted on a bare stage (no furniture, one level), then with furniture (whatever chairs, benches, stools seem useful), and finally on a stage with the floor broken up into three different levels (but without furniture).
8. Demonstrate different ways of "listening" on the stage.

Bibliography

Theory

Calvert, Louis, *Problems of the Actor,* New York: Henry Holt & Company, Inc., 1918. Good on "Listening" and on "Doing Nothing."

Gillette, William, *The Illusion of the First Time in Acting,* New York: Dramatic Museum of Columbia University, 1915.

Lewes, George Henry, *On Actors and the Art of Acting,* New York: Brentano's, 1875. See particularly the chapter on "Natural Acting."

Also previously cited books by Albright, Lees, Dolman, and Selden.

Plays

See collections of plays previously cited.

CHAPTER 19.

THE PRACTICE OF ACTING:
CASTING, REHEARSAL, PERFORMANCE

$\mathcal{M}$uch of the material in the preceding chapters on acting can be applied when the actor is working by himself or with a few others, but a good deal of it cannot be applied until the actor has been cast in a particular part, rehearsed it with other actors and with the help of the director, and performed it for an audience. Since the director is the co-ordinator of the actors, and in case of dispute the final arbiter, this chapter is presented from the director's point of view.

Casting

The selection of the actors to play the parts in a particular play may be done by a committee, but it is probably best made the sole responsibility of the director. In any case, casting, in the nonprofessional theatre at any rate, is ordinarily done with two aims: to insure as good a production as possible, and to provide actors with needed experience.

As long as admission is charged, the first aim must be given considerable weight. People pay to be entertained, not to watch the painful results of dramatics used to combat personality defects. Therefore, casting must be done a good deal according to physical and personality type, and the most demanding roles must be given to the most experienced actors. Nevertheless, if in the course of a season or of several seasons the audience is to be given the best acting possible, inexperienced actors must be broken in on the smaller parts and worked up to the larger ones. This is especially true in the school theatre, which loses actors each year through graduation, but even in the community theatre audiences get tired of seeing the same actors year after year in the leading roles.

Casting should aim not only to train inexperienced actors but also to widen the range of those who may be called experienced. Although we have said that casting must be done pretty much to type, type should not be interpreted narrowly. Every actor is naturally limited by his physique and personality, but most actors nevertheless can acceptably play a considerable variety of roles. The comic actor may be capable of serious roles, and the juvenile type, with the aid of makeup, may be capable of character parts, and so on.

TRYOUTS

In order to cast a play, one must be familiar with the appearance, voice, speech, personality, and probable ability of all those who may be interested in acting. Except in very small schools or clubs, where the director may be familiar enough with all the available actors to cast directly, some kind of tryout is necessary. Even when a tryout is not really necessary, it may be advisable in order that every candidate may feel that he has been given a chance to show what he can do.

General methods. One method is to hold general tryouts at the beginning of the school quarter, semester, or production season, to keep careful records of the results, and to cast particular plays from these records. This method is economical in time and energy and permits the director to choose the plays more definitely with the available acting talent in mind. However, this method makes heavy demands on the director's memory and imagination.

A second method is to select the play or plays first, and then to hold tryouts for the particular parts. Except for the added time required, there is no reason why the two methods cannot be combined: general tryouts before the program of plays has been decided upon, followed by special invitational tryouts for each play.

Essential information. Whatever the system, the director should gain from the tryout the following information about each candidate: name, address, telephone; height, weight, age, complexion, hair color, general physical appearance (thin, stout, etc.); personality (vivacious, stolid, etc.); theatre type (ingénue, juvenile, character, old, child, comic, serious); the volume, pitch, and quality of the voice; characteristic diction; vocal expressiveness (reading) and bodily expressiveness; and previous acting experience (types of parts played). It is sometimes useful to know also what musical instrument, if any, the candidate can play, whether he can sing well enough for stage purposes, and if he can do any kind of stage dancing.

Some of this information is supplied by the candidate, some by the director during the tryout. Probably the best way of handling this data is to have printed or mimeographed a card with spaces for recording each piece of information (see the form). The candidate can fill out his part beforehand and give it to the director as he appears to try out. The director can fill out the rest, and the card can then be filed for consultation whenever needed.

(To be filled out by the candidate)

NAME: TELEPHONE:

ADDRESS:

Height: Weight: Age: Color Hair:
Complexion:

If you play a musical instrument or sing well enough to do so on the stage, specify:

Indicate previous acting experience (types of parts) on the back of this card.

(To be filled in by the director)

Voice: Physical Type:

Speech: Personality:

Reading: Stage Type:

Pantomime: Possible Roles:

General Estimate:

Procedures. Particular procedures will vary with the time available, the particular circumstances, and with the director's temperament.

In general tryouts, each candidate may be required to act, complete with movement, a scene which he has memorized.

Offhand this might seem a good procedure, but it has two serious drawbacks. Unless one is willing to take anything that is offered (and the taste of the candidates is sometimes not of the best), one must prepare and make available several days beforehand a variety of suitable selections. One will almost surely have to hear the same selection many times and one's judgment may be dulled after a while by the tediousness of repetition. A more serious drawback is that few of the candidates will really memorize their selections, so if one wishes to hear them all, the rest must be allowed to read from the script.

Another procedure in general tryouts is to hand each candidate a copy of a play with a passage marked, or to allow the candidate to select one of a large number of such selected passages. After he has had time to read the selection silently long enough to get the general drift of it, he can be asked to get up on the stage and read the dialogue (all characters) without attempting to perform the pantomime. It is true that this procedure puts a premium on immediate responsiveness. Nevertheless a careful observer will get considerable notion of the candidate's probable acting ability.

In specific tryouts, the name of the play can be announced in time so that anyone who really wants to do so can read the play before the tryout and have some idea what characters he wishes to try. Moreover, if the tryout is for a particular play, one can have group readings of scenes involving several candidates so as to get an idea not only of each candidate's suitability for the particular role but also an impression of how he will look and sound on the stage in relation to candidates for the other parts. In most of the procedures suggested above, the candidate reads from a script, and as a result he will be able to act very little with his body. Nevertheless, one can tell something about his probable bodily expressiveness. By observing how the candidate walks across the stage and how he stands, one can get a general impression of poise and ease of movement or of nervousness and awkwardness. If one observes closely, one will be able to see whether the body reacts to the reading (although necessarily on a limited scale), and thus make a good guess regarding his probable ability in pantomime.

Some directors advise and use a much more elaborate procedure in tryouts: the separate testing of voice, diction, reading, pantomime, imagination, and characterization. This may be desirable if there is time and if everybody has the necessary patience. Long drawn out tryouts are hard on all concerned, however.

No procedure, however elaborate and painstaking, will prevent occasional errors of commission or of omission. Some actors who look good in tryout never get any better, and some actors of ability always make a poor tryout.

Whatever the tryout procedure, candidates should be required to take off outdoor clothing and remove their glasses for the time they appear on the stage. If a candidate needs his glasses to read the script, he should be asked to take them off for a moment when he has finished reading so that the director can see how he looks without them. If the candidate or candidates are reading from scripts, they should face full front most of the time so that they are fully visible to the director.

Ensemble considerations. We have been considering casting almost entirely as if it were a matter of individual actors and individual parts, but the actors are to appear on the stage together and must therefore be considered as a group.

Variety is a major factor in projecting the play and in holding audience attention, and a good deal of variety can be secured through casting: variety in the height, weight, coloring (hair and complexion), general physical appearance, voice quality, pitch range, rate of utterance, and even in the diction of the actors. The play should suggest such differences, if it does not specify them.

On the other hand, extreme differences (particularly in height and in diction) should be avoided, unless the play calls for comic or grotesque effects. And in some plays it may be desirable to use physical resemblances to suggest blood relationships between certain characters.

Understudies. Whenever possible, the director should choose a complete second cast, which will provide not only the essential insurance against emergencies but also experience for more actors. If an entire second cast cannot be mustered and held together through rehearsals (and this is difficult unless a performance is scheduled for the second cast), there should be understudies for all the principal roles.

Rehearsal

The actor can do much through individual study before rehearsals begin and outside rehearsals to create a pattern of movement and speech which will project the character, but the greater part of his work must be done in rehearsals because acting is a group art requiring the collaboration of other arts and because it takes place in a theatre before an audience. The period of rehearsal permits the testing of the actor's voice and movement under conditions which approach those of performance.

The work of his fellow actors may force modifications of his own characterization, and their mere presence on the stage will inevitably affect the particular form of his creation. The projection of his pattern of movement must be tested by the sightlines of the particular theatre, the projection of his vocal pattern by the acoustics. His imagined creation must be modified according to the costumes, the setting, the properties, and the lighting. Then the whole revised pattern of expression must be learned so that it can be repeated at will any number of times with little variation.

Rehearsal begins with emphasis on the individual actor, but emphasis soon shifts to the actors as a group, and in the final stages the focus has spread to include all the other materials of production. If a unified production is to be achieved, the whole rehearsal period must be supervised by the director.

TIME

The number and length of rehearsals will vary with the difficulty of the particular play, the experience of the cast, the length of time available, and probably with the patience of the director. For a full-length play, one may say as a rough guide that five weeks of five or six two-and-a-half to three hour rehearsals per week should be adequate. If the play is an easy one and the cast experienced, three weeks of daily rehearsal may be enough. A more difficult play with an inexperienced cast may require six weeks or more.

The individual rehearsal probably should not be less than two hours long, and two and a half or three hours is better.

Five or six rehearsals a week for five weeks is better than three rehearsals a week for eight or nine weeks. In any case a complete rehearsal schedule should be agreed upon at the first meeting of the cast. Changes can be made later if necessary, but a definite schedule saves a great deal of time and trouble.

METHODS

Early stages. If there is plenty of time, the first meeting of the cast may be devoted to a reading of the play by the director followed by an explanation of his conception of its meaning, form, style, and structure, and of the means by which these are to be realized in the theatre, particularly in terms of acting. In the experience of the writer, the reading has not seemed to be worth the time and energy it takes, and good results have come without it. The explanation should be followed by a discussion by the cast ending in an agreement regarding the main outlines of the production and the place of each character in the general scheme.

The next meeting is often devoted to a reading of the play by the cast seated around a table, with pauses for discussion and for suggestions designed to strengthen each actor's grasp of the play and his understanding of the function of his role in the whole pattern. This too takes considerable time, and two or three meetings can easily be devoted to it.

Rehearsals proper begin with a blocking out of the action for the first act as the director has imagined it. The plan of the setting should be marked out exactly on the floor of the stage or rehearsal room, and dummy furniture should be used for all the pieces of furniture required by the action. The actors read the lines without special attention to vocal expression and walk through the pattern of movement which the director has prepared beforehand.

The director should test all groupings according to the theatre sightlines. Some mistakes will very likely become apparent in this first walk-through, and he will make necessary changes, entering them or having them entered by the stage manager in his promptbook.

The actor should note his positions and movements in his script so that he can learn them along with his lines.

Blocking out is a long and tedious business requiring patience on the part of actors and director. No more than one act should be attempted in a single rehearsal, and if the rehearsal must be short a smaller unit is better. The pattern of movement should be run through at least twice. Ordinarily the next few rehearsals are devoted to learning this pattern of movement, and to the beginning of work on line reading.

When the first act is beginning to take shape both visually and vocally, a rehearsal should be devoted to blocking out the movement of the second act, and thereafter for about a week both acts may be handled in each rehearsal, running through one once and working intensively on the other, or they may be handled in alternate rehearsals. When the second act is out of the first rough stage, the third act should be blocked out. For a time it is probably best to alternate rehearsals devoted to act three only with rehearsals in which one works on both the earlier acts. Later one may wish to alternate rehearsals of act one and act three with rehearsals of act two and act three.

Soon after work has begun on the second act, the actors should know their first-act lines, and soon after work has begun on the third act they should know their second-act lines. *All lines should be memorized two weeks before performance.* Theoretically, the best way for the actor to learn his lines is indirectly: through repetition as he develops his vocal pattern in rehearsals. Thus he learns movement, words, and expression all together with little chance for conflict between words and vocal expression. The actor who is able to use this method should check his lines periodically against the text to be sure that he has not unwittingly departed from it.

Some actors, however, prefer to memorize their lines as quickly as possible in order to be rid of the script, which they feel hampers them in rehearsal, and often limited time *requires* that lines be memorized outside of rehearsals. In some cases this results in setting up mistaken vocal patterns that are difficult to change, but most actors are flexible enough to make necessary adjustments with little difficulty.

As soon as the actors begin to work without their scripts a prompter is needed, and indeed it is desirable to have the prompter hold the book from the first rehearsal, so that he will be thoroughly familiar with the script and with the acting of it before he undertakes to prompt. In the professional theatre, prompting is only one of the duties of the *stage manager* (see

Chapter 15). As prompter, he holds the book, notes changes in lines and action, prompts the actors, and "reads in" parts when necessary.

As soon as the actors are able to work without scripts, a full set of hand properties—the actual ones if possible, if not, adequate substitutes—should be used at each rehearsal.

Middle period. The early rehearsals are concerned with general outlines, the middle ones with giving the performance solidity by re-creating the structure, form, mood, and style of the play and thus expressing its meaning. The basis of the structure of most plays is the opening exposition. The director will try to see that every bit of information necessary to audience understanding of the initial situation is clearly presented with special allowance for the unfavorable conditions which will attend the first ten minutes of performance. In the logically constructed play, he will try to see that each scene is built to its individual peak of tension, with the entire series of scenes leading to the play's major crisis. In the episodic play, he will try to see that each scene is played for its full value in the pattern of the play as a whole, with particular regard for elements of likeness and difference, repetition and contrast which will give the performance unity. He must see the performance as a whole and help the actors to realize the rhythmic pattern of the written play.

Although he is concerned with the whole, the director is likely to get best results by concentrating on one aspect of acting for a whole rehearsal or at any rate for a definite part of each rehearsal. He may, if he wishes to concentrate on improving the reading of the lines, turn his back on the stage in order to rule out the visual element, and during an entire scene or act note readings which need to be improved. He will want also to test intelligibility from every part of the auditorium.

At another run-through he may ignore the reading and concentrate on improving the groupings and movements, seeking to make them more expressive and testing them for visibility.

An entire rehearsal may be devoted to characterization, to helping the actor build up a full understanding of his role and a clear image of the physical means by which it may be projected. Good characterization in the cast as a whole means variety of individual characterization.

Similarly, a rehearsal may be devoted to building up the mood of the act: horror and suspense, pity and fear, gaiety, or whatever may be required. Mood grows out of general similarities.

If the play is abstract or fantastic, style will be another focus, perhaps of several rehearsals.

For a revival, it may be desirable to spend one or more rehearsals on certain historical characteristics of acting or playwriting, the use of the fan and handkerchief in Restoration comedy, the handling of long speeches in verse in Shakespeare.

Entrances and exits provide another focus, and an extremely important one, because a good entrance means that a scene has started well, and a good exit usually means that a scene has reached a firm conclusion.

A rehearsal may be devoted very largely to stimulating the actors to pick up their cues. The tendency, of the beginner especially, is to speak his lines too rapidly, and to be slow in picking up his cues, a combination which makes for an effect of extreme dullness. Cues are almost bound to be slow if the actors are not reacting to each other. A session devoted to emphasizing the necessity of listening and reacting will result in a livelier picking up of cues and generally improved expression.

When the acting is flabby and directionless, as it usually is just after the lines have been memorized, a session devoted to motives and objectives will give backbone to the performance. In each situation what does each character want, and why? If motive and objective are imagined strongly enough, lines and movement which have seemed empty and tedious will take on meaning and vitality.

Important and complicated pieces of business will need special attention: the setting of a table, serving and eating a meal, playing a game of cards, packing a suitcase, writing a letter, a fight—all such activities need careful planning and careful rehearsal if they are to be co-ordinated with the lines and if they are to take their proper place in the performance as a whole.

When the actors are still fumbling for their lines, the director can feel free to stop the rehearsal frequently in order to suggest changes and to repeat bits, but as soon as the actors are able to run through an act or some smaller unit fairly smoothly, they should be allowed to proceed with the minimum of interruptions, in order that they may get a feeling for the unit as a whole. The director should cultivate the ability to sit in the auditorium and take detailed critical notes for distribution to the cast when the act or scene is over. Bits may be repeated afterwards, or the whole act may be repeated, this time with stops for work on particular spots.

Special rehearsal for laughs is sometimes desirable with a comedy, especially if the actors are inexperienced. Actors should be instructed to "pause and act"—hold the lines but act with the body until the laughter thins out—and then to come in strongly with the next line. A buzzer or bell may be used as a substitute for audience laughter. If the director buzzes at different times in several rehearsals, requiring the actors to pause and act, he can give them some actual training in the necessary response.

Throughout rehearsals, the director should remember that an actor can absorb only so many suggestions in a single rehearsal. The director should be prepared to make the same suggestions several times before the actor is able to incorporate them in his performance.

Discipline. Rehearsals should be businesslike. Actors should be required to be prompt and rehearsals should begin on time. Except when unforeseeable circumstances make this impossible, rehearsals should end at the time agreed upon. There should be absolute quiet in the auditorium while the rehearsal is in progress. Actors not actually needed on the stage for any length of time had better be banished to an adjoining room with provisions for calling them in time for their entrances.

There is at best a good deal of waiting around at rehearsals, so that anything which can be done in planning them to save time for actors who appear in only one or two scenes or acts will make for better morale.

Visitors. The problem of outsiders at rehearsals is troublesome. In the professional theatre, outsiders simply are not admitted. Some directors make it a policy never to admit a spectator except with the agreement of the cast. On the other hand, it is not easy to keep out friends and relatives of the actors. The actors may be unduly self-conscious in the presence of strangers, and the outsider, unable to evaluate what he sees in rehearsal, sometimes gets a false impression of the play and spreads harmful reports. On the whole, before the production is in final or nearly final shape, the fewer outsiders, the better.

Final rehearsals. The last week of rehearsals should be devoted to polishing the acting and to fitting together acting, setting, light, costume, sound, and makeup into a smoothly running, unified production. During these final rehearsals, the actors should be allowed to proceed from the beginning through the whole play, with halts only between the acts. If bits must be re-done they should be done at the end of each act. Even this should be kept at a minimum. The actors need to get a feeling of the play as a whole, and this can be acquired only by rehearsals which as nearly as possible approximate performance.

All practical parts of the setting should be complete a week before performance, so that the actors can adjust to them early. The actual properties should be in use for several rehearsals. Costumes, if modern, should be worn in the last two rehearsals. However, any quick changes of costume probably should be rehearsed earlier. Period or fantastic costumes should be worn during the whole last week of rehearsals, if possible. If sound effects figure prominently, these should be worked in early in the final week. As soon as the setting is complete, light should be added. Unless the makeup presents unusual problems, it may be left to the last rehearsal.

A detail sometimes overlooked, one which is too important to be left to the last moment, is the pulling of the front curtain. This should be practiced during at least one rehearsal during the final week and not left for the final dress rehearsal. Opening or raising the curtain is less important than closing it, but there is technique involved in both. The draw curtains should open slowly at first, but gather speed, reaching their full spread with decision. The curtain man should be sure he has got them open all the way. The drop curtain should rise fairly rapidly and evenly. The method of drawing or dropping the curtain should be adjusted to the mood of the scene it punctuates. The scene which ends in tension or in sorrow seems to call for a slow curtain. The scene which ends with surprise, a violent act, or a punch line is likely to be better served by a fast curtain. In most cases, the slow curtain should speed up some at the end. A falling drop curtain once it gets down to the level of the actors gives a bad picture, and the draw curtain often needs a little extra pull on the end to make sure that the two halves close completely.

Dress rehearsal. The last rehearsal is traditionally known as the "dress rehearsal," and traditionally it is an occasion marked by chaos and frenzy. If, as too often happens, acting, setting, costumes, light, sound, and makeup are all put together for the first time in this final rehearsal, chaos and frenzy are inevitable. However, if the actors have been properly rehearsed, and if the other materials of production have been added one at a time in previous rehearsals, the dress rehearsal can be a smooth run-through, perhaps with an invited preview audience, at which the director is free to note details still to be improved. If the proper groundwork has been laid, he should be able to sit in the auditorium making notes for the actors and for the heads of the production departments. As far as the actors are concerned, he should not in this last rehearsal attempt to correct the reading of individual lines, nor should he make major changes in movement and grouping; he should be concerned with correcting awkward details which are a result of co-ordination with the other materials of production, and with the larger flow of the action and the projection of the play as a whole.

One legitimate concern of the final rehearsal is the preparation of curtain calls; these should be rehearsed if they are to be taken in performance. The character of the curtain call will depend considerably on the play and the style of the production. In a revival of a nineteenth-century melodrama, the final tableau or a special tableau with each character in typical posture might be used and individual calls taken in character. In the Broadway production of *Life With Father*, the curtain calls were designed to suggest daguerreotypes. In general, the curtain call is best planned to have somewhat the same tone as the end of the play.

Morale. In order to get the best possible performance from a group of actors, their morale must be kept high. This means that they must be constantly interested in the work and eager to do well. As might be expected, the methods by which directors maintain morale vary considerably. Some depend almost wholly on adverse criticism, seldom meting out praise. If the director never criticizes without suggesting how the actor may improve, this method may not be bad. However, some actors will wilt under it.

Other directors succeed largely through praise and exhortation, concealing adverse criticism under bouquets of encouragement. This method may get no results at all from the self-satisfied actor.

As in many things, the happy medium, a judicious mixture of praise adapted to the individual, with endless suggestions for improvement, is likely to work best with the largest number of people.

Performance

If the play is really ready, the director on opening night, after he has inspected the actors in costume and makeup, should be able to leave the running of the production to the stage manager. He should be able to take a seat in the auditorium, where he can observe the audience reaction. He will want to make notes of details which may still be improved and to formulate general advice for the actors.

Relatively inexperienced actors frequently do surprisingly well in their first performance, and then slump badly in the second. Warning may help prevent such undue relaxation. If the slump is very bad, an extra rehearsal may be necessary. If performances are separated by several days, one or two rehearsals will be needed in the interval to keep the acting at a high level. In long runs, seldom a problem in the nonprofessional theatre, the actors frequently get stale and their performance mechanical and lifeless. Cues are slow, points are missed, and the play is no longer being projected. When this happens, a rehearsal should be called and the actors stimulated to pay attention once more to the play.

Questions

1. What should be the two principal aims in casting?
2. What are the advantages and the disadvantages of general tryouts?
3. What are the advantages of specific tryouts?

4. What information about each candidate should be gained from the tryout?
5. What are the ensemble considerations in casting?
6. About how long should a full-length play be rehearsed?
7. What is meant by "blocking out?"
8. What is the advantage of memorizing the lines in rehearsal?
9. Under what circumstances will it be necessary to memorize lines outside of rehearsal?
10. State the duties of the prompter in rehearsals.
11. What are some of the special problems to which a whole rehearsal may be devoted?
12. Why are so many dress rehearsals chaotic?
13. What are the legitimate concerns of a good dress rehearsal?
14. What should the director do during performance?

Exercises

1. Hold tryouts for parts in a one-act play, using the members of the class as candidates.
2. Cast the play and give reasons for your selections.
3. Hold a reading by the cast.
4. Hold a first rehearsal, blocking out the action.

Bibliography

Theory

Dean, Alexander, *Fundamentals of Play Directing*, New York: Farrar & Rinehart, Inc., 1941.

Dolman, John, Jr., *The Art of Play Production*, New York: Harper & Brothers, rev. ed. 1946.

Drummond, A. M., *A Manual of Play Production*, Ithaca, N. Y.: published by the author, 1939.

Shaw, George Bernard, *The Art of Rehearsal*, New York: Samuel French, pamphlet, 1928.

See also previously listed books by Heffner, Selden and Sellman, Gassner, and Downs.

Plays

See anthologies listed in Bibliographies to Chapters 3 and 7.

CHAPTER 20.

COSTUME DESIGN

*A*lthough a play exists first in written form and people are likely to think of the spoken word as the principal means of expression in the theatre, the series of pictures which a play presents to the eyes of the audience can be of great importance also in conveying the play's message. Settings and costumes should not be so compelling that they distract the attention from the words, but they can do much to emphasize the effect of the spoken lines and to interpret the locale and mood of the play. If the play is well costumed and well set the audience should accept the visual effect almost unconsciously. Furthermore, the audience should be so absorbed in the development of the play itself that it is not aware that lighting, setting, and costumes are actively helping it sense the meaning of the lines through suggestion and the psychological use of color and line.

The Training of a Costume Designer

Relatively few people read plays because, for one reason, many cannot visualize the stage picture as they read the lines. It is for the costume designer and scenery designer to produce visual images so compelling and "right" that the audience not only accepts them but is aided by the settings and the costumes in understanding the spoken lines and the action.

To be able to do this the costume designer needs broad training in the theatre and in art. He must be familiar with stage history, especially as it affects settings and the architecture of theatres. He must intimately know the history of costume and be able to produce a Louis XVI court costume or an Egyptian slave's habit on short notice, for the theatrical worker is always pressed for time. He must understand color psychology and the basic principles of design so that he can create significant costumes which will help interpret the play. He also needs a knowledge of art history, especially in the fields of architecture,

407

These costumes illustrate simplification and interpretation of period to suit individual characters. **Top.** These pictures from Canfield's *Lackeys of the Moon* suggest haughty sophistication. Plum colored, gold-trimmed sateen was used for the Duchess. The gentleman wore lavender kneebreeches and a white sateen coat, painted with flowers and leaves in pink, green, gold, and black outline. **Bottom.** These designs from Canfield's *The Duchess Says Her Prayers* show salient elements of a period, exaggerated or simplified. Slashed and puffed sleeves, doublet, and shoes (typical Renaissance) are used almost to excess so as to "place" them in the audience's mind.

furniture, and painting, so that he can interpret the most significant periods when great art flourished.

The costumer may be either a man or a woman; in fact, some of the most notable designers for both stage and moving pictures are men. Robert Edmond Jones and Lee Simonson have created countless costumes for their varied productions, and "gowns by Adrian" or by Travis Banton are familiar to all movie fans. The designer need not be a dressmaker or tailor, but he should understand clothing construction so that his design will be both practical and wearable and so that he can supervise the cutting and fitting of the garments that he has conceived. And finally, to all of this he must add all the imagination and daring that he can muster so that his creations will not be drab, commonplace clothes but exciting, personal embodiments of the spirit of the actor who is interpreting the play itself.

The Procedure of the Costume Designer

Before doing any costuming, the designer must be familiar with the play and with the way in which it is to be presented on the stage. Often the director of the play is not the designer, and whenever this is the case, whoever is chosen to design the costumes and settings must collaborate closely and constantly with the director, so that the visual interpretation of the play will be in the same spirit as the acting and the reading of the lines.

The following outline of procedure may prove helpful to the costume designer of any given play.

Read the play. Try to visualize the setting, the characters, and the costumes as you read, and try to analyze the characters themselves so that you can interpret their characteristics in their costumes. Do certain characters play together or express like attitudes or qualities? If so, their costuming by similarity of color, line, or texture may help to express their likenesses. Characters who oppose them should be costumed to express this opposition in color, line, and texture.

Consult the director. Find out how he plans to interpret the play and what style of staging he intends to use: realism, expressionism, and so on.

Learn the light plot. Find out what his light plot is so that the colors you plan for individual costumes or group effects will not be killed or changed disagreeably by colored light which you had not anticipated. The director should be able to tell you whether he plans a scene in full light, in amber, blue, or rose, and whether he plans special color effects for a portion of the scene, such as a certain light near a window in which a character will be "spotted." Too often costumes are executed as if to be used under full stage light or under flattering pastel tints and it is discovered too late that they will be seen under amber or blue, with the result that the entire scheme of color relations and sequences is changed for the worse or completely disrupted.

Learn stage grouping and playing pattern. Learn from the director where each character will be placed on the stage and in close proximity to what other characters, so that colors of costumes seen together will not unintentionally clash and "kill" each other. Sometimes a leading character plays all over the stage, first with one group of actors and then with another and his costume should be planned in relation to all of them.

Design individual costumes. Now, and not before, design each individual costume for each actor. Some will need several for one play, and each must be suited to the actor and his environs in the scene in which it is to be worn. Before making a design, study the character as found in the play; learn how the director interprets the character; recall in what light or lights he will appear; and then design a costume which in line, color, and texture will interpret that character.

Buy or procure materials for the costumes. Do not worry about not finding materials which will match your colored costume sketches. If you shop in bargain basements and decorator's departments, you should be able to find the colors you need, and if all else fails, there is the dye pot. Color is more important than texture, and often inexpensive materials of the right color can substitute for more expensive ones of heavier weight or finer weave. If possible, obtain large enough samples, or borrow a bolt of the material to try under the stage lights, as some textures are enhanced by colored light and others go dull and lifeless under artificial illumination.

Left and middle. These costumes for Titania and the Fairies from *Midsummer Night's Dream* illustrate how imagination can be used to vary traditional renderings of accepted characters. Instead of fluffy tarlatan skirts, wings, and wands, Titania was clad in clinging bluegreen, ornamented with silver paper stars and tinsel streamers, and the fairies wore green voile skirts sheathed in silver buckram. **Right.** Thisby in *Midsummer Night's Dream* is a comic character and illustrates the use of humor in a costume. The colors are garish, the garment ill-fitting and clumsy, and the striped stockings and big, silly, artificial flowers on her head are intended to be foolish and amusing.

Cut and make costumes. Cut out the costumes, allowing for plenty of fullness and for ample seams that will not tear out. Try them on the actors when basted or sewed, and alter to fit the wearer. Arrange for suitable fastenings, whether they be safety pins, hooks and eyes, or buttons.

Try costumes under stage light. Be sure that the actors wear the costumes once, if possible, before the dress rehearsal so that their effect under the play's lights may be seen. Any necessary change can then be made easily before the production night. Costumes should be worn before the dress rehearsal in order also that the actors may become familiar with the feel of them and learn to carry themselves with ease well before the first performance. This is especially true of period costumes, which are often so different from those in use today that the actors not

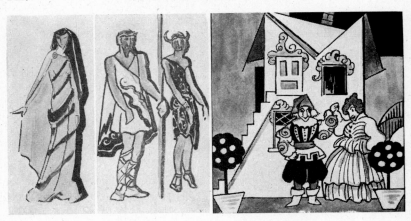

Left and middle. Ham's wife from *Noah's Flood* and Theseus and Hippolyta from *Midsummer Night's Dream* illustrate interpretation of historic costume to suit the period and character. **Left.** This shows a simplified version of a medieval costume planned to be seen on a large stage where it will appear as a unified spot of color. This costume was rendered in bright blue with yellow stripes. **Middle.** This makes use of Greek motifs but greatly enlarged in scale and used as a border design on Theseus' tunic. Hippolyta's garment was dyed and painted to suggest a spotted skin, similar to that of a leopard. **Right.** All too often costumes and scenery do not harmonize in spirit. In Thorndike and Arkell's *The Tragedy of Mr. Punch* the scenery was conceived as a stylized set of flatly painted cut-out "props." The design shown includes Mr. Punch's house and two cut-out potted trees. The entire setting was painted bright reds, yellows, and blues. Against this, all the costumes were solid, full, intense colors. Mr. Punch wore magenta and purple. His wife wore bright orange and a vermilion wig. Both costumes and setting were frankly painted and stylized in design so as to appear as a perfect visual unit.

only feel self-conscious in them but often have to practice how to walk or sit in them or how to handle capes or swords.

If this procedure is followed, the costume designer is free at the dress rehearsal to see the total stage picture and to concentrate on the ensemble color effect as seen against the scenery. Minor changes of color or accessory can then be made if desired. In one play, the leading lady was supposed to wear a white and gold-brocaded gown. It was not ready in time for the first dress rehearsal and she wore a plain white robe instead. The other

actors were in colorful, patterned fabrics and the designer realized that the gold-brocaded garment would not stand out from
the others at all, whereas the plain white was exactly right. So a
white gown was substituted for the more elaborate one originally planned.

Color

The successful designer needs to understand color as the physicist, the artist, and the psychologist use it.

COLOR AS LIGHT

There are important differences between color in light and
color in pigment, and although the costumer works with color
in pigment, he must be equally concerned with color in light,
because the apparent color of pigment depends to a great extent
on the light under which it is seen. This means that the costumer should have some knowledge of the practices of stage
lighting as described in Chapter 13, and particularly of the effect
of light upon pigments as described on page 256.

COLOR AS PIGMENT

In obtaining his color effects the artist works with paints or
dyes and needs to know the laws governing their harmonies.
There are several color theories, but the one most frequently
used recognizes yellow, red, and blue as *primary colors* and orange, green, and violet as *binary colors* (each one made up of
two primaries, as yellow and red together making orange). There
are also six other colors between the primaries and binaries,
making a spectrum circle of twelve hues. This is illustrated by
the chart on page 426.

COLOR PROPERTIES

Each color has three properties—hue, value, and intensity—
and is possible of an infinite number of variations.

Hue is the personal name of a color, such as *red, green,* or
yellow-orange.

Value is the amount of dark or light in the color tone, as *light*

The costumes shown here and on page 415 for the "Ballet of the Seven Deadly Sins" from Christopher Marlowe's *Dr. Faustus* were conceived in black, grays, silver, and white. The cut and texture of each costume was chosen to emphasize the characteristics of the "Sin." **Top left.** *Pride.* **Top right.** *Envy* wore expensive looking, modish draperies. **Bottom left.** *Gluttony* wore dull, heavy, lumpy shapes attached to his baggy costume.

blue or *dark blue,* that is, the amount of white or black it contains.

Intensity is the amount of brilliance in the color tone, such as *bright yellow* or *neutral yellow.* The intensity of a color is lowered by adding its complementary color.

A *normal* color is any hue at its fullest intensity, such as the *reddest red* or *bluest blue.*

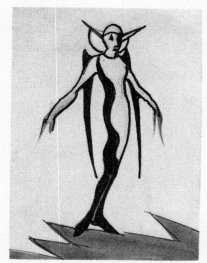

Top left. *Wrath* was all angles and contrasts, sharp and staccato in design. **Top right.** *Evil Angel* wore white tights which were painted with poison green and black motifs. Even his makeup was green and shadowy. **Bottom right.** *Lechery* wore thin, slinky, revealing draperies.

A *tint* is a color tone lighter than a normal color. Tints of red include *pink* and *flesh*.

A *shade* is a color tone darker than a normal color. A shade of blue would be *navy* or *midnight*.

Any hue has many possible *values* and *intensities* which include the tints and shades. In matching a sample of material it is often difficult to find just the right variation of the color. There may be two dozen bolts of blue material but only one that is right in hue, value, and intensity.

COLOR HARMONIES

There are certain color combinations which are recognized as *harmonies* and the costume designer can make excellent use of these in planning a single costume or a group of costumes which will look well when seen together. There are two basic kinds of harmonies: those of similarity and those of contrast.

Harmonies of similarity. A *one-mode* harmony consists of any one hue on the spectrum circle and its variations in value and intensity. Example: two tints of orange, a normal orange, and three shades of orange (which includes browns).

An *analogous* harmony consists of adjacent hues on the spectrum circle, not including two primaries. Each hue may vary in value and intensity. (Analogous colors are colors which have something in common. Any combination including two primaries would contain one color unrelated to the rest.) Example: yellow, orange, and red-orange, and their variations in value and intensity. All of these colors have some yellow in them and therefore are related or analogous.

Harmonies of contrast. A *complementary* harmony consists of any two hues which are directly opposite on the spectrum circle and their variations in value and intensity. Example: orange and blue.

A *double complementary* harmony consists of any two adjacent hues on the spectrum circle and their respective complements. Each hue may be varied in value and intensity. Example: green and blue-green and red and red-orange.

A *split complementary* harmony consists of any hue on the spectrum circle and the hue on either side of its complement. Example: yellow, red-violet, and blue-violet. These may vary in value and intensity.

There are four *triad harmonies*: a *primary triad,* which is always yellow, red, and blue, and their variations in value and intensity: a *binary triad,* which is always orange, green, and violet, and their variations in value and intensity. There are also two *hue triads,* one of which consists of red-orange, yellow-green,

Ben Jonson's *Masque of Oberon* contains many wood spirits such as Satyrs and Sylvans. **Top left.** The spiral on the Satyr shown here was painted on the skin, before each performance, with black grease paint. **Top right, Bottom left and right.** These costumes for the Sylvans from the *Masque of Oberon* illustrate imaginative interpretation of woodland characters.

and blue-violet, and the other of yellow-orange, blue-green, and red-violet, and their variations in value and intensity.

Other types of harmony. Any hues, in any value or intensity, may be harmonized if used with a *predominating background area of neutral tone.* Since the neutral background tone is a larger area than any color used upon it, and since it is not a color, it serves as a harmonizing agent. The neutrals are black, white, gray, and sometimes gold and silver. Other colors may serve as harmonizing background areas if they are sufficiently low in intensity and value.

Any *group of hues of the same value* tend to harmonize.

Neutral colors, such as gray-blue, olive-green, dull brown, etc., will harmonize because of their common element of neutrality.

All hues may be used together if combined with sufficient *black and white accents* in each costume. *Gold and silver accents* produce the same harmonizing result.

If all colors to be used together are "keyed" to some one color used in the group, the result will be particularly harmonious. "Keying" may be obtained best by dyeing or by the use of colored light. If all materials used for costumes for a certain scene are dyed the desired colors and a little dye of one color put into each other dye bath, keying will result. A single gelatin or a single colored-light effect thrown over all the costumes and scenery will key them in much the same way that dyeing will.

Uniformity of texture gives a degree of harmony; e.g., using only rough textures together or all shiny fabrics in a single scene.

COLOR PSYCHOLOGY

As explained in Chapter 11, people are often unconsciously susceptible to color because they are conditioned to certain reactions. Red suggests danger or fire; blue is generally restful; purple is somber; yellow is gay; and orange is almost as stimulating as red. White usually suggests innocence and purity; purple suggests royalty or tragedy. Some colors are gay, others somber; some are obvious and some subtle.

If certain colors affect people in definite ways, color can be used to produce emotional effects upon an audience. By proper selection and arrangement of color in costume, as in scenery, particular emotional effects can be achieved. A costume can thus be made to express the mood of the character who wears it, the mood of the scene, or the mood of the play as a whole.

In the Leslie Howard production of *Hamlet,* Ophelia, in the mad scene, was dressed in black velvet, although the usual costume for the scene is white. The black signified that she was in mourning for her father, but it also hinted at her death, which follows so swiftly upon that scene.

Design

The costume designer as well as the designer of settings needs to be familiar with the basic principles of design, for just as color can be used to produce psychological reactions on the part of the audience, so lines, areas, and textures can be used to produce calculated effects.

FUNDAMENTALS

Of primary importance to design is an understanding of line, contrast, scale, and texture.

Line. The eye follows the path of least resistance and is therefore attracted to and follows with ease an unbroken line, whether it be straight or curved. It has been pointed out in Chapter 11 that a setting which uses many vertical lines produces an emotional feeling of loftiness and exaltation on the part of the spectator, while one consisting of all horizontal lines or planes produces a completely different impression. In the same way, a costume designed with predominatingly vertical lines makes the actor look more stately—and taller and more slender as well. It may also augment the effect of a lofty setting by creating the same feeling of loftiness and exaltation as that expressed by the set.

Horizontal lines on a costume, as in a room, give the illusion of width. Slanting or diagonal lines, especially if they make sharp angles, show movement, unrest, excitement, and action. The eye will follow broken lines, but more slowly, as it has to

Top left and right. These two designs show different interpretations of a Devil. **Top left.** This design was rendered in red and yellow, with huge fingernails of cardboard and a horned headdress and wings of red flannel. **Top right.** This Devil was dressed in white tights with red wings and a twisted shiny, metal tail. The **top left** figure is almost a traditional rendering, the **top right** is more original. **Bottom left.** This shows a modern interpretation of Mayan Warrior costumes adapted from stone carvings on Mayan temples. The headdresses were made of painted buckram. **Bottom right.** This shows an interpretation of medieval costume rendered in lavender, with deep-purple sleeves and skirts, the cuffs lined with magenta crepe paper and the veils rendered in turquoise voile.

bridge the gaps; therefore, too many broken lines used together tend to produce a confusing effect which is irritating to the spectator.

Contrast. No matter how beautiful or pleasurable a thing is, too much of it is cloying to the taste and creates a craving for contrast or variety. This is especially true on the stage where dramatic situation follows dramatic situation and an entire play is built upon a succession of contrasts. Costume, too, should contain contrast so that it will be noticed and so that it will hold attention on the actor. Black and white used together are the strongest contrasts, but more subtle ones can be used with equal effectiveness. Perhaps an actor or a group of actors will be costumed in light, closely related colors so as to contrast with a deep, ominous background. In one production of *Twelfth Night,* the entire play was produced in black and silver, with but a single note of color relief—Viola's red wig.

Scale or proportion. The relative size of objects or areas seen together can produce in the spectator an effect independent of other characteristics, such as color and texture. Too great similarity in size is monotonous, and too great difference in size may be grotesque or definitely unpleasant. A room in which the wallpaper is patterned with diminutive rosebuds and the draperies with immense poppies and huge leaves will affect many people unpleasantly. Regardless of the colors, the two decorative patterns are too different in scale to harmonize. When there is difference in size, but not too great difference, a harmonious and pleasing effect is achieved. Good proportion, or scale, cannot be secured by mathematical formulae; a sound feeling for it must be developed through critical observation.

Texture. Of great importance to the costume designer is a feeling for texture. Just as in the case of scale relations, certain fabrics and weaves combine more dramatically and aesthetically than others. In general, rough textures look well together and smooth and shiny textures harmonize with each other, but too much similarity is monotonous and some contrast in textures is desirable. Here again, one's personal sensitivity to textural combinations is valuable. No one would think of combining burlap and chiffon in a single garment, yet burlap and cheesecloth

Here are shown examples of costumes worn by a chorus of Mayan Priests in a musical extravaganza. A most interesting effect was produced by designing the costumes in such a way that the front of each costume was identical, but when seen from the back, each cloak was different in color and pattern, producing an element of surprise. Since there were twenty-four in the chorus, the total stage picture was completely changed in color whenever the priests changed position.

might be used together effectively. The actor and his stage personality must also be considered. A smooth, sophisticated character costumed in jersey, heavy crepe, or satin would, by the costume's texture, reflect the personality demanded by the play. Robert Edmond Jones is supposed to have said, concerning texture for individual characters, that he introduced his actors and materials to each other and if they didn't get on together one of them had to be given up.

DESIGN PRINCIPLES

To plan costumes that are interesting and harmonious and psychologically correct for a given character, the following design principles are useful.

Opposition. A design consisting of straight lines meeting at angles, usually right angles, is said to be in *opposition*. Such a design is strong, harsh, direct, and basic. A plaid is an example of opposition.

Transition. A design consisting of straight lines, to which curved lines have been added to soften the opposition is known as a design in *transition*. It may also consist entirely of curved lines. A column is an example of transition, for the capital and base are transitional members softening the austere line of the shaft where it meets roof and ground.

Repetition. Repetition is achieved in a design when some element such as line, area, shape, value, or color is repeated at regular or irregular intervals. Frequently, one element is repeated and another varied within a single design. For example, the unit of design in an all-over pattern may be repeated exactly but the colors may be changed in some of the units, or color may be repeated but the size of the unit may be modified.

Balance. There are two kinds of balance: (1) *symmetrical* and (2) *asymmetrical* or *occult*. *Symmetrical balance* is obtained when both sides of a design—on either side of an imaginary center axis—are identical. *Asymmetrical* or *occult balance* is obtained when unequal attractions balance at unequal distances on either side of an imaginary center axis, the larger object being nearer the axis. A large, plain area on a dress, by its very size, may balance a small detail strategically placed, such as a large button, a pocket, a bow or sleeve ornamentation.

Movement. Slanting lines are exciting to the eye and when followed create a feeling of movement, life, and tension. In a costume, slanting lines can be placed so as to direct the attention to any part of a garment—the neck, the waist, or the ankles— and so can dramatize even a robe, a cloak, or a headdress.

Radiation. A wheel, the sun, a rose window in a cathedral, and a fan are all examples of the principle of radiation, by which a design spreads out from a central spot or area. Like movement, because the resulting design is made up of slanting lines, it can concentrate interest or divert it from a particular area.

Emphasis. A good composition, whether it be a painting, a costume, or the façade of a building, should have a center of interest, or a point of emphasis. In a landscape it may be the red roof of a barn which attracts the eye; in a costume it may be an embroidered vestee or a contrasting belt; in a building it is probably the entrance or a group of windows over the main doorway. By using contrast in size, color, or shape, and by subordinating all other elements, the important area is stressed and emphasis is obtained.

Rhythm. The principle of rhythm incorporates many of the preceding ones, for rhythm may be obtained by using straight or curved lines, separately or in combination. It always includes a certain amount of repetition—usually of line or area. Its aim should be a balanced design with a good center of interest, and it is full of movement. Rhythm implies certain pleasing similarities of line and shape. It may be strong, vibrant, marching; slow, lazy, undulating; staccato, with broken areas; or gay and skipping, with repeated curves of varying lengths.

The costume designer should be able to recognize all these design principles not only when they are found in clothes but everywhere: in nature, architecture, painting, sculpture, industrial design, textiles, and so on.

Period or Historical Costume

Before anyone can plan a costume or a setting for a historical play he must know something of the visual aspects of the age which the play depicts. There are many excellent books dealing with historical costume, and a designer can best interpret a particular play by studying several of them for the period and country which the play demands. Famous paintings that show portraits of a given period and groups of figures costumed in the style of a certain time can be most useful to the designer, not only in showing details and textures of clothing fashionable in that age, but because such paintings often indicate how the clothes should be worn: the typical silhouette, the tip of a hat or headdress, the drape of a cloak, the bunched fullness of an overskirt, or the length of a wig.

In costuming any specific period, one will seek to express the characteristics peculiar to the period and avoid falling into certain pitfalls. Almost any period can be better rendered by a slight exaggeration of cut and color than by too literal a reproduction, which may result in authentic but dull costume. The following paragraphs attempt to point out the high spots of the most important periods and certain practices to avoid in costuming them.

EGYPTIAN

There is an austerity to Egyptian clothing which is best interpreted by slightly stiff materials or by transparent or semitransparent fabrics, plaited and hanging close to the figure. Avoid skimpy skirts or robes, but also avoid bunchy fullness that disguises the contour of the figure. Collars, wristbands, girdles, and headdresses may be ornately patterned and full of strong colors and gold. Wigs should be made of heavy strands of candlewick dyed black or midnight blue. A blue-black will appear blacker under stage light than will a true black.

GREEK AND ROMAN

Drapery is the keynote of the Greek and Roman periods; for the human figure was clothed with material that was draped, tied, and pinned about it in graceful folds and cascades. All classic costume was not white, but it was of solid colors, often with small patterns dotted over the surface, or with larger patterns forming contrasting borders at the edges. Bands of solid color also formed borders, and scarfs and capes offered another possible note of color contrast. Any thin material is suitable for these costumes, and unbleached muslin, if cut amply, can be made to fall in graceful lines, especially if the dressing has been washed or dyed out of it. Old sheets are ideal for togas and classic robes.

Armor and helmets for Greek and Roman warriors can be made from oilcloth, painted gold, silver, or brown with metallic or oil paint, and cut and fastened together with brass paper fasteners which will not tear out as stitched seams will. Stiff buckram can be cut and sewed to form helmet shapes, greaves for the legs, and cuffs for the arms. The edges should be bound with adhesive tape to prevent chafing the skin of the wearer. Shields and swords can be made of wallboard and wood, cut with jigsaws and painted in appropriate designs.

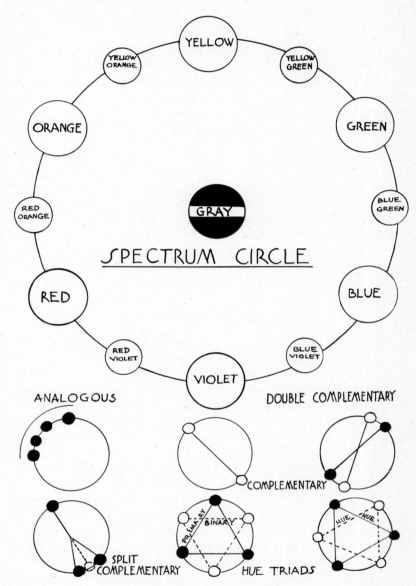

By referring to this chart, more harmonious and unusual color schemes can be planned for individual costumes and for total stage pictures.

BYZANTINE AND NEAR EASTERN

Lavish color, intricate patterns, and much gold, silver, and semiprecious stones characterize Byzantine and Near Eastern costumes. Robes for both men and women are cut, not draped. They hang from the neck and have sleeves sewed into them. They fit easily but are not too full or clumsy. Suitable patterned materials are often impossible to find, but any plain colored fabric can be painted or stenciled with the authentic textile motifs. Bands of embroidery set with semiprecious stones can be simulated with appliquéd strips of gold and silver foils and papers and gems from the dime store. Velvets and brocades can be suggested by dyed outing flannel, stencilled with metallic paint.

MEDIEVAL AND RENAISSANCE

During the Middle Ages and the Renaissance, costuming was elaborate in cut and detail. The materials worn were heavy woolens and linens; velvets; and brocades adorned with fur, semiprecious stones, and, in the Renaissance, with lace and ruchings. These materials are expensive, but substitutes such as the following goods have been found satisfactory.

Woolen fabrics can be simulated by burlap, monk's cloth, and outing flannel, all of which dye well. Velvets and brocades can be suggested by sateens, rayons, and dyed outing flannel. Unbleached muslin doubles for linen and, when dyed, can pass for woolen goods. Fur can be indicated by cotton, or by padded bands of outing flannel, dyed brown, gray, or black. For certain lace effects shelf paper or paper doilies can be used; for other effects crocheted lace stiffened with starch is effective.

For elaborate medieval headdresses, buckram or cardboard frames covered with material are serviceable and cheap. Shoes made of sateen or any strong fabric can be worn over slippers or hose and with padded pointed toes or wide slashed toes can represent medieval or Renaissance footgear.

The long hair worn by men in the Middle Ages is difficult to copy, and wigs for every member of a cast are expensive. One solution is to let as many of the male characters as possible wear hats during all scenes, and to drape the back and sides of the hat or headdress with material enough to cover the back of the head and neck. In one production of *Richard of Bordeaux* only the leading actors wore wigs; all the supporting cast was swathed in scarfs about the ears.

The silhouettes of any period should be studied, but this is particularly true of the Middle Ages and Renaissance. Paintings and sculpture are excellent guides to historic silhouettes. The infanta paintings by Velasquez show the wide-skirted silhouette of the Spanish court, which is a distinct contrast to the bell-shaped skirt of Italy and France and the bulbous farthingale of Queen Elizabeth's England.

Men's clothing during these two periods followed an upward trend. During the Middle Ages, long robes to the ankles or at least below the knee were worn. By the end of the age, these had become knee-length or shorter. During the Renaissance, the skirt of the tunic shrank still more until it was a mere frill about the hips. With the shortened tunic were worn long hose and short, baggy trousers, pushed up above the knee. The trousers were padded. A simple substitute may be made by sewing a band of padded cotton or roll of soft cloth to a pair of the actor's shorts and then making big, full, short trousers with elastic top and bottom to wear over the padded shorts.

SEVENTEENTH AND EIGHTEENTH CENTURY

During the seventeenth and eighteenth centuries, silhouettes changed less than in the preceding periods, and a tight bodice, low neck, short sleeve, and full skirt became the foundation costume for women. Variations occurred in a diversity of materials, colors, trimmings and accessories. In general, court costumes in the reigns of Louis XV and Louis XVI were more delicate in color and more feminine in detail than those worn in the earlier reigns.

Men's clothes were as ornate as the women's and made just as much use of satin, lace, ruffs, and brocade. Plumes, curled wigs, gloves, muffs, lace, frills, and embroidered waistcoats were in vogue. Silk hose and buckled shoes set off the satin knee breeches and wide-skirted coats.

Both men's and women's costumes of this era can be interpreted in sateens and rayons as well as in chintz, cretonne, and other flowered cotton fabrics chosen for their suitability of pattern and color.

OPPOSITION TRANSITION REPETITION

EQUAL
BALANCE

UNEQUAL
BALANCE

RADIATION
AND EMPHASIS

This shows design principles applied. In the example of **repetition**, the stripes are the repeated element but for variety they have been modified in width. In the example of **radiation and emphasis**, two principles have been illustrated in a single design. Emphasis implies some one area that attracts the attention, and in this costume the motif is at the waist.

NINETEENTH CENTURY

In the nineteenth century, costume developed in two directions. There was still the elaborate clothing worn by the nobility and by people of wealth, but middle class dress took on its own character and importance. Walking clothes, street outfits, and riding habits appeared. Men's clothing began to conform to a pattern which it still retains. Satins and velvets were discarded for dark, serviceable colors. Coats, trousers and cloaks in plum, bottle-green, gray, and tan cloth were worn with high crowned hats of similar colors.

Women's costumes of this century can be made fairly easily, but men's clothing should be rented or made by a dressmaker or tailor, as cut and line are important and makeshifts will not do.

TWENTIETH CENTURY

Twentieth century fashions are perhaps the hardest to reproduce today. They are so close to many of us that every detail is remembered, yet they are not old enough to have been treasured by individuals and so are hard to find. Old fashion magazines or illustrated books, published between 1900 and 1950 are the designer's most reliable source of inspiration.

Clothing Construction

The costume designer should know the rudiments of clothing construction, for without such knowledge much material is wasted and results are often disappointing. He should be able to use a paper pattern and to lay it out so that the material may be cut economically, with the long portion of the garment on the long grain of the goods. The material should always be cut generously, allowing for larger seams than the pattern demands, so that garments can be taken in or let out to fit the wearer and so that vigorous movement will not rip a seam.

Because actors and actresses when seen on a stage are usually slightly above the eye level of the audience, all skirts, tunics and short robes should be made slightly longer than customarily worn, and slips should be correspondingly adjusted.

It is not necessary to sew costumes for the stage with the same accurate finesse that is demanded of other garments, but it is necessary that they be sewn for strength and hard wear. Unless the material ravels badly, seams need not be bound. For a large theatre, nonfraying material need not even be hemmed. A stage costume often has more style if sewn for effect rather than for perfection, but it is not practical unless it can withstand frequent trying on, hasty changes, and general wear and tear.

PRACTICAL STAGE MATERIALS

In the section on "Historical Costume" (page 427), certain materials were mentioned that under stage light simulate expensive fabrics. In this section materials that are most adaptable for stage costumes are listed.

Transparent materials. *Cheesecloth* comes in many colors or may be dyed. It takes light well and when made up with ample fullness is a most effective transparent material.

Voile is a thin fabric too expensive for most costumes but is very graceful when plaited for skirts, sleeves, and capes.

China silk is another thin fabric too expensive for general use but most attractive for flowing effects. It can be dyed any color.

Tarlatan is made in a wide variety of colors. Any color that cannot be found can be produced by using a layer of one color over a layer of another thereby blending the color effect to produce the desired shade, as a layer of yellow over a layer of red to produce orange. Tarlatan also makes excellent ruffs and ruffles, and at a distance it simulates lace edgings.

Opaque materials. Virtually all opaque or closely woven fabrics can be stenciled or painted upon if patterned effects are desired.

Unbleached muslin is adaptable to many uses. It can be dyed any color and can simulate linen, cotton goods, and woolen fabric.

Cambric and *percale* can be used with either the shiny or the dull side out, according to the effect desired.

Cotton crepe and *seersucker* are made in many colors and take light well.

Rayon satin, taffeta, and *sateen* are useful materials that may be found in a wide variety of colors and textures. Because rayon ravels easily, ample seams should be made and bound or sewn down so that the garment does not fray. Hems must be carefully sewn so that raveling will not hang down. These materials can be stenciled or painted with dyes, showcard poster paints, and metallic paints.

Outing flannel is a most useful material which can always be bought in white, pink, blue, and dark gray. White outing flannel takes dye exceptionally well and when made up into a costume, especially if it is draped into deep folds, resembles velvet, when seen under artificial light.

Oilcloth may be used in any of the colors in which it is made or it may be painted with oil or metallic paint on either side. It makes excellent armor, belts, and costume accessories. It should be sewn by hand, since machine seams tend to tear like perforated paper. It may also be held together in strategic spots by pronged paper fasteners. Raw edges should be turned and sewed, or should be covered with cloth or adhesive tape to avoid chafing the actor's skin.

Rubber sheeting falls in heavy, graceful folds and gives a sculptured quality to a costume.

Buckram is stiff and is very useful for the foundations of headdresses, panniers, or wings, for it can be cut, sewed, or painted.

Crepe paper comes in every color and can be used for entire costumes or parts of costumes. It can also be sewed flat on a piece of material of contrasting color and thus provide interesting facings for skirts, sleeves, tunics, etc. When sewed on material in this way, it will not tear easily. Too much crepe paper in a single costume will tend to make it rattle, therefore its use is likely to be limited to pageants, dance dramas, and musical productions where music provides a background that will drown out the swish of the paper.

Metallic foils and *papers* are excellent as trimmings, for they glitter and sparkle and may be cut out in any shape and either glued or sewed to the costume. Small bits of foil crunched up and sewed in place suggest mounted jewels.

Cellophane may be used as fringe or as accessories on costumes and headdresses.

Cardboard, pliable and of medium weight, is useful in constructing headdresses, wings, and other accessories. For it can be cut, fitted, sewed together, covered with fabric, painted, and pasted.

Plastic materials add texture contrast and color range.

APPLYING COLOR

Dyeing. Any color may be obtained by dyeing, and streaky dyeing often gives greater depth of effect, under light, than evenly dyed cloth. Cotton materials are harder to dye than silk, which picks up the dye immediately. Therefore, cotton goods require a longer dipping and boiling process than does silk. Be sure to rinse the material after dyeing so that it will not rub off on the actors or on other clothing with which it comes in contact.

Painting. It is difficult to find patterned goods in cheap materials that may be used for period costumes. It is therefore better to buy plain-colored material and paint or stencil it with a typical design of the period desired. If dyes are used for painting the material, they will leave it as soft as it originally was. Showcard poster paints, oil paints, and metallic paints stiffen the material where they are applied to it. If showcard paints are used, an undercoat of plain color or white will form a ground for the final painting and the color will not soak into the material. Oil paints leave an edge of oil around any painted area which often acts as an outline or border effect to the painted surface, giving it accent and character. In fact, a line of black or dark blue paint a half-inch wide, painted alongside a neck line, or outlining trimming, gives depth to the costume when seen across the footlights.

SCALE

Everything must be exaggerated slightly so as to "carry" to the audience. Therefore, larger buttons, ribbons, coarser-patterned lace or trimming, and even larger stitches are desirable. Safety pins will not show from the audience if the theatre is a large one.

The scale of design for both scenery and costume is governed by the size of the stage and auditorium. A small intimate stage, where the audience sits close to the players, demands better workmanship and smaller patterns in the costumes than a large stage. A large stage in a large auditorium will call for simpler costumes of plain colors—one color to an individual.

Care of Costumes

Any theatre which gives frequent productions will in time accumulate costumes, accessories, and properties. To be useful, these must be stored and cared for in a room devoted to that purpose. Many costumes can be remade, modified, disguised, or combined with parts of other costumes and thus used for several plays, thereby reducing the cost of each new production. All costumes should be cleaned before being stored, and any which may attract moths should be packed with moth repellents.

If all complete costumes are hung on hangers from rods and are arranged in chronological order, they are easily found at some future date. Irrespective of how they were combined in any given play, all aprons, belts, blouses, collars, gloves, hose, robes, shirts, shoes, skirts, tights, trousers, and tunics should be stored in special, labeled boxes. Large or small pieces of uncut material, if sorted by color and kept in labeled boxes are easily found when new costume projects arise. New yard goods, in large quantities, may be kept folded on shelves, as in a store. Trimmings, "jewelry," fans, metallic lace, cloth, or veiling if kept in separate boxes will be available when needed. Woolen clothing, fur, or any costume which is inviting to moths should be especially packed with moth preventives.

Renting and Borrowing

If costumes are not made by a costume crew they must be rented or borrowed. Rented costumes are often more beautiful in texture than those made by a committee, but they are impersonal and not always sympathetic to a given character. A stage full of rented costumes is colorful but heterogeneous, since the costumer may want three cloaks of blue to fit in with the rest of the color scheme and may find that the costume company has but one blue, one red, and one brown. Cloaks are required, so these three are taken, but the color picture is broken.

RENTING

Cost. Rented costumes are expensive and their cost must be estimated against the other costs of production and the probable proceeds from the play. The rental per costume varies with the quality of the costume and with the company from which it is secured, the average rental ranging from $3.00 to $10.00.

For a production of *Henry IV, Part* I, given at a university theatre, rented costumes were used. The costume company from which costumes were usually rented had none of the particular period needed—all their costumes were of later date. Therefore, a New York company that specialized in that period provided them. They were beautiful and the armor was of the correct cut, but the bill was $625 for a total of two performances, and it ate up all the theatre's profits of the season. Even with less expensive rented costumes, the cost is high and should be anticipated.

Measurements. If costumes are rented, the costume committee must first procure accurate measurements for each actor so as to be able to choose clothing that will fit him with the least possible alteration. Rented costumes should be procured at least one week before the performance and two weeks if possible. This gives sufficient time for fitting the actors and for wearing the clothes in at least two dress rehearsals so that the wearer may feel at home in them by the night of production.

Care. The committee should keep a close watch over rented costumes and check after each wearing to see if every garment and accessory is in place. It is easy to mislay a glove, a chain, or a scarf in a theatre auditorium or an amphitheatre during rehearsal. Care should be taken of the costumes between rehearsals. The costume committee should check each costume in each dressing room after each rehearsal to see that it is properly hung up on hangers and not thrown in a heap; the committee should insist that hats with feathers or ribbons are hung so as not to crush perishable trimmings. If this is done, less pressing of garments is necessary.

Co-ordination. For some productions only a few costumes are rented and the rest are made or borrowed. When this is done, those not rented must be of a quality to harmonize in texture and workmanship with the rented ones. In a nineteenth-century play, the women's costumes may be made or borrowed, but the men's should be actual coats, trousers, waistcoats, cloaks, beaver hats, and so on.

BORROWING

Some plays can be completely costumed in borrowed clothes. This necessitates a knowledge of the town or city and an acquaintance with persons who have the needed clothing and will agree to loan it to the theatre. The costume committee must be willing to collect, care for, and return the garments in the same condition they were in when they were borrowed, and any damage to them through accident or wear must be repaired before their return.

Usually clothing that is just out of date is hard to rent and is most easily found by borrowing from friends of the theatre. Plays like O'Neill's *Ah! Wilderness* and Ruth Gordon's *Years Ago* call for twentieth-century clothes but not of this year's cut. Middy blouses, pointed shoes, sailor hats, and blazer jackets help create the mood of such plays and are needed to put them across successfully.

Organization of a Costume Committee

For every successful production there must be an efficient backstage organization and one of its busiest branches is the costume committee. Such a committee should be headed by a reliable person, usually a girl or woman who knows how to cut and make clothes, who is a good organizer, and who works well with people and can make them work—for both tact and coercion will be needed before dress rehearsal night. If the costumes are to be made she should have plenty of assistants, but she should personally supervise all work and check to see if it is being done up to schedule so as to be ready on time.

PRELIMINARIES

As soon as a cast is chosen, the costume committee chairman and her assistants should take the measurements of each actor and record them for future reference. She should be given the costume designs by the director. She may be commissioned to purchase the materials from which the costumes are to be made or she may be given the materials and shown how to allot them for individual costumes or parts of costumes. For example, she may have twelve yards of goods with which to make two dresses and one skirt, and the scraps may have been planned to be used for trimmings of other costumes.

She, or one of her committee, should be responsible for buying sufficient thread, needles, pins, elastic, tape, and any other essentials needed. Thread need not match every colored costume; black and white will serve for almost every purpose.

A room which can be locked when not in use should be provided for costume construction. It should contain one or more sewing machines, tables, chairs, and shelf space on which to store unfinished work. It should also contain a rod from which finished costumes or those in progress can be hung. It should be equipped with several electric outlets so that irons can be plugged in to press costumes before performances. (An ironing board is another essential.) A wall bulletin board is needed on which the chairman of the costume committee can post a schedule of costumes, when they are due, and who is responsible for each one, as well as a list of appointment times for actors to appear for fittings. Several pairs of scissors on long tapes tied to the tables or sewing machines may be convenient; an alternative is to make each member of the committee responsible for her own scissors, pincushion, and tape measure.

Warnings: Be sure that electric irons are disconnected and the electric lights turned off before the room is closed and locked. Do not allow smoking in the room, for it is a firetrap as long as so much necessary but inflammable material is about—especially if cotton, crepe paper, cellophane, and so on are used.

Finally the chairman should make a list of all costumes to be made and should assign to each member of the committee a certain actor or a group of actors for whose costumes each is responsible.

REHEARSAL AND PERFORMANCE

When all costumes are made, the committee's work is still far from done. All costumes should be pressed and hung in readiness for dress rehearsal. Since photographs of the show are usually made during dress rehearsals, the pressing is necessary before rehearsal; a photograph will reveal rumpled material and unpressed hems with cruel accuracy.

Whether costumes are made or rented, a member of the committee should be assigned to each actor, or small group of actors, to be of assistance in fastening clothing, adjusting cloaks, and checking the angle of hats and headdresses before they appear on the stage.

If all these procedures have been followed, the chairman of the costume committee should be free to sit in the auditorium during dress rehearsal and look over each scene with a critical eye. She should look first at the total stage picture as a color unit and see if it is harmonious or whether the substitution of a different colored scarf or cloak would improve the ensemble effect. Next she should check on the appearance of each individual costume to see if it is a success or whether it needs modification. Stage light is revealing, and it should be the responsibility of the costume chairman to see that actresses are wearing sufficient underwear, brassieres, girdles, and so on. She should provide herself with a notebook and make notes of any changes she wishes to effect before the night of production. It will be helpful if one of her committee sits next to her at rehearsals, ready to run errands or take messages to actors, so that she may stay in front and see the whole show as a unit.

As has already been mentioned, after each dress rehearsal and after each performance the costume committee is responsible for checking costumes, seeing that they are hung up, and locking dressing rooms.

By production night everything should be in a state of routine, with no problems to be solved. One member of the committee should always be backstage during a production, provided with needle, thread, and safety pins so as to be able to repair unforeseen damages and tears which may occur during a performance. Accidents will happen, but if all the foregoing precautions are taken, the costume end of a production should run off smoothly.

Creating a Mood Through Costume

If a designer has sensitivity and imagination and a sense of humor, the resulting costumes will not only clothe the actors but will enhance the mood of the play. As we said earlier in this chapter, clothing should express the wearer, and stage costume especially should help build the character through skillful design that incorporates color psychology and design principles.

INTERPRETATION

If the designer has a knowledge of architecture, furniture, and costume of the country or period in which the play is set, then he may *interpret* and make the materials he uses express the mood of the play and the characteristics of the specific character. Nothing is more deadly than a historically correct production in which no interpretation or imagination has been employed. Interpretation may even be incorrect (not authentic) and yet be not only more interesting than accurate reproduction but completely "right" for the mood of the play. *Carmen Jones* was a perfect example of inspired, interpreted, imaginative, and even humorous costuming which helped set the tone of the production.

Opera costumes are too often lavish and authentic, but dull, uninspired, and completely lacking any spark of interpretation. With vision, school or experimental theatre productions often outstrip professional performances in artistry and "eye appeal."

The modern dance has proved what imagination and interpretation can do to individual and group costumes of a more or less basic cut. Modern dance costumes show infinite variety even when conforming to a general pattern of long sleeves, tight bodices, and full skirts.

AUTHENTICITY

To be able to interpret in costume the mood or theme of a play and its characters, the designer must know what authentic costume of the country or period looks like—what colors and textures were worn—and whether the character is wealthy, of average means, or poor.

In Jules Romains' *Dr. Knock* a number of the lesser characters are peasants who come to the doctor for treatment. In one school production a new committee was entrusted with the costuming and carried out the designs for each costume to the letter, but bought shiny sateen for each garment with the result that the mass effect of the peasants was of a group of well-to-do citizens in satin breeches, blouses, and tunics. This was not discovered until the dress rehearsal, when it was too late to make new outfits, so all costumes were worn inside-out, with the dull surface suggesting homely, inexpensive fabrics rather than expensive silks.

EXAGGERATION

Having become aware of the correct costume for each character, the designer should play with the design a little and exaggerate the salient elements. Just as lines and gestures are heightened on the stage so as to carry across the footlights, so costume may be exaggerated for the same reason. Larger buttons, ribbons, bigger patterns, coarser lace or trimmings, more daring color, and even larger accessories such as purses, fans, and wallets may be desirable.

COLOR

Since individuals react spontaneously and often unconsciously to color, it becomes one of the most important factors in the interpretation of both costume and scenery. In Act I, scene 3 of Robert Edmond Jones' production of *Othello,* at the Central City Opera House in Colorado, everyone was awaiting the entrance of the Moor. The setting showed a large stone hall; the costumes of the doges and attendants were in pinks, magentas, and reds; the main doorway through which the entrance would be made was a well of blue-black darkness on either side of which was set a gilt and silver *torchère*. Into that scene came the swarthy Othello, dressed in mustard yellow and completely enveloped in a huge, white, woolen, hooded cape. The mustard harmonized with his dark skin, and the white cape framed him in the dark doorway as effectively as a white mat frames and brings out the beauty of a painting.

Many stage effects are ruined by thoughtless color grouping of actors. If a scene calls for only one or two characters on the stage at a time, there is no problem, but if large groups of characters are used and if there is much movement from group to group, the most careful planning of color sequences is necessary. Pattern seen against pattern is confusing and uninteresting; therefore, a safe and artistic rule to follow is to costume the leading characters in plain colors and costume the supporting cast in patterned fabrics. Another way to handle this situation is to dress the leading characters in patterned costumes and the supporting players in solid colors or in color effects varied by the use of a blouse of one color and a skirt of another; trousers of brown and doublet of green.

For certain effects keying a whole scene to one color may be effective, with the leading characters wearing the brightest or lightest or else the darkest version of the hue used. In a production of Dunsany's *Golden Doom* all costumes except the High Priest's were in variations of yellow, orange, gold, henna, copper, and brown. For emphasis and relief, the High Priest was robed in turquoise blue, gold, copper. The setting was in gold, copper, and browns.

In a production of *Twelfth Night* a striking color plot was followed. Settings for all scenes were midnight blue and silver. All the comedy characters wore reds, oranges, and yellows. All the romantic characters wore dull greens, blues, and violets. Maria, who played with both groups, wore yellow and violet. Viola wore peacock green, which not only harmonized with both groups but accented her in any grouping.

Contemporary Costume

Contemporary costume creates as much of a problem for the designer as do period clothes. Finding just the right suit or dress or hat, a coat that shows that it is shabby or a little out of date, or a blouse that is too fussy for the occasion, is just as important as creating the proper throne dress for Elizabeth or creating a leafy garment for Puck.

A play often contains a charwoman, a poor relation, or a tramp, like Sparrow in *Liliom,* whose clothes must be deliberately seedy and unpressed to carry out the illusion of the characterization. Even a housedress poses a problem. A miner's wife in a one-act play talks about how little money she and her husband have and how she is about to make herself a new dress for less than a dollar. The dress she is wearing is old, faded but clean. On the first night of one production, the young girl who played the wife appeared just before the curtain time in a brand-new, frilly, starched housedress, with her hair elaborately waved. The director was horrified, for the girl no longer expressed the plucky but poor wife of a miner. There was only one thing to be done. The dress was taken off, rumpled and soiled enough to make it look faded; the girl's hair was recombed more simply, and the play went on.

Unifying Costume and Setting

The costume designer must work in close harmony with the scene designer so that costumes and set may blend into an artistic unity. If the scenery is conceived as gay and boldly expressionistic, costumes of intricate detail and conservative cut and color will clash with it and destroy the unity of the stage picture. This is why, at times, rented costumes, although superior in quality and workmanship, do not fit into the play as conceived by the director. Too often rented costumes, while historically correct, are of all colors, and so cannot be made to harmonize with a prearranged color and light plot as can costumes made for the production itself. In the days when the star was allowed to choose her own costume and appeared becomingly gowned no matter what her part might be, the same incongruity often existed between her costume and the scenery designed for the play.

Fantasy

All costume can be classified as realistic, abstract, or fantastic, with historical accuracy one of the considerations in most costume design. But a more practical classification for the costumer is as follows: contemporary, historical, and fantastic. Fantastic costumes are used in fantastic plays, in some pageants, in dance dramas, and in musical extravaganzas and revues. They are the designer's delight, for any amount of imagination, daring, and humor may be used in their creation. They do not need to conform to any known period, pattern, texture, or color. Exaggeration, contrast, surprise, and invention can be used to the fullest extent. They are often used under a variety of colored lights and should be so planned that none of the lights under which they may be seen will kill their color or design.

Such costumes may be planned for a chorus of a number of singers or dancers. If an entire chorus is costumed identically, the mass effect is extremely pleasing, especially if the star, in a contrasting costume, sings or dances in front of this human stage setting. A chorus in which each member is costumed differently may be effective or may appear simply a kaleidoscopic mass of colored spots when viewed from the audience.

In a revue or pageant several costume changes may be necessary for one actor, dancer, or singer, and the design should be such that a quick change can be made. This involves planning easy fastenings and a costume as nearly in one piece as is practicable so that it may be slipped on and off with ease.

A test of a good costume designer is the costume he creates for a well-known character such as Red Riding Hood, Napoleon, Titania, Queen of the Fairies, or Santa Claus. For each of these the audience has a preconceived notion of the character's appearance. The designer's problem is to create a costume which is recognizable but with a new twist that will catch the attention of the audience and yet not divert its attention from the play.

Although the setting of a play may be definite and static, the costumes are moving bits of color which should complement the general mood created by the setting and at the same time help interpret the complex pattern of the developing dramatic action. Moving costumes on a stage help to balance the total picture as well as to form a rhythmic flow of line, mass, and color throughout the scene. A stage costume has an important role to play, and it is the designer who must meet the challenge.

Questions

1. What colored lights are most trying to costumes?
2. How can a stage effect be keyed to one color?
3. What are the attributes of a good costume designer?
4. How do light and pigment primaries differ?
5. How does a knowledge of color psychology help a designer?
6. What is "scale"? Give an example of its use.
7. Should all costuming be authentic? Why?
8. Describe the characteristics of Egyptian and Renaissance male costume.
9. Name six materials that are useful for costumes, and indicate in what periods they could be used.
10. Why is interpretation such an important factor in costuming?
11. How may a costume be humorous, and where may humorous costume be used?
12. Define a "split complementary" harmony and describe a costume which makes use of it.

13. How do fantastic costumes differ from others?
14. How does a designer create a mood through costuming?
15. Why should the costume and scene designer work in collaboration?
16. How is costume design affected by the size of the theatre?
17. What are the duties of a costume committee chairman?
18. What is the costumer's problem at a dress rehearsal?
19. How does the construction of stage costume differ from the construction of other clothing?
20. What qualities should dance drama costumes have?

Exercises

1. Design a costume for a medieval jester; a Greek matron; a Roman senator; and an eighteenth-century dandy.
2. Design a costume for Mrs. Lincoln in Drinkwater's *Abraham Lincoln*. Let the design be an afternoon dress that will express her character.
3. Plan a costume for Mrs. Roberts in Galsworthy's *Strife*. Choose the scene in which that lady is sitting before the fire in a chair, wrapped in a rug. Try to express her personality and her mental and physical condition by the costume that you plan.
4. For the Idol who has lost his eye in Dunsany's *Night at an Inn* the stage directions say: "Stony steps are heard. Enter a hideous Idol." Plan a costume for this character that is awe-inspiring and hideous, that seems to be of stone, and yet is a practical costume that can be worn by a man and in which he can walk.
5. Design three costumes for a dance drama in which the period is Egyptian, or for a dance drama in which the period is Italian Renaissance.
6. Plan a color scheme for a cowboy chorus for the musical *Oklahoma!*, designating the color of shirts, chaps, etc. so as to render them attractive when seen under amber light.
7. Design costumes for characters representing Greed, Famine, Spring, Science, Moses, Shadow, and Puck.
8. Design costumes for a Grecian warrior, an angel, Captain Kidd, Napoleon, a sorcerer, the Queen of Hearts.
9. Plan a keyed color scheme for a scene in which there is a group of peasants, two Franciscan priests, and a medieval king. List the colors to be used in each costume.
10. Plan a series of three costumes in which red is the predominating color. Let the three costumes interpret Flame, War, and Carmen.

Bibliography

Art Principles

Burris-Meyer, Elizabeth, *Color and Design in the Decorative Arts,* New York: Prentice-Hall, Inc., 1935.

Collins, M. R. and Riley, O. L., *Art Appreciation,* New York: Harcourt, Brace & Company, 1933.

Faulkner, Ray, *Art Today,* New York: Henry Holt & Company, Inc., 1941.

Gardner, Helen, *Art Through the Ages,* New York: Harcourt, Brace & Company, 1936.

————, *Understanding the Arts,* New York: Harcourt, Brace & Company, 1932.

Goldstein, Harriet, *Art in Everyday Life,* New York: The Macmillan Company, 1940.

Color

Birren, Faber, *The Story of Color,* Westport, Conn.: Crimson Press, 1941.

Bossert, H., *Encyclopedia of Color,* Berlin: Wasmuth, 1928.

Burris-Meyer, Elizabeth, *Historical Color Guide, Primitive to Modern Times,* New York: Helburn, 1938.

Graves, Maitland E., *The Art of Color and Design,* New York: McGraw-Hill Book Company, Inc., 1941.

Jacobson, Egbert, *The Science of Color,* American Photo-Engravers Association: Chicago, 1937.

Luckiesh, Matthew, *The Language of Color,* New York: Dodd, Mead & Company, 1918.

Maerz, A. and Paul, M. R., *Dictionary of Color,* New York: McGraw-Hill Book Company, 1930.

Munsell, A. H., *Color Notation,* Baltimore: Munsell, 1923.

Costume

Bartas, Y., and Spicer, D., *Latin American Costumes,* New York: Hyperion Press, 1941.

Brooklyn Public Library, *Reading and Reference List on Costume.*

Calthrop, D. C., *English Costume,* London: A. & C. Black, 1906.

Detroit Public Library, *Costume, a List of Books,* n.d.

Earle, A. M., *Two Centuries of Costume in America,* New York: The Macmillan Company, 1903.

Evans, Mary, *Costume Throughout the Ages,* Philadelphia: J. B. Lippincott Company, 1930.

Fischel, Oskar and Boehn, Max, *Modes and Manners of the Nineteenth Century,* New York: E. P. Dutton & Co., 1909.

Flemming, Ernest, *Encyclopedia of Textiles,* London: Ernest Benn, Ltd., 1928.

Giafferri, P. L., *Feminine Costume of the World,* Paris: Editions Nilsson, 1926.

————, *L'histoire du Costume Feminine Française,* Paris: Editions Nilsson, 1922.

Haire, F. A., *The Folk Costume Book,* New York: A. S. Barnes, 1926.

Halouze, Edouard, *Costumes of South America,* New York: French & European Publications, Inc., 1941.

Hottenroth, F., *Le Costume chez Les Peuples Anciens et Moderns,* Paris: A. Guerine, 1896.

Kretschmer, A., *Costumes of All Ages, Ancient and Modern,* Leipzig: J. G. Bach, 1887.

McClellan, E., *Historic Dress in America,* Philadelphia: McCrae Smith, 1910.

Merida, Carlos, *Mexican Costume,* Chicago: Pocahontas Press, 1941.

————, *Carnival in Mexico,* Mexico City: Talleres gráficos de la nación, 1940.

Parsons, F. A., *The Psychology of Dress,* New York: Doubleday & Company, Inc., 1920.

Planche, J. R., *Cyclopedia of Costume,* London: Chatto & Windus, 1876–79.

Price, J. M., *Dame Fashion,* New York: Charles Scribner's Sons, 1913.

Racinet, A., *Le Costume Historique,* Paris: Firmin-Didot et Cie, 1888.

Rhead, G. W., *Chats on Costume,* New York: F. A. Stokes & Co., 1906.

Robida, A., *"Yester-Year," Ten Centuries of Toilette,* New York: Charles Scribner's Sons, 1891.

Roediger, V., *Ceremonial Costume of Pueblo Indians,* San Francisco: University of California Press, 1941.

Tilke, Max, *Oriental Costumes,* New York: Brentano's, 1922.

Traphagen, Ethel, *Costume Design and Illustration,* New York: John Wiley & Sons, 1918.

Webb, W. M., *Heritage of Dress,* New York: McClures, 1908.

Wissler, Clark, *Indian Costumes in the United States,* New York: American Museum of Natural History, 1926.

Louis Braun and others, editors, *Zur Geschichte der Kostüme,* Munich: Braun & Schneider, 1909.

CHAPTER 21. ~~~~~~~~~~~~~~~~~

MAKEUP

*T*he function of makeup is to increase the actor's expressiveness. Applied primarily to the face but also to any other parts of the body not covered by the costume, makeup helps to overcome the yellowing effect of artificial light and the blurring effect of distance. Positively, it is used to alter the actor's skin coloring and apparent facial structure to conform better to the requirements of the particular character in the particular play.

Modifying Factors

THE PLAY

The general character of makeup will be set by the mood, style, and theatrical form of the particular play, and of these the style is the most important consideration.

Style. In the realistic play, since the aim is to express something through the creation of an illusion of real life, makeup should be designed to produce natural effects. Like the other materials of production, it should not call attention to itself but should achieve the necessary alterations in the appearance of the actors by subtle means. In the abstract play, makeup will be less detailed, more stylized, and freer to accentuate the actor's features which seem to express the essence of the character he is playing. In the fantastic play, makeup is free of the limitation of naturalness, and can be exaggerated or distorted to express the mood and meaning of the play. The makeup for *Pelleas and Melisande,* for instance, which seems to picture a twilight-world shadowed by a terrible and inescapable doom, might be uniformly pale with long lines and modeling suggestive of sadness.

Theatrical form. The representational play requires consistency in makeup, whether the style is realistic, abstract, or fantastic, because the characters must seem all to belong to the

Shown here is realistic makeup for a Greek play. Laurence Olivier as Oedipus in the Old Vic Company of London production has his nose built up with putty.

same world of the play. The presentational play, since it is not concerned with creating an illusion of this kind, permits and sometimes requires freedom in the use of makeup. Realistic and fantastic makeup might be used in the same play or in the same scene as long as the requirements of the characters were met. The style of the particular makeup will depend upon the degree to which the particular character is abstracted or distorted from life.

Greek tragedy and comedy were originally performed by actors who wore masks. These masks were sometimes abstractions

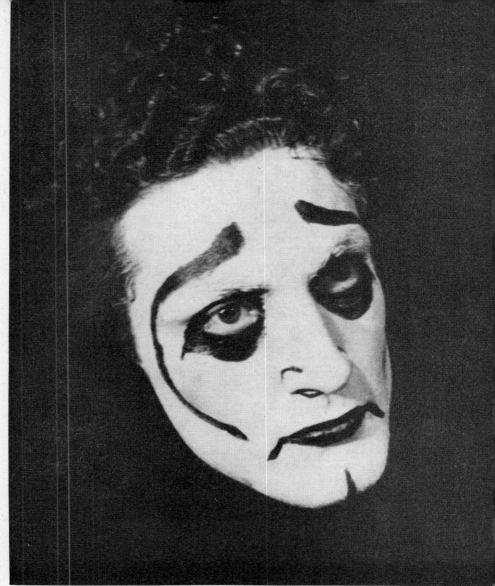

Richard Redden

This shows abstract makeup for the Greek play, *The Agamemnon*, University of Chicago Theatre. George Blair, director; makeup by John Bensen.

of the features and emotion of the character; sometimes they were grotesque distortions. It may not be practicable today to use masks in producing Greek drama, for great skill is required to make good ones, and neither actor nor audience is accustomed to them. Makeup used in their stead should employ the same kind of abstraction or distortion.

Of the medieval drama, the mystery and morality plays require abstraction and distortion in makeup, but to a lesser degree. A study of medieval paintings, altar pieces, and book illuminations will reveal how the Biblical characters and the type characters of the moralities were stereotyped in physiognomy as well as in costume.

English Restoration comedy on the other hand, although it is equally presentational, is primarily concerned with ridiculing the manners and behavior of a particular social class. The makeup, like the costume, will attempt to exaggerate what are already exaggerations. The makeup for young women, and to an extent the makeup for young men, will seek to give the effect of artificiality: abnormally creamy complexions, obvious rouge, exaggerated eyeshadows, and of course the inevitable beauty spots. The aged misers, cuckolds, and the representatives of the nonleisure classes, servants, doctors, merchants, lawyers, etc., should be given abstract or even grotesque makeups designed to express their stupidity, vanity, hypocrisy, or whatever dominating characteristic the playwright has endowed them with.

Molière's comedies are much broader in their scope, focusing on the foibles of no particular class. Most of the characters are broadly abstracted from life, sometimes to the point of fantasy, and they are clearly related to the highly conventionalized comic types of the Commedia dell' Arte, the Italian improvised comedy. The makeup should be abstracted and exaggerated in the same manner and degree to express as far as possible the naïvete, or hypocrisy, or pretentiousness, or stinginess of the particular character. This can be done without regard for considerations of realism.

In Shakespeare's tragedies we are accustomed to seeing realistic makeup, but his plays offer considerable scope for more direct expression through simplification and exaggeration. The comedies often mingle farcical and romantic elements. In *Twelfth Night* for example, Toby Belch, Aguecheek, and Malvolio might well be given grotesque makeups, while the Duke, Olivia, Viola, and Sebastian might be given relatively natural makeups.

Nineteenth-century melodrama is considerably more realistic in style than the earlier presentational drama, but its characters

Grotesque makeup on Dennis King as He in the Theatre Guild revival of *He Who Gets Slapped*.

are so obviously conventionalized types that this conventionalization will to some extent appear in the makeup. The heroine is always sweet and beautiful, the hero handsome and brave, and the villain oily and menacing.

Modern presentational plays like *The Adding Machine, From Morn to Midnight,* and *The Hairy Ape* seem to call for extremely artificial makeup or for masks.

THE THEATRE

The conditions of production, which are determined by the theatre building and its lighting facilities, affect certain other general characteristics of makeup.

Distance. The distance at which the actor must be seen is one of the important factors. Some elements of makeup would be unnecessary if all the spectators sat within ten or twelve feet of the actors. In many theatres no one sits that close to the stage, and some spectators sit sixty or seventy feet away. Consequently, some standard elements in makeup are designed to overcome the effect of distance and to make the actor's face carry by accenting its planes and by exaggerating such expressive features as the eyes, nose, and mouth. The larger the theatre, the stronger and sharper the makeup must be, even if a realistic effect is the aim. In very large theatres, makeup strong enough to carry and look natural from the farthest seats may look extremely artificial from the front rows. A compromise may be the best solution to this problem: makeup strong enough to carry to most of the seats and not so strong that it looks too artificial from the front rows. Of course, grotesque makeup must be more and more exaggerated the larger the theatre.

In the very small theatre, if natural effects are desired, the elements designed to emphasize the features should be used subtly or entirely omitted. Exaggeration suitable for abstract and fantastic plays can also be more subtle. This is particularly true of the salon type of arena theatre in which the actors are very close to the spectators.

Light. The intensity of illumination has a marked effect upon makeup. If the light on the actors is dim, makeup must be strong and sharp if it is to carry. Under bright light, makeup designed to produce natural effects must be subtler, the contrasts not so great.

The type of illumination also has its effect on makeup. Most plays today are produced under artificial electric light, which contains less red and more yellow than does sunlight. Consequently, one whole aspect of most makeup is designed to overcome the yellowing effect of electric light by reinforcing the natural red in the skin, cheeks, and lips. Good stage lighting today helps the makeup artist by using, whenever possible, tints of red on the acting areas. When this is done, less red reinforcement is required in the foundation color. Occasionally a scene is played in a blue or largely blue light, under which red tends to look black. For such a scene red should be omitted from the makeup (lips and cheeks) if possible. If the makeup must be worn in ordinary stage light also, it should be toned down with powder for the scene in the blue light.

Makeup to be worn in daylight, as in some outdoor theatres, requires considerable modification. Reinforcement of the red in the skin, lips, and cheeks must be done subtly, as for street wear in life. If natural effects are to be achieved, much greater subtlety must be exercised, though the factor of distance may counteract the clearer visibility under natural illumination. In small outdoor theatres, the water makeups may be more useful for realistic effects.

THE ROLE

The general character of makeup is determined largely by the style and form of the play and by the conditions of production, but its particular character is determined largely by the nature of the role. What is the character's function in the play? What kind of person is he—sad, happy, lively, lethargic, stupid, or intelligent? etc? How old is he? What is the state of his health? What is his occupation? What kind of life does he lead—active or restricted, outdoor or indoor? The answers to some or all of these questions will provide helpful clues to the specific form of the individual makeup.

THE ACTOR

Since makeup must be worn by human beings, it is limited by the general character of the human face, and although considerable transformation or distortion is possible, makeup, in comparison with setting, for instance, must be comparatively realistic. Makeup for the particular role will be determined in part by the appearance of the actor who is to play it. If the actor looks the part reasonably well, only *straight* makeup will be needed to counteract the yellowing effect of electric light and to accentuate his own features and normal expression so that these will carry to the farthest seats.

However, makeup will frequently be called upon to modify the actor's appearance by making him look older or younger, fatter or thinner, healthier or sicker than he is, or to give his face lines and planes suggestive of grief, or gaiety, or serenity. Or the role may require a mustache or a beard which the actor does not possess. Makeup thus designed to alter the actor's appearance in any considerable way is usually called *character* makeup. The changes which can be achieved with color, within the realistic style, are distinctly limited. The very thin, long face can be made with greasepaint, rouge, highlight, and shadow to look less long and thin, but it cannot be made to look round and fat. Likewise, the round, fat face can be made to look less round and fat, but it cannot be made to look long and thin. More can be done with plastic or three-dimensional makeup: beards and mustaches, nose putty, and cotton and gauze constructions, but as long as realism is an aim, the degree of change remains limited.

Greater changes are possible both with color and with plastic makeup for abstract and fantastic characters. The picture of the Priest in *The Flies,* on page 334, and of the character in *Agamemnon,* page 449, illustrate different degrees of abstraction, and the picture of Dennis King as He in *He Who Gets Slapped* illustrates a common type of grotesque makeup.

The Makeup Artist

Anyone who wishes to become an artist in makeup should study the different facial types he meets in life as a basis for his practice of makeup, remembering that simplification and exaggeration are necessary except for makeup for realistic characters in small theatres. Sculpture and painting may be even more rewarding, especially for the beginner, because the sculptor or painter has already done much of the simplification and exaggeration. The planes of the face, an understanding of which is essential to character makeup, are best studied as they are represented in three-dimensional sculpture. From the paintings of men like Rembrandt, Hals, Jan Van Eyk, Titian, and others who have represented types of the human face on canvas, one can learn how to use color, line, highlight, and shadow to suggest different types required for the stage.

This study provides a sound basis for experiment and practice with the materials of makeup under the conditions of production. Facility will come only with considerable practice.

MATERIALS

Cold cream: Used to clean the face before applying grease-paint foundation and to remove grease-paint makeup.

Foundation colors: Used to give the basic skin color to face, neck, hands, arms, and occasionally legs. There are two types: grease paint, which is sold in relatively hard, thick sticks, and in a softer form in tubes, and water paint, which is sold in cakes. The grease paints come in a great variety of colors, the water paints are more limited.

Lining colors: Used for highlights and shadows, for accenting the eyebrows, etc. They have a grease base and are sold in a variety of colors in hard, thin sticks and, in a softer form, in small tins.

Rouge: Ordinary lipstick rouge may be used, but a soft grease rouge, called *moist rouge,* for theatrical makeup, is sold in glass jars in four shades: light, special, medium, and dark. *Dry rouge,* used to touch up color in the cheeks either after powder has set the grease makeup or on top of water makeup, comes in cakes and in half a dozen tints and shades.

Powder: Dry theatrical powder used to set grease makeup is sold in large tins in about twenty different tints and shades. Liquid powder, used largely for body makeup, is sold in bottles and in a variety of skin colors.

Lining brushes, paper liners, and *toothpicks:* Used for applying lining colors and lip rouge.

Powder puffs: Large ones for applying powder.

Powder brushes: For removing excess powder.

Rabbit's foot: For applying dry rouge. A small powder puff may be used for this, but a rabbit's foot is better.

Crepe hair: For beards, mustaches, and sideburns. It is sold braided by the foot or yard and in an adequate variety of hair colors.

Spirit gum: Used to fasten crepe hair and some other kinds of plastic makeup to the face. It is sold in small bottles with applicator cork.

Rubbing alcohol: Used to clean makeup off the face before applying spirit gum, and also to dissolve the spirit gum when removing crepe hair.

Sharp scissors (barber type): For cutting crepe hair.

Facial tissue: For removing grease or water paint.

Absorbent cotton and *silk gauze:* Used to build up large parts of the face.

Nose putty: Used for small three-dimensional constructions, particularly to build up the nose.

Specific Practice
STRAIGHT MAKEUP

Grease paint. If grease paint is used, cold cream is first rubbed thoroughly into the skin of the entire face, including the eye-sockets and lids, the ears, and all of the neck not to be covered by the costume. The excess cold cream is then wiped off, so that the surface is left dry. If there is no street makeup to be removed, and if the soft form of grease paint is used, this first step may be omitted.

A foundation color is then selected according to the complexion and age of the actor or of the character he is playing: very light pink for extremely pale complexions, light pink for pale, blonde young girls and small boys, medium pink or a pinkish tan for brunette young women and young men, and dark pink mixed with some brown for middle-aged men and women.[1] This is applied in streaks or dabs on forehead, cheeks, nose, chin, ears, and neck, and then it is blended with the fingers until it is perfectly smooth and even over the whole surface.

Moist rouge (light for women with light complexions, medium for brunette women and most men, and dark for the dark complexion) is applied in a small circle or triangle at the highest point of each cheekbone and is blended by drawing the edges out with the fingertip toward the eye, toward the temple, toward the nose, and down toward the jaw until there is a subtle grada-

[1] The colors mentioned are descriptive; they do not refer to particular foundation colors sold by any manufacturer of makeup.

The above sketches show blending of rouge for a woman and for a man.

tion of red, strongest on the cheekbone and growing weaker as
it moves away, until it disappears completely in the foundation
color. Cheek coloring in women is ordinarily more localized
than in men, and the blending of the rouge in women's makeup
should therefore not be carried so far up on the temple nor so
far down toward the jaw as in men's makeup. However, the end
of the rouge even for women should not appear as a line, unless
one wishes the effect of badly applied makeup.

The lips should be accented with the same rouge applied with
brush or fingertip. Rouge is applied also very lightly to the upper orbit of the eye and in faint touches above the eyebrows, on
the bottom and on the sides of the nose, the lobes of the ears
and on the neck in order to lessen the contrast between the
foundation color and the accentuated lips, eyes, and eyebrows.

Because distance and the brightness of the foundation tend to make the eyes look smaller, the eyes are accented. A light area looks larger and closer when it is surrounded by dark areas. The eyes are therefore outlined with a shadow of the appropriate color, ordinarily chosen according to the color of the hair (*blonde:* blue or blue-gray; *brown:* light brown or red-brown; *brunette:* dark brown, dark red, or purple-red; *red:* blue-green, green, or brown). The color is taken on the end of brush, stump, or toothpick, and a line is drawn from the inner corner along the lower lid to a point a quarter of an inch beyond the outer corner, a little heavier in the middle than at either end. This is then blended downward about an eighth of an inch. The upper lid is shadowed in the same way but the line is blended up. These two lines are seen as heavy eyelashes. To insure against smudging when the eye is opened, the shadow on the upper lid should be powdered as soon as it has been blended. If the rest of the upper lid now appears too light, it should be darkened slightly with violet liner or with a mixture of dark gray and crimson. Two bright red dots, about a sixteenth of an inch in diameter, one near the inner corner of each eye, are supposed to give added sparkle to the eyes.

Unless eyebrows are unusually dark and thick, they should be accented with the appropriate lining color (light brown for blondes, brown or brown mixed with red for red hair, and dark brown or black for dark hair). This is applied with brush, stump, or toothpick, keeping the color strongest near the center and relatively light near the ends.

The nose may be accented by drawing a light, straight line of very pale pink or white down its length and shadowing the sides faintly with violet. A dab of bright red inside each nostril is also a traditional part of straight makeup.

The whole makeup is set with powder of a lighter color than the foundation: light pink for young women, and dark pink or brunette for dark women and for men. The powder should be patted on lightly but profusely and evenly over the whole makeup. The excess is then carefully brushed off. The powder sets the makeup so that it will not run or smudge easily, takes off the shine of the grease, and reduces the contrasts between rouge, foundation, and lining colors.

After this makeup has been powdered, little can be done to alter it. However, if the cheek rouge has been toned down too much by the powder it can be brightened with dry rouge of the same color, and eyebrows can be darkened and lips rerouged without destroying the whole makeup.

Greaseless makeup. No cold cream is used for a greaseless makeup. Cheek rouge, eye lines, highlights, and shadows are applied on the clean, dry face with grease makeup as described above but somewhat more heavily. Liquid base of the proper color is then patted on very lightly with a damp sponge and blended carefully. The aim should be to let just the right amount of rouge, highlight, and shadow show through the base. If too much of the rouge has been covered, the cheeks may be touched up with dry rouge applied over the base. It is easier to use dry rouge on the cheeks, applying it on top of the base, but the effect thus achieved is less subtle and lifelike. Eyebrows and lips are made up last, and no powder is necessary except to set these.

CORRECTIVE MAKEUP

It is often desirable to use makeup to correct facial defects or blemishes—that is, to make the actor's face conform more closely to the conventional notions of beauty. Complexion defects are taken care of by the foundation. Any undesirable depressions can be made largely invisible by a heavier application of the foundation color or by application of a lighter color. Prominences can be depressed by using less foundation on them or by shadowing them with a darker color.

Face. If the face is too wide, a darker foundation applied lightly on its sides, and rouge kept nearer the nose and blended more vertically than horizontally will make it look less wide. If the face is long and narrow, a lighter foundation on the sides of the face and rouge applied further from the nose and blended more horizontally than vertically will minimize the apparent length.

Eyes. If the eyes protrude too much under the upper lids, the prominence can be reduced by shadowing with violet or a mixture of dark gray or crimson. If they are deeply sunk, the upper lids should not be shadowed but perhaps highlighted with a light foundation.

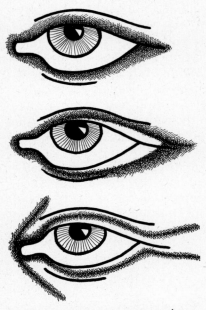

These sketches show eye makeup. **Top**, ordinary shadowing; **Middle**, extension of the cornea; and **Bottom**, lining to make eyes look farther apart.

Small eyes can be made to appear larger by drawing out the eyelines to meet beyond the outside corner of the eye and by filling in the small triangle between them and the eye with white tinged with blue to imitate the cornea. Further enlargement can be achieved by leaving a space of about an eighth of an inch between the eyelines and the edge of the lid all the way along and filling in this space with the cornea color.

Eyes set too close together can be made to look further apart if several lines are drawn from the inner corner of the eye slanting up and away from the nose and if two lines are drawn from the outside corner at an acute angle. The illusion will be strengthened if the eyebrows are blocked out near the nose with the foundation color and extended at the other ends. This pattern may be reversed to make wide-set eyes look closer together.

Brows. Eyebrows may be blocked out in whole or in part with foundation color and drawn in as desired with the lining color.

Nose. The long nose can be made to appear shorter by shadowing the tip, applying a broad short highlight to the ridge, and by lowering the eyebrows.

To increase the apparent length of the nose, a narrow highlight can be drawn down the ridge and over the tip, the sides shadowed to this highlight, the eyebrows raised.

The wide nose can be narrowed by shadowing heavily up to a thin highlight on the ridge.

The thin nose can be thickened with a broad highlight down the ridge.

The crooked nose can be straightened by drawing a highlight where the ridge should be and shadowing heavily any part of the actual ridge which is out of line.

A hump can be reduced by light shadowing, and the snub nose can be somewhat corrected by highlighting the depression and shadowing the tip.

Chin. The chin can be treated in similar fashion: a long chin can be shadowed at the tip; a short chin can be given a vertically blended highlight at the tip; the broad chin can be shadowed at the sides.

Ears. Prominent ears can be made less prominent by shadowing.

Mouth. Irregular mouths can be corrected with foundation and rouge. Thin lips can be thickened and the small mouth can be extended at the corners with rouge. Thick lips and a large mouth can be reduced by bringing in the foundation color somewhat at the top, bottom and corners. Turned-down corners can be highlighted with foundation and made to turn up with rouge; similarly, corners can be turned down with rouge and foundation.

CHARACTER MAKEUP

The commonest character makeup is designed to give an illusion of old age. Age produces certain fairly definite effects in all people: it changes the color and texture of the skin, making it coarser and either sallower or ruddier; it makes the face either fatter and flabby or thin and sunken; and it takes the color out of the hair.

The foundation color must be chosen or mixed according to physical type and according to age. A yellowish foundation is used for the sallow type, less for middle age, more for old age. A reddish-yellow foundation or a reddish-brown foundation is used for the ruddy type and the amount increases with the age to be represented. The effect of thinness or fatness is achieved with highlight and shadow.

Thin old age. To emphasize thin features, the bony structure of the face is accented with highlights lighter than the founda-

The patterns of highlight and shadow in thin old age are shown here.

tion color: the frontal bone above the nose and eyebrows, the ridge between the eye socket and the temple depression, the cheekbone, the point of the chin, and the line of the lower jaw.

The facial depressions are then shadowed with brown, dark brown, dark gray, violet, or crimson and gray mixed, depending on the sallowness or robustness desired. The eyesocket gets the heaviest shadow. The hollow below the cheekbone, irregularly triangular in shape with concave sides, should be somewhat less heavily shadowed, and darkest at the center. The hollows at the temples get a lighter shadow. A still lighter shadow, elongated and darker at the center, above the highlight on the forehead, gives the shallow frontal depression between the frontal eminence and the supercilliary arch. Still lighter shadows go at the root of the nose just under the supercilliary arch, at the sides of the nose, in the depressions which run from the nose past the corners of the mouth, at the corners of the mouth, on the sides of the chin, and underneath the jaw.

Then the shadows should be carefully blended toward the highlights without destroying their essential angularity, and the highlights toward the shadows. An emphasis on the vertical rather than the horizontal will increase the effect of leanness.

Rouge should not be used at all in the thin makeup. On the cheeks it destroys the skeletal pattern of highlight and shadow, and it makes the lips look full instead of thin and pale.

For advanced age, naturally red lips may need to be toned

down with the foundation color. Lips can be made to look shrunken by alternating vertical streaks of highlight and shadow.

A few of the shadows described above will be long and thin enough to be called lines, but the above method of modeling the face in highlight and shadow rather than drawing in a large number of sharp lines, each consisting of a long thin sharp shadow flanked by two thin lines of highlight, produces much more natural effects of age. For large theatres the contrast between highlight, shadow, and foundation should be sharp; the blending should be slight. For small theatres, the contrasts should be less marked and the whole more subtly blended.

The whole makeup should be set with a light powder, flesh or brunette. The old-age powders cover up too much of the makeup.

Fat old age. The effect of fatness is achieved almost entirely by means of a pattern of large, roughly spherical highlights, separated and accentuated by relatively small, slight, and curved shadows. Curves should be flattened toward the horizontal for a broadening effect.

After the ruddy foundation color has been applied all over (especially heavy on any natural hollows, including the sockets of the eyes), the shadows necessary to the illusion of fatness are drawn in with dark red or violet liner. The apple cheek is outlined with a crescent shadow which begins on the cheekbone under the middle of the eye, curves out toward the ear, and down and back roughly parallel to the jaw (it is heaviest near the ear), and by a smaller crescent curving in the reverse manner between the nose and the cheekbone. If these two crescent shadows were allowed to meet top and bottom they would form a somewhat flattened circle enclosing the cheek.

The forehead is shadowed for half an inch to an inch below the hairline all the way round and down the temple. Two convex shadows on the sides of the roots of the nose will make the bridge appear broader, and a circular shadow around the tip will make the tip look wider and fuller.

Light red shadows on the inner and outer corners of the eyelids help to produce a swollen effect. Eyebrows drawn out as far as possible give greater breadth.

A convex shadow curving down on both sides from the center

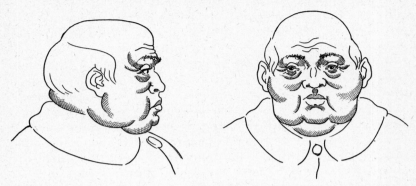

The patterns of highlight and shadow in fat old age are shown here.

of the lower lip rounds the chin, two concave shadows drawn from the center of the chin down and out, and two similar shadows on either side of the jaw suggest jowls. A large red mouth with a concave shadow at each corner and a slight downward curving shadow cutting the vertical line of the declivity in the upper lip complete the pattern of shadow.

Highlights of a foundation or liner that is lighter than the base color are required as follows: a bright circle on the center of each cheek; a large but not so bright circle on each side of the forehead above each eyebrow; an ellipse of medium brightness on the upper half of the eyesocket; small dabs on the central parts of the eyelids; a quarter-inch wide area under each eye for puffiness; a small dab on the middle of the tip of the nose; two small dabs on the chin between the upper and lower shadows; a wide horizontal highlight on the base of the chin; a light stroke on the lower front portion of each cheek to suggest a jowl below the main bulge of the cheek; a dab on each wing of the nose; and two small dots on the lower lip.

If rouge is used on the cheeks, it should be light enough not to have the effect of shadow and should be applied lightly, so as not to upset the pattern of highlight and shadow.

Highlights and shadows should be blended towards each other, accentuating the generally spherical and horizontal character of the pattern.

The makeup is set with a light powder of a pinkish cast.

The steps described above are those used for grease-paint makeup. Character makeup with a water base is done with highlight and shadow also, but the highlights and shadows are applied first on a clean, dry face somewhat more heavily and with less blending. The foundation color is then patted on with a sponge and blended carefully, allowing the pattern of highlight and shadow to show through. If the pattern has been too much obscured, highlights and shadows can be touched up somewhat with lining color on top of the base and these grease areas set with powder lightly applied. Subtle effects useful in very small theatres can be achieved with greaseless foundation, but considerable skill and experience are necessary to judge in advance the effect the base will have on the modeling.

Hair. Eyebrows are grayed by rubbing them the wrong way with white liner. If a wig is not worn, the hair can be grayed with aluminum powder, corn starch, white powder, liquid powder, or liquid white mascara. Streaks of gray can be put in easily with white grease paint.

Body. Hands can be made up with the foundation color used on the face, modeled for age with the same highlights and shadows, and the whole set with powder. When arms, legs, back, and chest must be made up, it is best to use liquid powder of the proper shade.

Mustaches, beards, etc. Mustaches, beards, and side whiskers in brown or red add to the appearance of maturity, and in gray or white to the appearance of age. They are made of crepe hair, and unless they are very elaborate and to be used in many performances, they are best built up on the face for each performance like the rest of the makeup. Crepe hair comes tightly braided and must be pulled out, dampened, and pressed to take out the curl before it can be used for most purposes. The rest of the makeup is ordinarily done first, but the skin to which hair is to be attached must be clean of grease.

For a mustache of the brush type, take a piece of prepared crepe hair, pull it to the desired thickness, cut one end on a curve to fit one side of the upper lip, and bevel the thickness so that the ends of the hair may be attached to the curve of the lip, with the hair extending out and down. Paint the surface to which the hair is to be attached with spirit gum, let it dry a few seconds, then press the beveled ends of the hair to the gummed surface so that the ends of the hairs are fastened to the lip. Press

Beveling the hair to fit the face is shown above. **Top,** brush mustache; and **Bottom,** pointed mustache.

down with a damp cloth for a few moments. Cut off most of the excess, leaving, however, more than will be needed for the finished product. Bevel the excess piece to fit the other side of the lip, and apply it in the same way as the first. Then trim both sides to suit, remembering that hair is usually cut on the bias, not straight.

For a long, pointed, or turned-up mustache, the crepe hair is pressed into cylindrical shape and given a bias cut about an inch long. The bias surface is attached to the lip so that the hairs extend more toward the side and less downward. This makes it easier to twist out the ends of the mustache. Ends can be stiffened with a little spirit gum.

Side whiskers are made in the same way as the pointed mustache, except that a thicker cylinder of crepe hair is usually necessary. The bias cut is as long as the surface from which the whiskers are to appear to grow. The crepe hair is fastened to the side of the face, beginning just under the actor's own rudimentary side whiskers and continuing down to and along the line of the lower jaw. The hair should appear to grow out and down.

A full beard may be made in five sections. A wide piece of crepe hair is cut in a V and beveled slightly so that the middle can be fastened just above the larynx and spread up and out on either side toward the ears with the hair projecting out and a little up.

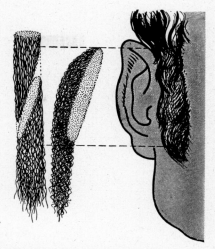

Beveling the hair to fit the face for side whiskers is shown here.

A second section is cut and beveled to fit above this just under the chin with the hair projecting out and down. Then two pieces are cut like side whiskers, but long enough and with enough bevel so that they can be fastened all the way from the natural hairline on each side, down and along the jaw onto the chin. The final piece, the façade, should be fitted to follow the curve of the lower lip, beveled to project largely downward, and fastened so as to cover the union of side and under pieces. The addition of mustaches will give greater volume and a different effect. When all the pieces are firmly fastened and pulled together so that the beard looks all of one piece, it can be trimmed to the desired shape.

Smaller beards are constructed of fewer pieces attached to a smaller area of the face. Some makeup artists prefer to build up even a large beard out of many more pieces, thus achieving a more homogeneous creation, but the principle is the same.

The traces of real beard on the face will provide some added guidance. One should remember that hair grows out of the face, usually not straight but partially parallel to the surface. Crepe hair stuck flat on the face will look unnatural and the top layers will come off because they are not fastened to the face. Plenty of crepe hair should always be attached; if it is too long it can be trimmed, but if too short it must be washed off with alcohol and a longer piece substituted. If one gently pulls apart pieces

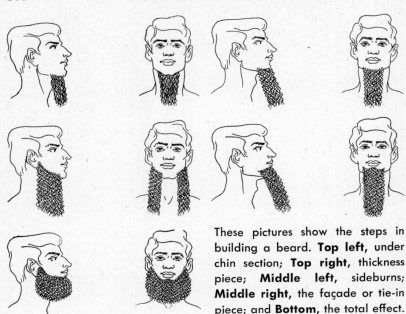

These pictures show the steps in building a beard. **Top left,** under chin section; **Top right,** thickness piece; **Middle left,** sideburns; **Middle right,** the façade or tie-in piece; and **Bottom,** the total effect.

of hair to be used in constructing a beard, one gets a natural thinning of the pulled ends more effective than can be achieved with scissors.

It is not necessary that the beard match exactly the hair on the head, because natural facial hair is seldom exactly the same color, but either a little darker or a little lighter.

Wigs. The wig needs to be fitted to the actor to be sure that it will be completely satisfactory. This is particularly true of wigs used for serious characters and in realistic plays. A poorly fitting wig may be seriously distracting. Wigs for comic characters, especially in nonrealistic plays, may be rented without fitting on the basis of head size. Simple nonrealistic wigs, for instance for servants in Elizabethan comedies, may be made by sewing crepe hair to the lining of a man's hat.

PLASTIC MAKEUP

The face is sometimes built up with plastic wax, nose putty, or absorbent cotton and gauze, but elaborate plastic makeups are difficult to execute and are likely to interfere with facial expression. They are most useful in large theatres and in fantastic plays.

Alfred J. Balcombe

Nose putty. For building up the nose or chin, nose putty is used. It is pressed onto the dry surface of the skin and modeled with the fingers into the desired shape. If it does not stick firmly the skin should be painted with spirit gum. After the putty has hardened it may be colored with foundation rubbed on carefully with the fingers. Plastic wax is softer than nose putty and not so adhesive but is sometimes used for the same purpose and is applied in the same fashion.

Here is a wig, beard, and putty nose worn by Sir Toby Belch in *Twelfth Night*, Dramatic Workshop of the New School, New York. Erwin Piscator, director.

Absorbent cotton. Absorbent cotton, fastened to the face with spirit gum and given a hard surface with spirit gum or diluted collodion, is used for larger constructions, and when the whole side of the face is built up, layers of absorbent cotton are covered with a piece of silk gauze fastened down all around the edges with spirit gum.

The contours of the cheeks can be changed also by placing rolls of cotton gauze inside the mouth between the teeth and the cheek.

RACIAL TYPES

Arabic. The Arab complexion varies from nearly white or light pink (in women) through brownish yellow to brown. The face tends to be broad, with a high and wide forehead and a broad and flat nose. The eyes may slant upwards at the outer corners, or they may be set horizontally with the lower lid nearly straight. The upper part of the eye socket, instead of receding markedly from the brow, drops more or less vertically and is consequently prominent. The eyebrows are inclined to be short and straight. Most of these features can be suggested with highlight and shadow. If necessary, the nose can be broadened with putty.

Chinese. The skin color of the Chinese varies from almost white to a strong yellowish-brown. The most common shade might be described as olive with a yellowish cast. Chinese women in general are lighter than men. The face is broad with prominent cheekbones, and the eyes appear slanting or almond-shaped. The latter effect can be achieved by slanting the eye lines upward toward the temple or by pulling the skin at the outside corners of the eyes upward with adhesive tape. The brow tends to be high and the upper lip broad. The nose is somewhat broad and flat.

Egyptian. The ancient Egyptians were apparently copper or bronze complexioned, with high cheekbones, high forehead, and aquiline nose. The face was squarish with full lips. Women made up their eyes with black and used rouges on the lips. Eyebrows were long, straight, and horizontal.

Greek. The ancient Greek was much like the modern Caucasian. He had a fair complexion, a straight or aquiline nose, and high cheekbones.

Indian. The American Indian is reddish, yellow, olive, or deep brown in complexion. The cheekbones and brow are prominent, the nose broad and aquiline. The eyes are usually small and deepset. The face is squarish, but the features are sharp.

The Asiatic Indian varies in complexion from light to dark brown. High foreheads, large aquiline noses, and thick lips are common.

Japanese. The Japanese are somewhat less yellow of complexion than the Chinese. The upper classes tend to resemble Caucasians; the lower classes are similar to Mongolian Chinese in facial structure. Geisha girls use a stylized makeup—large eyebrows drawn in bold arches and doll-like circles of rouge on the cheeks.

Negro. The Negro has a dark brown or almost black skin, a flat nose, thick protruding lips, a long skull, and receding hair.

The upper lip is lighter than the general skin coloring, and the lower lip sometimes shows some pink. In modeling, black should be used for shadows, and light brown or light brown mixed with light pink for the highlights. The palms of the hands are usually very light and with considerable pink in them.

Organization

Except for unusually elaborate jobs, every actor should be able to do his own makeup; but in the nonprofessional theatre, this is seldom the case. If the actors are to make themselves up, each should be supplied with directions including the general character of the makeup plus the color foundation and lining colors with a description of highlight and shadowing and of any mustache, sideburns, or beard. Makeup is best done under light approximating the stage lighting, and dressing rooms or a makeup room are sometimes equipped with lights which can be fitted with different colored gelatins for this purpose. Makeup of all characters should be inspected by the director or by a makeup manager before the curtain goes up.

MAKEUP MANAGER AND CREW

Unless the makeup is furnished by the individual actors, there should be a manager of makeup, who is supplied with a copy of the makeup chart and is responsible for checking the makeup on hand and for purchasing any necessary additions. If, as is frequently the case in the nonprofessional theatre, the actors are not capable of making themselves up, the manager of makeup will be responsible also for assembling a crew to do the makeup, for giving the members any necessary instruction, and for supervising their work in rehearsal and performance.

Rehearsal. Except for extremely elaborate jobs, one makeup rehearsal is usually enough, and this is likely to be the final dress rehearsal, because the makeup cannot be judged until the lighting has been set. The makeup manager, and if possible the whole makeup crew, should see the results of their work from the house and note any changes to be made for performance.

Performance. During performance, actors should be required to be on hand early enough so that their makeup can be done without rushing. Makeup may be done either before or after getting into costume. If done before, the actor must take care not to smear his makeup or dirty his costume when he dresses. If done afterwards, the costume must be completely covered with a large full apron to protect it from the makeup.

Questions

1. What is the function of makeup?
2. How does it accomplish its function?
3. How is makeup affected by the style of the play?
4. How might makeup for Greek tragedy differ from makeup for Restoration comedy? Why?
5. What elements in makeup are designed to overcome distance?
6. What elements in makeup are designed to counteract the effects of artificial light?
7. What modifications should be made in makeup that is to be worn in a predominantly blue light?
8. What questions should the makeup artist ask about the character?
9. What special studies will be useful to the makeup artist?
10. Outline the steps in applying a straight grease makeup for a woman.
11. What differences would there be in a straight makeup for a man?
12. How can eyes be made to look larger?
13. How can the nose be made to look thinner? Thicker?
14. Outline the steps in applying a thin grease-paint makeup for thin old age.
15. How will the fat old age makeup differ from the thin old age?
16. What is a disadvantage of elaborate plastic makeup?

Exercises

1. Plan a realistic character makeup.
2. Plan an abstract character makeup.
3. Plan a grotesque makeup.
4. Prepare a makeup plan for a one-act play.
5. Execute a straight grease-paint makeup.
6. Execute a character makeup.
7. Put on a crepe hair mustache.
8. Put on a crepe hair beard.
9. Execute an Indian, Negro, or Chinese makeup.

Bibliography

Baird, John, *Make-up,* New York: Samuel French, 1930. A good practical manual.

Corson, Richard, *Stage Make-up,* New York: D. Appleton-Century-Crofts, Inc., revised edition, 1949. A good, up-to-date book.

Parsons, Charles S., *A Guide to Theatrical Make-up,* London: Pitman, 1932.

Strenkovsky, Serge, *The Art of Make-up,* New York: E. P. Dutton Co., 1937. The most comprehensive book.

Strauss, Ivard, *Paint, Powder and Make-up,* New Haven, Conn.: Sweet & Son, 1936. A good guide, well illustrated.

GLOSSARY

THE COMMON STAGE TERMS

APRON: The portion of the picture-frame stage which projects into the auditorium—very shallow in most modern theatres, deep in Restoration and eighteenth-century English theatres.

BACKDROP: See *drop*.

BACKING: A flat, a combination of flats, or a drop, used to limit the audience's view through an opening (e.g., a door or window) in a setting; *i.e.*, to mask the backstage area.

BATTEN: A length of rigid material, usually of wood or pipe, hung or fastened in a horizontal position. Lights, drops, and other pieces of scenery are fastened to *battens* so that they may be hung from the flies.

BOOMERANG: A rolling platform of two or more levels on which scene painters may stand to gain better access to tall scenery. Also a similar but smaller device designed to carry heavy lighting units.

BORDER: A short drop with no batten at its lower edge, hung above the stage parallel to the proscenium arch, to mask the flies. A *sky border* is painted to look like the sky and was a standard part of the exterior setting composed of wings and backdrop. A *kitchen border* was painted a dirty brown; it represented the ceiling of a humble dwelling in interior settings composed of wings and backdrops. A *fancy border* represented the ceiling in rich interiors. A *cut border* is one that is cut to represent architecture or foliage. A *foliage border* is cut and painted to represent overhanging branches and leaves.

BORDERLIGHTS: Sections of lights, in a trough or in individual compartments, hung above the stage to give general illumination to the acting area from above.

BOX SET: The standard form of interior setting in realistic production; it is usually composed of back wall, two side walls, and ceiling.

BUNCH LIGHT: An older type of floodlight, consisting of a metal boxlike reflector with sockets for a number of low-wattage lamps. It is useful for lighting through windows, etc., when widely diffused light is needed over a large area from a particular direction.

CEILING: A canvas-covered frame, hung on two or three sets of lines so that it rests on the tops of the three walls of the box set to complete the set at the top and to mask the flies.

COLOR FRAME: A metal or wood frame designed to hold a color medium for insertion in a spotlight or other type of lamp.

COLOR MEDIUM: Any medium, such as gelatin or glass, placed in front of a source of illumination to provide colored light.

CONCERT BORDERS: The borderlights hanging immediately upstage of the teaser.

CONNECTORS: Fiber blocks used for connecting cable to lighting units: one, the *male,* contains a pair of brass pins; the other, the *female,* is fitted with brass sleeves into which the pins fit.

CORNER BLOCK: A small piece of $\frac{3}{16}''$ three-ply veneer board, cut in the shape of a triangle and used to reinforce joints in units of scenery.

COUNTERWEIGHT SYSTEM: A method of rigging in which each batten to be flown is permanently attached to a cradle running on wires at the side of the stage, in which *counterweights* (heavy iron bars) may be placed to balance the weight of scenery or lights attached to the batten, so that the batten and its load can be raised with little effort.

CUE: The words or action in a play which constitute the signal for the next action, line, or effect.

CURTAIN LINE: The line across the stage behind the proscenium which marks the position of the front curtain when it is closed. Also the final speech of an act, the line which cues the curtain.

CUT BORDER: See *border.*

CYCLORAMA: A large curtain of canvas or other material, hung from a horizontal U-shaped frame, and suspended from the flies so as to enclose at back and sides most of the playing area.

DIM DOWN: To reduce the intensity of light. To *dim up* is to increase the intensity of light.

DIMMER: A device for reducing the flow of electricity through an electrical circuit, and thus for controlling the intensity of illumination provided by a lamp or lamps connected in that circuit.

DOCK: Usually the space under the stage, but also any storage space. A *scene dock* is a rack for the storage of flats.

DOOR FLAT: See *flat.*

DOOR FRAME: A solid wood door frame made to fit into the opening in a door flat.

DOWNSTAGE: In the direction of the audience.

DRAPES: Large curtains hung in folds from battens so as to mask the offstage area and provide a neutral background for actors, properties, or units of scenery.

DROP: A large sheet of cloth (usually canvas), its top and bottom edges each fastened to a batten, hung by a set of lines from the gridiron so that the lower edge touches the stage floor and the upper edge is hidden by the borders. A *backdrop* is a full-stage drop used to mask the backstage area in a drop-and-wing setting. It is usually painted to represent a landscape, a street, or the sky. A *cut drop* has sections cut out to permit scenery behind it to show through, as in a grove of trees. A *leg drop* has its center cut out so that only narrow strips (usually the two outer edges) touch the floor. These *legs* are usually painted and shaped in profile to represent tree trunks, columns, buttresses.

DUTCHMAN: (1) A narrow board hinged between two of the flats of three-fold or four-fold unit to permit folding. (2) A strip of cloth glued over the crack between two flats joined edge to edge to form a continuous wall. (3) A fitting containing an extra condensing lens used to adapt a plano-convex lens spotlight for projecting slides or moving effects.

ELEVATION: The view of an object looking from the front, side or rear, without perspective. Settings are usually drawn in front elevation.

FIREPLACE FLAT: See *flat.*

FLAT: A unit section of flat scenery, made of a light wood frame covered with muslin, duck, or canvas, and designed to form in combination with other flats the side and back walls of settings. An *arch flat* has an arched opening, a *door flat* an opening for a door frame, a *fireplace flat* an opening for a fireplace, and a *window flat* an opening for a window.

FLIES: The space above the stage between the top of the proscenium arch and the gridiron.

FLIPPER: A narrow piece of flat scenery hinged to a wide piece of flat scenery.

FLOODLIGHT: A single light unit consisting of a large reflector and one or more lamps, designed to light a relatively large area. It may be hung from a batten above the stage, stood in the wings on a stand, or set on the floor behind a ground row.

FLOOR CLOTH: See *ground cloth.*

FLOOR PLAN: See *ground plan.*

FLOOR POCKET: See *pocket.*

FLY: To raise scenery or lights above the level of the stage floor by means of lines running from the gridiron.

FLY GALLERY: A narrow platform found in some theatres along the side wall of the stage some distance above the stage floor; from it are worked the lines used for flying scenery. Some theatres do not have a fly gallery; in these the lines are worked from the stage floor.

FOLIAGE BORDER: See *border*.

FOOTLIGHTS: Sections of lights sunk in the floor of the stage in front of the front curtain, designed to provide general illumination for the playing space from below.

FORESTAGE: The part of the stage near the audience when the stage is divided into two parts by an inner proscenium.

FORMAL SETTING: A permanent, plastic setting in which the elements have been reduced to simple masses so that change of scene may be effected by changing the light and the properties.

FRESNEL: A compact, highly efficient spotlight with a corrugated lens that throws a soft, diffused beam.

GRAND DRAPE: A decorative or neutral, shallow drape or curtain hung at the top of the proscenium in front of the front curtain to dress the top of the proscenium opening and to reduce its height.

GRIDIRON OR GRID: The framework of wood or steel beams above the stage. It supports the rigging for flying scenery.

GROUND CLOTH or FLOOR CLOTH: A large piece of waterproof duck or canvas usually used as a permanent covering for the stage floor.

GROUND ROW: A cut-out profile representing shrubbery, rising ground, a stone wall, or distant hills, etc., designed to hide the meeting place of sky drop and floor in an exterior setting.

HALL BACKING: A backing, usually of two-fold flats, painted to look like a hall and set behind a door opening.

HAND PROPS: Small articles necessary to the play, which are used by the actors.

HEAD BLOCK or LEAD BLOCK: Three or more sheaves framed together and attached to the gridiron directly above the pin rail.

IN ONE: The stage area (about six feet deep) which in the wing type of setting was included in the first pair of wings and a backdrop immediately behind them. *In two* was the area included in two sets of wings and their backdrop.

JOG: (1) A narrow flat, usually one foot or less wide. (2) To move part of the wall of a set on stage by inserting a *jog* perpendicular to the line of the wall.

KEYSTONE: A small piece of $\frac{3}{16}''$ three-ply veneer board cut in the shape of a keystone and used to reinforce joints in units of scenery.

KITCHEN BORDER: See *border*.

LASH: To tie two pieces of scenery (usually flats) together by means of sash cord and an arrangement of cleats.

LEAD BLOCK: See *head block*.

LEKO: An ellipsoidal reflector spotlight of high intensity and sharpness whose beam can be shaped with great precision.

LEG DROP: See *drop*.

LIGHT PLOT: A complete plan for lighting a setting or all the settings in a play.

LOFT BLOCK: A single sheave in a steel frame bolted to the gridiron to carry a fly rope.

MASK: To conceal from view of the audience. A *masking piece* is a piece of scenery used thus to conceal some part of the stage or offstage area.

OFFSTAGE: Outside the playing area.

OLIVETTE: A floodlight with a single high-wattage lamp.

ONE STEP: A step unit with one riser and one tread. A *two step* has two risers and two treads, and so on.

ONSTAGE: Within the playing area.

PARALLEL: The collapsible frame which supports a standard platform.

PIN HINGE: A hinge whose connecting pin may be withdrawn and the two halves separated. It is used for joining pieces of scenery as well as for hinging.

PIN RAIL: The double rail at one side of the stage floor or in the fly gallery; it holds belaying pins to which fly ropes are tied off.

PLASTIC: Built in three dimensions rather than painted on a flat surface. Used also of light which reveals the three-dimensionality of objects and of a stage which brings the actors into the midst of the audience rather than showing them behind a proscenium frame.

PLAYING SPACE: The portion of the stage used by the actors in performance, usually enclosed on three sides by the scenery and bounded on the remaining side by the proscenium arch.

POCKET: A square hollow porcelain-lined electrical receptacle containing heavy contact plates to accommodate a stage plug. It is sunk in the stage floor or wall and has a metal cover.

PORTAL UNIT SET: An arrangement of scenery consisting of a permanent frame, in front of and behind which units are changed to provide settings for a number of different scenes.

PRACTICAL: Usable. A *practical door* is one that can be opened and closed by the actor. A *practical window* is one that can be raised and lowered by the actor.

PROPERTY PLOT: A diagram of a stage setting, showing the location of all furniture and other articles necessary to the production.

PROPERTIES or PROPS: All furniture and furnishings necessary to the action or to dress the stage and all objects used by the actors in the course of the action.

PROSCENIUM: The wall which divides the stagehouse from the auditorium in the picture-frame theatre.

PROSCENIUM ARCH: The opening in the proscenium, which frames the playing space in the picture-frame theatre.

RAIL: A cross-piece in the frame of a flat.

RAKE: To set on a slant, either horizontally or vertically.

RAKING PIECE: A piece set on a slant. A *ramp* is a common type of *raking piece*. Also a short ground row.

RAMP: An inclined platform sloping up from the level of the floor.

RETURN: A flat used to run the side wall of a setting off stage behind the tormentor. It is set parallel to the proscenium and fastened to the downstage edge of the side wall.

REVEAL: Any thickness piece. When a door unit is used in a door flat, the door frame serves as a thickness piece, but when a door flat is used as an arch without the door unit, the sides and top of the opening must be given wall thickness by fastening to them *reveals* made of wall board or veneer board.

ROSENE: A resinous adhesive which will not curl, used for applying scrim, gauze, and netting to cut drops or borders.

SCENE DOCK: See *dock*.

SCENE PLOT: A chart showing the location of all units of scenery on stage for each setting.

SCRIM: A loose-weave, large-thread material used for "disappearance" and "dissolving wall" effects. When illuminated from in front it appears opaque; when objects behind it are illuminated they can be clearly seen through it.

SET PIECE: A three-dimensional piece of scenery which stands without hanging or bracing.

SET PROPS: Properties such as chairs, tables, pictures, etc., which are on the stage when the curtain goes up, as distinguished from *hand props* which are carried on by actors in the course of the action.

SHEAVE: A pulley wheel. A *block* contains one or more *sheaves*.

SHIFT: To move one setting with its properties off and another setting on stage.

SHORT LINE: In each set of three rigging lines, the one nearest the pin rail. The line farthest from the pin rail is the *long line;* the third is the *center line*.

SIMULTANEOUS SET: A setting which serves without changes for several different scenes.

SKY BACKING: A small drop or two-fold flat, painted to look like sky and used behind window or door openings.

SKY DROP: See *drop*.

SPACE STAGE: An abstract setting consisting of platforms and steps, and sometimes simple architectural pieces, backed by a sky drop or cyclorama.

SPOTLIGHT: A lighting unit consisting of a ventilated housing, a single, concentrated-filament lamp, and a condensing lens. The spotlight is designed to provide specific illumination in a relatively small area.

STAGE BRACE: An adjustable device made of two lengths of wood clamped together, with a pair of metal horns at one end designed to fit into a brace cleat on the back of a flat, and with an iron rocker on the other end which can be fastened to the floor with a stage screw. It is used to support scenery from behind.

STAGE CABLE: A pair or more of heavy, flexible electric wires, bound together and armored with jute to withstand hard wear.

STAGE LEFT: The actor's left as he faces the audience. *Stage right* is the actor's right as he faces the audience.

STAGE PLUG: An electrical connecting unit consisting of a fiber block carrying heavy copper contact strips with set screws to which cable may be attached and a clamp for securing the cable. It is used to plug into a pocket.

STAGE SCREW or PEG: A large, tapered screw with a handle, used to fasten toe irons and stage braces to the stage floor.

STILE: Any long, vertical piece. The side pieces in the frame of a flat are *stiles*.

STREET BACKING: Flats or a drop painted to look like the fronts of buildings, used behind window or door openings.

STRETCHERS: The horizontal crosspieces in the frame of a flat. They are also called *rails*.

STRIKE: To remove from the playing area.

STRIP LIGHT: A unit containing a row of low-wattage lamps in a trough or compartments, hung above door openings or on the backs of flats to light backings, or laid on the floor behind a ground row to light the bottom of a drop.

SWITCH: A device for opening and closing an electrical circuit and thus turning lights on and off.

SWITCHBOARD: The panel containing all switches and dimmer controls necessary to stage lighting.

TEASER: A neutral-colored border hung just upstage of the front curtain. It masks a part of the flies and can be raised or lowered to vary the height of the proscenium opening.

TOGGLE RAIL: The stretcher in a flat frame, which is mounted about five feet from the floor so that a stagehand may grasp it to *toggle* the flat into position.

TORMENTOR LIGHT: Any light unit used from a position behind the tormentor. Usually it is clamped to a pipe stand set up to hold a number of light units.

TORMENTORS: Two-fold flats of neutral color which stand one

on either side of the playing area just upstage of the proscenium. They serve to mask a part of the wing space and, since they are movable, to vary the width of the proscenium opening.

TRAP: A trap-door in the floor of the stage.

TRAVELER: A track on which draw curtains are hung.

TWO-FOLD: Two flats hinged to fold together. A *three-fold* is three flats hinged to fold together.

UNIT SET: Any setting in which a large part of the scenery is re-used to form a new scene.

UPSTAGE: Away from the audience.

WINDOW FLAT: See *flat.*

WINDOW FRAME: A solid wooden window made to fit into the opening in a window flat.

WINGS: Two-fold flats designed to mask the offstage space when set in pairs along opposite sides of the playing area. They are usually painted and shaped to look like the walls of a room, a forest, street fronts, etc. Also the offstage space left and right.

WING SETTING: A setting composed of wings, backdrop, and borders.

INDEX

DATE DUE

DEMCO 38-297